Art and Artifact in Austen

Art and Artifact in Austen

Edited by
ANNA BATTIGELLI

University of Delaware Press
NEWARK
DISTRIBUTED BY THE UNIVERSITY OF VIRGINIA PRESS

University of Delaware Press
© 2020 by Anna Battigelli
All rights reserved
Printed in the United States of America on acid-free paper

First published 2020

978-1-64453-174-7 (cloth)
978-1-64453-175-4 (paper)
978-1-64453-176-1 (e-book)

9 8 7 6 5 4 3 2 1

Library of Congress Cataloging-in-Publication Data is available for this title.

Cover art: Cassandra Austen, portrait of Fanny Knight, 1808, watercolor on paper. (Jane Austen's House Museum, Chawton, UK)

Contents

List of Illustrations   vii
Acknowledgments   ix
List of Abbreviations   xi

Introduction: The Intimate Ironies of
Jane Austen's Arts and Artifacts   1

Portraiture as Misrepresentation in the Novels
and Early Writings of Jane Austen   24
PETER SABOR

Jane Austen's "Artless" Heroines:
Catherine Morland and Fanny Price   44
ELAINE BANDER

Legal Arts and Artifacts in Jane Austen's Persuasion   61
NANCY E. JOHNSON

Jane Austen and the Theater? Perhaps Not So Much   76
DEBORAH C. PAYNE

Everything Is Beautiful: Jane Austen at the Ballet   93
CHERYL A. WILSON

Jane Austen, Marginalia, and Book Culture   109
MARILYN FRANCUS

Gender and Things in Austen and Pope   126
BARBARA M. BENEDICT

"A Very Pretty Amber Cross": Material Sources
of Elegance in Mansfield Park   146
NATASHA DUQUETTE

Religious Views: English Abbeys in Austen's
Northanger Abbey and Emma   165
TONYA J. MOUTRAY

Intimate Portraiture and the Accomplished Woman Artist in Emma   189
JULIETTE WELLS

"Is She Musical?" Players and Nonplayers in Austen's Fiction"   206
LINDA ZIONKOWSKI AND MIRIAM HART

What Jane Saw—in Henrietta Street   224
JOCELYN HARRIS

Bibliography   239
Contributors   257
Index   261

Illustrations

1. Cassandra Austen, copy of an engraving of George Morland's *Pedlars*, 1808 — 25
2. Cassandra Austen, portrait of Fanny Knight, 1808 — 26
3. Cassandra Austen, *Edward IV*, in Jane Austen, "The History of England," 1791 — 28
4. Henry Bunbury, *Recruits*, 1780 — 29
5. Cassandra Austen, *Henry V*, in Jane Austen, "The History of England," 1791 — 30
6. J. M. W. Turner, *Fishing Boats Entering Calais Harbour*, 1803 — 39
7. Jane Austen's inscription of Vicesimus Knox, *Elegant Extracts* (ca. 1782–83) — 111
8. Jane Austen's marginalia in "The Character of Mary Queen of Scots," in Vicesimus Knox, *Elegant Extracts* (ca. 1782–83) — 112
9. Jane Austen's marginalia in "The Character of Queen Elizabeth," in Vicesimus Knox, *Elegant Extracts* (ca. 1782–83) — 113
10. Jane Austen's marginalia in "The Character of Mary Queen of Scots," in Vicesimus Knox, *Elegant Extracts* (ca. 1782–83) — 114
11. Marginalia in Mary Brunton, *Self-Control* (1811) — 118
12. Remnant of cut page in Frances Burney D'Arblay, *The Wanderer* (1814) — 120
13. Angelica Kauffmann, *Self-Portrait*, 1787 — 155
14. Johann Zoffany, *The Family of Sir William Young*, 1767–69 — 162
15. William Gilpin, *Tintern Abbey I*, from *Observations on the River Wye* (1782) — 170
16. William Gilpin, *Tintern Abbey II*, from *Observations on the River Wye* (1782) — 171
17. J. M. W. Turner, *Tintern Abbey: The Crossing and Chancel, Looking towards the East Window*, ca. 1794 — 172
18. John Constable, *Netley Abbey by Moonlight*, ca. 1833 — 174
19. William Gilpin, *Tintern Abbey I*, from *Observations on the River Wye* (1800) — 182
20. William Gilpin, *Tintern Abbey II*, from *Observations on the River Wye* (1800) — 183

Acknowledgments

An edited volume is a group effort. I am deeply fortunate to have worked on this project with so many talented and amiable scholars and colleagues. The essays in this volume expand and enrich a dialogue begun at SUNY Plattsburgh's 2017 bicentenary conference "Jane Austen and the Arts." Conference participants, both those presenting papers and those responding to them, engaged in discussions that continued long after the conference and eventually resulted in this volume. Nancy Johnson, Deborah Payne, Natasha Duquette, Kym Taylor, Paul K. Johnston, James A. Winn, Paula Backscheider, Mary-Nell Bockman, and my splendid colleagues and students in the English Department at SUNY Plattsburgh provided skilled and incisive support leading up to conference. Two former students—Kym Taylor and Megan Throne—were crucial to the conference's success, both through their rich understanding of Jane Austen's work and through their personal contributions to the conference. The revised essays benefited from the incisive readers' reports provided by the University of Delaware Press. A semester at the University of Tulsa as the Bell Visiting Professor of Anglican Studies provided valuable editing time. Lisa B. Nurme and Giovanna Battigelli offered indispensable help regarding permissions. Mario Battigelli continued his work as an invaluable research assistant. Special thanks to the contributors, whose good cheer and Austenian attention to detail made them a delight to work with—as did their facility in meeting deadlines, offering crucial suggestions, and producing the stimulating essays in this volume.

Conferences cannot happen without an institution's financial support, and SUNY Plattsburgh's bicentenary conference was sponsored in part by the SUNY Conversations in the Disciplines Program of the State University of New York. It also received support from SUNY Plattsburgh, particularly from Dean Andrew Buckser, Provost James Liszka, and President John Ettling. The skilled and efficient staff members of Feinberg Library's interlibrary loan office—Ethel Facteau and Mila Su—made this volume possible. The members of the editorial staff at the University of Delaware Press were unfailingly helpful. The Metropolitan Museum of Art and the Morgan Library generously provided images for use at the conference. Staff from Chawton House and the Jane Austen's House Museum generously fielded queries regarding Austen's art and artifacts.

Abbreviations

E	Austen, Jane. *Emma*. The Cambridge Edition of the Works of Jane Austen. Edited by Richard Cronin and Dorothy McMillan. Cambridge: Cambridge University Press, 2005.
J	Austen, Jane. *Juvenilia*. The Cambridge Edition of the Works of Jane Austen. Edited by Peter Sabor. Cambridge: Cambridge University Press, 2006.
Letters	Austen, Jane. *Jane Austen's Letters*. Edited by Deirdre Le Faye. 4th ed. Oxford: Oxford University Press, 2011.
LM	Austen, Jane. *Later Manuscripts*. The Cambridge Edition of the Works of Jane Austen. Edited by Janet Todd and Linda Bree. Cambridge: Cambridge University Press, 2008.
MP	Austen, Jane. *Mansfield Park*. The Cambridge Edition of the Works of Jane Austen. Edited by John Wiltshire. Cambridge: Cambridge University Press, 2005.
NA	Austen, Jane. *Northanger Abbey*. The Cambridge Edition of the Works of Jane Austen. Edited by Barbara M. Benedict and Deirdre Le Faye. Cambridge: Cambridge University Press, 2006.
P	Austen, Jane. *Persuasion*. The Cambridge Edition of the Works of Jane Austen. Edited by Janet Todd and Antje Blank. Cambridge: Cambridge University Press, 2006.
P&P	Austen, Jane. *Pride and Prejudice*. The Cambridge Edition of the Works of Jane Austen. Edited by Pat Rogers. Cambridge: Cambridge University Press, 2006.
S&S	Austen, Jane. *Sense and Sensibility*. The Cambridge Edition of the Works of Jane Austen. Edited by Edward Copeland. *The Cambridge Edition of the Works of Jane Austen*. Cambridge: Cambridge University Press, 2006.

Art and Artifact in Austen

Introduction

The Intimate Ironies of Jane Austen's Arts and Artifacts

Jane Austen was immersed in the arts. She loved dancing. She was a proficient pianist who practiced daily and collected and transcribed piano scores.[1] Her characteristically neat handwriting can be seen in her letters, manuscripts, and musical transcriptions. "In everything that she attempted with her fingers," writes her nephew, "she was successful."[2] Her letters reveal the inescapably social nature of the arts in Georgian and Regency England. The tightknit and gregarious Austen children grew up in the company of boys boarding with the family to receive lessons from their clergyman father. They learned early how to cultivate and enjoy the company of others. For them, art was an indispensable component of social interaction. They amused themselves by reading to one another and by putting on amateur theatrical performances. Both Jane and Cassandra took drawing lessons as children, "probably from the water-colourist John Claude Nattes."[3] Jane Austen delighted her family with her witty and parodic juvenile writings and with her impromptu storytelling.[4] Cassandra contributed clever caricatures to Jane Austen's "History of England." Mrs. Austen presented poems to her husband's boarders, playfully encouraging them in their studies. Henry and James Austen collaborated at Oxford to launch the weekly periodical the *Loiterer*, to which the young Jane Austen may have contributed.[5] Manuscripts of her novels were read aloud within the family. As an adult, Austen attended concerts, plays, and art exhibits in London. She and her family sat for affordable silhouettes from leading practitioners.[6] She subscribed to libraries, read voraciously, and commented in her letters on novels and sermons, even as she described bonnets, textiles, window blinds, quilts, and balls. That the family transmitted its love of the arts to the next generation of Austens is evident in the manuscripts sent to her by her nephew James Edward Austen and her nieces Anna Lefroy, Fanny Knight, and Caroline Austen—all aspiring novelists. For the extended Austen family as for others during the long eighteenth century, creating art and domestic artifacts was an indispensable means of understanding and engaging with one's world.

Introduction

Playing the piano, singing, dancing, or drawing provided entertainment in Regency and Georgian England, but more humble domestic arts were also essential to the practical and emotional ordering of daily life.[7] Even with "the decline in home-based economic production" and the rise of the consumer revolution, a staggering number of household essentials were made, altered, embroidered, mended, or trimmed at home.[8] These included dresses, shirts, shifts, socks, bonnets, gloves, rugs, shawls, handkerchiefs, head-dresses, purses, wall decorations, fire screens, chair and sofa covers, tablecloths and linens, quilts, curtains, and footstools. Handmade gifts, such as needle cases, or embroidered items constituted what one critic calls a "freemasonry among women, a delicate recognition of shared activity."[9] In addition to the practical, decorative, and social functions of domestic art, the skill it required served significant psychological purposes: it helped one manage unruly energies and coexist with others in crowded spaces. Losing oneself in work, whether at the piano or by mending gloves, provided occupation during long winter evenings and offered solace or needed distraction during trying times. When Austen wearied of her nephews' hunting mania, she gave them nets to mend for the next day's hunt. Amused by her success in quieting the young hunters, she compared their concentrated effort with that of her brother Frank: "they are each about a rabbit net, & sit as deedily to it, side by side, as any two Uncle Franks could do" (*Letters*, 244).[10] Animal spirits could be channeled into artistic activities to produce artifacts for a hunt—or a ball. Just as Samuel Richardson's Clarissa Harlowe labors "to compose [her] angry passions to [her] Harpsichord," so, too, do Austen's heroines often use their art as a means of subduing and organizing chaotic feelings.[11]

In conduct books and sermons, such accomplishments were encouraged as part of a young woman's preparation for marriage. Elsewhere, however, women's education in the arts was viewed as both subordinating and debasing. Mary Wollstonecraft objected to the "smattering of accomplishments" that impeded the more rigorously intellectual education necessary for independence of mind.[12] For different reasons, Hannah More objected to "the phrenzy of accomplishments" that rendered women "unfit[]" "for the active duties of their own very important condition."[13] Austen's ironies encompass and complicate these arguments, in part because she wrote novels, not didactic treatises, but also because she never lost sight of the utility of arts and crafts for creating psychic space in confined quarters. Yet her letters to Cassandra also show that her understanding of the value of women's work did not preclude her willingness to parody her own domestic skills. There

Introduction

she parades her command of fabrics, gauzes, sleeve lengths, cap trimmings, gowns, and stockings, comically performing her role as an English woman dutifully adhering to her culture's insistence that women excel at domestic work. As Cassandra surely perceived, her sister's chatter about fashion trends and fabric prices also conveyed more intimate pains and depths of emotion that she was intended to share.[14] Similarly, in Austen's novels, women's work briefly stalls narrative action to convey the emotional undertow it masks or regulates. The writer who transformed narrative technique by powerfully intensifying its capacity to represent mental activity through free indirect discourse also learned a great deal in the parlor by observing how visual cues revealed inner thought. As friends and family members alternately worked in contented concentration or threw down and picked up objects in restless unease, Austen stockpiled mental images demonstrating how people unwittingly expose their states of mind as they take up needles, sharpen a pen, or open and then close a book.

It should not surprise us, then, that in her novels Austen uses a broad range of arts and artifacts, from sewing needles to estates, both to zoom into a character's subjective mental experience and to zoom out to the larger social and political world of Regency and Georgian England. Her emphasis on interiority makes her novels intellectually and emotionally atmospheric: characters "think," "feel," "reflect," "judge," and "consider." Computer analysis of Austen's language confirms what we already know: her vocabulary fingerprint consists of the largely abstract language of thought and feeling.[15] By contrast, material arts and artifacts appear sparingly.[16] That very infrequency, however, concentrates their power to signify feeling. Austen's art is that of a miniaturist, and when she famously described her novels as "the little bit (two inches wide) of Ivory on which I work with so fine a Brush, as produces little effect after much labour," she was referring to the painting of portrait miniatures onto ivory (*Letters*, 337). It follows that in her mature novels, small responses to artifacts telegraph much larger meaning: when Elinor Dashwood recognizes Edward Ferrars's likeness in the portrait miniature that Lucy Steele hands her, her response is to "return[] it almost instantly."[17] Elinor's "'allergic' reaction" to the portrait, as one critic calls it, gives expression to her unspeakable emotion.[18] In more mundane ways, Henry Tilney's voluble knowledge about muslin in *Northanger Abbey* marks him as not only fashionable but also belonging to "a new masculine identity based upon conspicuous consumption rather than inherited or landed wealth . . . [and to a] consumerist identity developed in response to Britain's imperial expansion, which had engendered the importation and eventual domestication of Indian muslin."[19] Lydia Bennet's purchase of a hat she dislikes just so she can "pull it to pieces" and remake it denotes her unreflective participation in that same consumer economy.[20] More grotesquely, Robert Ferrars's baroque design for a toothpick case made of ivory, gold, and pearls identifies him as a consumer obsessed with showcasing wealth, not taste. Lady Bertram's myopia in reducing her nephew's dangerous voyage to the East Indies to the shawl he might acquire for her there is contrasted with the generosity and thoughtfulness of Captain Harville, who, though "no reader" himself, builds "very pretty shelves" for Captain Benwick's books.[21] Larger artifacts, such as estates, landscapes, and gardens are also put to use. Elizabeth Bennet is stunned by the view of Pemberley, which is situated so as to surprise and impress visitors. The road leading to the estate constitutes a narrative experience through which visitors like Elizabeth arrive "at the top of a considerable eminence, where the wood ceased," only to have their "eye" "instantly caught by Pemberley House, situated on the opposite side of a valley, into which the road with some abruptness wound" (*P&P*, 271). The estate's visual beauty forces Elizabeth to reconsider her assumptions regarding Darcy's character in ways she cannot yet understand, let alone articulate. Repeatedly, the way characters respond to or treat art and artifacts telegraphs their state of mind or aligns them with cultural habits of thought that Austen invites us alternately to sympathize with or to judge.

If the physical and geographical constraints on women made recourse to artistic activity psychologically and spiritually necessary, for unmarried women in particular the arts were essential to creating a sense of belonging and community that was otherwise difficult to establish. For them, "home" was often temporary or tenuous, less a physical structure than a collection of artistic and social activities that provided a sense of purpose.[22] When Austen's most homeless protagonist, Anne Elliot, sits down at a keyboard to produce country dances for the Musgroves "by the hour together," she both wins their gratitude and creates a temporary shelter for herself from her exhausting itinerary (*P*, 51). The invalid and impoverished Mrs. Smith demonstrates how the arts allowed a woman rendered invisible by society to forge a sense of self-worth and belonging. She knits "little thread-cases, pin-cushions and card-racks," which Nurse Rooke sells so as to provide money for the poor, thereby finding dignity and establishing a role for herself in a world that would rather not see her (*P*, 168).[23] Similarly, Jane Fairfax's disciplined artistry with music is a necessity required for what appears to be the inevitability of her future as a governess.

Introduction

More darkly, Austen's use of arts and artifacts can signal moral decline and manipulative calculation. Caroline Bingley's effort to attract Mr. Darcy's attention by feigning interest in reading is exposed when she picks up the second volume of a title that Mr. Darcy is reading. Fanny Dashwood eschews labor altogether by purchasing needlebooks "made by some emigrant" for the Steele sisters, cheaply sidestepping the labor that, as David Selwyn points out, would make such a gift meaningful (*S&S*, 288).²⁴ Significantly, the most stylish and artful character of *Mansfield Park*, Mary Crawford, uses artistry not to subdue but to assert her will. She constructs a beautiful tableau of literal and figurative domestic harmony by playing her harp while her half sister embroiders on a "tambour" or large embroidery frame that craftsmen produced to cater to wealthier women in search of fashionable materials for their artwork. The narrator calls attention to the effectiveness of Mary's tableau:

> A young woman, pretty, lively, with a harp as elegant as herself, and both placed near a window, cut down to the ground, and opening on a little lawn, surrounded by shrubs in the rich foliage of summer, was enough to catch any man's heart. The season, the scene, the air, were all favourable to tenderness and sentiment. Mrs. Grant and her tambour frame were not without their use; it was all in harmony; and as everything will turn to account when love is once set going, even the sandwich tray, and Dr. Grant doing the honours of it, were worth looking at.²⁵

The aesthetic appeal of this scene with its artistically accomplished women, summer weather, and sandwiches masks the moral relativism that renders Mary Crawford unfit for life as a parson's wife. Her musicianship and accomplished dramaturgy in staging harmonious domestic order is eventually exposed as mere show after she urges Edmund to dismiss her brother's adultery with Maria Rushworth "as folly, and that folly stamped only by exposure" (526). Her staged tableau is more insidious than the staging of Inchbald's play *Lovers' Vows* because it seems more natural: she counterfeits a gift for domestic order that her moral relativism negates. Her staging is of a kind with Lucy Steele's less elegant work on a filigree basket to win Lady Middleton's favor. Indeed, in *Mansfield Park* artistic effort is never unshackled from the dark undertones of manipulation. Even Fanny Price's good-natured patience in arranging Lady Bertram's needlework and her skill in decorating the chilly East Room with cast-off amateur art constitute little acts of conquest that sit uneasily in a novel that criticizes colonial encroachment. As she makes herself more central to the estate's family life, she eerily mirrors her uncle's struggle to control estates overseas. The estate's hold on Fanny's character becomes evident when she is banished to Portsmouth. Faced with the material disorder and claustrophobic unease of poverty, Fanny forgets the humiliation, pain, and moral disorder of Mansfield and identifies it, not Portsmouth, as her real home. So vexed is the moral resonance of the estate of Mansfield Park that it has been described as "the principal character in the novel."[26] It, more than Northanger Abbey, exerts gothic power. Far from constructing a satisfying love story, Fanny's marriage to Edmund absorbs her in the estate's moral quagmire. Austen clearly grew dissatisfied with the fairy-tale beauty of *Pride and Prejudice*, in which the marriage of Elizabeth Bennet and Mr. Darcy "satisfies our desire to believe that what is right socially and ethically can also be stylish and beautiful."[27] By the time she wrote *Mansfield Park*, Austen was interested in a marriage that was neither particularly stylish nor unambiguously socially or ethically right—despite her heroine's good intentions.

Austen's estates, gardens, and landscapes resonate with meaning, serving as "metonym[s] of an inherited culture," but they also provide the settings through which character unfolds and the means through which characters move through time.[28] Scholars have aligned Austen with Anna Barbauld, "who imagines the experience of reading *Clarissa* as akin to moving through a landscape, which is the novel itself."[29] Conscious of the narratological value of traveling through landscapes, Austen placed Elizabeth's journey with the Gardiners on the exact route that the picturesque theorist William Gilpin describes in *Observations, Relative chiefly to picturesque beauty, made in the year 1772, on several parts of England, particularly the mountains and lakes of Cumberland and Westmoreland* (1786).[30] Well-managed estates, such as Pemberley or Donwell Abbey, offer characters a space in which they can traverse the barriers distancing disparate social groups.[31] It is meaningful that the Gardiners of Gracechurch Street in London meet Darcy on the grounds of Pemberley. Similarly, the view from Donwell Abbey embraces the Abbey Mill farm, the home of the farmer Robert Martin. True to her clergyman father's experienced ease with people from a broad range of social classes, Austen rejected the class segregation effected by the landscape designer Humphry Repton. Repeatedly, his designs "disguise churches, remove cottages, and place shrubberies in churchyards to counter the disgusting images of mortality."[32] Only Austen's most flawed characters embrace Reptonian class erasure. Maria Bertram finds relief in the distance between Sotherton and its church, and Henry Crawford suggests plantings at Thornton Lacy to "shut out the blacksmith's shop" (*MP*, 281). Never one to be outdone in

Introduction

meanness, Mrs. Norris reports having wished to use plantings to shut out the churchyard from the parsonage at Mansfield Park. For his part, General Tilney's enthusiasm for improving his estate with his succession houses and pinery reflects his sense that importing plants or rich wives for his son are interchangeable ways to plan for the future.[33] When he learns that Catherine Morland is less wealthy than he had imagined, he summarily ejects her from Northanger Abbey.

As these examples suggest, Austen's readers become skilled at watching characters negotiate boundaries. They know to attend to the play of perspective afforded by windows, doors, and gates, on the one hand, and portraits, both large and small, on the other hand. Austen knew that the novel—like landscape design and like portraits—relies on "technologies of perspective."[34] She found analogies for the way that narrative conveys and frames a character's point of view in these two arts. When Charlotte Lucas looks out of an upper window of Lucas Lodge to spy Mr. Collins approaching, she permanently contracts her vision by deciding to provide "the most flattering" reception for his courtship (*P&P*, 136). Her experience gazing through a window is the opposite of Elizabeth's expansion of perspective at Pemberley as she notices approvingly that "from every window there were beauties to be seen" (*P&P*, 272). The beauty Elizabeth perceives is not diminished by its origin in tricks of perspective. Such tricks as the ha-ha, a ditch that serves as a boundary without obstructing the view, were related to narrative tricks, particularly free indirect discourse's almost imperceptible boundary between narrator and character.[35] Readers experiencing Austen's free indirect discourse expand their minds to encompass the mental states of Austen's characters. They absorb Fanny Price's shock as she warns Maria Bertram not to slip through the locked iron gate at Sotherton and register the hysterical pitch of her warning: "you will certainly hurt yourself against those spikes—you will tear your gown—you will be in danger of slipping into the ha-ha" (116). Fanny fully understands the moral and material significance of the boundary Maria crosses when she passes through the gate. She also sees that Maria is intentionally blind to the danger she incurs. Later, when Fanny turns her back to those playing at the piano to gaze out a window at nature, she rhapsodizes about the effects of the view: "When I look out on such a night as this, I feel as if there could be neither wickedness nor sorrow in the world; and there certainly would be less of both if the sublimity of Nature were more attended to, and people were carried more out of themselves by contemplating such a scene" (*MP*, 132). Here Austen invites us as readers to experience the frames of the window as keys to the aesthetic experience embedded in her novel. As we experience Fanny's transport and her engagement with picturesque theory, we sense the impossibility, and certainly the unattractiveness, of escaping the perspectives offered through the arts.[36]

Portraits, too, play tricks not just in representing someone who is absent but in inviting the reader to see beyond the portrait.[37] In *Northanger Abbey*, Catherine Morland stares uncomprehendingly at the portrait of Mrs. Tilney, mystified that no likeness to her children can be detected. Catherine is too admiring of the Tilney children to consider the worrisome possibility that they resemble their father. In *Mansfield Park*, the younger generation disregards the portraits of Rushworth ancestors, a sign of their narrow presentism. In that novel, only Fanny's perspective encompasses both the historical past and distant geographies, as we learn from her possession of a book recounting Macartney's embassy to China and her willingness to ask questions about slavery. For her, the arts serve as windows through which to see the world more clearly; for the Rushworth sisters, the arts are simply a means of winning attention. In *Persuasion*, Anne Elliot's elegance of mind consists in part of her skill at descrying contrasting points of view. When she visits the Great House at Upper Cross, she imagines the portraits of Musgrove ancestors "staring in astonishment" at the "modern minds and manners" of Henrietta and Louisa, who have scattered the room with a pianoforte, a harp, flower stands, and little tables: "Oh! Could the originals of the portraits against the wainscot, could the gentlemen in brown velvet and the ladies in blue satin have seen what was going on, have been conscious of such an overthrow of all order and neatness!" (*P*, 43).[38] As characters interact with art and artifacts, the reader, too, is challenged to follow Austen's game of perspective to see more expansively, more sympathetically, and more ironically.

The essays in this volume draw upon three distinct areas in recent scholarship to examine Austen's use of art and artifacts. The first is the materialist turn within Austen studies, which has focused on Georgian and Regency objects and their role in an increasingly commercialized and commercializing culture.[39] The second is work by art historians such as Marcia Pointon and Ann Bermingham, and literary critics who have drawn on these works, such as Alison Conway and Joe Bray.[40] The third is new scholarship on Austen's attitude toward arts such as music or the theater.[41] Thanks to such work, we are poised to see more fully how the domestic spaces Austen creates in her fiction function as theaters of consciousness in which characters telegraph

Introduction

their cognitive activity through their use of art. Arts are discussed together with artifacts because of the increasing association between amateur artists and consumer activity during Austen's lifetime. In the era before mass production, "a screen painted at home by an Elinor Dashwood would not have looked very different from a similar item bought in a shop."[42] Entrepreneurs responded to the growing class of amateur artists by creating emporia that offered supplies to enhance their work. Consumer goods often traded in the arts. Portrait miniatures, for example, could be parts of snuffboxes, necklaces, watchcases, lockets, or pearl bracelets. The portrait miniature's association with jewelry linked it to luxury and consumer activity. Like many artifacts, portrait miniatures were "sentimentally invested artifact[s]" presented as gifts to announce and cement social relationships.[43] In Austen's hands, however, the permanence promised by such objects proves illusory. Captain Benwick's portrait, lovingly commissioned for one woman, winds up reframed as a token of love for another woman. The friendship commemorated by the watercolor portrait of Harriet Smith in *Emma* begins to fade the moment it is hung above the mantelpiece. The shared passion for music that Marianne Dashwood views as emblematic of her love for Willoughby only intensifies her heartbreak after he leaves. Additionally, interpretive confusion and misunderstanding triggered by art often allows us to understand a character's mental world more clearly. Banished to Portsmouth, Fanny Price feeds on books from a circulating library in an effort to preserve the elegantly ordered lifestyle she has cultivated at Mansfield Park; in the process, she seems to forget that estate's moral disorder and infliction of pain. Admiral Croft's bemusement at a painter's rendition of sailors appearing "at their ease" in a "shapeless old cockleshell" of a ship in a stormy sea, reminds readers of the proximity of shipwreck, an image that underlies his expressed concern regarding Frederick's marital future (*P*, 184, 183). Austen never merely uses the arts or artistic accomplishment to signal idealized femininity in the manner of sentimental novelists. When her characters turn to the arts, we see their minds at work, including their confusions and misperceptions.

Barbara Benedict reminds us of the false divide between private galleries and public emporia by focusing on the thriving exchange of consumer goods during Austen's lifetime. Following Ann Bermingham's account of the rise of the amateur artist, Benedict examines the rise of a consumer society that specialized in amateur needs. In shops such as Rudolph Ackermann's Emporium, S. & J. Fuller's Temple of Fancy, Lackington Allen & Co.'s Temple of the Muses, and Josiah Wedgewood's showrooms, all manner of artistic

Introduction

supplies could be found: transparencies, tracing paper, framed miniatures, paintings, paper, crayons, chalks, watercolors, pencils, camel's hair brushes, and figures on silk for needlework. Ackermann's magazine, *Repository of the Arts*, helped women navigate twin worlds of fashion and art as they considered the many items he offered for sale. Many of these emporia were social venues. They provided drawing lessons, offered tea, and lent books. Benedict capitalizes on this merger of art and consumer culture to trace similarities between Austen's and Alexander Pope's satire of consumerism. Both writers satirize characters' self-representation through objects they carry about them or wear. Pope's *The Rape of the Lock* serves as a shadow text for Austen's *Sense and Sensibility*, with Willoughby imitating the Baron's zeal for collecting women's locks. Benedict's specific interest, however, is the way in which objects in turn possess their possessors. Just as both the Baron and Belinda become defined by the objects they use or wear, characters in Austen's novels risk having their self-understanding reduced to the books they read or to the fashionable items they wear. Mrs. Allen assesses her self-worth exclusively through the quality and style of her gowns. Isabella Thorpe anticipates hungrily the envy she can arouse by the sight of hoop rings on her fingers. Mrs. Norris in *Mansfield Park* exposes her greed through the many objects she pilfers. In *Sanditon*, Sir Edward Denham conceives of himself as a reincarnation of Samuel Richardson's Lovelace. Significantly, as Benedict points out, the shop called "The Library" in *Sanditon*, like the emporia in London, offers both books and consumer goods. Austen and Pope wrote insightfully about how women and men could commodify themselves by surrendering their identity to consumer goods. In Austen's world, hoop rings, hot pressed paper, books, dresses, and other material goods threaten to subsume both judgment and self-understanding.

Austen's understanding of the arts and their relation to gender was influenced by her household's defiance of the gendered segregation of the arts. Although the needle was "an archetypally female instrument," Jane Austen's sailor brothers, Francis (or Frank) and Charles would have had to sew for themselves at sea.[44] Francis Austen, a successful naval commander, was particularly appreciated by family members for his meticulous precision and handiness; he was not above "making very nice fringes for the Drawingroom-Curtains" in Southampton a month before taking up his post as commanding officer of the HMS *St. Albans* (*Letters*, 128).[45] A year earlier, he undertook the task of making clothing for his first child, cutting the fabric, according to his sister Jane, "to admiration" (*Letters*, 120). His extensive and precise practical skills included woodworking, and when early

Introduction

on he learned how to use a lathe, he immediately "turned a very nice little butter-churn for [his niece] Fanny" (*Letters*, 7). Later, he wondered whether "parts of Capt Harville's were drawn from myself," adding that "at least some of his domestic habits, tastes and occupations bear a strong resemblance to mine."[46] But Austen may have owed more to her brother's gender reversals than the inspiration for Captain Harville. Henry Tilney's playful familiarity with the price and quality of muslin in *Northanger Abbey*, Mrs. Croft's comfort living in her husband's naval ships, her skill at adjusting the reins of her husband's carriage to prevent it from overturning, and even Lady Susan's imitation of aspects of Richardson's male rake, Lovelace—each of these reversals owes a debt to Austen's experience of brothers who could engage deftly and cheerfully in domestic arts considered by most to be women's work.

Austen's most remarkable transformation of gender roles can be seen in her generic celebration of the novel itself as a site in which women's mental worlds could be celebrated in tandem with the domestic work that structured their days. In her hands, women's manual and intellectual dexterity is as central to social order as it is to national identity. Nancy Johnson argues in this volume that in *Persuasion*, Anne Elliot supplants the male authority inscribed in both the *Baronetage* and the *Navy Lists*. Sir Walter Elliot finds self-worth in his social representation in the pages of the *Baronetage*, which he displays as he might a portrait. More sympathetically, Frederick Wentworth's activities are inscribed in the *Navy List*, which Anne Elliot uses to trace his naval success. But the authority exemplified by these texts is subordinated, Johnson argues, to the moral authority of the novel's clear-headed heroine, Anne Elliot. Her poise, her "elegance of mind," her endurance as she fights successfully for survival in a dispiriting family environment parallels the more publicly celebrated heroism of Frederick Wentworth. It is Anne who becomes the novel's ruling moral authority, supplanting the masculine authority embodied by both the *Navy List* and the *Baronetage*. Johnson notes that Anne's moral authority results from her consistently cool-headed judgment and rationality, gifts she inherits, significantly, from her mother. Her mother's legacy of good judgment provides Anne with a rich inner life; as a result, she takes pleasure in the beauties of poetry, Italian music, and nature. Her judgment gives her the steadiness and insight necessary to create domestic order, and her devotion to domestic order, far from marginalizing her as subordinate, makes her symbolically central to national character in the novel's closing sentences. By equating Anne's rational judgment with Wentworth's naval success, Austen transforms the concept of the heroine into something more substantial than a cluster of feminine accomplishments. Anne's rational judgment and deep feeling help transform the novel as a genre into a vehicle for depicting both the artfully inflected richness of women's mental worlds and the centrality of that richness to national character.

If we turn from visual artifacts to music, we encounter Austen's complex attitude toward women and music. On the one hand, musical training was almost a given in Austen's day. As Leon Plantinga explains, music was "woven into the very fabric of social interaction: it was part of the system of signs by which people communicated with each other."[47] On the other hand, Austen's three most accomplished pianists—Marianne Dashwood, Georgiana Darcy, and Jane Fairfax—allow their passions to lure them into compromising pacts with men. Austen evidently understood that music's mimetic power represented and intensified feeling.[48] As such, music's affective power posed both dangers and strengths for young women. Though Marianne Dashwood prides herself on her sensibility to the arts and on her depth of feeling, her piano playing becomes a metonymy for her self-indulgence. Her gift for music ought to provide her with a means of needed consolation during heartbreak, but she uses it instead to indulge and intensify her sorrow.[49] The similarly musical Georgiana Darcy and Jane Fairfax allow their passions to lead them into reckless agreements with men. Georgiana is rescued by her brother, but Jane Fairfax's fate remains in question, shadowed by Frank Churchill's prima donna bluster. That Frank is himself an enthusiastic musician, like the more knowingly calculating John Willoughby, seems significant. Yet however concerned Austen was with music's power to intensify the passions, she does not seem to agree with Charles Burney's trivialization of music as "an innocent luxury, unnecessary, indeed, to our existence, but a great improvement and gratification of the sense of hearing."[50] For Austen, music remained a valued resource. As Linda Zionkowski and Miriam Hart explain in their essay in this volume, Austen treads a fine line in her novels when she depicts women's engagement with music. Mary Bennet's violation of decorum in showing off her hard-earned pedantry seems to conform to warnings against the public display of talent in conduct manuals. Yet those characters who either reject a musical education or fail to cultivate their talents—Catherine Morland, Fanny Price, and Emma Woodhouse—"restrict their possibilities for growth." Much less sympathetically, Mrs. Elton's noisy fuss about marriage interfering with her piano exposes her as a poseur more interested in claiming skill than cultivating it. Lady Catherine, too, poses as a hypothetical piano prodigy by making the

Introduction

absurd claim that "if I had ever learnt, I should have been a great proficient" (*P&P*, 194). Like motherhood in Austen's novels, a character's attitude toward her own real or imagined talent amplifies personal traits, for better and often for worse.

Like music, theater, too, stirs ambivalence in Austen. Deborah C. Payne applies her knowledge as a theater historian to sidestep arguments over whether Austen was anti-theatrical or pro-theatrical in order to consider Austen's remarkable prescience in deciding early to turn from writing plays to composing novels. As Payne points out, "dramatic form by its very nature decenters authorial voice, while the demand for completion in performance undermines any sense of ownership or proprietary relationship to the text." Tellingly, Austen's use of dialogue diminished over the course of her career as she increasingly exploited the possibilities offered by narrative. Payne builds on work by Kathleen E. Urda to place firmer generic boundaries between novelistic and theatrical approaches to character. Within *Mansfield Park*, the threat that drama might subsume the novel form is suggested by the stage's physical expansion into Sir Thomas's study, which significantly involves displacing a bookshelf. But this threat is overturned. Like Urda, Payne agrees that by staging rehearsals for Elizabeth Inchbald's *Lovers' Vows* but refusing to stage the actual performance of the play, Austen sidelines drama, replacing it with a much richer venue for interiority—narrative.[51]

Cheryl A. Wilson draws on ballets and stage dance pieces that were typically performed at the theater to suggest that Austen was drawn to the ballet's increasing attention to female physicality to telegraph character and tell stories through movement. The rise of the ballerina placed new emphasis on women's bodies, an emphasis Austen replicates when she depicts Darcy's physical attraction to Elizabeth Bennet, whose eyes and complexion are brightened by her vigorous walk to Netherfield. Both Darcy and Elizabeth must be shaken out of their habitual role as spectators into embodied actors. Like Elizabeth, Darcy is reluctantly drawn into performance. His first performance—his initial proposal of marriage—is a spectacular failure. Eventually, however, both Elizabeth and Darcy learn to trust one another enough to abandon mere guarded observation for embodied interaction. Wilson documents the ballets Austen might have seen and correlates them to Austen's growing interest in women's physicality in her novels.

Two essays examine the intersection of morality and aesthetics. Natasha Duquette examines the significance of the amber cross given to Fanny Price by her sailor brother William in *Mansfield Park*. For Duquette, the cross richly complicates the kind of elegance that Fanny Price acquires. Intended to elevate her socially, the cross entangles her with Henry Crawford, who arranges for his sister to provide her with a matching chain. Fanny is rescued from the debt of using Henry's chain for the cross by the convenient fact that the chain will not fit the cross's bail. Instead, she uses a chain given to her by Edmund. When she wears the cross to the ball that Sir Thomas throws for her, her elegance is confirmed. But for Duquette, Fanny Price's true elegance, unlike the Bertram sisters' false elegance, is telegraphed by the amber cross, with its beauty and its association with suffering. For Austen, elegance, like sensibility, is not good in and of itself. By linking Fanny's simple elegance to her moral virtue, Austen sides with Mary Wollstonecraft's criticism of the dangers posed by fashionable cults of ignorance and beauty.

Elaine Bander turns to Austen's two artless heroines: Catherine Morland and Fanny Price. For all their differences, both Catherine and Fanny use their moral judgment to defy their family and friends. Their artlessness takes different forms: Catherine is merely ignorant and willingly takes lessons in the picturesque from the Tilneys, but Fanny actively resists a training in the arts. But in both cases, the fusion of artlessness and clear moral judgment overturns Shaftesbury's moral theory, which, particularly after it was transmuted through Hume's empiricism, Adam Smith's theory of sympathy, and Rousseau's emphasis on "natural" goodness, threatened to deny rational access to truth. For Shaftesbury, "What is beautiful is harmonious and proportionable, what is harmonious and proportionable is true, and what is at once both beautiful and true is, of consequence, agreeable and good."[52] By contrast, Austen's two artless characters segregate aesthetic and moral judgment. Catherine's moral sense precedes any illumination she acquires from the Tilneys about taste or the picturesque. Fanny shows no Shaftesburian conflation of aesthetics and ethics. Bander concedes Lorrie Clark's observation that Fanny's dialogic moral thought owes a debt to Shaftesbury's concept of soliloquy—that self-scrutinizing power of internal debate used to reason through moral problems.[53] Significantly, however, Fanny's moral soliloquies are not contingent on aesthetic appreciation. She can discriminate between the fine taste and deficient moral judgment of Henry and Mary Crawford. Bander concludes that Austen used the arts "strategically to surprise her readers out of habitual categorical judgments" into using their reason.

That Austen was accustomed to surprising readers is evident, as Marilyn Francus demonstrates by reviewing Austen's reading habits, which were often undertaken with pencil in hand. Scouring copies of books that Austen read, Francus identifies the reading practices illuminated by her notes.

Introduction

Austen was clearly a resistant reader who questioned and even caricatured the historical narratives that books provided. But reading—even private reading—was also part of an extended social practice through which members of the Austen family recorded their responses to particular passages for subsequent readers to find. Looking at the collection in Edward Austen Knight's library at Godmersham, Francus finds a matrix of readers responding to the same text—and to one another. For the Austen family, reading was a collective, social activity. Like Darcy's library in *Pride and Prejudice*, the Godmersham library "is the work of many generations," both through its acquisition of books and also through the marginal comments left for subsequent readers (*P&P*, 41). Francus reads the marginal notes to speculate about inscribers' states of mind, literary criticism, and reading practices.

Tonya Moutray reminds us that Austen's appreciation for the arts extended beyond strictly literary texts to landscape theorists and their paintings. She finds that Austen's depictions of abbeys in *Northanger Abbey* and *Emma* are rooted in aesthetic and discursive models of abbeys provided in William Gilpin's travel writing, in which abbeys appear enmeshed in English history, rooted in English soil, and thus naturalized in ways that for Gilpin diminished their Catholic identities. In *Northanger Abbey*, the gothic menace for which Catherine searches in the Tilney home is only ironically subdued by her acceptance of Henry's rational authority. In *Emma*, however, Austen presents an abbey largely freed from gothic resonances. Managed by the forward-looking Mr. Knightley, Donwell Abbey represents English national identity extracted from its vexed Catholic past. Its depiction as a structure integrated into a characteristically English picturesque landscape follows Gilpin's practice in his aquatints of subordinating or erasing the Catholic resonances of the structures he depicted.[54] The result of this excision in Austen's novels is a new British pastoral landscape that subordinates the violent history of the Reformation to forge an English national identity in which monastic ruins signal Englishness.

Austen's use of the arts is most dramatically complex when she uses the visual arts, particularly portraits, which she almost always deploys to complicate hermeneutic certainty. Far from presenting portraits as reliable likenesses of their sitters, Austen's use of portraits confirms Joe Bray's general claim that in eighteenth-century novels, portraits "often result not in accuracy and clarity of meaning, but rather misunderstanding and confusion, complicating rather than elucidating character."[55] Peter Sabor's essay in this volume revisits Bray's claim as a rich launching point for his own review of

Introduction

how portraits trigger both representation and misrepresentation in Austen's novels.[56] Most famously, Elizabeth Bennet stands transfixed before Mr. Darcy's full-length portrait at Pemberley, which has the effect of causing her to consider the glowing recommendation of the housekeeper, whose name—Mrs. Reynolds—recalls the age's greatest portrait painter, Sir Joshua Reynolds. As Elizabeth gazes, the portrait exerts or oversees a transformation in Elizabeth's mental concept of Darcy, which "softens" as she feels "a more gentle sensation towards the original, than she had ever felt in the height of their acquaintance" (*P&P*, 277). Catherine Morland is similarly entranced by the portrait of Mrs. Tilney, but her surprise that her portrait does not resemble the faces of her children signals her similar misunderstandings about family ties and inheritance. A more public discussion of portraits, this one a portrait miniature, occurs in *Persuasion*, when Anne Elliot and Captain Harville argue over whether men or women are more loyal to lost love. The miniature he holds in his hands directly contradicts his argument, but the discussion it inspires also reaffirms Wentworth's constancy, which fulfills Sabor's claim that Austen uses portraits to overturn expectations and unsettle both the characters who view the portraits and the readers who participate in the characters' experiences of portraits.

Juliette Wells also examines the misunderstandings instigated by portraits by turning to the portrait episode in *Emma*. Wells discusses Emma's portrait of Harriet Smith in the context of two concepts that help us see the dynamics of power behind portrait painting. The first is Marcia Pointon's concept of "portrait contract" between artist, viewer, and sitter; the second is the "intimate portrait" concept behind the lavish 2009 British Museum exhibition that was catalogued by Stephen Lloyd and Kim Sloan. Emma's gender and amateur status realign the power dynamics of the portrait contract so that she, rather than a paying patron, decides the effects of the portrait. Additionally, because her portrait of Harriet is an "intimate portrait" designed for a private family space that she largely controls, Emma has an exaggerated sense of control over her portrait's intended effects. Her expectations are overturned when instead of weaving Harriet into the Woodhouse family, the portrait leads to misunderstanding and confusion. Its enhancements of Harriet's likeness activate obligations, confusions, and friction within the social world for which it is created. As characters comment on Emma's portrait, they reveal more about themselves than they do about either Harriet or the portrait. Significantly, the novel concludes with Emma's marriage to the man whose portrait is missing from her portfolio of portraits, Mr. George Knightley. For Wells, this move from portrait painting to marriage signals Emma's willingness to let go of the artistic control she exerts through her portrait painting in order to engage in the occupations of wifehood and motherhood and the new creative challenges they present.

Jocelyn Harris makes a compelling argument for Austen's exposure to and appreciation of the Regency art of caricature. Austen's letters reveal her eye for visual satire and its exaggeration of physical, moral, and temperamental excess. Using her extensive knowledge of the Regency art world, Harris reads Austen's letters in order to correlate her frequent trips to London with the many shops and streets in which satirical prints were sold or otherwise displayed. The proliferation of visual satire in Regency London would have resonated with Austen's playful and sometimes bawdy humor. In fact, reading Austen's novels against the transgressive world of Regency caricature with its dark humor, cruelty, and sexual knowingness highlights similar strains in Austen's novels. Harris also puts to rest claims that Austen was apolitical by demonstrating how Austen channeled political satire through characters such as John Thorpe or William Walter Elliot. Viewing Austen's satire within the context of James Gillray's caricatures helps us see more clearly how Austen absorbed and adapted the visual satire flooding London into her own verbal satire.

Art was for Austen an everyday activity. Its givenness in women's lives helped her use it to create intimate portraits of women at work, transforming literary characters into identities that readers experience as real. As we follow their journeys, we are invited to see the rich complexity of their mental worlds. Austen asks us to see beyond surface exhibition to the psychological needs motivating artistic engagement. As characters channel sorrow or distress, calm and focus an anxious mind, or engage with or retreat from the noise, confusion, and disorder of their social worlds, they expose a complex interiority that both complicates and enriches Austen's representations of Englishness. Like her developments in narrative technique, her use of the arts forever changed the English novel. When Catherine Morland opens a chest of drawers, when Marianne Dashwood or Anne Elliot sit at the keyboard, when Fanny Price neatly arranges her aunt's needlework, we see their minds in action, just as when we open a novel by Jane Austen, we cross a psychological threshold sure to transform us as well.

Introduction

Notes

1. See Kathryn L. Libin, "Daily Practice, Musical Accomplishment, and the Example of Jane Austen," in *Jane Austen and the Arts: Elegance, Propriety, and Harmony*, ed. Natasha Duquette and Elisabeth Lenckos (Bethlehem, PA: Lehigh University Press, 2014), 3–20; and Linda Zionkowski and Miriam Hart, "'Aunt Jane Began Her Day with Music': Austen and the Female Amateur," *Persuasions* 37 (2015): 165–85.

2. James Edward Austen-Leigh, *A Memoir of Jane Austen: And Other Family Recollections*, ed. Kathryn Sutherland (Oxford: Oxford University Press, 2008), 77. The Austen family's musical transcriptions are preserved at Chawton House in Hampshire, England, and at the Hampshire Record Office in Winchester. They have also been digitized by the University of Southampton's Hartley Library and are available at https://archive.org/details/austenfamilymusicbooks.

3. David Selwyn, *Jane Austen and Leisure* (London: Hambledon, 1999), 78; Deirdre Le Faye, *Jane Austen: A Family Record* (Cambridge: Cambridge University Press, 2004), 50.

4. Deirdre Le Faye, "Anna Lefroy's Original Memories of Jane Austen," *Review of English Studies* 39, no. 155 (1988): 418.

5. Park Honan and others identify as Jane Austen the "Sophia Sentiment" who chided the male authors of the *Loiterer* for their disregard for women's point of view. She would have been about thirteen at the time that Sophia Sentiment expressed her exasperation: "Only conceive, in eight papers, not one sentimental story about love and honour. . No love, and no lady" (*Loiterer* [Dublin, 1792], no. 9 [March 28, 1789]; and Park Honan, *Jane Austen: Her Life* [London: Phoenix, 1997], 60–61).

6. Honoria D. Marsh, *Shades from Jane Austen* (London: Parry Jackman, 1975), xv–xxii.

7. For a discussion of the gendered divisions between arts and crafts, see Clive Edwards, "'Home Is Where the Art Is': Women, Handicrafts and Home Improvements 1750–1900," *Journal of Design History* 19, no. 1 (spring 2006): 11–21. Edwards distinguishes between "crafts," which were associated with women's work, and "art," which was associated with men's activities (12). For the purposes of this essay, "art" refers broadly to both domestic art, such as needlework, and professional work, such as portrait painting and landscape design. See also Rozsika Parker, *The Subversive Stitch: Embroidery and the Making of the Feminine* (London: I. B. Tauris, 2010).

8. Edwards, "Home Is Where the Art Is," 12. See also Judith S. Lewis, "When a House Is Not a Home: Elite English Women and the Eighteenth-Century Country House," *Journal of British Studies* 48, no. 2 (2009): 336–63; and Antje Blank, "Dress," in *Jane Austen in Context*, ed. Janet Todd (Cambridge: Cambridge University Press, 2005), 234–51.

9. Selwyn, *Jane Austen and Leisure*, 68. Selwyn includes photographs of a needle case made by Jane Austen for Mary Lloyd, 67. See also Tiffany Potter, who traces the sometimes hazy distinction between artifacts belonging to "popular culture" and art created in elite culture in *Women, Popular Culture, and the Eighteenth Century* (Toronto: University of Toronto Press, 2012), 6.

10. Jane Austen, *Jane Austen's Letters*, ed. Deirdre Le Faye, 4th ed. (Oxford: Oxford University Press, 2011). All references to Austen's letters refer to this edition and will be provided parenthetically in the text.

Introduction

11. Samuel Richardson, *Clarissa*, ed. Angus Ross (New York: Penguin, 1985), 231. See also Joe Bray, *The Portrait in Fiction of the Romantic Period* (New York: Routledge, 2016); Alison Conway, *Private Interests: Women, Portraiture, and the Visual Culture of the English Novel, 1709–1791* (Toronto: University of Toronto Press, 2001); and Juliette Wells, "'In Music She Had Always Used to Feel Alone in the World': Jane Austen, Solitude, and the Artistic Woman," *Persuasions* 26 (2004): 98–110.

12. Mary Wollstonecraft, *A Vindication of the Rights of Woman*, in *Works of Mary Wollstonecraft*, ed. Marilyn Butler and Janet Todd (Abingdon: Pickering and Chatto, 1989), 148.

13. Hannah More, *Strictures on the Modern System of Female Education*, 2 vols. (London, 1799), 1:62, 63. See also Gary Kelly, "Education and Accomplishments," in *Jane Austen in Context*, ed. Todd, 252–61. As Devoney Looser concludes, Austen "has been and remains a figure at the vanguard of reinforcing tradition *and* promoting social change" (Looser, *The Making of Jane Austen* [Baltimore, MD: Johns Hopkins University Press, 2017], 3).

14. For a full development of this insight, see Suzanne Juhasz, "Bonnets and Balls: Reading Jane Austen's Letters," *Centennial Review* 31, no. 1 (1987): 90.

15. David Andrews Graves provided an early account of computer-generated analysis of word frequency in *Emma*: "Reading the computer-generated list of most frequently used words reveals a high incidence of words about feelings (both positive and negative), cognition, judgment, discourse, and relationships. These words appear frequently in all of Austen's novels, and make a significant portion of her vocabulary fingerprint" (Graves, "Computer Analysis of Word Usage in *Emma*," *Persuasions* 21 [1999]: 208). See also Raksangob Wijitsopon, "A Corpus-Based of the Style in Jane Austen's Novels," *Manusya: Journal of Humanities Regular* 16, no. 1 (2013): 41–64; Jeffrey A. Nigro, "Visualizing Jane Austen and Jane Austen Visualizing," *Persuasions* 29, no. 1 (winter 2008); Sarah J. Kerr, "When Computer Science Met Austen and Edgeworth," *NPPSH [New Perspectives: Postgraduate Symposium on the Humanities]: Reflections* 1 (2017): 38–52; and the remarkable website by Laura White and others, Austen Said: Patterns of Diction in Austen's Major Novels, http://austen.unl.edu.

16. For Norman Page, Austen's "deliberate playing-down of the surface of life" intensifies "the localized and limited world of the novel to those wider issues of conduct which are, for her, all-important, and which alone justify the claim of the novel to be taken seriously." The effect, he argues, is to focus attention "upon speech and action, and the analysis of their implications." The essays here contribute to Page's attention to language, though they find greater significance than he allows in Austen's economical but significant use of art and artifacts (see Norman Page, *The Language of Jane Austen* [1972, repr., New York: Routledge, 2013], 58–59).

17. Jane Austen, *Sense and Sensibility*, ed. Edward Copeland (Cambridge: Cambridge University Press, 2006), 151. Subsequent references are to this edition and will be supplied parenthetically within the text.

18. Jessica A. Volz, *Visuality in the Novels of Austen, Radcliffe, Edgeworth and Burney* (London: Anthem, 2017), 41. Volz argues that Austen uses visual cues "alongside free indirect discourse" to create correspondences between characters and the estates they inhabit or the material arts they own or experience (85). Volz's claim that "visuality,

Introduction

more than free indirect discourse, provided women novelists with a discreet means of shifting views and viewpoints in order to show that even if their heroines conformed outwardly, they were beginning to see and think in ways that called appearances and patriarchal authority into question" may overstate the merits of visuality over free indirect discourse, but her emphasis on the significance of visuality in Austen's novels is worthy of additional exploration (22).

19. Lauren Miskin, "'True Indian Muslin' and the Politics of Consumption in Jane Austen's *Northanger Abbey*," *Journal for Early Modern Cultural Studies* 15, no. 2 (spring 2015): 6.

20. Jane Austen, *Pride and Prejudice*, ed. Pat Rogers (Cambridge: Cambridge University Press, 2005), 242. Subsequent references are to this edition and will be supplied parenthetically within the text.

21. Austen, Jane, *Persuasion*, ed. Janet Todd and Antje Blank (Cambridge: Cambridge University Press, 2006), 106. Subsequent references are to this edition and will be supplied parenthetically within the text.

22. As Amanda Vickery points out, an unmarried woman "had to be poised to collect her things together and move on, nesting in a corner of someone else's house," adding that "continuity and familiarity lay in the tea tray, the ornaments and the linens, not in bricks and mortar." She concludes that "the comfort of home inhered in what she could take with her" (Vickery, *Behind Closed Doors: At Home in Georgian England* [New Haven, CT: Yale University Press, 2009], 230; see also 207–30).

23. For a more cynical reading of Mrs. Smith, see Karen Bloom Gevirtz, *Life after Death* (Newark: University of Delaware Press, 2005), 156–57.

24. Selwyn, *Jane Austen and Leisure*, 68.

25. Jane Austen, *Mansfield Park*, ed. John Wiltshire (Cambridge: Cambridge University Press, 2005), 76. Subsequent references are to this edition and will be supplied parenthetically within the text.

26. Nigel Everett, *The Tory View of Landscape* (New Haven, CT: Yale University Press, 1994), 188.

27. A. Walton Litz, "The Picturesque in *Pride and Prejudice*," *Persuasions* 1 (1979): 13–24.

28. Alistair M. Duckworth, *The Improvement of the Estate: A Study of Jane Austen's Novels* (Baltimore, MD: Johns Hopkins University Press, 1971), 71.

29. Anne Toner, "Landscape as Literary Criticism," *Critical Survey* 26, no. 1 (2014): 12. As Toner notes, Anne K. Mellor argues that Barbauld started "the study of what we now call narratology" (10). See also Mellor, *Mothers of the Nation: Women's Political Writing in England, 1780–1830* (Bloomington: Indiana University Press, 2000), 94.

30. Toner, "Landscape," 9. See also Jocelyn Harris, *Jane Austen's Art of Memory* (Cambridge: Cambridge University Press, 1989), 34–47. For Alice Drum, Austen understood the "'vertical' ascendancy of the new professional class, as opposed to the 'horizontal' acquisition of power and status that marked the landed classes in the pre-industrial world" (Drum, "Jane Austen and the Professions," *College Literature* 36, no. 3 [2009]: 110).

31. Rosemary Bodenheimer, "Looking at the Landscape in Jane Austen," *Studies in English Literature, 1500–1900* 21, no. 4 (1981): 605–83. See also James Brown, "Jane Austen's Mental Maps," *Critical Survey* 26, no. 1 (2014): 20–41; Roger E. Moore, *Jane*

Introduction

Austen and the Reformation: Remembering the Sacred Landscape (Burlington, VT: Ashgate, 2016); and Peter Knox-Shaw, *Jane Austen and the Enlightenment* (Cambridge: Cambridge University Press, 2011).

32. Everett, *The Tory View of Landscape*, 188.

33. For additional discussions of General Tilney's horticultural interests, see Deidre Shauna Lynch, "'Young Ladies Are Delicate Plants': Jane Austen and Greenhouse Romanticism," *ELH* 77, no. 3 (2010): 689–729; and Claire Lamont, "Domestic Architecture," in *Jane Austen in Context*, ed. Todd, 225–31.

34. Julie Park, "What the Eye Cannot See: Interior Landscapes in 'Mansfield Park,'" *Eighteenth Century* 54, no. 2 (2013): 170. See also Ruta Baublyté Kaufmann, *The Architecture of Space-Time in the Novels of Jane Austen* (New York: Palgrave Macmillan, 2018).

35. Park, "What the Eye Cannot See," 175.

36. A fuller discussion of the difficulties the reader experiences identifying Fanny's authentic feeling can be found in David Marshall, *The Frame of Art: Fictions of Aesthetic Experience, 1750–1815* (Baltimore, MD: Johns Hopkins University Press, 2005), 72–90. See also Doug Murray, "Spectatorship in *Mansfield Park*: Looking and Overlooking," *Nineteenth-Century Literature* 52, no. 1 (1997): 1–26.

37. See Lance Bertelsen, "Jane Austen's Miniatures Painting, Drawing, and the Novels," *Modern Language Quarterly* 45, no. 4 (1984): 357. See also Joe Bray, "Belinda, *Emma*, and the 'Likeness' of the Portrait," *Nineteenth-Century Contexts* 33, no. 1 (2011): 1–15.

38. Laura Mooneyham White opens *Jane Austen's Anglicanism* (Burlington, VT: Ashgate, 2011) with this image (3).

39. Since Claudia L. Johnson's groundbreaking *Jane Austen: Women, Politics, and the Novel* (Chicago: Chicago University Press, 1988), critics have probed Austen's novels for their references to her world. Janine Barchas, Margaret Doody, and others have recently documented the precision with which Austen constructed fictional worlds within precise temporal, spatial, and linguistic contexts, demonstrating her dense artistic enmeshing of those worlds in English history. Similarly, Paula Byrne has shown how objects in Austen's novels reflect her themes. A series of essay collections have focused on Austen's interaction with her material world. See Janine Barchas, *Matters of Fact in Jane Austen: History, Location, and Celebrity* (Baltimore, MD: Johns Hopkins University Press, 2012); Paula Byrne, *The Real Jane Austen: A Life in Small Things* (New York: Harper, 2013); Margaret Doody, *Jane Austen's Names: Riddles, Persons, Places* (Chicago: University of Chicago Press, 2016); Duckworth, *The Improvement of the Estate*; Claudia L. Johnson and Clara Tuite, eds. *A Companion to Jane Austen* (Malden, MA: Wiley-Blackwell, 2009); Le Faye, *Jane Austen: A Family Record*; Le Faye, *Jane Austen: The World of Her Novels* (New York: Abrams, 2002); Selwyn, *Jane Austen and Leisure*; Kathryn Sutherland, ed., *Jane Austen: Writer in the World* (Oxford: Bodleian Library, 2017); and Todd, ed., *Jane Austen in Context*.

40. See Ann Bermingham, *Learning to Draw: Studies in the Cultural History of a Polite and Useful Art* (New Haven, CT: Yale University Press, 2000); Joe Bray, *The Portrait in Fiction of the Romantic Period* (New York: Routledge, 2016); Alison Conway, *Private Interests: Women, Portraiture, and the Visual Culture of the English Novel, 1709–1791* (Toronto: University of Toronto Press, 2001); and Marcia Pointon, *Hanging the Head: Portraiture and Social Formation in Eighteenth-Century England* (New Haven, CT: Yale University Press, 1993).

Introduction

41. See, particularly, the essays in Duquette and Lenckos, eds., *Jane Austen and the Arts*. See also Kathryn Libin, "Music, Character, and Social Standing in Jane Austen's *Emma*," *Persuasions* 22 (2000): 15–30; Selwyn, *Jane Austen and Leisure*; Lawrence Lipking, *The Ordering of the Arts in Eighteenth-Century England* (Princeton, NJ: Princeton University Press, 1970); Wells, "In Music"; Juliette Wells, "A Harpist Arrives at Mansfield Park: Music and the Moral Ambiguity of Mary Crawford," *Persuasions* 28 (2006): 101–14; Gillen D'Arcy Wood, *Romanticism and Music Culture in Britain, 1770–1840: Virtue and Virtuosity* (Cambridge: Cambridge University Press, 2010), and "Austen's Accomplishment: Music and the Modern Heroine," in *A Companion to Jane Austen*, ed. Johnson and Tuite, 366–76; and Zionkowski; "Aunt Jane Began Her Day with Music."

42. David Selwyn, "Consumer Goods," in *Jane Austen in Context*, ed. Todd, 216. See also "Ariane Fennetaux, "Female Crafts: Women and *Bricolage* in Late Georgian Britain, 1750–1820," in *Women and Things, 1750–1950: Gendered Material Strategies*, ed. Maureen Daly Goggin and Beth Fowkes Tobin (Burlington, VT: Ashgate, 2009); and Deborah Simonton, "Threading the Needle, Pulling the Press: Gender, Skill and the Tools of the Trade in Eighteenth-Century European Town," *Cultural History* 1, no. 2 (2012): 180–204.

43. Marcia Pointon, "'Surrounded with Brilliants': Miniature Portraits in Eighteenth-Century England," *Art Bulletin* 83, no. 1 (2002): 48.

44. Vickery, *Behind Closed Doors*, 238.

45. See also Selwyn, *Jane Austen and Leisure*, 70.

46. Le Faye, *Jane Austen: A Family Record*, 274. See also Jocelyn Harris, *A Revolution Almost beyond Expression* (Newark: Delaware University Press, 2007), 308.

47. Leon Plantinga, "The Piano and the Nineteenth Century," in *Nineteenth Century Piano Music*, ed. R. Larry Todd (New York: Routledge, 2004), 3; see also Gillen D'Arcy Wood, "Austen's Accomplishment," in *A Companion to Jane Austen*, ed. Johnson and Tuite, 366–76.

48. Lipking, *The Ordering of the Arts*, 218–24.

49. As Stuart Tave remarked long ago, "The potency of Marianne's sensibility makes her morally impotent; her small degree of fortitude is overcome, she is without any power because she is without any desire of command over herself and the slightest mention of anything relative to Willoughby overpowers her in an instant" (Tave, *Some Words of Jane Austen* [Chicago: Chicago University Press, 1973], 81).

50. As cited in Lipking, *The Ordering of the Arts*, 280.

51. Kathleen E. Urda, "Why the Show Must Not Go On: Real Character and the Absence of Theatrical Performances in *Mansfield Park*," *Eighteenth-Century Fiction* 26, no. 2 (winter 2013/2014): 281–302.

52. Anthony Ashley Cooper, Third Earl of Shaftesbury, *Characteristics of Men, Manners, Opinions, Times*, ed. Lawrence Klein (Cambridge: Cambridge University Press, 1999), 415.

53. Lorrie Clark, "Shaftesbury's Art of 'Soliloquy' in *Mansfield Park*," *Persuasions* 24 (2002): 59–70.

54. Moutray's depiction of Austen's interest in abbeys differs from that offered by Roger E. Moore, *Jane Austen and the Reformation* (Burlington, VT: Ashgate, 2016); and Beth Kowaleski Wallace, "'Penance and Mortification For ever': Jane Austen and the

Ambient Noise of Catholicism," *Tulsa Studies in Women's Literature* 31, no. 1–2 (2012): 159–75.

55. Bray, *The Portrait in Fiction*, 1.

56. Peter Sabor's essay in this volume presents a significant revision of claims he articulated in an earlier essay, "'Staring in Astonishment': Portraits and Prints in *Persuasions*," in *Jane Austen's Business: Her World and Her Profession*, ed. Juliet McMaster and Bruce Stovel (Basingstoke, UK: Palgrave Macmillan, 1996), 17–29.

Portraiture as Misrepresentation in the Novels and Early Writings of Jane Austen

PETER SABOR

Jane Austen, according to her brother Henry in his "Biographical Notice of the Author," "had not only an excellent taste for drawing, but, in her earlier days, evinced great power of hand in the management of the pencil."[1] Regrettably, no such pencil drawings by the novelist are known to be extant. In a letter of November 17–18, 1798, to her sister Cassandra, then visiting their brother Edward and his family at Godmersham Park, Austen refers to a gift that she has sent to one of their nephews, Edward's three-year-old son George. "I hope," she writes, "George was pleased with my designs. Perhaps they would have suited him as well had they been less elaborately finished; but an artist cannot do anything slovenly." At the end of the letter, Austen adds, "I shall send George another picture when I write next."[2] If these lost sketches could be recovered, they might throw light on Austen's use of portraiture in her novels, the subject of this essay.

When, nineteen years later, Henry wrote his memoir of Jane Austen, he might have recalled "elaborately finished" pictures such as these as signs of her artistic powers. He would have been able to judge their merits, since he was an amateur artist himself: in 1805, he was giving drawing lessons at Godmersham to his sister-in-law Harriet Bridges, as Fanny Knight records in her diary for May 27.[3] Of the Austen siblings, however, it was neither Jane nor Henry who was best known for artistic prowess but rather Cassandra. In a letter of January 3–5, 1801, when Cassandra was at Godmersham and Jane was helping their parents pack up the family's belongings at Steventon rectory before they moved to Bath, Jane assures her sister that while most of the paintings and prints in the house will be left to the rectory's new incumbents, their elder brother James and his family, "Your own Drawings will not cease to be your own" (*Letters*, 70).

One of Cassandra's later compositions, a quite accomplished watercolor, is taken from an engraving by James Fittler of a painting entitled *Pedlars* by

Portraiture as Misrepresentation

Fig. 1. Cassandra Austen, copy of an engraving of George Morland's *Pedlars*, 1808, watercolor. (Collection of Chris Viveash)

George Morland (fig. 1). It depicts a group of agricultural workers with a young child and bears Cassandra's initials, "CEA," and the date of 1808, when she, Jane, and their mother were living in Southampton.[4] Other sketches by Cassandra are now at Jane Austen's House Museum. Of particular interest is a watercolor portrait of her niece Fanny, eldest daughter of Edward Austen, undertaken, according to Fanny's diary, on September 3, 1805, four months before her thirteenth birthday (fig. 2). It depicts, in the words of Fanny's biographer Margaret Wilson, "a slender young girl in a simple high-waisted dress with medium brown hair swept up at the back in a comb. In profile she has a pleasant face with a fairly sharp nose, as she sits at a table with a paint-box beside her, absorbed in doing a painting herself."[5] It is this latter detail that makes the portrait so intriguing. What might the subject of the portrait be portraying: Cassandra the artist, herself the sitter, or something else entirely? And if the portrait in the artist's portrait is of Cassandra, is she here experimenting with a *mise en abîme* technique, making the portrait more complex than it might seem at first glance?

That Cassandra was interested in unconventional portraiture is further suggested by her two depictions of Jane: the first a rear-view sketch, still in private hands, and the second the famous sketch at the National Portrait Gallery. The earlier of the two is a watercolor, like Cassandra's portrait of

Fig. 2. Cassandra Austen, portrait of Fanny Knight, 1808, watercolor. (Jane Austen's House Museum, Chawton)

Fanny Knight, executed a year earlier in 1804 and bearing the date and Cassandra's initials on the back. In a letter of August 8, 1862, Austen's niece Anna Lefroy refers to it as follows: "I would give a good deal, that is as much as I could afford, for a sketch which Aunt Cassandra made of her in one of their expeditions—sitting down out of doors on a hot day, with her bonnet strings untied."[6] Although R. W. Chapman gallantly claims that "it shows the graceful outline of a seated lady,"[7] it has caused much vexation to Austen biographers wishing to see their subject's face. Park Honan, for instance, terms it a "rather demure back-view watercolour of Jane Austen, who sits in blue and white with her face hidden by a poke bonnet as if the watercolourist had wished to reveal very little."[8] For David Nokes, "this curious, unprepossessing sketch" shows "a plump, dumpy woman seated on a tuft or stool, gazing away from us into a white vacant blankness," while revealing "the merest hint of a plump, pink child-like curve of cheek."[9] Such concealment, however, was very much in tune both with Cassandra's portraiture and with Jane Austen's complex treatments of portraiture in her novels.

Cassandra's better-known pencil and watercolor sketch of her sister, unsigned and undated but probably drawn in about 1810, when its subject was in her mid-thirties, is equally enigmatic. For Chapman, it was merely a "disappointing scratch."[10] Other critics, however, have been struck by the sitter's apparent belligerence. Park Honan, for instances, notes the "defiant, slightly aloof expression," Valerie Grosvenor Myer finds that "the mouth . . . looks small and mean," while Margaret Kirkham writes that "the arms and hands, crudely drawn, are crossed in an uncompromising manner and the whole attitude of the sitter appears somewhat confrontational."[11] In its Victorian refashioning by a professional portraitist, James Andrews of Maidenhead, who furnished a painting based on the sketch that in turn was engraved as a frontispiece for James Edward Austen-Leigh's *Memoir of Jane Austen* (1870), Cassandra's sour sketch is sweetened. As Kathryn Sutherland remarks, "the face is softer, its expression pliant, and the eyes only pensively averted."[12] It is the far more suggestive original drawing that reveals both Cassandra and Jane Austen's interest in the capacity of portraiture to do something other than merely flatter its subject, as the painting by Andrews does so egregiously.

Austen's fascination with portraiture, and with the power of art to deceive, is manifested in one of the satirical pieces that she wrote as a teenager, "The History of England," dated November 26, 1791, three weeks before her sixteenth birthday. It was conceived in collaboration with her sister, who provided thirteen medallion portraits of the monarchs who feature in Austen's text, all but one grandiloquently signed "C. E. Austen pinx" (painted, *pinxit*, by Cassandra Elizabeth Austen). They are, as Deirdre Le Faye observes, "as deliberately misleading as the text, portraying the monarchs not as royal heads of state but as contemporary and sometimes disreputable-looking people."[13] Like most of her early writings, Austen's miniature history is a parody. She wrote it as a mocking response to a huge, four-volume history of England by Oliver Goldsmith, who claimed to narrate his story in a detached, impartial fashion. Austen, in contrast, aided by her sister, set out to write an overtly arbitrary and bigoted account, with the Stuarts as the heroes and Elizabeth I as the principal villain of her story.

In Austen's history, portraiture makes its way quite literally into the text, with each section of the manuscript headed by one of Cassandra's witty and allusive watercolor portraits.[14] On two occasions, Austen refers specifically to these illustrations. Of Edward IV, she declares ironically, "This Monarch was famous only for his Beauty and his Courage, of which the Picture we have here given of him, and his undaunted Behaviour in marrying one

Fig. 3. Cassandra Austen, *Edward IV*, in Jane Austen, "The History of England," 1791, ink and watercolor. (British Library Board, Add. MS 59874, f. 7)

Woman while he was engaged to another, are sufficient proofs."[15] Cassandra's portrait of Edward in contrast, with its protruding lips, turned-up nose, and staring eyes, makes him among the least attractive of the monarchs (fig. 3). He is dressed like an eighteenth-century farmer rather than a fifteenth-century king, and he looks more like a country bumpkin than the nation's sovereign. And heightening the joke is that Cassandra, in this instance, merely copied her portrait of Edward IV from a satirical print by Henry Bunbury, *Recruits* (1780):[16] the model for Cassandra's oafish king was a caricature, designed to ridicule the wretched state of the British army (fig. 4). The illustration contrasts comically with Austen's reference to Edward's "Beauty and his Courage," taken from Goldsmith's *History of England*, which declares that "his best qualities were courage and beauty."[17] Cassandra also made use, in Bunbury's print, of a young officer examining the recruits, who furnished her with a sly portrait of Henry V (fig. 5). In her text, Jane Austen remarks that Henry V "turned his thoughts to France, where he went and fought the famous Battle of Agincourt" (177), but it is hard to imagine Cassandra's monarch, with his somewhat quizzical gaze, fighting anyone, let alone defeating the mighty French army in battle. Further complicating matters here is a sly allusion by Cassandra to her and Jane's brother Henry, then serving in the Royal Regiment of Artillery: as Christine Alexander notes, Henry V is wearing Henry Austen's military uniform.[18]

Fig. 4. Henry Bunbury, *Recruits*, 1780, stipple engraving. (Library of Congress Online)

Austen's second reference to her sister's illustrations in "The History of England" is wonderfully surreal. Her two-sentence account of Edward V, much the shortest in her history, begins with the remark that "This unfortunate Prince lived so little a while that no body had time to draw his picture" (*J*, 179). Despite this mock claim, however, Goldsmith's *History* contains a portrait of the youthful monarch. And although Cassandra did not provide an illustration, Austen left space for one in her manuscript, together with an incomplete caption, "Edward the" (459n31). The textual lacuna parallels the absence of the image: "Edward the [blank]" is a perfectly apt title for a void in search of an illustration.

Austen's fascination with art, and its power to deceive, emerges on another occasion in her juvenilia, which she collected in three notebooks, entitled,

Fig. 5. Cassandra Austen, *Henry V*, in Jane Austen, "The History of England," 1791, ink and watercolor. (British Library Board, Add. MS 59874, f. 4)

as though they formed a novel, "Volume the First," "Volume the Second," and "Volume the Third." The second of two items in "Volume the Third," "Catharine, or the Bower," dated August 1792, is the longest of these early writings. It contains a discussion between the impoverished heroine and her false friend, Miss Stanley, who is bent on singing the praises of the wealthy and "quite delightful" Maria Halifax: "Maria is one of the cleverest Girls that ever were known—Draws in Oils, and plays anything by sight. She promised me one of her Drawings before I left Town, but I entirely forgot to ask her for it—. I would give anything to have one" (*J*, 257). Miss Stanley is a forerunner of hypocritical young women such as Lucy Steele in *Sense and Sensibility* and Isabella Thorpe in *Northanger Abbey*, whose characteristically hyperbolic rhetoric betrays their blatant insincerity. Despite her ability to use oil paint, requiring greater proficiency than the use of watercolors, Maria Halifax's drawings are of so little significance that her supposed admirer, Miss Stanley, has somehow forgotten to ask for one. And Catherine, for all her naivety, readily sees that the words "I would give anything to have one" mean just the opposite: that Miss Stanley would give nothing. A sharp reply that Austen subsequently deleted reveals Catherine's understanding of both the emptiness of Miss Stanley's protestations and the worthlessness of Maria's productions: "Why indeed, if Maria will give my Friend a drawing, she can have nothing to complain of, but as she does not write in Spirits, I suppose she has not yet been fortunate enough to be so distinguished" (*J*, 257).

Portraiture as Misrepresentation

In her illuminating study of eighteenth-century portraiture, *Hanging the Head*, Marcia Pointon observes that "the portrait has no unproblematic referent; it cannot be explained as a correlative to the text of a subject's life."[19] Her remark throws light on many of the passages in Austen's novels that I wish to consider here; portraits repeatedly prove to be far more disturbing than the characters who create, sit for, or admire them might wish them to be. Consider, for instance, the scene that concludes volume 1 of *Sense and Sensibility* (1811) in which Lucy Steele, in a tense conversation with Elinor Dashwood, reveals the secret of her engagement to Edward Ferrars. Both here and in Austen's final completed novel, *Persuasion* (1817), a prized miniature plays a crucial role: in this case a portrait of Edward that Lucy displays as an emblem of her exclusive rights to its subject. "To prevent the possibility of mistake," she tells Elinor, "be so good as to look at this face. It does not do him justice to be sure, but yet I think you cannot be deceived as to the person it was drew for.—I have had it above these three years."[20] The likeness of the portrait is not in question, but the significance of possessing it certainly is. As Kazuko Hisamori observes: "The tension between the two shifts from a verbal to a visual one. Elinor is forced to look at her lover's 'face.' Like a photograph one might put in a present-day mobile phone, a miniature is portable. Lucy's nasty trick may be likened to showing off to one's rival an intimate photograph stored in a mobile phone. Elinor returns Edward's miniature "'almost instantly.' She cannot bear to look at it any longer."[21] After Elinor is compelled to acknowledge that the subject is Edward, Lucy piles on the pressure with her next remark:

> "I have never been able," continued Lucy, "to give him my picture in return, which I am very much vexed at, for he has always been so anxious to get it! But I am determined to sit for it the very first opportunity."
> "You are quite in the right," replied Elinor calmly. (*S&S*, 151)

Lucy has already told Elinor that she and Edward have been engaged for four years; her claim to have lacked any opportunity to have her portrait taken thus rings ludicrously false. Miniatures, at this time, could be obtained quite cheaply in rural areas, although fashionable London portraitists would charge much more.[22] Lucy, though, seems to have been unwilling to invest any money at all in commissioning a miniature to give to her fiancé.

In another power move, Lucy next shows Elinor a letter from Edward, knowing that the handwriting will be readily recognizable: "You know his hand, I dare say, a charming one it is" (*S&S*, 154). Finally, she returns to the miniature which, she claims, gives her "comfort," while "poor Edward has not even *that*. If he had but my picture, he says he should be easy" (154). By the end of the novel, though, Lucy is ready to return the portrait to its subject at "the first opportunity" (414)—the same meaningless phrase she had used in announcing her intention of sitting for her own portrait. All this foreshadows Austen's use of the miniature in *Persuasion*, in which Lucy's crass inconstancy gives way to Captain Benwick's much more subtle, and sympathetic, mutability.

A less prominent passage in *Sense and Sensibility* involves the youngest Dashwood sister, Margaret, who tells Elinor of her conviction that Marianne will soon be married to Willoughby: "'You have said so,' replied Elinor, 'almost every day since they first met on High-church Down; and they had not known each other a week, I believe, before you were certain that Marianne wore his picture round her neck; but it turned out to be only the miniature of our great uncle'" (70–71). That Marianne wears around her neck a portrait not of her beloved Willoughby but rather of her great uncle, the "old Gentleman" who figures prominently in the opening chapter of the novel, is an intriguing point. He is, after all, the relative who had willed his fortune not to the needy Mrs. Dashwood and her daughters but to John Dashwood, who is readily persuaded by his appalling wife to give his half sisters nothing at all. As Janet Todd observes, "the usual reason why a person would wear a miniature of an old relative is in hope of inheriting or in gratitude for having done so; the detail suggests Marianne's refusal to enter the system of money relationships in which her worldly lover Willoughby is enmeshed."[23] Marianne, then, is the antithesis of both Lucy and Captain Benwick; rather than discarding her prized miniature in response to changing circumstances, she chooses to wear it with no obvious reason for doing so.

In *Pride and Prejudice* too, pictures are used to afford insights into their subjects and their viewers. Caroline Bingley, for instance, mocks Darcy about his interest in Elizabeth Bennet by belittling her uncle's position as a lowly attorney: "Do let the portraits of your uncle and aunt Philips be placed in the gallery at Pemberley. Put them next to your great uncle the judge. They are in the same profession, you know; only in different lines. As for your Elizabeth's picture, you must not attempt to have it taken, for what painter could do justice to those beautiful eyes?"[24]

While Miss Bingley's sarcasm is intended to disparage Elizabeth's appearance, suggesting that her eyes and her looks in general are nothing out of the ordinary, her remark supports both Jane and Cassandra Austen's view of portraiture. In Austen's fiction, portraits do not "do justice" to their models; what makes the pictures interesting is the extent to which they are not purely representational.

Pride and Prejudice also contains the best-known portrait scene in any of Austen's novels. Elizabeth here is being led around the great house at Pemberley by Darcy's housekeeper, the aptly named Mrs. Reynolds. Here she sees miniatures of Wickham, described by Mrs. Reynolds as "very wild," of Darcy, "a very handsome gentleman," and of his sister Georgiana, "the handsomest young lady that ever was seen; and so accomplished!" (273, 274). Elizabeth is then shown a picture gallery with "many good paintings" (276), which, knowing nothing about art, she finds less interesting and intelligible than some crayon drawings by Georgiana. All this pales, however, before a second, larger portrait of Darcy, depicted "with such a smile over the face, as she remembered to have sometimes seen, when he looked at her." Elizabeth is captivated by this portrait, "and as she stood before the canvas, on which he was represented, and fixed his eyes upon herself, she thought of his regard with a deeper sentiment of gratitude than it had ever raised before; she remembered its warmth, and softened its impropriety of expression" (277).

Particularly striking here is the phrase "fixed his eyes upon herself," aptly described by Isobel Armstrong as "an amazing moment of syntactic ambiguity."[25] The indeterminate syntax allows both Elizabeth and the portrait of Darcy (and by extension Darcy himself) to be fixing his eyes upon her; either Elizabeth is becoming Darcy, looking at herself through his eyes, or she finds herself unable to avoid his gaze. And thanks to this ambiguity the portrait ceases to have a straightforward function: it does much more than merely represent its subject, taking, instead, an active role in Elizabeth's growing fascination with Darcy. Further ambiguities in this passage are noted by Joe Bray, who observes that the noun "regard" signifies "both [Darcy's] esteem for [Elizabeth] and, in a more literal sense, his view of her." And similarly, as Bray notes, "the phrase 'impropriety of expression' refers both to Darcy's countenance in the painting and to his first proposal and the condescending and 'improper' way in which he then expressed his 'regard' for her."[26]

Portraiture also plays a small but significant part in *Mansfield Park*. Mr. Rushworth's seat, Sotherton, contains, we are told, an abundance of pictures, some of them good, "but the larger part were family portraits, no longer any thing to any body but Mrs. Rushworth."[27] Rushworth himself, characteristically, takes no interest in these family memorials, any more than he regrets having cut down "three fine old trees . . . that grew too near the house," which, he opines, "opens the prospect amazingly" (65). Austen counterbalances the Sotherton family portraits, on open display but unwanted, with the items that constitute Fanny Price's "nest of comforts" in the East room at Mansfield Park: "three transparencies, made in a rage for transparencies, for the three lower panes of one window, where Tintern Abbey held its station between a cave in Italy, and a moonlight lake in Cumberland; a collection of family profiles thought unworthy of being anywhere else, over the mantlepiece, and by their side and pinned against the wall, a small sketch of a ship sent four years ago from the Mediterranean by William, with H.M.S. Antwerp at the bottom, in letters as tall as the mainmast" (178–79). Maria and Julia Crawford, who presumably created these once fashionable transparencies, have lost interest in their work; Fanny, however, notoriously untraveled and ignorant of geography, treasures them for affording glimpses of worlds unknown to her. It is significant that the transparencies are described more fully than the much grander family portraits on display at Sotherton. So too is the sketch of a ship, evidently one on which he had served, by Fanny's sailor brother William. Austen creates a telling contrast between this sketch and Mary Crawford's fatuous advice to Fanny, in the preceding chapter, that she should "get his picture drawn before he went to sea again" (173). Fanny, of course, lacks the means to commission even the cheapest kind of professional portrait of her brother, but she delights in the amateur drawing that he has created himself.

Emma too contains a set-piece portrait scene, in which the heroine's whole-length watercolor portrait of Harriet Smith is subjected to the scrutiny of her family and friends. Mrs. Weston, who as Emma's former governess is well aware of her shortcomings, contends that the picture flatters Harriet, who has "not those eye-brows and eye-lashes. It is the fault of her face that she has them not." Mr. Knightley, more bluntly, declares, "You have made her too tall." Mr. Woodhouse, forever hypochondriac, finds fault with the model's "sitting out of doors, with only a little shawl over her shoulders—and it makes one think she must catch cold."[28] Mr. Elton, exclaiming, "I never saw such a likeness" (49), deftly applauds the skill of the artist while also, ostensibly, admiring the beauty of her sitter. As Emma's undeclared admirer, he must defend her artistic prowess against the criticism of Mrs. Weston, Mr. Knightley, and Mr. Woodhouse. Thus he ascribes the full eyebrows and eyelashes of the portrait, absent in the sitter, to "the effect of shade"; the exaggerated height to the fact of Harriet's sitting down, and the supposed "proportions, foreshortening" that this entails; and the light clothing in an outdoor setting to "the naiveté of Miss

Smith's manners" (49, 50). Emma is well aware that Elton protests too much; she knows, for example, that she has made her subject too tall, "but would not own it" (49). Harriet, we have already been told, is "short, plump and fair" (22); Emma, in contrast, is tall and elegant. The portrait thus creates an image that resembles Emma as much as its ostensible subject, while misrepresenting both.

This strange, hybrid portrait, both Emma and Harriet and yet neither, creates further confusion as Elton takes it to London to be framed, exclaiming as he receives it from Emma, "What a precious deposit!" (*E*, 51). The deluded artist is left to imagine a scene in which Elton shows the pictures to his admiring mother and sisters as a means of introducing Harriet to them while declaring "how much more beautiful is the original" (59), when doubtless he is using it instead to introduce Emma, and declaring how much more beautiful the picture is than its unworthy subject. Finally the portrait, source of so much misunderstanding, returns framed to hang in Emma's sitting room, where Elton ambiguously "sighed out his half sentences of admiration just as he ought" (73). Intriguingly, as Juliette Wells observes in her fine essay in this volume, Austen does not reveal Emma's final assessment of her work; the heroine may or may not be satisfied with what she has accomplished. And neither, as Wells points out, does Austen choose to inform us about the portrait's final destiny; it will surely not hang on the walls of Hartfield after Emma discovers how mistaken about Elton's, and Harriet's, desires she has been.

In *Northanger Abbey* Austen again makes substantial use of a portrait, in this case as part of the heroine's emotional entanglements at the Abbey. Rapidly persuaded of General Tilney's cruelty to his late wife, Catherine Morland asks his daughter Eleanor whether he keeps Mrs. Tilney's portrait in his room, while "blushing at the consummate art of her own question." Eleanor replies: "'No;—it was intended for the drawing-room; but my father was dissatisfied with the painting, and for some time it had no place. Soon after her death I obtained it for my own, and hung it in my bed-chamber—where I shall be happy to shew it you;—it is very like.'—Here was another proof. A portrait—very like—of a departed wife, not valued by the husband!—He must have been dreadfully cruel to her!"[29] Austen here uses the technique of free indirect discourse to convey Catherine's thoughts to the reader; these are not the narrator's perceptions, but the incoherent ideas running through Catherine's mind.

When she is later shown the portrait in Eleanor's room, Catherine's expectations are disappointed. The painting, we are told, represented a very lovely woman, with a mild and pensive countenance, justifying, so far, the expectations of its new observer; but they were not in every respect answered, for Catherine had depended upon meeting with features, air, complexion, that should be the very counterpart, the very image, if not of Henry's, of Eleanor's;—the only portraits of which she had been in the habit of thinking, bearing always an equal resemblance of mother and child. A face once taken was taken for generations. But here she was obliged to look and consider and study for a likeness. She contemplated it, however, in spite of this drawback, with much emotion; and, but for a yet stronger interest, would have left it unwillingly. (*NA*, 196)

Catherine's being obliged to "look and consider and study" epitomizes the whole course of her experiences at the abbey. Most of her assumptions there are found wanting; in this case, her belief that mothers will resemble their daughters and sons is undermined. Faces are not, as she had supposed, taken for generations; hereditary and family ties, as well as portraiture itself, are less straightforward than this.

In *Persuasion*, as in *Pride and Prejudice* and *Northanger Abbey*, the heroine contemplates a portrait at length. The scene takes place at the White Hart Inn in the penultimate chapter, one of two Austen wrote to replace the original conclusion. Captain Harville here shows Anne Elliot a miniature painting of Captain Benwick. It is to be presented to Benwick's new fiancée, Louisa Musgrove, but Harville recounts its origins to Anne "in a deep tone":

"It was not done for her. Miss Elliot, do you remember our walking together at Lyme, and grieving for him? I little thought then—but no matter. This was drawn at the Cape. He met with a clever young German artist at the Cape, and in compliance with a promise to my poor sister, sat to him, and was bringing it home for her. And I have now the charge of getting it properly set for another! It was a commission to me! But who else was there to employ? I hope I can allow for him. I am not sorry, indeed, to make it over to another. He undertakes it—(looking towards Captain Wentworth) he is writing about it now." And with a quivering lip he wound up the whole by adding, "Poor Fanny! she would not have forgotten him so soon!"[30]

Miniature portraits, as Janet Todd and Antje Blank observe, were "approximately three inches wide, . . . usually painted with watercolors on ivory, [and] were popular memorabilia in the late eighteenth and early nineteenth centuries." They add that they were "often given as tokens of love to and from men who left to fight in the Napoleonic War."[31] Captain Benwick, while serving as first lieutenant of the *Laconia*, had had a miniature portrait of himself painted when the ship was stationed at the Cape of Good Hope. On his return to England he was promoted to captain and appointed commander of the *Grappler*. He intended to give the miniature to his fiancée, Frances Harville, Captain Harville's sister, but she had died three months earlier, as Captain Wentworth had the task of telling his old friend. For some five months, while Benwick was in mourning, the portrait had remained in his possession. Now that he has become engaged to Louisa Musgrove, it is time to have it set: either as a locket to be worn round her neck, or as an ornament to a necklace. And Harville, as he tells Anne at the White Hart, has been charged with making the necessary arrangements, so that Benwick can present it to Louisa before he sets sail again.

The origin of the portrait, bringing the Cape of Good Hope unexpectedly into the geographical range of the novel, is of interest in itself. Jocelyn Harris suggests that Austen is alluding to her brother Francis, whose miniature portrait in his captain's uniform might also, she believes, have been painted at the Cape. Harris contends that the "clever young German artist" in Captain Harville's account can be identified as Jacob Frieman or Fruman, who resided at the Cape in 1807–9 and placed a newspaper advertisement, stating that he was "open to take miniatures." Harris also finds a resemblance in style between the portrait of Francis Austen, extant in private hands, and five miniatures by Frieman at the Victoria and Albert Museum, and proposes Frieman as the painter both of the actual portrait of Captain Austen and the imaginary portrait of Captain Benwick.[32]

My interest in Benwick's miniature is of another kind, leading into the text of the novel rather than outward to Austen's world. Captain Harville's sorrow over his friend's inconstancy, inspired by Benwick's transferring the miniature portrait from one fiancée to another, as though they were somehow interchangeable, leads to the famous debate between Anne and Harville over the respective constancy of men and women in love. While Harville believes that his sister Fanny, had she been the survivor, would have remained faithful to the memory of her beloved, Anne goes much further, suggesting that no woman who "truly loved" (*P*, 253) could act in the manner of Benwick. Their discussion, of course, is overheard by Wentworth, and Anne's words inspire him to write the letter that brings about their reunion. But the miniature does not merely facilitate the unfolding of the plot; it remains as a disturbing emblem not of constancy, its intended role, but of inconstancy. It will be "properly set" for Louisa, but it could then be reset, and reset again. Its subject, Captain Benwick, is already on enforced leave from the navy and will eventually be compelled to retire; the miniature, in contrast, freezes him in time as a dashing young captain at the outset of a promising career, and as a man in love with a woman who is no longer alive.

Austen is concerned with portraiture as misrepresentation: the disparity between visual images and the lives they purport to display. The miniature, with its changing functions, gives a new cast to the many previous references to Captain Benwick's devotion to Fanny Harville, which now take on a poignant irony. When we first hear of the couple, for example, we are told that "Captain Wentworth believed it impossible for man to be more attached to woman than poor Benwick had been to Fanny Harville" (*P*, 104): the penultimate chapter reveals how wrong Wentworth can be. He has, it seems, projected his own continuing devotion to Anne onto his friend's putative devotion to the memory of his beloved. Later, he expresses astonishment to Anne when he hears of Benwick's engagement to Louisa: "A man like him, in his situation! With a heart pierced, wounded, almost broken! Fanny Harville was a very superior creature; and his attachment to her was indeed attachment. A man does not recover from such a devotion of the heart to such a woman!—He ought not—he does not" (199). All of this, while true of Captain Wentworth and Anne Elliot, has little to do with Captain Benwick and Fanny Harville. In the penultimate chapter of *Persuasion*, Wentworth is made implicitly to acknowledge as much, when we see him writing his letter about the setting of the miniature, a task that Captain Harville has found too painful to undertake. With his passion for the poetry of Scott and Byron, Benwick seems to be in love with love itself rather than with either Fanny or Louisa.

Captain Benwick's miniature is not the only example of painting as misrepresentation in *Persuasion*. Shortly before the scene at the White Hart Inn, Anne Elliot encounters Admiral Croft as she walks up Milsom Street. He is standing alone at a print-shop window, gazing in astonishment at a composition which he urges Anne to examine for herself:

> But what a thing here is, by way of a boat. Do look at it. Did you ever see the like? What queer fellows your fine painters must be, to think that any body would venture their lives in such a shapeless old cockleshell as that. And yet, here are two gentlemen stuck up in it mightily at their ease, and looking about them at the rocks and mountains, as if they were not to be upset the next moment, which they certainly must be. I wonder where that boat was built!.. I would not venture over a horsepond in it. (183–84)

The model for Austen's imagined print might have been a painting by the greatest English painter of the sublime, J. M. W. Turner, such as his *Fishing*

Portraiture as Misrepresentation

Fig. 6. J. M. W. Turner, *Fishing Boats Entering Calais Harbour,* 1803, oil on canvas. (Frick Collection, New York)

Boats Entering Calais Harbour, executed in 1803 and first published as a print by Turner himself in January 1816—making it a timely piece for the Bath print-shop's window display (fig. 6).[33] The two figures at the center of Turner's painting seem to be almost enamored of the dangers confronting them. This type of painting, as Lorrie Clark observes in a stimulating essay, is that of the "'sublime' school ... popular from 1750 to 1850, where the annihilation of boats and men at sea by mountainous waves and threatening rocks is a recurrent motif."[34] Clark also suggests that the admiral is a poor interpreter of the painting—but I disagree with her here. His bluff, pragmatic response seems to me entirely justified: the "two gentlemen ... mightily at their ease, and looking about them at the rocks and mountains," should surely be taking emergency measures to save themselves, not indulging their taste for the Romantic sublime at the obvious risk of their lives.

There is, I believe, an implicit link between these sailors' indifference to their peril and that of Louisa in her famous walk along the Cobb at Lyme. Louisa rashly insists on jumping down the steep steps leading from the high path to the lower into the arms of Captain Wentworth, just as she habitually jumps down to him on crossing stiles during their country walks: the sensation, as the narrator observes drily, "was delightful to her." Disaster ensues:

> The hardness of the pavement for her feet, made him less willing upon the present occasion; he did it, however; she was safely down, and instantly, to shew her enjoyment, ran up the steps to be jumped down again. He advised her against it, thought the jar too great; but no, he reasoned and talked in vain; she smiled and said, "I am determined I will:" he put out his hands; she was too precipitate by half a second, she fell on the pavement on the Lower Cobb, and was taken up lifeless! (*P*, 118)

The higher the jump, the greater the thrill for Louisa; just as for the two men on the ocean, the mightier the waves, the more their sublime pleasure. And with her critical stance toward the men's solipsistic delight, Austen surely endorses the rational objections of Captain Wentworth to jumping on the unforgiving Cobb and of Admiral Croft to setting to sea in a storm equipped with only a "shapeless old cockleshell" of a boat.

In January 1817, Austen began work on *Sanditon* but was able to write for less than two months before her fatal illness forced her to stop, leaving the manuscript in fragmentary form. At the end of the novel as Austen left it, the heroine, Charlotte Heywood, and her friend, Mrs. Parker, have been ushered into the grand sitting room of Lady Denham. Charlotte sees, centrally placed above the mantelpiece, a full-length portrait of Lady Denham's late husband, Sir Harry Denham; in another part of the room, crowded inconspicuously among a group of miniatures, is the portrait of a previously deceased husband, Mr. Hollis. The passage concludes with a witty narratorial observation, forming the last fictional sentence that Austen ever wrote: "Poor Mr. Hollis!—It was impossible not to feel him hardly used; to be obliged to stand back in his own house and see the best place by the fire constantly occupied by Sir Harry Denham."[35] The episode plays an important part in *Sanditon*. Mr. Parker has previously given Charlotte an account of the rivalry among the various claimants to Lady Denham's fortune of thirty thousand pounds, telling her that of the three competing camps, "Mr. Hollis' kindred were the *least* in favour and Sir Harry Denham's the *most*" (*LM*, 152). Now the rivalry is visually embodied in the respective placing of Mr. Hollis's miniature and Sir Harry's whole length-portrait, which seems to reveal Lady Denham's evaluation of the respective merits of her two late husbands.

I have, however, changed my view of how this scene contributes to the novel fragment. I used to think that the lowly positioning of the miniature, as well as its inferior size, was a sign that popular opinion about who was most likely to inherit Lady Denham's wealth was right. I now believe that Austen could well be planting false clues here, as she seems to be doing so often in *Sanditon*. It is quite possible that the Hollis descendants, although overshadowed for now by those of Sir Harry Denham, could emerge triumphant at the end—or that neither one will prevail. We have, after all, been told of a third claimant to Lady Denham's fortune: the members of her own family. They too, presumably, figure among the "many miniatures" hanging in an inconspicuous part of her living room, without being so as much as named, yet this could well indicate that their prospects of inheriting Lady Denham's wealth have been underrated, just as Sir Harry Denham's prized place over the fire, in the form of a full-length portrait, is by no means a sure sign that the Denhams will triumph.

In conclusion, I shall return briefly to Captain Benwick's miniature, soon to be "properly set for another." This should support Anne's contention in her great debate with Captain Harville that a woman's love is deeper and more immutable than a man's. "Your feelings," she declares, "may be the strongest . . but the same spirit of analogy will authorise me to assert that ours are the most tender. Man is more robust than woman, but he is not longer-lived; which exactly explains my view of the nature of their attachments." "All the privilege I claim for my own sex," she concludes, "is that of loving longest, when existence or hope is gone" (*P*, 253–54, 256). At this point, even her adversary is moved: "'You are a good soul,' cried Captain Harville, putting his hand on her arm quite affectionately. 'There is no quarrelling with you.—And when I think of Benwick, my tongue is tied'" (256).

But Anne does not get the last word. Her former suitor, Captain Wentworth, has not been idle during the debate, writing not only his business note about the setting of the miniature but also his far more personal letter to Anne: "Dare not say that man forgets sooner than woman, that his love has an earlier death. I have loved none but you. Unjust I may have been, weak and resentful I have been, but never inconstant" (*P*, 258). His words, which are nothing if not persuasive, call into question the lesson that the history of the miniature had seemed so neatly to provide. Austen, I believe, uses visual images in her fiction not to provide us with representations of reality but rather to unsettle us, thwart our expectations, and make us question much of what we might wish to believe.

Notes

1. James Edward Austen-Leigh, *A Memoir of Jane Austen and Other Family Recollections*, ed. Kathryn Sutherland (Oxford: Oxford University Press, 2008), 139. Somewhat mysteriously, in his "Memoir of Miss Austen" (1833), a revised and generally expanded version of the earlier piece, Henry omits this sentence about his sister's artistic prowess (see *A Memoir of Jane Austen*, 149).

2. Jane Austen, *Jane Austen's Letters*, ed. Deirdre Le Faye, 4th ed. (Oxford: Oxford University Press, 2011), 21.

3. Deirdre Le Faye, *Fanny Knight's Diaries: Jane Austen through Her Niece's Eyes* (Chawton: Jane Austen Society, 2000), 9.

4. The sketch was acquired by David Gilson in 1993; see his "Cassandra Austen's Pictures," *Jane Austen Society Report for 1993*, 17, and illustration, 18. For further discussion of the sketch, now in the possession of Chris Viveash, see Adrienne Bradney-Smith, "Art and the Austen Family," *Jane Austen Society Report for 2008*, 135; and Janine Barchas, "Artistic Names in Austen's Fiction: Cameo Appearances by Prominent Painters," *Persuasions* 31 (2009): 153.

5. Margaret Wilson, *Almost Another Sister: The Story of Jane Austen's Favourite Niece* (Maidstone: George Mann, 1998), 39.

6. R. W. Chapman, *Jane Austen: Facts and Problems* (Oxford: Oxford University Press, 1948), 213.

7. Chapman, *Jane Austen: Facts and Problems*, 214.

8. Park Honan, *Jane Austen: Her Life* (London: Weidenfeld and Nicolson, 1987), 290.

9. David Nokes, *Jane Austen: A Life* (New York: Farrar, Straus and Giroux, 1997), 246.

10. Chapman, *Jane Austen: Facts and Problems*, 212.

11. Honan, *Jane Austen: Her Life*, 291; Valerie Grosvenor Myer, *Jane Austen: Obstinate Heart* (New York: Arcade, 1997), 69; Margaret Kirkham, "Portraits," in *Jane Austen in Context*, ed. Janet Todd (Cambridge: Cambridge University Press, 2005), 69.

12. Kathryn Sutherland, *Jane Austen's Textual Lives: From Aeschylus to Bollywood* (Oxford: Oxford University Press, 2005), 112.

13. Jane Austen, *The History of England*, ed. Deirdre Le Faye, introd. A. S. Byatt (Chapel Hill, NC: Algonquin, 1993), xi.

14. Here and on a few subsequent occasions, I have drawn on a previous essay, "The Strategic Withdrawal from Ekphrasis in Jane Austen's Novels," in *Icons—Texts—Iconotexts: Essays on Ekphrasis and Intermediality*, ed. Peter Wagner (Berlin: de Gruyter, 1996), 213–35.

15. Jane Austen, *Juvenilia*, ed. Peter Sabor (Cambridge: Cambridge University Press, 2006), 178. Subsequent references are to this edition and will be supplied parenthetically within the text.

16. This was first noted by Jan Fergus (see *The History of England*, ed. Fergus et al. [Edmonton, Canada: Juvenilia Press, 1995], iv).

17. Oliver Goldsmith, *The History of England* (1771), 2:250.

18. *Love and Friendship and Other Youthful Writings*, ed. Christine Alexander (London: Penguin, 2014), xxvi.

19. Marcia Pointon, *Hanging the Head: Portraiture and Social Formation in Eighteenth-Century England* (New Haven, CT: Yale University Press, 1993), 4.

20. Jane Austen, *Sense and Sensibility*, ed. Edward Copeland (Cambridge: Cambridge University Press, 2006), 151. Subsequent references are to this edition and will be supplied parenthetically within the text.

21. Kazuko Hisamori, "Facing a Portrait of the 'Lover': *Frankenstein*'s Monster and the Heroines of *Sense and Sensibility* and *Pride and Prejudice*," *Persuasions On-line* 32, no. 1 (2011).

22. In his edition of the novel, Copeland notes that miniatures were "in country areas procurable for as little as three pounds from travelling artists" (*S&S*, 467).

23. Janet Todd, ed., *The Cambridge Introduction to Jane Austen* (Cambridge: Cambridge University Press, 2006), 52.

24. Jane Austen, *Pride and Prejudice*, ed. Pat Rogers (Cambridge: Cambridge University Press, 2006), 57. Subsequent references are to this edition and will be supplied parenthetically within the text.

25. Isobel Armstrong, introduction to *Pride and Prejudice*, ed. James Kinsley and Frank W. Bradbrook (Oxford: Oxford University Press, 1990), xxi.

26. Joe Bray, *The Portrait in Fiction of the Romantic Period* (London: Taylor and Francis, 2016), 127.

27. Jane Austen, *Mansfield Park*, ed. John Wiltshire (Cambridge: Cambridge University Press, 2005), 99. Subsequent references are to this edition and will be supplied parenthetically within the text

28. Jane Austen, *Emma*, ed. Richard Cronin and Dorothy McMillan (Cambridge: Cambridge University Press, 2005), 49, 50. Subsequent references are to this edition and will be supplied parenthetically within the text.

29. Jane Austen, *Northanger Abbey*, ed. Barbara M. Benedict and Deirdre le Faye (Cambridge: Cambridge University Press, 2006), 185. Subsequent references are to this edition and will be supplied parenthetically within the text.

30. Jane Austen, *Persuasion*, ed. Janet Todd and Antje Blank (Cambridge: Cambridge University Press, 2006), 252. Subsequent references are to this edition and will be supplied parenthetically within the text.

31. See their note on miniatures in *Persuasion*, 389–90. In a letter of December 16–17, 1816, four months after writing her new conclusion to *Persuasion*, Austen made a famous comparison between herself and a miniaturist painter in a letter to her nephew James Edward Austen, telling him of the "little bit (two Inches wide) of Ivory on which I work with so fine a Brush, as produces little effect after much labour" (*Letters*, 337).

32. Jocelyn Harris, *A Revolution Almost beyond Expression: Jane Austen's Persuasion* (Newark: University of Delaware Press, 2007), 84.

33. In "The Strategic Withdrawal" (226–27), I suggested that the admiral might have been contemplating a print from Turner's famous sea-piece *Shipwreck* of 1805. There, however, the sailors are struggling against their imminent fate, rather than delighting in their fate.

34. Lorrie Clark, "Transfiguring the Romantic Sublime in *Persuasion*," in *Jane Austen's Business: Her World and Her Profession*, ed. Juliet McMaster and Bruce Stovel (Basingstoke, UK: Palgrave Macmillan 1996), 30.

35. Jane Austen, "Sanditon," in *Later Manuscripts*, ed. Janet Todd and Linda Bree (Cambridge: Cambridge University Press, 2008), 209. Subsequent references are to this edition and will be supplied parenthetically within the text.

Jane Austen's "Artless" Heroines
Catherine Morland and Fanny Price

ELAINE BANDER

Most of Jane Austen's heroines are reasonably adept at music or drawing. *Sense and Sensibility*'s Elinor Dashwood draws with great taste, according to her sister Marianne, while Marianne herself plays the pianoforte and, the narrator assures us, sings well.[1] *Pride and Prejudice*'s Elizabeth Bennet and *Emma*'s Emma Woodhouse, clever women both, lack discipline to pursue art to perfection, but their performances please their admirers. In *Persuasion*, Anne Elliot is a truly accomplished woman even by Mr. Darcy's exigent criteria.[2] Only two Austen heroines, Catherine Morland in *Northanger Abbey* and Fanny Price in *Mansfield Park*, lack artistic accomplishments, for they neither draw, nor sing, nor act on stage, nor write clever rhymes, nor play the harp or the pianoforte. They are, alone among Austen's heroines, artless.

They share two additional traits that distinguish them from Austen's other heroines. First, they are the least liked of her heroines. For two hundred years readers and critics have dismissed Catherine as "silly,"[3] a "fool,"[4] or "fatuous,"[5] while Fanny has been called "morally detestable."[6] Generations of readers may have fallen in love with Elizabeth Bennet, Tony Tanner claims, "but nobody falls in love with Fanny Price."[7] Lionel Trilling agrees: "Nobody, I believe, has ever found it possible to like the heroine of *Mansfield Park*."[8]

Catherine and Fanny share a second distinguishing characteristic: they actively resist when friends and family to whom they owe loyalty or obedience urge them to do what they believe to be wrong. No other Austen heroines challenge a beloved family member who urges them to act against their principled judgment. Admittedly, Elizabeth Bennet defies her mother's order to marry Mr. Collins, but she does so with the doting support of her father, nor is her courageous defiance of Lady Catherine complicated by any obligation of duty. When handsome, clever, rich Emma Woodhouse dismisses Mr. Knightley's brotherly advice, she is motivated by convenience, not conscience. Anne Elliot, in breaking her engagement to Captain Wentworth eight years before *Persuasion* opens, chose filial duty over love.

Jane Austen's "Artless" Heroines

Only Catherine Morland and Fanny Price defy family members who urge them to act against their conscience.

Catherine's heroic moment comes when her brother James and the Thorpes press her to cancel her engagement with the Tilneys in order to drive with them to Clifton. While Isabella dabs her eyes, James Morland calls his sister "unkind" for not making the "sacrifice," chiding her for her intransigence: "you were not used to be so hard to persuade; you once were the kindest, best-tempered of my sisters."[9] Catherine resists this painful, unjust attack: "'I hope I am not less so now,' she replied, very feelingly; 'but indeed I cannot go. If I am wrong, I am doing what I believe to be right.'" After Thorpe announces that he has canceled Catherine's appointment with the Tilneys, Catherine declares: "I cannot submit to this. I must run after Miss Tilney directly and set her right" (*NA*, 101). When James and the Thorpes physically restrain Catherine, continuing to argue with her, Catherine insists, "'If I could not be persuaded into doing what I thought was wrong, I will never be tricked into it.' And with these words she broke away and hurried off" to find the Tilneys (101). Catherine may be naïve, but she has heroic courage to act upon principle in the face of emotional blackmail and even physical restraint.

Fanny twice resists the importunities of the Bertram family, to whom she is very aware that she owes gratitude and filial obedience. The first occasion is her refusal to act in *Lovers' Vows* despite the demands of her cousins and aunts. With elder-son privilege, Tom insists, "Indeed but you must, for we cannot excuse you."[10] Her aunt, cousins, and their friends are ranged against her. Only Edmund supports her: "Let her choose for herself as well as the rest of us.—Her judgment may be quite as safely trusted." Mrs. Norris replies, "I shall think her a very obstinate, ungrateful girl, if she does not do what her aunt and cousins wish her—very ungrateful indeed, considering who and what she is" (*MP*, 172). In response to these attacks, Fanny spends an anguished morning in the East room examining her conscience in order to assure herself that her motives are not selfish ones: "But ... she had begun to feel undecided as to what she *ought to do*; and as she walked round the room her doubts were increasing. Was she *right* in refusing what was so warmly asked, so strongly wished for? ... Was it not ill-nature—selfishness—and a fear of exposing herself?" (179). When Edmund accepts a role to spare Miss Crawford's feelings, and Mrs. Grant joins the players, Fanny "was full of jealousy and agitation. ... But reflection brought better feelings" (187). Then, minutes before Sir Thomas's unexpected return home upstages the theatrical project, she reluctantly agrees to *read* Mrs. Grant's part during a rehearsal (201). To oblige her cousins, Fanny "must yield" on that occasion despite her deep personal reluctance (201), but she never agrees to *perform* the role.

Her second, more consequential, resistance occurs after Henry Crawford's proposal, when her uncle comes to the East room intending to congratulate her upon so brilliant a match, only to learn that she has chosen to "Refuse Mr. Crawford!" (364). To Sir Thomas, Fanny's decision is unfathomable: Cinderella does not reject the Prince!

> "I am half inclined to think, Fanny, that you do not quite know your own feelings."
> "Oh! yes, Sir, indeed I do. His attentions were always—what I did not like." (365)

Since Fanny "could scarcely dare mention" Henry's flirtations with her cousins and must hide her own transgressive love for Edmund from her uncle's piercing gaze—"She would rather die than own the truth, and she hoped by a little reflection to fortify herself beyond betraying it" (365)—her behavior appears to him inexplicable, or worse, undutiful: "you have now shewn me that you can be willful and perverse, that you can and will decide for yourself, without any consideration or deference for those who have surely some right to guide you—without even asking their advice. . You do not owe me the duty of a child. But, Fanny, if your heart can acquit you of *ingratitude*—" (367–68). Fanny must endure not only her uncle's Lear-like accusations but also Henry's persistence, Mary's pleading, and even beloved Edmund's solicitation on Henry's behalf, all the while guarding her secrets. Her resolve never falters, for "she trusted, in the first place, that she had done right, that her judgment had not misled her; for the purity of her intentions she could answer" (374). In the face of Bertram pressure, Crawford charm, and Portsmouth exile, she stands her ground.

While Catherine and Fanny are unpopular Austen heroines who act courageously in order to do what they believe to be right, these two "artless" heroines have little else in common besides their youth at each novel's opening. Catherine, created early in Austen's career, is simple, direct, and completely transparent, at least to the Tilneys. She is "artless" as Johnson defined it: "Void of fraud; as, an *artless* maid."[11] Fanny, on the other hand, the first of Austen's mature "Chawton" heroines, is by no means "artless" in Johnson's sense, for she is complex, reserved, and exceptionally guarded, consciously masking her deepest feelings—love for Edmund, jealousy of Mary, mistrust of Henry—from those she lives among. Thus Fanny is *not* entirely guileless, despite her cousin Edmund's characterizing her as "the heart that knew no guile" (*MP*, 527).

Moreover, while Catherine's artlessness is not essential to her character, Fanny's most certainly is. Catherine's ignorance of the arts serves a burlesque function, distinguishing her from the clichéd novel heroine against whom the ironic, quixotic narrator in *Northanger Abbey* keeps measuring her.[12] Indeed, shortly before her death Austen was still mocking that conventional novel heroine in her burlesque "Plan of a Novel." A heroine created according to the advice of her friends and critics, Austen wrote, would have to be "very highly accomplished, . . . particularly excelling in Music—her favourite pursuit—& playing equally well on the Piano Forte & Harp—& singing in the first stile."[13] In fact, Catherine has no objections to the arts; she is simply untutored or indifferent. Fanny's rejection of the performative arts, however, goes deeper. She consistently resists acquiring the forms of display practiced by "accomplished" young ladies such as Maria and Julia Bertram and Mary Crawford. Catherine's artlessness is a consequence of her simplicity; Fanny's is a conscious choice.

Austen's creation of these two vulnerable but different young heroines who possess both principled heroism and "artlessness" was a deliberate strategy, part of her lifelong project to interrogate and to remake the English novel. She began in childhood, burlesquing absurd novel conventions and sententious novel conclusions. When she came to write her own novels, she domesticated those conventions, testing them against the conditions of everyday experience while ironically inverting or subverting the didactic sentence. Austen's development as an artist, moreover, was recursive: she frequently revisited themes and character types from earlier works, always writing against the grain of readerly expectations while challenging her own readers (who participate, as they read, in the same trials facing her heroines) to read carefully, to reflect seriously, and to judge for themselves rather than lazily to follow coded signs or to anticipate conventional tropes.[14] Unlike many of her contemporaries, therefore, Austen does not use a heroine's artistic accomplishment as a conventional marker for her gentility or her virtue. By the time she published *Mansfield Park*, in fact, this association between artistic skill and moral virtue was already outdated. The opening paragraphs of Sir Walter Scott's *Waverley*, published in 1814, the same year as *Mansfield Park*, burlesque sentimental novels' improbably accomplished heroines, like Charlotte Smith's Emmeline:

> If I had rather chosen to call my work a "Sentimental Tale," would it not have been a sufficient presage of a heroine with a profusion of auburn hair, and a harp, the soft solace of her solitary hours, which she fortunately always finds the means of transporting from castle to cottage, although she herself be

sometimes obliged to jump out of a two-pair-of-stairs window, and is more than once bewildered on her journey, alone and on foot, without any guide but a blowsy peasant girl, whose jargon she can hardly understand?[15]

Despite this apparent disclaimer, Scott later tempts his readers as well as his naïve hero Edward Waverley with the vision of a Highland heroine, Flora Mac-Ivor, singing and playing her harp against the romantic backdrop of a mountain waterfall. While Edward grows besotted, Scott warns readers that "Edward was . . . in the fair way of creating a goddess out of a high-spirited, accomplished, and beautiful young woman."[16]

So, of course, is Edmund Bertram in *Mansfield Park*. Like the comically sentimental harp-playing heroine of Scott's opening pages of *Waverley*, Mary Crawford "fortunately . . . finds the means of transporting her harp" to Mansfield Parsonage, where she has the same effect upon Edmund Bertram as harp-playing Flora has on Edward Waverley, but in contrast to Flora in her Highland glen, Mary poses in front of a prosaic parsonage window: "A young woman, pretty, lively, with a harp as elegant as herself; and both placed near a window, cut down to the ground, and opening on a little lawn, surrounded by shrubs in the rich foliage of summer, was enough to catch any man's heart" (76). Readers, however, who expect the hero to marry the romantic harpist are invited by authorial irony in both novels to reexamine their conventional expectations.

Maria Edgeworth was not one of those readers. She admired Scott's Flora, but not the harp-playing scene. In a letter to Scott congratulating him upon the publication of *Waverley*, she took exception to "the appearance of Flora and her harp" as "too like a common heroine," adding, "she should be far above all stage effect or novelist's trick."[17] Edgeworth's own 1814 novel, *Patronage*, like *Mansfield Park*, contrasts two sets of cousins: wealthy, showy, predatory Falconers on the one hand, and virtuous, hardworking Percys on the other.[18] Buckhurst Falconer claims that his cousin, the modest heroine Caroline Percy, "sings and plays like an angel, fifty times better than our two precious sisters, who have been *at it* from their cradles, with all the Signor *Squalicis* at their elbows." He adds, significantly, that "Caroline Percy never exhibits in public."[19] Like Fanny Price, Caroline Percy does not act or perform—but unlike Fanny, she is an accomplished musician and actress. Even for the new generation of novelists, then, the sentimental association of female accomplishments with refinement and virtue was slow to die.

Frances Burney also depicted a harp-playing heroine in her 1814 novel, *The Wanderer*. Born in 1752, Burney belonged to an older generation and aesthetic than did Austen, Scott, and Edgeworth. Moreover, between 1802 and 1812 she had been in forced exile in France. The complex novel that she published upon her return to England is in some respects a throwback to the sentimental tales that Scott burlesques in *Waverley*. Burney's aristocratic heroine, Juliet Granville, experiences adventures strikingly similar to Scott's burlesque plot, but while nameless and penniless, her impeccable gentility, beauty, refinement, and virtue are revealed through her performance of the arts. Early in the novel, thinking herself alone in the wealthy household in which she has found temporary shelter, she is overheard playing the harp by her wealthy patrons: "They stopped, and distinctly heard a harp; they listened, and found that it was played with uncommon ability. . 'Hist! dear ladies,' said Harleigh; ''tis some exquisite performer'"[20] (Burney, 73–74). Everything Juliet dare not reveal about herself directly, she conveys through music. Harleigh is amazed "to find in her all the delicately acquired skill, joined to the happy natural talents, which constitute a refined artist" (75). Her voice "was varied, with the nicest discrimination, for the expression of every character" (80). Urged to perform as musician or actress, she declines (81). Nevertheless compelled to step into the lead role of Lady Townly in *The Provoked Husband*, her "beauty, figure, and dress" and her brilliant acting "created a surprize so powerful, and a delight so unexpected, that the play seemed soon to have no other object than Lady Townly" (94). Only when thus *impersonating* an elegant woman of fashion does Juliet appear, briefly, in her true aristocratic guise. Juliet requires her admirers because, despite her correct behavior, she must repeatedly be rescued by others: she does not resist authority except through retreat. For Austen's heroines, in contrast, artistic proficiency is neither a necessary ingredient of, nor an essential marker for, their gentility and virtue. They are defined not by their art but by their actions.

Yet Austen did not, as did Evangelical Bluestocking author Hannah More, condemn women's cultivation of artistic accomplishments as a frivolous distraction from their more rigorous moral and religious duties.[21] In her 1798 *Strictures on the Modern System of Female Education*, More exhorts English women to use their influence, gifts, and charms not to "captivate" men but to reform them.[22] She deplores the modern "phrenzy of accomplishments" in female education as, at best, a shocking waste of a young woman's time better spent on reading and domestic or charitable pursuits, and, at worse, a corrupting influence upon morality.[23] "A young lady," she warns, "may excel in speaking French and Italian, may repeat a few passages from a volume of extracts; play like a professor, and sing like a syren; have her dressing room decorated with her own drawings, tables, stands, screens, and cabinets; nay, she may dance like Sempronia herself, and yet may have been very badly educated."[24] Austen might have had this passage in mind when she wrote her concluding chapter of *Mansfield Park*, in which Sir Thomas reflects upon his daughters' faulty education (*MP*, 535).[25] Certainly Austen's conclusion seems to vindicate More's warning that "when a man of sense comes to marry, it is a companion whom he wants, and not an artist. It is not merely a creature who can paint, and play, and dress, and dance; it is a being who can comfort and counsel him; one who can reason, and reflect, and feel, and judge, and act, and discourse, and discriminate; one who can assist him in his affairs, lighten his cares, sooth his sorrows, purify his joys, strengthen his principles, and educate his children."[26] *Mansfield Park*, however, is only one among Austen's six published novels. *Emma* and *Persuasion*, novels that followed *Mansfield Park*, present Emma Woodhouse and Anne Elliot as both accomplished and virtuous. Clearly Austen neither embraced Evangelical austerity nor opposed the arts in principle.

Rather than making each of her heroines accomplished artists in the outdated sentimental manner or condemning the performative arts as moral hazards, Austen deploys the arts strategically to surprise her readers out of habitual categorical judgments, encouraging them to become women "who can reason, and reflect, and feel, and judge, and act, and discourse, and discriminate."[27] Often that challenge requires characters (and readers) to distinguish between aesthetics and ethics, taste and morality, the pleasant and the good.[28] In making those distinctions, Catherine Morland and Fanny Price, who may not always strike readers as "pleasant," model true heroism.[29]

Both Catherine and Fanny are ignorant little girls when we first meet them, and neither has much inclination to become "accomplished" in art or music. Of Catherine, we are told: "Her mother wished her to learn music; and Catherine was sure she should like it, for she was very fond of tinkling the keys of the old forlorn spinet; so, at eight years old she began. She learnt a year, and could not bear it. . . . The day which dismissed the music-master was one of the happiest of Catherine's life. Her taste for drawing was not superior" (*NA*, 6). By the time she arrives in Bath at age seventeen, the narrator assures us, "She knew nothing of drawing—nothing of taste" (112). But while Catherine is Austen's most naïve, ignorant heroine, she does not reject the arts; rather, she is simply untutored, disinclined to practice the arts herself. She is a willing enough pupil for the Tilneys to enlighten as they walk together on Beechen Cliff, where Catherine, bewildered by the counterintuitive criteria of the picturesque employed by the Tilneys, is "heartily ashamed of her ignorance" (112). Without guile, however, "she confessed and lamented her want of knowledge; declared that she would give any thing in the world to be able to draw; and a lecture on the picturesque immediately followed, in which [Henry Tilney's] instructions were so clear that she soon began to see beauty in every thing admired by him, and her attention was so earnest, that *he became perfectly satisfied of her having a great deal of natural taste*" (112–13, emphasis mine). Catherine may never become an artist, or even a sophisticated reader of history and novels, but under Henry's tutelage, she appears (to Henry at least) to have "a great deal of natural taste"—by which Henry, invoking the early eighteenth-century ideas of Rousseau and Shaftesbury, means an innate but cultivated ability to judge works of art, although by the end of the century the idea of "taste" was entrenched in ordinary discourse and had come to mean different things to different people.[30]

Fanny Price at age ten is equally ignorant, but unlike Catherine she consistently resists acquiring the performative arts. Soon after her arrival at Mansfield, her cousins Maria and Julia report: "Dear Mama, only think, my cousin . . does not know the difference between water-colours and crayons! . . . Do you know, she says she does not want to learn either music or drawing" (*MP*, 20–21). Fanny's childhood resistance persists as she matures; when pressed to take a small part in *Lovers' Vows*, she recoils in horror: "Indeed you must excuse me. I could not act any thing if you were to give me the world. No, indeed. I cannot act" (171). Whether Fanny, like Hannah More, has a principled Evangelical objection to acting or simply a personal distaste for public display is irrelevant, because Austen, who *did* act, does not intend Fanny's *preferences* to be exemplary. Rather she is endorsing the reflective *process* Fanny undergoes to arrive at her decision.[31] Lorrie Clark extends Shaftesbury's term "soliloquy" to describe Fanny's dialogic reflective process, arguing that Fanny's dialogues with "her other self" Edmund constitute Shaftesburean soliloquies.[32] According to Clark, in *Mansfield Park* Austen "explores the two most powerful influences traditionally on 'manners' or *mores*: religion, and art or aesthetics—'the pulpit' and 'the theatre'— and comes up with a third alternative," "soliloquy," or reflection.[33] For an Austenian heroine, art is optional, but reflection is essential, for she must, to return to Hannah More's terms, "reason, and reflect, and feel, and judge, and act" not upon a theatrical stage but as an independent moral agent.

Moreover, Fanny, like Catherine, prefers nature to art. Austen repeatedly contrasts Fanny's taste for nature with Mary Crawford's indifference. During the drive to Sotherton, Fanny closely observes the countryside and all its features, but Miss Crawford "had none of *Fanny's delicacy of taste*, of mind, of feeling; she saw nature, inanimate nature, with little observation; her attention was all for men and women, her talents for the light and lively" (*MP*, 94, emphasis mine). Later, as Fanny and Edmund stand together at the window at Mansfield watching the mild summer evening descend upon the park while the other young people are behind them in the drawing room preparing to sing glees, she declares: "Here's harmony! . . . Here's what may leave all painting and music behind, and what poetry can only attempt to describe" (132). Edmund offers to take Fanny out onto the lawn to view the constellation Cassiopeia, but then the glee begins, and he turns away from her to join Mary at the piano, rejecting the harmony of Nature for the harmonies of Mary's singing.[34]

Later the narrator contrasts the two women's responses to nature while they sit together in the parsonage shrubbery. Fanny "rhapsodizes" at length over the shrubbery, contemplating "the operations of time, and the changes of the human mind!" (*MP*, 243), while "Miss Crawford, *untouched and inattentive*, had nothing to say" (243, emphasis mine). "Fanny, perceiving it, brought back her own mind to what she thought must interest" (243), but Miss Crawford has no more interest in "The evergreen!" than she has in Fanny's speculations about time and memory (244). Fanny confesses: "When I am sitting out of doors, I am very apt to get into this sort of wondering strain. One cannot fix one's eyes on the commonest natural production without finding food for a rambling fancy" (244).[35] For Fanny, the book of God's works is legible and inspirational, but Mary cannot read it, any more than she seriously reads the Book of God's word.

Although Fanny resists practicing art, she does not reject art, for while she resolutely refuses to perform herself, she is drawn to the performances of others, and, like Catherine, she appears to have a great deal of natural taste—that is, a discriminating responsiveness to other people's performances of art. And while Edmund has educated and formed her taste for history and poetry as well as for nature, much as Henry Tilney begins to form Catherine's taste, the talented Crawfords provide her first real education in the world of artistic performance. Early in the visit of the Crawfords to Mansfield, Edmund asks, "And how do you like Miss Crawford *now*?" Fanny responds, "She entertains me; and she is so extremely pretty, that I have a great pleasure in looking at her" (*MP*, 74). Fanny's early approbation of Miss Crawford is entirely aesthetic. She yearns almost as much as Edmund to hear Mary Crawford's harp (77), a gratification that she finally receives after Maria's marriage, when Fanny is the only young person remaining at Mansfield and rain forces her to take shelter at the parsonage.

Mary is "happy to have a new listener, and a listener who seemed so much obliged, so full of wonder at the performance, and who shewed herself *not wanting in taste*" (241, emphasis mine).

Just as Fanny can appreciate Mary's prettiness and harp-playing without liking her, so too she is able to judge Mr. Crawford's talents fairly without liking him. Fanny, in fact, observes the Mansfield actors as though *they* were characters in a play while they argue among themselves over what to perform: "Fanny looked on and listened, not unamused to observe the selfishness which, more or less disguised, seemed to govern them all, and wondered how it would end. For her own gratification she could have wished that something might be acted" (*MP*, 154). During the rehearsals of *Lovers' Vows*, she reflects on her own pleasure in observing the rehearsals: "Fanny believed herself to derive as much innocent enjoyment from the play as any of them;—Henry Crawford acted well, and it was a pleasure to *her* to creep into the theatre, and attend the rehearsal. . . . As far as she could judge, Mr. Crawford was considerably the best actor of all; he had more confidence than Edmund, more judgment than Tom, more talent and taste than Mr. Yates.—She did not like him as a man, but she must admit him to be the best actor" (193–94). After Fanny has "refused Mr. Crawford," she must endure his presence in the drawing-room, where her innate "taste" does justice to Henry Crawford's talents while he reads from *Henry VIII*:

> All her attention was for her work. She seemed determined to be interested by nothing else. But taste was too strong in her. She could not abstract her mind five minutes; she was forced to listen; his reading was capital, and her pleasure in good reading extreme. To *good* reading, however, she had long been used; . . . but in Mr. Crawford's reading there was a variety of excellence beyond what she had ever met with. . . . It was truly dramatic.—His acting had first taught Fanny what pleasure a play might give, and his reading brought all his acting before her again; nay, perhaps with greater enjoyment, for it came unexpectedly, and with no such drawback as she had been used to suffer in seeing him on the stage with Miss Bertram. (389–90)

So powerful is the charm of Crawford's acting that Fanny's eyes, which have "studiously" avoided him all day, now rise involuntarily to watch him as her needle falls from her hands—until he closes the book "and the charm was broken" (390). The talent for speaking lines, which in *The Wanderer* reveals the worthiness of Juliet's character to discerning listeners, serves Crawford only as a temporary charm. His talents alone will not win Fanny's heart nor persuade her head that he is worthy of her love.

Fanny does not confuse aesthetics and ethics. Mary can be pretty and musical, Henry can be a talented actor, without either of them being good or likeable. Her ability to distinguish between art and morality is crucial. Throughout the long eighteenth century, as aesthetic criteria shifted from a dependence upon the older Aristotelian, neoclassical "rules" to a more subjective, empirical emphasis upon innate "taste," moral philosophers and critics who saw parallels between "rules" in art and "principles" in ethics probed the tension between feelings and rules as a basis for judgment. Karen Valihora locates the birth of these ideas in Shaftesbury's *Characteristics*, which she claims is about "common sense," not "received ideas."[36] Shaftesbury, she argues, "set the terms for the project of moral philosophy in the eighteenth century when he grounded it in aesthetics."[37] Vivasvan Soni calls this tension between ethics and aesthetics the "fundamental crisis of judgment that plagues eighteenth-century thought."[38]

In Austen's first published novel, *Sense and Sensibility*, Marianne Dashwood confuses moral and aesthetic taste when she falls in love with John Willoughby, reading his "manly beauty" (51) as an outward manifestations of his inner worth, and trusting that since "their taste was strikingly alike," so too must be their moral values (56).[39] Later Marianne defends her transgressive visit with Willoughby to Allenham by invoking Shaftesbury's concept of "moral taste": "If there had been any real impropriety in what I did," she assures Elinor, "I should have been sensible of it at the time, for we always know when we are acting wrong, and with such a conviction I could have had no pleasure" (80). Edward Copeland glosses this speech in his Cambridge edition by citing Shaftesbury: "No creature can maliciously and intentionally do ill, without being sensible at the same time, that he deserves ill" (80n9).[40] Valihora, however, points out that Shaftesbury did not defend feelings devoid of reflection as a basis for judgment. On the contrary, she argues, "moral and aesthetic judgments turn, for him, around the spontaneous feeling of pleasure or pain, but only because this feeling provides the occasion for a second, more distanced, reflection, one that involves setting one pleasure (or pain) against another."[41] Not all aesthetic responses are moral. Marianne concedes to her sister, "Perhaps, Elinor, it *was* rather ill-judged in me to go to Allenham" (80).[42] Eventually, after reflection, Marianne becomes a better judge, learning to temper her aesthetic and moral taste with what Austen calls "principles."

Mary Crawford, musically adept, pretty, and witty, is ignorant of those principles. Her own are entirely worldly: marriage, for her, is a take-in.

Eldest sons are preferable to younger. Town is better than country. A clergyman is nothing. Even "the *really good feelings* by which she was almost purely governed" (*MP*, 173, emphasis mine) do not save her from a life of dissatisfaction, but she never understands why she is dissatisfied because her judgment is dominated by feelings, not reflection, and certainly not by any absolute moral or religious principles. For Mary, Henry and Maria's elopement is a social gaffe rather than a grievous moral transgression. To what Edmund and Fanny consider a serious sin she gives "no harsher name than *folly*" (526). Her wit and talent and really good feelings cannot help her to find a path through the wilderness.

The contemporary picturesque theorists whom Austen read and admired also commented upon parallels between taste and morality and debated criteria for judgment. The practical landscaper Humphry Repton, for example, argued in 1803 that "the man of good taste . . . knows that the same principles which direct taste in the polite arts direct the judgment in morality; in short, that a knowledge of what is good, what is bad, and what is indifferent, whether in actions, in manners, in language, in arts, or science, constitutes the basis of good taste."[43] Repton was skeptical about established landscape theorists Richard Payne Knight and Uvedale Price applying aesthetic theories of fine art (painting and sketching) to practical landscape gardening.[44] On the other hand, Knight's influential 1805 work, *An Analytical Inquiry into the Principles of Taste*, attacked Repton's position that judgments should be based upon fixed rules: "Critics have done nearly the same in taste," Knight complained, "as casuists have in morals; both having attempted to direct by rules, and limit by definitions, matters, which depend entirely on feeling and sentiment."[45] For Knight, "benevolent" feelings were to be trusted more than rigid rules.[46] Indeed, the sacrifice of natural feelings of humanity "to an abstract principle or opinion," he argued, had led to "the atrocious and sanguinary passions" of men like Marat and Robespierre.[47] Clearly Shaftesbury's ideas, however transformed, were still thriving in the new century.

Jane Austen was having none of it. Musical herself, a theater-lover, a keen observer of both pictures and nature, and of course, a superb writer, Austen nevertheless resisted this fashionable conflation of moral and aesthetic taste. In a letter written from London in 1815, Austen recounts a conversation with her brother Henry's friend, the surgeon Mr. Haden: "I have been listening to dreadful Insanity.—It is Mr Haden's firm beleif [sic] that a person *not* musical is fit for every sort of Wickedness. I ventured to assert a little on the other side, but wished the cause in abler hands."[48] It is "dreadful Insanity" in Austen's view to suggest that aesthetic taste is an essential component of ethical behavior.

Austen, an artist, did not believe that to be "artless" was to be wicked. She would have been much more in sympathy with the views of Rev. Samuel Hall, who, in 1782, read a paper before the Literary and Philosophical Society of Manchester entitled "An Attempt to shew that a Taste for the beauties of nature and the Fine Arts, has no influence favourable to morals." Refuting the arguments of Shaftesbury's *Characteristics* and Lord Kames's later *Elements of Criticism* (1762), Hall argues: "The man of taste admires the beauty and expression exhibited in the works of a Raphael, or a Michael Angelo, without feeling the slightest wish to become an artist, and to rival these great masters. May he not, in like manner, view the charms of virtue, and of moral conduct, without making one single effort to become a moralist, or a virtuous man?"[49] He may indeed, if his name is Henry Crawford.

Henry, certainly a man of taste, envies the professional skill and courage of William Price and the professional eloquence of Edmund Bertram without wishing to exert himself in either field, and he is attracted to Fanny's virtue without wishing to practice virtue himself. Significantly, the only time Austen uses Shaftesbury's term "moral taste" is in relation to Henry Crawford. Henry, the narrator tells us, "had too much sense not to feel the worth of good principles in a wife, though he was too little accustomed to serious reflection to know them by their proper name" (*MP*, 341). When Henry sees Fanny reunited with her brother William—"the glow of Fanny's cheek, the brightness of her eye, the deep interest, the absorbed attention, while her brother was describing" his adventures at sea—the narrator assures us that "it was a *picture* which Henry Crawford had *moral taste* enough to value" (274, emphasis mine), even if, like his sister, he lacks the words with which to describe those virtues. Henry possesses a natural "moral taste" just as his sister Mary possesses really good feelings, but moral *taste* and good *feelings* are not enough, even if gilded by glittering accomplishments, as Sir Thomas comes to realize about his daughters' education: "He feared that principle, active principle, had been wanting, that they had never been properly taught to govern their inclinations and tempers, by that sense of duty which can alone suffice. . . . To be distinguished for elegance and accomplishments—the authorized object of their youth—could have had no useful influence that way, no moral effect on the mind" (536). Fanny Price, who refuses to perform art or music, has both a powerful sense of duty and the dialectical skill for the ethical deliberation necessary to identify and obey that duty, a skill nourished by her hours of reflection in the East room.

Curiously, what Austen calls Fanny's "heroism of principle" alludes not to her two acts of principled resistance (against acting and against Henry's proposal) but to her secret struggle to repress her feelings for Edmund before her ball: "It was her intention, as she felt it to be her duty, to try to overcome all that was excessive, all that bordered on selfishness in her affection for Edmund. . She had all the *heroism of principle*, and was determined to do her duty" (*MP*, 307, emphasis mine).[50] So, in reality, "artless" Fanny can and does "act." Her performance is an example of what Paula Byrne calls the "social role-playing" essential to the functioning of polite society.[51] Just as Juliet Granville performs her actual aristocratic refinement in *The Wanderer* when she acts the role of Lady Townly in *The Provoked Husband*, so too Fanny performs her authentic heroic courage when she strives to overcome her "excessive" feelings for Edmund. Unlike Miss Andrews, whose social role-playing of being "in" or "out" had so confused Tom Bertram, Fanny's principled behavior, her performance of duty even though no one else can perceive or appreciate the performance, is not "'acting upon motives of vanity,'" as Edmund had said of Miss Andrews: Fanny does not wear her duty like a close bonnet (58).

Readers who dismiss Catherine Morland as a foolish girl and Fanny Price as a passive prig fail to recognize these characters' "heroism of principle" and thus also fail to meet the challenge that Austen constructs for her readers. In Jane Austen's novels, not every heroine needs to be an accomplished artist, but every heroine, like every reader, must be prepared to judge for herself, guided by principle, and to act upon what she believes to be right. Thus equipped, even a powerless, artless young woman may be heroic if she dares to do her duty.

Notes

1. Jane Austen, *Sense and Sensibility*, ed. Edward Copeland (Cambridge: Cambridge University Press, 2006), 20, 41. Subsequent references are to this edition and will be provided parenthetically within the text.

2. To be considered accomplished, declares Miss Bingley, "a woman must have a thorough knowledge of music, singing, drawing, dancing, and the modern languages" as well as "a certain something in her air and manner of walking," to which Mr. Darcy adds the need for "the improvement of her mind by extensive reading" (Jane Austen, *Pride and Prejudice*, ed. Pat Rogers [Cambridge: Cambridge University Press, 2006], 42–43).

3. Wayne C. Booth, *The Rhetoric of Fiction* (Chicago: University of Chicago Press, 1961), 186.

4. Brian Southam, "*Sanditon*: The Seventh Novel," in *Jane Austen's Achievement*, ed. Juliet McMaster (London: Macmillan, 1976), 12.

5. Anne Henry Ehrenpreis, introduction to *Northanger Abbey*, by Jane Austen (Harmondsworth, UK: Penguin, 1972), 16.

6. Martin Amis, "What Became of Jane Austen?," in *Jane Austen: A Collection of Critical Essays*, ed. Ian Watt (Englewood Cliffs, NJ: Prentice-Hall, 1963), 142.

7. Tony Tanner, "Jane Austen and 'The Quiet Thing': A Study of *Mansfield Park*," in *Critical Essays on Jane Austen*, ed. Brian Southam (London: Routledge, 1970), 137.

8. Lionel Trilling, "*Mansfield Park*," in *Jane Austen: A Collection of Critical Essays*, ed. Watt, 128.

9. Jane Austen, *Northanger Abbey*, ed. Barbara M. Benedict and Deirdre Le Faye (Cambridge: Cambridge University Press, 2006), 99. Subsequent references are to this edition and will be provided parenthetically within the text.

10. Jane Austen, *Mansfield Park*, ed. John Wiltshire (Cambridge: Cambridge University Press, 2005), 171. Subsequent references are to this edition and will be provided parenthetically within the text.

11. "Artless," def. 2, *Johnson's Dictionary* (1785). I, however, am using the word here not in Johnson's sense but, rather, to mean "not practicing any of the fine arts."

12. See, for example, the eponymous heroine of Charlotte Smith's *Emmeline* in *The Works of Charlotte Smith*, ed. Judith Stanton, vol. 2, *Emmeline, the Orphan of the Castle* (London: Pickering and Chatto, 2005): an orphan, supposedly illegitimate, raised by the kindly housekeeper of a decayed, remote castle, Emmeline manages to acquire "a taste for poetry, and the more ornamental parts of literature" (5), and later, through her friendship with accomplished Mrs. Stafford, quickly becomes adept at drawing, French, and Italian (42–43).

13. Jane Austen, "Plan of a Novel, according to hints from various quarters," in *Later Manuscripts*, ed. Janet Todd and Linda Bree (Cambridge: Cambridge University Press, 2008), 226.

14. My dissertation, "Jane Austen's Readers" (PhD diss., McGill University, 1981), makes these arguments throughout.

15. Sir Walter Scott, *Waverley*, ed. Claire Lamont (Oxford: Oxford University Press, 1986), 4.

16. Scott, *Waverley*, 143.

17. Maria Edgeworth to Walter Scott, October 23, 1814, in *Life and Letters of Maria Edgeworth*, 2 vols., ed. Augustus J. C. Hare (London, 1894), 1:230. Edgeworth misses the invitation implicit in Scott's opening burlesque to view Flora ironically.

18. Edgeworth's sophisticated, realistic novel echoes the themes of the simpler, satiric and didactic 1796 moral tale of Elizabeth Inchbald, *Nature and Art*, which also contrasts the "natural" versus "artificial" upbringing and values of two generations (brothers and cousins) of a family.

19. Maria Edgeworth, *Patronage*, ed. Eva Figes (London: Pandora, 1986), 37.

20. Frances Burney, *The Wanderer*, ed. Margaret Anne Doody, Robert L. Mack, and Peter Sabor (Oxford: Oxford University Press, 1991), 72. Subsequent references are to this edition and will be provided parenthetically in the text.

21. See, however, Kathryn L. Libin's discussion of Hannah More's change of heart about musical education for young ladies, in "Daily Practice, Musical Accomplishment, and the Example of Jane Austen," in *Jane Austen and the Arts: Elegance, Propriety, and Harmony*, ed. Natasha Duquette and Elisabeth Lenckos (Bethlehem, PA: Lehigh University Press, 2014), 6–8.

22. Hannah More, *Strictures on the Modern System of Female Education*, 2 vols., 5th ed. (London, 1799), 1.1:2–4.

23. More, *Strictures*, 1.2:69.

24. More, *Strictures*, 1.4:105.

25. Natasha Duquette discusses the morally questionable objective of "elegance" of Sir Thomas's education of his daughters in this volume in "'A Very Pretty Amber Cross': Material Sources of Elegance in *Mansfield Park*." Duquette asks, "Why has Sir Thomas Bertram's parenting and educating of his own children at home led to 'elegant and agreeable' daughters without moral discernment?"

26. More, *Strictures*, 1.4:107.

27. More, *Strictures*, 1.4:107.

28. More complains, "There was a time when . . the words venerable, learned, sagacious, profound, acute, pious, ingenious, elegant, agreeable, wise, or witty, were used as specific marks of distinct characters." But in the fashionable world, "The word *pleasant* now serves to combine and express all moral and intellectual excellence" (More, *Strictures*, 1.1:12).

29. Vivasvan Soni also claims that Austen's novels "model for their readers a practice of judgment not beholden to any fixed criteria whatsoever. They even demand that readers engage in this practice of reflective judgment if they are to read the novels well" ("Preface: Jane Austen's Critique of Aesthetic Judgment," in *Jane Austen and the Arts*, ed. Duquette and Lenckos, xvii).

30. "Taste," according to James Noggle, was "the most potent evaluative term in eighteenth-century British culture" (Noggle, *The Temporality of Taste in Eighteenth-Century British Writing* [Oxford: Oxford University Press, 2012], 1). Peter Kivy, *The Seventh Sense: Francis Hutcheson and Eighteenth-Century British Aesthetics* (Oxford: Clarendon, 2003), surveys the philosophical evolution of the term "taste."

31. This is essentially Soni's argument (and was the argument of my 1981 dissertation): Austen endorses a reflective *process* rather than specific *criteria* for judgment (see note 29 above).

32. Lorrie Clark, "Shaftesbury's Art of 'Soliloquy' in *Mansfield Park*," *Persuasions* 24 (2002): 62.

33. Clark, "Shaftesbury's Art," 64.

34. Kathryn L. Libin's "Lifting the Heart to Rapture: Harmony, Nature, and the Unmusical Fanny Price," *Persuasions* 28 (2006): 137–49, examines Fanny's preference for nature over music. Lorrie Clark suggests that Fanny's pleasure in nature is both moral and aesthetic ("Shaftesbury's Art," 61).

35. Fanny meets picturesque theorist Richard Payne Knight's definition of philosopher: "To a mind richly stored, almost every object of nature or art, that presents itself to the senses, either excites fresh trains and combinations of ideas, or vivifies and strengthens those which existed before. . Every insect, plant, or fossil . . is, to the naturalist and philosopher, a subject of curious inquiry and speculation" (*An Analytical Inquiry into the Principles of Taste*, 2nd ed. [London, 1805], chap. 2, 143).

36. Karen Valihora, *Austen's Oughts: Judgment after Locke and Shaftesbury* (Newark: University of Delaware Press, 2010), 32.

37. Valihora, *Austen's Oughts*, 33.

38. Soni, "Preface," xvi.

39. Many critics have noted this. Soni, for example, attributes Marianne's false inference to her mistaken reliance on the "consonance between the love of beauty and the love of the good," arguing that *Sense and Sensibility* "urges us to see that the inference from good taste to virtuous behavior cannot hold" ("Preface," xvi).

40. Copeland cites the 1790 edition of *Characteristics*: "An Enquiry Concerning Virtue," pt. 2.

41. Vallihora, *Austen's Oughts*, 106.

42. Both Soni and Clark argue that Austen finds her own "third" alternative to prevailing ideologies by advocating for what Soni calls "autonomous judgment" ("Preface," xvi) and Clark, "soliloquy," or reflection ("Shaftesbury's Art," 64).

43. Humphry Repton, *Observations on the Theory and Practice of Landscape Gardening* (London: Constable, 1906), 67.

44. See Dorothy Dyck, "The Development of the Picturesque and the Knight-Price-Repton Controversy" (master's thesis, McGill University, 1991), 46–47.

45. Knight, "Analytical Inquiry," 233.

46. Knight, "Analytical Inquiry," 234.

47. Knight, "Analytical Inquiry," 235.

48. Jane Austen to Cassandra Austen, November 24, 1815, in *Jane Austen's Letters*, ed. Deirdre Le Faye, 4th ed. (Oxford: Oxford University Press, 2011), 312. Le Faye notes: "Mr Haden must have been quoting or paraphrasing *Merchant of Venice*, V.i" (*Letters*, 312n4).

49. Samuel Hall, "An Attempt to shew that a Taste for the beauties of nature and the Fine Arts, has no influence favourable to morals," in *Memoirs of the Literary and Philosophical Society of Manchester* (London, 1785), 1:229. He added: "Let taste . . "be cultivated, as the source of many elegant pleasures: but let it ever be cultivated, in subordination to sound morality. Taste can ill supply the want of moral discipline" (1:239).

50. Natasha Duquette sites Fanny's "heroism of principle" in a specifically Christian context, as the consequence of William giving her the amber cross and Fanny praying for Edmund's happiness (see "'A Very Pretty Amber Cross': Material Sources of Elegance in *Mansfield Park*" in this volume).

51. Paula Byrne discusses the various significances of the word "act" in this novel: "In the morally ambiguous world of *Mansfield Park*, Austen consistently puns on the words 'act' and 'acting' to blur the distinctions between role-playing and social conduct." She adds: "Far from proposing that acting encourages a kind of insincere role-playing in life, Austen suggests in her depiction of polite society that an ability to perform socially is often a necessity." Elinor in *Sense and Sensibility* is an example of such polite social acting (Byrne, *Jane Austen and the Theatre* [London: Hambledon and London, 2002], 203).

Legal Arts and Artifacts in Jane Austen's Persuasion

NANCY E. JOHNSON

In the original ending to Jane Austen's *Persuasion*, Admiral Croft compares Anne Elliot to "a little Judge." She has stopped by Kellynch Hall for a brief visit, and he begins to tease her about romantic intrigue: "'Why, Miss Elliot, we begin to hear strange things of you'—(smiling in her face)—'But you have not much the Look of it—as Grave as a little Judge." Upon hearing this remark, Anne blushes, and all is well again. "Aye, aye, that will do," utters Admiral Croft, "Now, it is right. I *thought* we were not mistaken."[1] The Admiral's observation, "as Grave as a little Judge," can certainly be read as a mere simile, and a common one at that, tossed out by an affable older man to a younger woman who is too serious for her own good.[2] However, in a novel that is about judgment, the casting of Anne Elliot as a figure of the law is important, particularly because, in the course of the novel, she will emerge as a juridical model. Whereas more formal representatives of the law, such as Sir Walter Elliot, an MP,[3] and Mr. John Shepherd, a lawyer, are engaged in the business of the law, which is often trivial or suspect, Anne will rise above the fray and become the voice of reasonableness and equity, not least in her success obtaining Frederick Wentworth's aid in resolving Mrs. Smith's legal troubles. Yet, because Anne must not be seen as transgressing into the domain of law, she must remain a young woman and occupy herself with the concerns of a young woman, such as finding a good husband. And thus the reader, like Admiral Croft, will be reassured by the blush that signals Anne's vulnerability, sensibility, and familiar status as an Austenian heroine.

I begin with this image of Anne Elliot, recovered from a canceled chapter, because it calls attention to a subtext. This subtext is embedded in the narrative of a cultural shift marked by the return of naval personnel after the war with France, which Brian Southam describes as a "social phenomenon of some magnitude."[4] When we see the *Baronetage* displaced by the *Navy List*, and we witness the ancestral home of Kellynch become a marketable property rented out to a naval family, we find the destabilization of two hallmarks of landed wealth, and we know that something in the social order has changed. These markers of change initially point to Sir Walter Elliot, William Walter Elliot, Admiral Croft, Captain Wentworth, and all the other "captains," but it is Anne Elliot who becomes the focal point of both transformation and stasis. Anne is cast as a Burney-like "nobody"[5] at the start of the novel; she was "nobody with either father or sister: her word had no weight; her convenience was always to give way;—she was only Anne" (*P*, 6).[6] Moreover, she remains in transit through most of the novel, on a *Cecilia*-like journey[7] as she comes to terms with her pivotal encounter with "persuasion"; that is, when Lady Russell persuades her not to marry Captain Wentworth (31–32). Her subjectivity is ephemeral and in flux. However, what I will suggest is that Anne is transformed from an apparent nobody to a figure of juridical authority, whose displacement sets her on a path to justice—a path that, notably, is not traveled by Sir Walter or Mr. Shepherd, or any formal representatives of the law. As she moves toward legal agency, justice will become detached not only from rank, landownership, and gender but also from its central legal art of persuasion. Persuasion will be exposed as a mere rhetorical art, and it is flawed; judgment is where integrity resides. On her journey, Anne's identity as a "nobody" will give her a degree of freedom to navigate and to explore, unnoticed and unthreatened. Additionally, she will be bolstered by the hint of subjectivity in this first statement of negation; in the apparent absence of "nobody" is "only Anne," which is a subjective presence. And "only Anne" is propelled forward by a form of judgment that she has inherited from her mother and attaches not only to her stoic virtue of fortitude and constancy but also to what she describes as a reasoned "elasticity of mind" that will inform her sense of justice (167).[8]

In the remainder of this essay, I will examine two sets of supporting legal artifacts, both of which elucidate Anne Elliot's journey and her symbolically significant emergence as a judge. The first set consists of John Debrett's *Baronetage of England*, undergirded by William Dugdale's *Ancient Usage*,[9] and juxtaposed with the *Navy List*. I treat the *Baronetage* as a legal artifact because it is a record of legal authority. Baronets stood as members of Parliament for the House of Commons (a site of legislation); some served in prestigious offices, such as that of the lord chief justice, and others were members of the Privy Council. The second set of legal artifacts consists of the estate, which is juxtaposed with the carriage and the ship. The estate is crucial to juridical agency—the foundation for it and the guarantee of its continuity. The carriage removes landowners and their families from the estate and puts them in motion; it also carries judges on the assizes. The ship might be seen as an antithesis to the estate. While the borders of an estate are meant to be preserved, like the borders of a nation, a ship crosses boundaries and moves in international waters.[10] Moreover, ships were under the jurisdiction of maritime law and the Courts of Admiralty, rather than the Courts of Common Law and the Courts of Equity. The Courts of Admiralty addressed violations by citizens of other nations and entered into diplomatic terrains, hearing cases that, like the ship, crossed national borders.[11] What we find embedded subtextually in these artifacts and their counterpoints—that is, why they are important—is the revelation of female agency and a concept of justice that is articulated by women.

The Baronetage

The *Baronetage*[12] is the opening image of *Persuasion*, and as nearly every scholar of *Persuasion* has noted, the indulgence in the *Baronetage* by the vain and provincial Sir Walter puts a comedic spin on the hypocritical and narrow-minded adherence to inherited rank, especially when it is espoused by the landed gentry. The diminishing significance of the *Baronetage* is marked by its physical smallness: the Elliot entry is confined to "two handsome duodecimo pages," pages that are "folded twelve times," and therefore, as Patricia Meyer Spacks explains, it would be the size of a contemporary paperback.[13] The *Baronetage* was an easy target because, although inherited, the title of baronet was not a peerage. Earliest mentions of baronets date back to the fourteenth century; however, the Order of Baronets, which is the source of Debrett's *Baronetage*, was created by James I in 1611 for the dubious purpose of increasing revenue. Compounding this tainted history was the fact that by the end of the eighteenth century baronets were growing in number. Thomas Keymer reports that approximately 233 new baronetcies were added between 1760 and 1800—a proliferation that created the need for Debrett's *Baronetage*.[14] Moreover, despite its solidity as an artifact—a bound and printed book—the *Baronetage* was meant to be updated and republished over time. It was a provisional text that could be written upon by Sir Walter himself as he updated and improved it by adding family details and events since its publication. Thus, when Austen pokes fun at both the *Baronetage* and Sir Walter's obsession, she is directing her critique at a book whose physicality is transient, and at a relatively modern creation of rank that has become less valuable as it has become more common.

As mentioned earlier, what makes the *Baronetage* a particular artifact of the law is its record of legal officeholders. But the honor of each of the positions outlined in the Elliot entry is compromised. The first office mentioned in the Elliot entry is that of the "High Sheriff," who was designated "the Crown's chief officer in a county" and was responsible for "the administration of justice."[15] It was an important position, but as Jocelyn Harris notes, the post of high sheriff was "unpopular" and often "unsought" because it frequently carried an expensive fee.[16] The second office mentioned is that of member of Parliament. The Elliots served in "three successive Parliaments," and while we have no record of their contribution to the governance of the country, our expectations are set by the example of the selfish and indulgent Sir Walter (*P*, 4). Finally, we learn that the Elliot baronetcy was created "in the first year of Charles II," 1660, which was another time when the number of baronetcies increased dramatically, and as Jocelyn Harris notes, often in exchange for cash, certainly in exchange for loyalty.[17] The "heirs" to this legacy, Sir Walter and Mr. Elliot, carry on the questionable honors attached to their title and only heighten our doubts about the value of these honors and these rankings. Sir Walter, an MP, and Mr. Elliot, who had been "engaged in the study of the law" (8), meet not only in the lobby of the House of Commons but also at Tattersal's, an auction house for horses and a site for betting.[18] Both are more interested in personal social and economic advancement than in service to the nation, and neither has the personal integrity that one would like to associate with rank and honor. Thus, the small, thick, cheap book that records the lineage of baronets perfectly introduces both men's compromised credentials as representatives of the law.

The *Navy List*, which documents meritorious accomplishments, is often seen as the counterpoint to the *Baronetage*. With two brothers in the British navy, Austen is forthright about her pride and faith in the honors of maritime bravery and effective action, over and above the supposed honors of rank—albeit, those of the landed gentry.[19] However, the opposition between the two texts is not as decisive as it might appear.[20] The *Baronetage* makes an effort to accommodate military and maritime honors as a means to bolster the status and value of its baronetcies. In the preface to the Debrett's 1808 edition of the *Baronetage*, which is the edition most scholars expect that Austen was referring to in *Persuasion*, the editor tells the story of the origin of the Order of the Baronet. "Ireland," he explains, "which had been long the theatre of a destructive war, was then in great measure brought to allegiance. For the alleged purposes of guarding and fortifying the subjection of that great province, of aiding its cultivation, and civilizing its people, James appealed to the loyalty and patriotism of the most respectable and wealthy commoners of ancient families in his realm, and ordained that such individuals of that description as were willing to maintain thirty soldiers in Ireland, for three years . . . should be exalted to the dignity in question."[21] In other words, baronets were enlisted in a "war effort" to subjugate, cultivate, and civilize the Irish. While they might not have served in combat, they made it possible for the British army to assert its dominance and maintain order.

Likewise, in an addendum to the preface, in the 1815 edition, the editor justifies the expansion of the *Baronetage* to include military and naval heroes who have been honored with a baronetcy: "Military and Naval services of a character heretofore almost unparalleled even in these realms, during an additional seven years, to a war before of unexampled length have claimed with the strictest justice, and received with a most due liberality, those purely honourable rewards, which his Royal Highness the Prince Regent, . . . has been pleased to allot to them. Long may their honours remain in their blood, and so long may their posterity emulate the bright example of such ancestors."[22] The absorption of more recent military and naval heroes into the baronetcy gives credence to those earliest of baronets enlisted to "fight" the Irish; the light of contemporary victories against Napoleon's France is cast back onto those wealthy and respectable commoners of ancient families, providing them with a more glorious, and updated, form of honor. This expansion of the baronetcy breaks down the apparent opposition between the *Baronetage* and the *Navy List* and becomes an example of social rank accommodating a social shift: the *Baronetage* is strengthened by its recognition of returning military and naval personnel who are altering the social landscape.

A more provocative opposition than that between the *Baronetage* and the *Navy List* might be discovered between the patrilineal inheritance of the *Baronetage* and the matrilineal inheritance of Anne Elliot and her mother. Whereas women in the *Baronetage* are described generically by Austen as "all the Marys and Elizabeths" whom the baronets have married, women outside the *Baronetage* are the caretakers and preservers of the British family and estates (*P*, 4). The case of the Elliots exemplifies this very breakdown of patrilineal inheritance. Sir Walter Elliot is the embodiment of biblical vanity, "vanity of vanities! All is vanity" (Ecclesiastes 1.2); for Sir Walter, "vanity was the beginning and the end" and he was himself "the constant object of his warmest respect and devotion" (*P*, 4). Obsessed by his family's place in the *Baronetage*, he fails to understand the humility of the biblical concept of generational passage: "A generation goes, and a generation comes, but the earth remains forever" (Ecclesiastes 1.4). The achievements documented by both the *Baronetage* and the *Navy List* are diminished in this context because they are seen to be merely part of a generational cycle that is replicated in nature: "The sun rises and the sun goes down, and hastens to the place where it rises. The wind blows to the south, and goes round to the north; round and round goes the wind and on its circuits the wind returns" (Ecclesiastes 1.5–6). The patrilineal model, based on ambition and achievement, gives way to the matrilineal model that is infused with humility. With the passage of generations represented by Lady Elliot's death and her legacy to Anne, we have a reaffirmation of the generational cycle of Ecclesiastes. While Sir Walter fails to produce a direct heir for his baronetcy, Lady Elliot delivers her heirs—and her legacy, in contrast to a hollow title, is sound judgment and conduct. Lady Elliot, we are told, "had been an excellent woman, sensible and amiable; whose judgment and conduct, if they might be pardoned the youthful infatuation which made her Lady Elliot, had never required indulgence afterwards" (*P*, 4). Alistair Duckworth is correct when he argues that *Persuasion* maintains "an allegiance to inherited moral and social structures";[23] however, I would further assert that it is an allegiance to matrilineal, over patrilineal, inheritance. Lady Elliot's daughter Anne, whose humility is manifest in her identity as "nobody," will fill the void of judgment left behind by Sir Walter, Mr. Shepherd, and William Walter Elliot, Esq., and she is poised to do so because of what she has inherited from her mother, not her father.

The Estate

With classic Austenian irony, immediately after we read of Sir Walter's indulgence in the *Baronetage*, we also learn that because of poor stewardship, he must rent his estate, Kellynch Hall. Thus the man who has failed to produce a male heir has also failed in his responsibility to maintain his family's estate, and to make matters worse, he is either oblivious to the implications of his failure, or he is indifferent. In legal discourse, the estate is a foundational metaphor that points to the stability and solidity of English law and the English nation. Sir William Blackstone in his *Commentaries on the Laws of England* compares English common law to "an old Gothic castle, erected in the days of chivalry, but fitted up for a modern inhabitant."[24] The image of the gothic castle invokes the Magna Carta of 1215, which was often cited as the source of British liberty; the gothic castle was then "fitted up for a modern inhabitant" when those liberties were later reconfirmed by the Declaration of Right in 1689. In political discourse, the estate is equally important. Edmund Burke returns to Blackstone's metaphor when he argues for the concept of liberty as contained in—and therefore protected by—an "entailed inheritance," bequeathed to us by our forefathers and intended to be transmitted to posterity. For Burke, our rights are likened to an "estate," and through "a constitutional policy, working after the pattern of nature, we receive, we hold, we transmit our government and our privileges, in the same manner in which we enjoy and transmit our property and our lives."[25]

Therefore, when Kellynch Hall is turned into a marketable—or more precisely, rentable—commodity by one who is supposed to be a steward of not just the estate, but the law and the liberties that the law is meant to protect, we see that he has neglected his obligations of citizenship. But, in the way that the *Baronetage* absorbs the *Navy List*, the British estate welcomes the Royal Navy into its fold, and Sir Walter rents his estate to Admiral Croft and his wife. When the Napoleonic Wars have ceased and naval officers return to land under the glories of victory and with the aid of accumulated wealth, they step in to provide the nation with the stability that baronets and members of Parliament, like Sir Walter, have failed to supply.[26] In fact, British stability was becoming increasingly reliant on trade and the Royal Navy, such that by 1815, according to Martin Robson, "the British Empire was not a territorial empire but a maritime trading empire based on free access to global trade routes, guaranteed by strategic positions and the Royal Navy."[27] Thus the habitation of Kellynch Hall by Admiral Croft and his wife is perfectly suitable to the rise of the Royal Navy in national importance.

Nonetheless, the Crofts are only renting Kellynch, and looming in the future is William Walter Elliot's ability to dispose of Kellynch.[28] Thus the solution to the destabilized estate has an impermanence to it that recalls the temporality of both the physical *Baronetage* and the *Navy List*. In addition, and perhaps most significant, once again the tension between inherited honor versus accomplished honor, as represented by the *Baronetage* and the *Navy List*, obscures an alternative third option: justice and national stability through the leadership of women. At the time we learn of Sir Walter's financial dilemma, we also learn that it was Lady Elliot who had kept the estate solvent while she was alive, and she managed to do so because under her watchful eye "there had been method, moderation, and economy." Despite her husband's lineage, she is the one who was the effective caretaker, the guardian of British law and liberty. With her passing was the loss of "all such right-mindedness," and Sir Walter, unleashed, drove the family into debt. Mr. Shepherd, "a civil, cautious lawyer," and Lady Russell, who was something of a surrogate mother to Lady Elliot's daughters, were to advise Sir Walter in economy; however, Mr. Shepherd sheds his responsibility and defers to Lady Russell (*P*, 9–10, 13). Lady Russell is impeded—in part by her indulgence of rank and consequence—and so she consults Anne. In Anne's response, we see the legacy of her mother: "Every emendation of Anne's had been on the side of honesty against importance. She wanted more vigorous measures, a more complete reformation, a quicker release from debt, a much higher tone of indifference for every thing but justice and equity" (13). In Anne's recommendations for retrenchment, we find her mother's competence, and in her adherence to justice and equity, we see a figure of the law. As we do for her mother, we recognize Anne's potential as a steward of British liberty.

Despite their efforts, neither Anne nor Lady Russell is able to convince Sir Walter and Elizabeth to economize. Consequently, the Elliots must abandon the estate and take to their carriages; Sir Walter and Elizabeth travel to Bath, while Anne goes to Uppercross Cottage, the home of her sister Mary and Mary's husband, Charles Musgrove. The carriages, which are a counterpoint to the estate, represent independence as well as prestige because they were expensive.[29] Horses, carriages, and armorial ensigns that might appear on the side of a carriage were all taxed, and these taxes were increased at the turn of the century to offset the expense of war.[30] The status-conscious Sir Walter is loath to give up his carriage, but he must, and so it was "the last office of the four carriage-horses" to take Sir Walter, Elizabeth Elliot and Mrs. Clay to Bath (*P*, 38). The horses that are fulfilling their final service to the Elliots provide a link back to Tattersal's, the site of horse trading and betting, and the place where Sir Walter had met William Walter Elliot. Both men are implicated by Tattersal's, which, with its emphasis on commerce and chance, sits in direct contrast to the rationality of the law and the responsibility of governance to which they are supposed to be attending. Austen draws attention to the central contradiction between chance and the law when she juxtaposes them in a single sentence: "'For they must have been seen together,' he observed, 'once at Tattersal's, and twice in the lobby of the House of Commons'" (8). The observation is made by Sir Walter, and "they" refers to Sir Walter and Mr. Elliot. However, we might read "they" as Tattersal's and the House of Commons, which we, unlike Sir Walter, see as dangerously linked "together."

The carriage as a counterpoint to the estate functions in a twofold manner for Anne Elliot: it carries her on her journey of displacement, and it enables her disbursement of justice. Considering Anne a figure of the law, we are reminded of the carriage that would transport a judge to the assizes or the quarter sessions. The carriage indicates movement, but it also signifies balance because it requires a certain distribution of weight to function; it is a balance that one might liken to the scales of justice. We also see both movement and balance in the first location to which the carriage takes Anne, the estate of Uppercross, inhabited by the Musgrove family. The name of the estate invokes the stability of a monument (a cross atop a pilaster), as well as the balance that is achieved in Uppercross's accommodation of the modern. The Great House is softened by the warmth and informality of family life, such that the portraits of passing elders "seemed to be staring in astonishment." But the Musgroves, we are told, "like their houses, were in a state of alteration, perhaps of improvement. The father and mother were in the old English style, and the young people in the new" (*P*, 43).

The carriage also takes Anne to Lyme, where the "estate" becomes the lodging rooms of the naval personnel returned from sea. The rooms of Captain and Mrs. Harville are small, but Captain Harville has created all kinds of "ingenious contrivances and nice arrangements" to turn the space to "the best possible account, to supply the deficiencies of lodging-house furniture, and defend the windows and doors against the winter storms to be expected" (*P*, 106). Both Brian Southam and Tony Tanner have likened the Harville's lodging to those of a ship in its size and efficiency, and in its collection of items "curious and valuable from all the distant countries" (*P*, 106).[31] The ship that is invoked in the Harvilles' lodging is another counterpoint to the estate, and a particularly provocative one for the novel. The estate is landlocked; it is dependent on boundaries, and it is a cornerstone to nationalism. In contradistinction, the ship moves along seas; it is meant to cross boundaries, and it must engage internationally; furthermore, it is the future of Great Britain. The ship reinforces the *Navy List*, and once again the members of the Royal Navy, more so than the landowners such as Sir Walter who are supposed to be the national caretakers, are the more accomplished protectors of British law and liberty, as demonstrated by their recent successes in the war with France.

Yet, as with the other counterpoints, embedded in the binaries of estate and ship, land and sea, is an assertion of the competency of women. Both Admiral Croft and Captain Wentworth, two naval heroes, are overshadowed by Mrs. Croft and Anne Elliot in their ability to handle critical situations. Mrs. Croft proves to be the formidable partner in negotiations for the rental of Kellynch. Mr. Shepherd describes her as "shrewd" and explains that she "asked more questions about the house, and terms, and taxes, than the admiral himself, and seemed more conversant with business" (*P*, 25). Mrs. Croft unapologetically occupies space on her husband's ship, and, challenging the predominance of the estate, declares that "women may be as comfortable on board, as in the best house in England" (74).[32] Finally, we see Mrs. Croft, in a particularly precarious moment in a carriage, take the reins from the Admiral and navigate them safely home. The image of Mrs. Croft skillfully guiding her husband and taking the reins of the carriage when necessary sets a precedent for Anne, who while in Lyme will have to step in and take charge when our naval heroes crumble. She counsels the heartbroken Captain Benwick, whose fiancée, Fanny Harville, died while he was at sea. And when Captain Wentworth, who showed remarkable bravery and resolve in "the action off St. Domingo" (28), falls apart at the sight of Louisa's fall, Anne takes control.[33] While she cares for Louisa, Anne issues commands for the others to take care of Captain Wentworth: "Go to him, go to him, for heaven's sake go to him. I can support her myself" (118). This is a triumphant moment for Anne, and a turning point on her journey toward juridical authority.

The extent to which Anne is transformed in Lyme becomes clear when she is once again in the carriage—this time with Captain Wentworth and Henrietta, as they return to Uppercross. Emboldened by her newfound authority in Lyme, Anne confronts persuasion. She has been the victim of persuasion and the object of Captain Wentworth's judgment because of her acquiescence. But now the tables have turned, and it is Captain Wentworth who is in a state of vulnerability and uncertainty, and Anne takes the opportunity to evaluate him. Persuasion is the central rhetorical art of the law, and it is just that: an art, as opposed to truth. It is the business of lawyers, who compete for the most convincing narrative. The judge must assess the rhetoric of persuasion to ascertain truth and arrive at a fair and equitable judgment. While in the carriage, Anne contemplates Captain Wentworth's view of persuasion and wonders "whether it ever occurred to him now, to question the justness of his own previous opinion as to the universal felicity and advantage of firmness of character; and whether it might not strike him, that, like all other qualities of the mind, it should have its proportions and limits" (*P*, 126). Anne is now acting as a judge, challenging Captain Wentworth's opinion and demarcating her perspective on justice from his. Captain Wentworth's view on the antithesis of persuadability—firmness of character—is bound by universality and rigidity, while Anne's is liberated by proportion and limitation. Notably, Captain Wentworth's judgment, which has been devoid of mercy and forgiveness, keeps the couple apart, whereas

Anne's will bring them together. In addition, Anne has transformed the carriage from a place where women are so often compromised in novels, to a site of juridical victory.

This victory is almost immediately followed by a sober scene in which Anne inhabits the estate of Uppercross mansion by herself. She has convinced the Musgrove family to go to Lyme to be with Louisa during her recovery. In the interval between their departure for Lyme and Anne's return to Lady Russell's, Anne is left to "the solitary range of the house" (*P*, 133). For a male character, this moment of inhabiting an estate would be symbolic of his power, especially on the heels of an ascendency, but for Anne, the scene is tinged with sadness. She is "the only remaining one of all that had filled and animated both houses, and, of all that had given Uppercross its cheerful character" (133). She imagines the rooms "now so deserted, occupied but by her silent, pensive self, might be filled again with all that was happy and gay, all that was glowing and bright in prosperous love, all that was most unlike Anne Elliot!" (133). The mood is a somber one, and the "thick" November rain obscures her vision and emphasizes the isolation of the estate. Here, she is the "grave little judge," and melancholy weighs down the victory she has just experienced. Therefore, her journey is not quite complete. She must be the "blushing" Anne who reassures Admiral Croft and the reader that she is still a young woman, and she must resolve her romantic dilemma to become a symbolically full representation of justice.

Thus, it is back to the carriage, and onward to Bath, where by the end of the novel nearly all of the characters of *Persuasion* have gathered to witness, and gossip about, multiple unions. The resolution embedded in Anne's and Captain Wentworth's reunion is about justice—a reckoning of how Anne, Captain Wentworth, and Lady Russell have engaged with persuasion. But it is Anne who now speaks firmly and comfortably as a judge. The first signal that indicates Anne's journey toward juridical authority is coming to a close is her rejection of a chair (a vehicle akin to a carriage) to carry her home. She chooses to walk, a decision that facilitates her reconciliation with Captain Wentworth and allows her to confront him about his faulty judgment. They are on an equal footing literally and symbolically, enabled by the mature love they have now discovered. With careful reasoning, bolstered by common sense, Anne explains that her capitulation to Lady Russell's persuasion was that of a nineteen-year-old girl acting out of a sense of filial duty. However, if she were to marry William Walter Elliot, a man to whom she was indifferent, "no duty could be called in aid here . . . all risk would have been incurred, and all duty violated" (*P*, 266). It would have been illogical.

Gender roles are reversed once again as Captain Wentworth admits that he could not reason about the situation as clearly as Anne because he was overwhelmed with emotion.

At this culminating point of her journey, Anne has been transformed from a nobody to a "steadfast and fearless" woman, who is also "glowing and lovely in sensibility and happiness" (*P*, 266, 267). The combination of constancy and courage on the one hand, and sensibility and happiness on the other, is important to the novel because it presents us with an image of the juridical woman, and it gives Anne the authority to articulate her judgment. "I have been thinking over the past," she admits, "and trying impartially to judge of the right and wrong, I mean with regard to myself" (267). And while the others consider how they erred, Anne concludes that she was right. "I was perfectly right," she asserts, "in being guided by the friend whom you will love better than you do now. To me, she was in the place of a parent" (267–68). In the process of becoming a judge—no longer the "grave little judge" but rather a woman who has reconciled her ability to reason with a capacity for joy and happiness—Anne discloses an understanding of justice that surpasses any of those formally affiliated with the law. She defines good judgment as "a quickness of perception . . a nicety in the discernment of character, a natural penetration" (271). Her definition is similar to that of sensibility, reminding us that the discernment and compassion of sensibility function at the heart of an otherwise rational process of the law. In reaching this conclusion about judgment, Anne transforms the pathos of the rhetoric of persuasion into the sensibility of justice. We are told that Anne will not be rewarded with an estate; however, there is optimism in her alternative association with the navy because the artifact of the ship promises a more enlightened future. When the ship takes the reader beyond the confines of the estate and outside the borders of the nation, it points the reader in the direction of international engagement, which is where British prospects lie. Neither the *Baronetage* nor the *Navy List* will ever account for Anne's advancements in the law, thus her record of justice must be chronicled in that site of women's accomplishments, the novel.

Notes

1. Jane Austen, *Persuasion*, ed. Janet Todd and Antje Blank (Cambridge: Cambridge University Press, 2013), 314–15. Subsequent references are to this edition and will be provided parenthetically within the text.

2. According to Brian Southam, Admiral Croft's position as a "Rear-Admiral of the White" would likely place him in his early to mid-forties (Southam, *Jane Austen and the*

Navy [New York: Hambledon and London, 2000], 268). Anne is twenty-seven years old when the novel opens (*P*, 31).

3. Sir Walter Eliot's status as an MP is suggested by his presence at the House of Commons. See also *P*, 338n25, where the editors note that he may have been there only to attend the debates. Given the predominance of law in the novel, I am assuming he is characterized as an MP.

4. Southam, *Jane Austen and the Navy*, 265.

5. The term "nobody" in eighteenth-century writing has become associated with Frances Burney, who dedicated her first journal to "Nobody." In an entry dated March 27, 1768, Burney writes: "To Nobody, then, will I write my Journal! since To Nobody can I be wholly unreserved" (*Early Journals and Letters of Fanny Burney*, 5 vols., ed. Lars E. Troide [Montreal: McGill-Queens Press, 1988], 1:2). In addition, Burney used the image of a female nobody in her novels (see Joanne Cutting-Gray, *Woman as "Nobody" in the Novels of Fanny Burney* [Gainesville: University Press of Florida, 1992]). For a broader discussion of the motif of "nobody" in eighteenth-century fiction, see Catherine Gallagher, *Nobody's Story: The Vanishing Acts of Women Writers in the Marketplace 1670–1820* (Berkeley: University of California Press, 1994).

6. Margaret Anne Doody notes that Austen typically uses the name "Anne" for "subordinate and inferior characters" who are marked by "shyness, weakness," and "social incapacity." But she also notes that the name "Elliot" is "sometimes connected with the Hebrew for 'the lord on high' or with 'Elias' (Hebrew prophet Elijah)" (Doody, *Jane Austen's Names: Riddles, Persons, Places* [Chicago: University of Chicago Press, 2015], 194–95). The combination of names reflects Anne's movement from a nobody to a judge.

7. In Frances Burney's novel *Cecilia* (1782), her protagonist, Cecilia, is a young woman cast adrift on a journey of self-realization. Kathryn Davis suggests that Anne's journey toward self-governance is a "trial" and that her judgments are grounded in spiritual fortitude (Davis, *Liberty in Jane Austen's Persuasion* [Bethlehem, PA: Lehigh University Press, 2016], 115–17). Similarly, Alistair Duckworth argues that Anne is on a journey "in search of spiritual stability" (Duckworth, *The Improvement of the Estate: A Study of Jane Austen's Novels* [Baltimore, MD: Johns Hopkins University Press, 1994], 185).

8. For more on Anne Elliot's virtue in the context of classical virtue, see chapter 7 of Sarah Emsley, *Jane Austen's Philosophy of the Virtues* (New York: Palgrave Macmillan, 2005), 145–58. For a discussion of *Persuasion* and Christian virtue, see Duckworth, *Improvement of the Estate*, 191, 194.

9. Sir William Dugdale, *The Ancient Usage in Bearing of Such Ensigns of Honour as Are Commonly Call'd Arms, with a Catalogue of the Present Nobility of England to which is Added a Catalogue of the present Nobility of Scotland and Ireland & c.* (London: Theater Dudley Davis, 1682). In his annotated edition of *Persuasion*, Robert Morrison notes that to be mentioned in Dugdale as having an "authentic" claim to a baronetcy lent legitimacy to Sir Walter's baronetcy (Morrison, *Persuasion: An Annotated Edition* [Cambridge, MA: Harvard University Press, 2011], 34n11).

10. I am indebted here to Paul Gilroy's metaphor of the ship in *The Black Atlantic: Modernity and Double Consciousness* (Cambridge, MA: Harvard University Press, 1995).

11. Sir William Holdsworth, *A History of English Law* (London: Methuen, 1903), 300–302, 306.

12. Editors of *Persuasion* concur that Austen is probably referring to the 1808 edition of Debrett's *Baronetage*, in two volumes, 2nd edition. The first of the Debrett baronetages was published in 1804 under the title of *A New Baronetage of England*, printed for William Miller, 1 volume, 12 mos. (see *Complete Baronetage: English Baronetcies, 1611–1625 and Irish, 1618–1625* [W. Pollard, 1900], 1:xiv). Janine Barchas suggests that Austen is referring to the third edition, published in 1815, which was enlarged to accommodate the many new baronets since 1808 (Barchas, *Matters of Fact in Jane Austen* [Baltimore, MD: Johns Hopkins University Press, 2012], 207).

13. Jane Austen, *Persuasion*, ed. Patricia Meyer Spacks (New York: Norton, 2013), 4n7.

14. Thomas Keymer, "Rank," in *Jane Austen in Context*, ed. Janet Todd (Cambridge: Cambridge University Press, 2005), 391.

15. *Persuasion: An Annotated Edition*, ed. Morrison, 34n12. Stephen K. Roberts offers details of the office in the seventeenth century: "The sheriff was responsible for collecting dues to the crown and played an important part in meetings of the assizes when the judges visited the county. He was the returning officer at parliamentary elections for the shire and was in charge of ensuring that writs and returns were made in elections for the boroughs" (Roberts, "Conclusion County Counsels: Some Concluding Remarks," in *The County Community in Seventeenth Century England and Wales*, ed. Jacqueline Eales and Andrew Hopper [Hatfield, UK: University of Hertfordshire Press, 2012], 125). It is important to note that women occasionally held the office of sheriff in the thirteenth and fourteenth centuries (British History online, "sheriff").

16. Jocelyn Harris, *A Revolution Almost beyond Expression: Jane Austen's Persuasion* (Newark: University of Delaware Press, 2007), 120.

17. Harris, *A Revolution Almost beyond Expression*, 120.

18. Harris, *A Revolution Almost beyond Expression*, 135.

19. Brian Southam also suggests that Austen was writing "a morale-boosting novel, a story designed . . to show the navy in its best light" because it had just suffered a series of defeats (Southam, *Jane Austen and the Navy*, 264–65).

20. Janine Barchas makes a similar argument, based on a study of names from the *Baronetage* and the *Navy List* (Barchas, *Matters of Fact*, 206–7).

21. *Baronetage of England: Containing their descent and present state . . .* , ed. John Debrett (London: F. C. and J. Rivington, 1815), iii.

22. *Baronetage of England*, ed. Debrett (1815), vii.

23. Duckworth, *Improvement of the Estate*, 184.

24. Sir William Blackstone, *Commentaries on the Laws of England*, 4 vols. (1765–69; Chicago: University of Chicago Press, 1979), 3:268.

25. Edmund Burke, *Reflections on the Revolution in France* (London: J. Dodsley, 1790), 47–48.

26. Two treaties ended the Napoleonic Wars with France. The first was signed on May 30, 1814. The second, which was necessitated by Napoleon's escape from captivity and a resumption of war, was signed on November 20, 1815. In regard to prize money, Brian Southam observes that "even the humblest of seamen and the youngest of Lieutenants could dream of winning riches, could hope to reap their reward in prize-money, the 'golden harvest' of the sea" (Southam, *Jane Austen and the Navy*, 121).

27. Martin Robson, *A History of the Royal Navy: The Napoleonic Wars* (London: I. B. Tauris, 2014), 232–33.

28. G. H. Treitel, "Jane Austen and the Law," *Law Quarterly Review* 100 (1984): 564; Duckworth, *Improvement of the Estate*, 203.

29. Paula Byrne notes that Anne Elliot "truly feels her independence" when she acquires her own "landaulette" (Byrne, *The Real Jane Austen: A Life in Small Things* [New York: Harper Perennial, 2013], 112–13).

30. G. E. Mingay, *English Landed Society in the Eighteenth Century* (New York: Routledge, 2013), 83; Stephen Dowell, *History of Taxation and Taxes in England*, 4 vols. (London: Longmans, Green, 1884), 3:221–29, 310–14.

31. Southam, *Jane Austen and the Navy*, 285; Tony Tanner, *Jane Austen* (Cambridge, MA: Harvard University Press, 1986), 224.

32. According to Brian Southam, the place of wives on board ship was controversial, and conditions were not necessarily comfortable (Southam, *Jane Austen and the Navy*, 276–79, 284).

33. Southam, *Jane Austen and the Navy*, 273.

Jane Austen and the Theater?
Perhaps Not So Much

DEBORAH C. PAYNE

That Jane Austen enjoyed the theater is without doubt. She penned playlets in her adolescence, she watched her family mount amateur theatricals, and, as an adult, she attended performances in Bath and London, nieces in tow. Whether or not these dabblings and outings exerted serious "artistic influence" on Austen's oeuvre, however, is questionable. Many of us take pleasure in art forms and pastimes that do not necessarily inform our own practices. I adore opera and have written about it, but one would be hard pressed to detect Gluck's musical phrasing shaping the cadences of my sentences. Nonetheless, scholarship intent on proving Austen's artistic indebtedness to the late eighteenth-century stage turns for evidence to material traces, such as her letters and juvenile writings. Cultural determinations, which are far more nebulous, comprise another form of evidence. Both have been invoked to argue "that her play-going and her reading of plays were a formative influence on her comic art."[1] From plays, Austen supposedly learned how to craft dialogue; from productions, how to stage domestic interiors; and from a highly theatricalized Georgian culture at large, how to present a "vision of the world" that was "intrinsically dramatic."[2]

Although it might seem perverse, especially in a volume that celebrates Jane Austen's relationship to the arts, to argue *against* influence, that indeed is the thrust of this essay. For one thing, the historical record suggests that Austen's interest in the theater was wholly unremarkable. Early nineteenth-century audiences were besotted with theatrical stars, and, unsurprisingly, during visits to London she also wanted to see the latest celebrities. Fandom does not necessarily betoken artistic indebtedness. Arguably, Austen's decision not to write plays for the stage reveals far more about her artistic aims than any passing reference to *The School for Scandal* or viewing of Sarah Siddons could disclose. Moreover, in repudiating playwriting, Austen forged a career path that would become all too familiar among writers by the mid-nineteenth century. While Regency theater specialized in crowd-pleasing productions, which included the extravagantly staged entr'acte entertainments, curtain tunes, and afterpieces that augmented the main drama, that very popularity put off writers of a more "literary" bent. And finally—and most importantly—writers choose forms precisely to exploit their structural attributes. Drama demands a penchant for collaboration and a comfort with bodies, props, and stagecraft, not to mention the demands of actors and managers. Austen wanted none of it. Instead, she turned to the novel, the literary form that best accommodated her desire for narrative control and psychological interiority.

Clearly, Austen took pleasure in theater from a young age. Beginning in 1782, when she was seven years old, her older brother James began directing family theatricals at the Steventon rectory, for which he also wrote prologues and epilogues. James recruited family, friends, and even neighborhood children to appear in these confections. We have no firsthand evidence of Austen's participation, but she did apparently watch the performances. Her nephew James Edward Austen-Leigh recalled that his aunt was "an early observer, and it may be reasonably supposed that some of the incidents and feelings which are so vividly painted in the *Mansfield Park* theatricals are due to her recollection of these entertainments."[3] If Austen-Leigh's recollection is accurate, then Austen would have seen family and friends perform plays such as Richard Brinsley Sheridan's *The Rivals*, Susanna Centlivre's *The Wonder: A Woman Keeps a Secret*, and David Garrick's farce, *High Life below Stairs*, as well as his adaptation of John Fletcher's Jacobean comedy *The Chances*. These family theatricals may have inspired several adolescent experiments with playwriting: an undated fragment called simply "The first Act of a Comedy"; another incomplete piece, *The Mystery*, probably composed when she was thirteen; and *The Visit*, written a year later. Paula Byrne thinks that "these were probably performed as afterpieces to the main play," but only *The Visit* is complete, making it the sole candidate for a family theatrical.[4] Byrne also follows Brian Southam and John Halperin in attributing to Austen a short five-act play based on Samuel Richardson's *Sir Charles Grandison*.[5] More recently, though, scholars have accepted what was long believed within the family, that her niece Anna Lefroy dictated the play to Austen, who wrote down "the stories she invented for herself long ere she could write."[6] As Janet Todd and Linda Bree point out in their introduction to the Cambridge University Press edition, "there seems little in 'Sir Charles Grandison' beyond the ability of an intelligent child between seven and ten since the few decent lines are in the original or based closely on it."[7]

As an adult, Austen continued to enjoy theater, but her participation, enthusiasm, and attendance have perhaps been overstated.[8] We know, for instance, of only one turn she took in a private theatrical: William Heathcote recalls her playing "with great spirit" the role of Mrs. Candour at a Twelfth Night presentation of *The School for Scandal*. Otherwise, she appears to have read plays aloud, as she did novels, with families and friends.[9] During trips to London, Austen pursued the pastimes common to her class. She shopped and browsed; she attended tea- and supper-parties; she viewed displays of curiosities and fine paintings; she listened to professional glee-singers and amateur harpsichordists; and, of course, she went to the theater. Her letters reveal a doting aunt, happy to accompany her brother and nieces to various theatrical venues around town, ranging from "illegitimate" playhouses, such as Astley's in Lambeth, to the patent playhouses, such as Covent Garden and Drury Lane. Her letters record attendance at seven performances in London, one in Southampton, and one in Bath. If we accept what Austen's niece claimed, that her sister Cassandra destroyed "the greater part" of their correspondence—perhaps three-quarters is a fair estimate—then in all likelihood additional instances of spectatorship vanished with the letters.[10] Even if these omissions are factored in, Austen's play-going would have been entirely conventional for gentry from the countryside visiting London.

Moreover, the nineteenth-century stage was very much an "actor's theater," and, like most women of fashion, Austen idolized Sarah Siddons and Edmund Kean, the stars of the London stage. Tellingly, when Austen attends the theater, she invariably comments upon the performers, never the quality of the script. Her theatrical tastes incline toward the blockbuster hits and celebrity turns that everyone else wanted to see, the same pattern followed today by out-of-town visitors to Broadway and London theater. Disappointed of securing a ticket for Siddons's performance of Constance in Shakespeare's *King John*—a coveted role for eighteenth- and nineteenth-century divas—Austen jokes to Cassandra that she "could swear at her [i.e., Siddons] with little effort for disappointing me" (*Letters*, 192). This quip accords with what Jocelyn Harris has recently argued, that Austen was an inveterate celebrity watcher, a cultural category comprised of well-known "writers, actors, politicians, naval men, heiresses, and 'exotic' individuals."[11] Again, her interest in this regard is unexceptional; as Charles Beecher Hogan points out in his introduction to part 5 of *The London Stage*, "Contemporary letters, journals, diaries constantly record the gossip of the stage."[12]

Outings in London were often proposed by her brother Henry, who resided in Sloane Square for several years and knew the city well. The theater numbered among the many "peremptory enthusiasms" he embraced and then abandoned.[13] As a result, plans frequently came to nothing, canceled at the last minute due to Henry's distractibility. Even when the family managed to organize themselves sufficiently to attend a performance, Austen did not always share her nieces' enthusiasm for the production: "Of our three evenings in Town one was spent at the Lyceum & another at Covent Garden;—the Clandestine Marriage was the most respectable of the performances, the rest were Sing-song & trumpery, but did very well for Lizzy & Marianne, who were indeed delighted;—but *I* wanted better acting.—There was no Actor worthy naming.—I believe the Theatres are thought at a low ebb at present" (*Letters*, 240). If bored or tired, Austen left early, an entirely understandable response given that performances, between entr'acte entertainments and afterpieces, could run upward of five hours, especially for operas. Austen records on one occasion spending four and a half hours at the Lyceum. The show began at 7:00 p.m., and the clan crawled home at 11:30 p.m., fortifying themselves with "Soup & wine & water" before retreating to their "Holes" (*Letters*, 227).

That considerable commitment of time sometimes dulled her appreciation even of celebrities she had long waited to see. Although thrilled finally to secure seats to see Edmund Kean's vastly popular portrayal of Shylock in *The Merchant of Venice,* she complained that his "part was too short" while the other "parts were ill filled & the Play heavy" (*Letters*, 268–69). Tired, she and the rest of the clan decamped early. The following night, they were to see Thomas Arne's opera *Artaxerxes* at Covent Garden. Austen worried the performance would "be very tiresome," a prediction borne out by the evening's performance: "I was very tired of Artaxerxes, highly amused with the Farce, & in an inferior way with the Pantomime that followed" (271). In this particular instance, she stayed the course; however, the lackluster performances and overly long program dulled her appetite for further outings during this particular trip to London. When Austen learned that John Plumptre and his family were eager to return to Covent Garden the following day, this time to see Charles Dibdin's comic opera, *The Farmer's Wife,* she confessed to Cassandra: "He is to try for a Box. I do not particularly wish him to succeed. I have had enough for the present" (272).

Just as the scant record of play-going is mined for evidence of Austen's embrace of all things theatrical, so too is her childhood reading. Byrne states she "was familiar with a wide range of plays," a statement echoed by Peter Sabor, who claims that the "young Austen . . . read contemporary fiction and drama voraciously."[14] Neither a catalogue of the five hundred books in her father's library nor childhood diaries exist that might confirm this familiarity.[15] Solely extant are the juvenilia, which reference numerous novelists: Samuel Richardson, Sarah Fielding, Henry Fielding, Charlotte Lennox, Frances Brooke, Frances Burney, Laurence Sterne, Oliver Goldsmith, Henry Mackenzie, Charlotte Smith, and, of course, Ann Radcliffe, whose *The Mysteries of Udolpho* she would parody in *Northanger Abbey*. If the juvenilia, as Vivien Jones suggests, functioned as a kind of adolescent sketchbook, allowing Austen to imitate and thus acquire "the idioms and tropes of popular fiction," it did not do so in the same manner for the drama.[16] Only a handful of dramatists are mentioned, most notably Nicholas Rowe, Richard Brinsley Sheridan, and Henry Fielding. Austen especially seems to have liked plays that mocked theatrical excess, such as Fielding's *Tom Thumb* and Sheridan's *The Critic*—hardly candidates for modeling dramatic dialogue. These comedies appear to have largely inspired attempts at literary spoofery, as when Austen borrowed from William Hayley's singularly bad verse comedy *The Mausoleum* the name of "Sophia Sentiment" for a satirical letter.[17]

Not once does the adult Austen record reading a play in solitude. Moreover, the largest library collection to which she had access contained little drama. Between 1798 and 1813, Austen made six visits over ten months to Godmersham Park, an impressive estate inherited by her brother Edward in 1798. During these stays, Austen availed herself of the library; she would, however, have read little drama.[18] The catalogue of 1,300 books, now digitized, reveals astonishingly few dramatic titles: the Pope and Bell editions of Shakespeare; the 1640 two-volume edition of Jonson's *Workes* (which would have included the major plays); the 1725 and 1761 editions of Congreve's *Works . . . Consisting of his plays and poems*; and French editions of Racine and Voltaire's plays.[19] And while eighteenth-century English drama is virtually absent, popular novels of the century are very much apparent: Fielding's *Tom Jones* and *Joseph Andrews*; Swift's *Gulliver's Travels*; Richardson's *Sir Charles Grandison*; Smollett's *The Adventures of Roderick Random*; Burney's *Evelina*; Edgeworth's *Patronage* and *Tales of Fashionable Life*; Scott's *Marmion*; and Sterne's *Tristram Shandy*. Histories, ancient and modern, constitute the bulk of the collection, followed by travel literature, novels, and theology. Overall, the library holdings dovetail with what the letters disclose about Austen's reading habits. Drama did not much interest Austen; rather, as Margaret Anne Doody claims in an influential article: "It is to novel reading that Austen brings her energies, her discrimination, her really serious judgment. Read aloud, then reread, novels formed her mind so that she could re-form the novel."[20] Even allusions to Shakespeare

are surprisingly few in Austen, especially given his enshrinement as the "national poet" by the late eighteenth century.[21]

Far more revelatory than her habits of play-going or reading was Austen's youthful decision not to pursue playwriting in adulthood; effectively, she *chose* a career path that failure forced upon her contemporaries. William Wordsworth, for instance, wrote when he was twenty-five his sole dramatic effort, the verse tragedy *The Borderers* (1795–97). He heard on December 14, 1798, that his play had been turned down, a rejection he blamed on "the depraved state of the theatre at the time." Furious, Wordsworth and Dorothy left London "in a huff the same day."[22] Years later, his estimation of the theater had, not surprisingly, soured considerably. Book 7 of *The Prelude* makes apparent a preference for the "casual incidents of real life" that

> [o]utweighed, or put to flight, the set events
> And measured passions of the stage, albeit
> By Siddons trod in the fulness of her power.[23]

Samuel Taylor Coleridge similarly attempted a verse tragedy, *Osorio,* in his youth. After Sheridan rejected it for Drury Lane, the play languished for sixteen years until actors assisted Coleridge with making extensive revisions. The new version, renamed *Remorse,* ran for twenty nights in 1813. Perhaps buoyed by this late success, he wrote two years later another verse play *Zapolya: A Christmas Tale.* It, too, was rejected by Drury Lane but finally had a feeble run at Thomas Dibdin's regional Surrey Theatre. Coleridge's other plays, including a painstaking translation from German manuscripts of Friedrich Schiller's *Wallenstein* trilogy, were never produced during his lifetime.[24] Lord Byron pursued a somewhat different course, spurning the box office and declaring that he wrote "without regard to the Stage." Instead, he targeted the "mental theatre of the reader," a strategy intended to free the text from the material constraints of production.[25]

Byron's sniffiness about stagecraft supposedly resulted from his "aristocratic," poetic outlook.[26] Nineteenth-century novelists of far more modest origins nonetheless shared his contempt for the limitations staging invariably imposes on the playwright. When the *Pall Mall Gazette* asked Thomas Hardy—the son of a stonemason—why he considered the novel a superior form to the drama "for bringing your ideas before the public whom you address," he ticked off a litany of complaints that would have seemed entirely familiar to Byron and likely to Austen as well: managers who refused "a truly original play"; scenes arranged "to suit the exigencies of scene-building"; parts fitted to actors, "not actors to the part." All of these material considerations inhibited "the presentation of human passions," whereas the novel gave the author unfettered freedom, both in the depiction of locale, the shifting of time, and the representation of interiority.[27] Hardy actually took it as a sign of artistic maturity when writers overcame a youthful predilection for drama, averring that "as they approach middle age .. they cannot by any possibility feel deeply interested in the regulation stage-presentation of life."[28]

David Kurnick argues that one of the dominant stories about the birth of the nineteenth-century novel has to do with its origins in theatrical failure, and striking indeed are the many novelists who turned aside from drama after experimentations that came to nothing.[29] George Eliot attempted a dramatic poem in scenes. Henry James tried his hand at one-acts written for periodicals; then, midcareer, he penned *Guy Domville*, a play so bad that the audience jeered when he took a bow at the end of the performance. He did not repeat the experiment. Robert Louis Stevenson, like Austen, wrote several juvenile dramas; however, *unlike* Austen, he mistook these youthful assays as prefigurations of future competence. Two of the resulting three plays were produced to tepid responses. Wilkie Collins coauthored with Charles Dickens, arguably the sole novelist to write successfully for the stage, an amateur play, *The Frozen Deep*. Despite Dickens's assistance, it was never produced by a professional company. Anthony Trollope had both of his plays, *The Noble Jilt* and *Did He Steal It?*—the latter an adaptation of his popular novel *The Last Chronicle of Barset*—rejected by theatrical management.

Austen, along with Sir Walter Scott (one of her favorite novelists) and the Brontë sisters, stands apart from this literary train wreck. Her acuity in not risking theatrical failure in adulthood is especially striking when measured against a contemporary like Coleridge, who persevered stubbornly in writing largely unproducible plays until he was forty, his judgment perhaps addled by opium. Austen, by contrast, never experimented further with scripts after the age of fourteen, and she abandoned rapidly her two brief excursions into epistolarity, *Lady Susan* and *Love and Friendship*, arguably the narrative form closest to drama.[30] Certainly, playwriting was an option for a woman. Austen clearly knew the work of Elizabeth Inchbald, the daughter of a gentleman farmer, whose play *Lovers' Vows*, based on August von Kotzebue's *Das Kind der Liebe* (1780), figures prominently in *Mansfield Park*. Inchbald made a good living from the theater: nineteen out of the twenty-three comedies, farces, and sentimental dramas she wrote were produced between 1784 and 1805. She additionally published two novels, became a theater critic, and compiled that twenty-five-volume monument to dramatic posterity, *The British Theatre* (1806-9). Fanny Burney, closer to Austen's gentrified origins, wrote four novels, eight plays, a biography, and twenty volumes of journals and letters. Burney eventually assumed the post of "Keeper of the Robes" at the court of George III, attesting to her respectability.

That Austen refrained from following in the theatrical footsteps of Inchbald and Burney can, of course, be attributed in part to her upbringing in a clergyman's household. Ellen Donkin and Tracy C. Davis have chronicled the onus that still attached to female playwrights, genteel of birth or not, perhaps explaining a similar reticence in the Brontës or even Mrs. Gaskell to write for the stage.[31] I want, however, to grant Austen the artistic agency we commonly accord to men rather than viewing her as largely shrinking from social censure. Put simply, Austen rejected professional playwriting because the form did not suit her artistic aims or intellectual interests. In this respect, Austen appears to have had far more self-awareness than her (largely) male counterparts and successors. She grasped by her midteens what circumstances determined for them far more brutally: few are the writers cut out temperamentally or artistically to write for the stage. Production entails collaboration with actors, designers, musicians, and managers. Dramatic form by its very nature decenters authorial voice, while the demand for completion in performance undermines any sense of ownership or proprietary relationship to the text. "No art," as the philosopher Alain Badiou points out, "is so little a *ktèma es aiei* (an *everlasting possession* or a *treasure forever*)." Everlasting possession, however, is precisely what the novel afforded Austen.[32]

Like Hemingway and Faulkner, Austen possesses a narrative voice so distinctive that it occasions both imitation and parody. When someone wants to "do" Austen, she mimics the arch, ironic, and oftentimes deadly observations issued by the narrator, not the dialogue which, especially in the early novels, comes precariously close to sounding like the narration. One is hard pressed, for instance, in *Sense and Sensibility* to distinguish Elinor's voice from that of the equally astute narrator. As Austen perfects her craft, she writes dialogue more expressive of individual character: Fanny Price, for instance, sounds nothing like Mary Crawford in *Mansfield Park,* nor does Emma Woodhouse vocally resemble Harriet Smith in *Emma*. It could be argued that drama taught Austen how to individuate voices, but the same could be said of the eighteenth-century novel. We know, for instance, that Austen adored Samuel Richardson, and part of the considerable pleasure in reading a novel like *Clarissa* derives not only from dueling outlooks but also from the two distinctive voices that dominate the epistolary narrative: Clarissa's penchant for self-reflection, heartfelt sincerity, and passionate exclamations (often marked by exclamation points) versus Lovelace's inclination for description, sarcasm, and cold analysis.

Overemphasis on "artistic influence" effaces craft, by which I mean the literary techniques acquired over years of painstaking work and deliberation. In the instance of female writers such as Austen, the story of "influence" equally risks casting them as daughters in need of their father's tutelage (and one of the reasons that feminist scholars since Elaine Showalter have emphasized matrilineal succession for female novelists).[33] Whether or not Austen "learned" to write dialogue from Richardson or Sheridan—and why could she not have taught herself?—revealingly, she reduces its presence in her novels over time. *Northanger Abbey* (1798–99) features 40 percent dialogue to 60 percent narration, a number that declines eighteen years later in *Persuasion* (1817) when she reduces dialogue to only 33 percent of the text. Additionally, more of the dialogue in *Persuasion* is indirect, detailing a character's internal thoughts. Minimized are exchanges in the present moment, the structural characteristic fundamental to drama. Austen's overwhelming preference for narration, even in her early years, departs considerably from contemporary novelists. Fanny Burney's *The Wanderer* (1814), which was published just three years before *Persuasion* and also came at the end of a literary career, reverses the numbers: 66 percent dialogue to 34 percent narration, a 2:1 formula that colleagues specializing in nineteenth-century fiction tell me is far more typical. These numbers not only reveal Austen to be an outlier but also that she exercised *more* narrative control, not less, as her career progressed.

Arguably, Austen sought to exploit the narratological capacity of the novel, the reason why she never penned a play in adulthood. Austen's narrators do not simply describe: they judge actions, they probe motives; and they reveal inner thoughts—a lot. Even *Mansfield Park,* the only novel in the Austen oeuvre to reference the theater at length, subsumes dialogue to narration, using the latter to nudge us away from Mary Crawford and toward Fanny Price, as occurs in the famous horseback riding scene in chapter 7 of volume 1. Austen assumes, of course, that her readers accept narrative efficaciousness; otherwise, she would not catalogue for nearly three pages the wrongs occasioned by Mary's use of Fanny's beloved little mare. First, the narrator relates how Edmund's thoughtlessness in borrowing the mare robs Fanny of the exercise necessary for her health. Then she details the emotional toll, especially how Mary's rapid mastery of horsemanship (she learns how to go from a walk to a canter in a mere two days) occasions feelings of jealousy and inadequacy in Fanny. Worst of all, as the narrator makes apparent, is Fanny's witnessing of physical contact between Mary and Edmund, a sight that causes the agitation conveyed through free indirect discourse: "he was evidently directing her management of the bridle, he had hold of her hand; she saw it, or the imagination supplied what the eye could not reach" (*MP*, 79). Only *after* narration has established both the external events and Fanny's ensuing misery does dialogue erupt into the scene, with Mary "apologizing" for her poor conduct: "I am come to make my own apologies for keeping you waiting—but I have nothing in the world to say for myself—I knew it was very late, and that I was behaving extremely ill; and, therefore, if you please, you must forgive me. Selfishness must always be forgiven you know, because there is no hope of a cure" (80).

Free indirect discourse in this scene conveys Fanny's interiority. When she watches Edmund seizing hold of Mary's hand to demonstrate the proper use of a bridle, she doubts her senses, not knowing whether she perceives reality or whether "the imagination supplied what the eye could not reach" (*MP*, 79). This line conveys metacognition with an economy the drama cannot rival outside of Shakespeare's brilliant monologues. Even so, the forms work differently. Shakespearean monologues encourage audience complicity with the dramatic action, a shared moment in the playhouse. Free indirect discourse, by contrast, promotes readerly sovereignty, a solitary and almost voyeuristic glimpse into the mental operations of a literary character. So innovative is Austen's technique in this regard that George Butte claims it changed the course of the English novel.[34] Lisa Zunshine largely concurs, pointing to how Austen's prose is "actively experimenting with readers' cognition."[35] Certainly, the horseback riding scene entails four levels of recursive mental embedment, which look something like this: Fanny is *aware* that Mary *understands* that she *pretends* not to *mind* the appropriation of the mare. Without the preceding three pages of narration, which establish the depth of Fanny's self-awareness, the dialogue conveying Mary's apology and Fanny's bland response (reported indirectly) reduces from four levels of mental embedment to two: Fanny *pretends* not to mind, and Mary *pretends* to apologize.

Were this a script for the stage, Fanny might come downstage and confess her feelings aloud in an aside or monologue, but the very act of doing so changes her character from a circumspect, painfully shy young girl to an overwrought heroine out of sentimental drama. Revealingly, Austen withholds dialogue from Fanny at moments when dialogic utterances might undermine what narrative technique has already established about her character. Fanny does not, for instance, respond to Mary's spoken "apology." Instead, the narrator *describes* Fanny's response, remarking simply that her "answer was extremely civil" (*MP*, 80). Had Fanny uttered her "extremely civil" reply immediately after Mary declares archly that "there is no hope of a cure" for selfishness, she would risk sounding equally insincere. These brief reported responses in *Mansfield Park* safeguard Fanny's depth of character; by contrast, long passages of witty dialogue underscore Mary's shallowness. In an attempt to dissuade Edmund from entering the church, Mary mocks—for nearly five pages—the life of a clergyman: "Oh! no doubt he is very sincere in preferring an income ready made, to the trouble of working for one; and has the best intentions of doing nothing all the rest of his days but eat, drink, and grow fat. It is indolence Mr. Bertram, indeed. Indolence and love of ease—a want of all laudable ambition, of taste for good company, or of inclination to take the trouble of being agreeable, which make men clergymen" (128). So caught up is Mary in performing witty albeit cruel banter that she ignores its effect on Edmund, who has, after all, chosen the very profession she derides. This scene anticipates the rehearsals two chapters later of *Lovers' Vows*, another instance where the excitement of performance—of being swept up in the pleasure of embodied display—similarly blinds the participants to the "real life" impact of the words they utter.

Mansfield Park not only renders highly theatrical dialogue suspect but also opposes social performance against more "authentic" behavior. Having discovered Edmund's admiration for nature and music, Mary stages herself carefully for his delectation by playing an instrument in a room that looks out upon landscape: "a young woman, pretty, lively, with a harp as elegant as herself; and both placed near a window, cut down to the ground, and opening on a little lawn, surrounded by shrubs in the rich foliage of summer, was enough to catch any man's heart" (76). Austen echoes this scene later in chapter 11; this time, however, Fanny and Edmund gaze through a window to nature beyond. Rather than posing herself in surroundings akin to a Georgian stage set, as does Mary in chapter 7, Fanny loses herself in "the scene without, where all that was solemn and soothing, and lovely, appeared in the brilliancy of an unclouded night, and the contrast of the deep shade of the woods" (132). With a heartfelt rapture worthy of a Romantic poet, Fanny "spoke her feelings," prompted by "the sublimity of Nature" (132). Fanny's ability to meld emotionally and imaginatively with a landscape that cannot confer social benefits, speaks to the novel's privileging of contemplation over performance and loss of self over calculated self-consciousness. As Julie

Park argues, Fanny "lives as much in the internal reflections of her mind as in the controlling structures of moral principles," thus pitting her against the theatrical dialogue and self-serving schemes that color less admirable characters.[36] Interiority and "controlling structures" also happen to be the very attributes at which novels such as *Mansfield Park* excel, thus identifying Fanny closely with Austen's overall narrative project.

Austen may have enjoyed theatrical outings in real life; however, in the world of *Mansfield Park*, the attempted performance by young, amateur players produces neither emotionally nor ethically efficacious outcomes. As narratological privileging of Fanny makes evident, the "internal reflections" of the mind rather than the temporal and affective flow of performance facilitate insight and empathy. The rehearsals of *Lovers' Vows* result in mixed signals, hurt feelings, and, in the case of Mary and Henry Crawford, personal ruin.[37] These repeat performances "consolidate suspect forms of autoethnography," as Daniel O'Quinn observes, in addition to aligning "quite explicitly with all the characters who enthusiastically take up Mr. Yates's self-aggrandizing desires."[38] Additionally, the roles in *Lovers' Vows* parallel in exaggerated fashion the roles characters play in the novel, thus dangerously blurring the distinctions between the dramatic world of the play and the social reality of the novel. Austen's amateur actors moreover do not even grasp the moral lessons acquired by the Kotzebue/Inchbald characters, a blindness Dvora Zelicovici takes as emblematic of the ethical "inefficacy" of the play.[39] I would put it somewhat differently. It is not so much the inefficacy of the play itself but, rather, that *Lovers' Vows* never realizes its *telos* in performance. Novels finalize authoritatively in print what rehearsal does endlessly, variably, and sometimes incompletely. Narrative fixedness functions like the landscape upon which Fanny gazes, providing an unchanging ground for contemplation—the literary aesthetic clearly preferred by Austen.

There might also be an element of one-upmanship in incorporating a popular contemporary play and then sidelining it, perhaps Austen's sly way of demonstrating how her novel accomplishes what a performance of *Lovers' Vows* cannot: the contemplative pleasure occasioned by a reading in one's closet rather than an evening in Drury Lane. This is not to say that Austen disliked theater—the evidence clearly suggests otherwise—but that her reaction was nuanced. In the hands of professionals, theater was a legitimate pleasure for which she (or, more likely, her brother) was willing to pay. And while it is tempting to read the amateur theatrical in *Mansfield Park* through a biographical lens, doing so effaces its fictional specificity. Austen drops flawed, self-absorbed young people into an emotionally fraught situation without the benefit of adult supervision, which was certainly not the case at the Steventon rectory. Arguably, the treatment of the amateur theatrical in *Mansfield Park* attests to Austen's guarded appreciation for the affective power of performance—a capacity so potent that it requires careful management by those who would attempt it. Professionals, of course, learn to control what proves otherwise combustible when attempted by self-centered young people, such as those represented in this novel. Indeed, even their selection of a play is an exercise in egotism. While watching the ensuing quarrel over the choice of script, Fanny was "not unamused to observe the selfishness which, more or less disguised, seemed to govern them all, and wondering how it would end" (*MP*, 154). Once rehearsals begin, so caught up are the players in the heady, affective flow induced by dramatic dialogue and action, they do not discern how these repetitions are affecting others adversely, even to the point of driving apart the formerly close Bertram sisters: "They were totally preoccupied. Tom was engrossed by the concerns of his theatre, and saw nothing that did not immediately relate to it. Edmund, between his theatrical and his real part . . was equally unobservant" (191).

Tellingly, Fanny alone among the amateur players retains the ability to feel *and* judge. During the rehearsals, she is capable of being moved by Henry Crawford's performance, but she still perceives his considerable deficits: "She did not like him as a man, but she must admit him to be the best actor" (*MP*, 193–94). While it is tempting to credit spectatorship—Fanny refuses to act in the play but agrees to be a prompter—the other spectators, such as Mrs. Norris and Lady Bertram, do not see how the rehearsals are riving relationships. Accustomed to "living in the internal reflections of her mind," Fanny brings that singular thoughtfulness to the act of watching a play. Ironically, it is Fanny's peculiarly narratological habit of mind—her capacity for metacognition and interiority, as well as for earnest emotions—that make her the ideal spectator. In that regard, she is not unlike a professional actress, who similarly brings to her job what amateurs cannot summon forth: the ability to negotiate cognitive and emotional realms simultaneously. There is nonetheless, a clear preference here for the literary form that does *not* realize its aesthetic ends through emoting (or maddeningly insensate) bodies and perceptive (or irritatingly oblivious) spectators. An extraordinary actor can certainly create a simulacrum of the inner life that drives Macbeth to exclaim, "O full of scorpions is my mind."[40] Austen, however, does not have to depend on the good graces of a Sarah Siddons to convey the interior world of Fanny's anguish, loneliness, and insecurity. For that she has narrative description, character bias, and free indirect discourse, the literary tools she chose to wield with absolute and memorable sovereignty.

Despite the misgivings expressed here, I suspect theatrical Austen will continue to sally forth in the criterial literature, largely to combat the dour spinster of earlier scholarship. As late as 2013, Paula Byrne in *The Real Jane Austen* still felt the need to correct the long-held view that "she disapproved of the theatre and drama."[41] Gone is the spinster aunt, dutifully caring for her brother's children and grabbing the odd moment to scratch out a few lines amid domestic duties; in her stead is the London sophisticate, swanning about playhouses and parties. Even Austen's childhood home has been reinvented in keeping with this new Boadicea of the boards. The Steventon parsonage, Penny Gay maintains, was "by no means divorced from things theatrical."[42] These recent, jolly constructions of Austen—fashion maven, gossip, gadabout, theater aficionado, and even, if we are to believe Helena Kelly, secret radical—certainly accord with the dynamic woman *we* want her to be.[43] Teleportation from the draughty corridors of Steventon to the fleshy warmth of Drury Lane thus renders cozy what might otherwise seem glacial to the twenty-first century. We are hardly unique in this regard; in her splendid study of Austen's afterlife, Devoney Looser traces how "many of us have adapted her, finding in her what best suits us."[44]

Additionally, the material turn in Romanticism has made nineteenth-century theater and performance—long ignored in literary studies—respectable, if not downright sexy, objects of critical interest. Austen's forays into the playhouse, infrequent as they were, suddenly seem timely given our current fascination with eighteenth-century celebrity and performance. Sometimes, though, in our eagerness to detect influence, we overlook authorial agency. Literary texts result as much from techniques honed and discarded as they do from the subjective determinations produced by history and biography. That Austen occasionally saw blockbuster hits in London should hardly surprise. So did everyone else of her class and education in the early nineteenth century. She is far more likely to reference fashionable watering holes in Bath and scenic countryside in Hampshire than anything to do with the theater; indeed, a veritable critical industry has sprung up devoted to identifying places, people, and even menus in her novels.[45] Rather, what startles is Austen's singular brilliance in grasping at a young age that drama would neither accommodate her specific formal interests nor give expression to her particular genius. This might be an old-fashioned argument, but it is still worth reiterating, that the very best writers like Austen invariably find a fit between form and talent. Had she embarked upon a playwriting career, I suspect we would not be contributing to this volume of essays.

Notes

1. Paula Byrne, *Jane Austen and the Theatre* (London: Hambledon and London, 2002), xi.
2. Byrne, *Jane Austen and the Theatre*, xi
3. James Edward Austen-Leigh, *A Memoir of Jane Austen*, ed. Kathryn Sutherland (Oxford: Oxford University Press, 2008), 49.
4. Byrne, *Jane Austen and the Theatre*, 12.
5. Byrne, *Jane Austen and the Theatre* , 26, 92–93; *Jane Austen's "Sir Charles Grandison,"* ed. Brian Southam (Oxford: Oxford University Press, 1980); John Halperin, *The Life of Jane Austen* (Baltimore, MD: Johns Hopkins University Press, 1984), 119–20.
6. Fanny Caroline Lefroy, "Family History," as qtd. in Jane Austen, *Later Manuscripts*, ed. Janet Todd and Linda Bree (Cambridge: Cambridge University Press, 2008), cxii.
7. Janet Todd and Linda Bree, introduction to *Later Manuscripts*, by Jane Austen, ed. Todd and Bree, cxvii.
8. Paul Byrne, for instance, claims that "Jane Austen was as avid a theatregoer as she was a participant in amateur dramatics," but we know of only one instance where she actually performed (Byrne, *The Real Jane Austen: A Life in Small Things* [New York: Harper Collins, 2013], 141).
9. As qtd. in Byrne, *The Real Jane Austen*, 27.
10. See preface to *Jane Austen's Letters,* ed. Deirdre Le Faye, 4th ed. (Oxford: Oxford University Press, 2011), xii–xiii. All subsequent references are to this edition and will be provided parenthetically in the text.
11. Jocelyn Harris, *Satire, Celebrity, and Politics in Jane Austen* (Lewisburg, PA: Bucknell University Press, 2017), xvii. Janine Barchas also traces Austen's interest in celebrity culture in *Matters of Fact in Jane Austen: History, Location, Celebrity* (Baltimore, MD: Johns Hopkins University Press, 2012).
12. *The London Stage, 1660–1800*, pt. 5: *1776–1800*, ed. Charles Beecher Hogan (Carbondale: Southern Illinois University Press, 1968), clxxvii.
13. David Nokes, *Jane Austen: A Life* (New York: Farrar, Straus and Giroux, 1997), 378.
14. Byrne, *Jane Austen and the Theatre*, 16; Jane Austen, *Juvenilia*, ed. Peter Sabor (Cambridge: Cambridge University Press, 2006), xxx.
15. In December 1800, Austen's father, George, announced his decision to retire from the Church of England, leave the Steventon rectory, and move the family to Bath. He also decided during this period to dispose of his library: several weeks later, Austen reported that her "father has got above 500 Volumes to dispose of;—I want James to take them at a venture at half a guinea a volume." We do not know how the volumes were actually dispersed (see *Letters*, January 16, 1801).

16. See Vivien Jones, "Jane Austen's Domestic Realism," in *The Oxford History of the Novel in English*, vol. 2: *English and British Fiction 1750–1820*, ed. Peter Garside and Karen O'Brien (Oxford: Oxford University Press, 2015), 280.

17. Austen, *Juvenilia*, xxx.

18. For a full account of Jane Austen's use of the library, see Peter Sabor, "Godmersham Park Library: Jane Austen's Paradise Regained," *Persuasions: The Jane Austen Journal* 39 (2017): 31–44.

19. See www.readingwithausten.com, a new website housed at McGill University's Burney Centre that digitally re-creates the library at Godmersham Park, the estate inherited by Edward Austen Knight. Visitors can access titles by searching the 1818 library catalogue or by exploring the digitally reproduced bookshelves.

20. Margaret Anne Doody, "Jane Austen's Reading," in *The Jane Austen Handbook*, ed. J. David Grey et al. (London: Athlone, 1986), 183. Doody expands on Austen's knowledge of history in part 1 of *Jane Austen's Names: Riddles, Persons, Places* (Chicago: University of Chicago Press, 2015).

21. For the standard discussion of how Shakespeare was established as the "national poet" by the end of the eighteenth century, see Michael Dobson, *The Making of the National Poet: Shakespeare, Adaptation, and Authorship, 1660–1769* (Oxford: Clarendon, 1992).

22. Ken Johnston, *The Hidden Wordsworth: Poet, Lover, Spy* (New York: Norton, 1998), 396.

23. William Wordsworth, *The Prelude, or Growth of a Poet's Mind* (London: Edward Moxon, 1850), 188.

24. Katharine Cooke, *Coleridge* (London: Routledge and Kegan Paul, 1979), 41.

25. As cited in Alan Richardson, "Byron and the Theatre," in *The Cambridge Companion to Byron* (Cambridge: Cambridge University Press, 2004), 136.

26. Peter Cochran, for instance, claims that "his distaste was motivated by feelings of class. Through most of his association with the theatre, Byron was driven by feelings of class-based elitism" (Cochran, "Byron and Drury Lane," in *Byron at the Theatre*, ed. Cochran [Newcastle, UK: Cambridge Scholars Publishing, 2008], 1).

27. Harold Orel, *The Final Years of Thomas Hardy, 1912–1928* (London: Macmillan, 1976), 99.

28. Orel, *The Final Years of Thomas Hardy*, 99.

29. See the introduction to David Kurnick's *Empty Houses: Theatrical Failure and the Novel* (Princeton, NJ: Princeton University Press, 2012).

30. Some scholars think that *Sense and Sensibility* and *Pride and Prejudice* may also have originated as epistolary novels; if so, telling is Austen's decision once again to put aside the form of narration closest to the drama (see B. C. Southam, *Jane Austen's Literary Manuscripts: A Study of the Novelist's Development through the Surviving Papers* [Oxford: Oxford University Press, 1964], 54–62).

31. Ellen Donkin, *Getting into the Act: Women Playwrights in London, 1776—1829* (London: Routledge, 1995); *Women and Playwriting in Nineteenth-Century Britain*, ed. Tracy C. Davis and Ellen Donkin (Cambridge: Cambridge University Press, 1999).

32. Alain Badiou, *Rhapsody for the Theatre*, ed. Bruno Bosteels (London: Verso, 2013), 13.

33. Elaine Showalter, *A Literature of Their Own: British Women Novelists from Brontë to Lessing* (Princeton, NJ: Princeton University Press, 1977); see also Nancy Armstrong, *Desire and Domestic Fiction: A Political History of the Novel* (Oxford: Oxford University Press, 1990).

34. George Butte, *I Know That You Know That I Know: Narrating Subjects from Moll Flanders to Marnie* (Columbus: Ohio University Press, 2004), vii.

35. Lisa Zunshine, "Why Jane Austen Was Different, And Why We May Need Cognitive Science to See It," *Style* 41, no. 3 (2007): 276.

36. Julie Park, "What the Eye Cannot See: Interior Landscapes in *Mansfield Park*," *Eighteenth Century* 54, no. 2 (2013): 178.

37. See, for instance, Syndy McMillen Conger, "Reading *Lovers' Vows*: Jane Austen's Reflections on English Sense and German Sensibility," *Studies in Philology* 85, no. 1 (1988): 92–113.

38. Daniel O'Quinn, "Jane Austen and Performance: Theatre, Memory, and Enculturation," in *A Companion to Jane Austen,* ed. Claudia L. Johnson and Clara Tuite (Chichester, UK: Wiley-Blackwell, 2009), 381.

39. Eric Gerald Stanley, "Jane Austen's *Mansfield Park* and Kotzebue's *Das Kind der Liebe, Lovers' Vows*: 'that we should have such a scene to play!'?," *Archiv für das Studium der neueren Sprachen und Literaturen* 157, no. 2 (2005): 309; Dvora Zelicovici, "The Inefficacy of *Lovers' Vows*," *ELH* 50 (1983): 531–40.

40. William Shakespeare, *Macbeth*, ed. Barbara A. Mowat and Paul Werstine, updated ed. (New York: Simon and Schuster, 2013), 3.2.41.

41. Byrne, *The Real Jane Austen*, 147.

42. Penny Gay, *Jane Austen and the Theatre* (Cambridge: Cambridge University Press, 2002), 1.

43. See Helena Kelly, *Jane Austen: The Secret Radical* (New York: Knopf, 2017).

44. Devoney Looser, *The Making of Jane Austen* (Baltimore, MD: Johns Hopkins University Press, 2017), 217.

45. See, for instance, Daniel Pool, *What Jane Austen Ate and Charles Dickens Knew* (New York: Simon and Schuster, 1993); and Roy Adkins, *Jane Austen's England* (New York: Viking Penguin, 2013).

Everything Is Beautiful
Jane Austen at the Ballet

CHERYL A. WILSON

For Maggie, Shelia, and Bebe in the 1975 Marvin Hamlisch musical *A Chorus Line*, "everything is beautiful, at the ballet." It is a place to escape the less-than-ideal aspects of daily life and slip into a fantasy where "graceful men lift lovely girls in white." Difficult family dynamics and personal insecurities are replaced with the guarantee of a romantic dreamlike happy ending. One might argue that Jane Austen's novels have a similar effect on contemporary readers. They can serve as a place of escape, accomplishing that function precisely because they are somewhat predictable—down to the graceful men and girls in white—in their guarantee of a happy resolution to the romance plot. Jane Austen's work has been adapted into ballet, which I discuss further below, yet those adaptations are very few. There are both contemporary and historical connections between Austen's writings and ballet, however, that can provide useful context for reading her novels. Whereas scholarship on Austen and social dance has expanded over the past decade, stage dance has received little attention, perhaps due to the lack of stage dancing in Austen's novels. Nonetheless, bringing stage dance, specifically late eighteenth- and early nineteenth-century ballet, into conversation with Austen's works helps highlight her strategies for representing bodies and the ways in which physicality could be used to develop and form both character and narrative.

Dance historians and interdisciplinary scholars of dance and literature traditionally differentiate between "stage" and "social" dance. Stage dancers are trained and perform in front of an audience, usually in a theatrical setting; social dance is performed in parlors and ballrooms by everyday people who may or may not have had any formal lessons. Stage dance is an art form, designed to entertain spectators; social dance is a form of ritual and courtship through which individuals and groups can articulate their own identities and their relationships to one another. The arguments for treating stage and social dance separately began in the eighteenth century with the professionalization of dance performance and dance training. However, as dance historian Theresa Jill Buckland points out in her 2011 book *Society Dancing: Fashionable Bodies in England, 1870–1920*, scholars can create limitations by separating the different forms of dance. Indeed, she argues that such distinction has done a disservice to social dance, which has "largely remained the Cinderella of dance studies" as stage dance has garnered the lion's share of critical attention.[1] Jane Austen and her contemporaries certainly would have recognized some overlap between stage and social dance. Despite the differences in performance venues and dancer training, the ballroom and the stage borrowed liberally from one another, and the stage costumes of the leading ballerinas even influenced the street fashions of middle- and upper-class women during the early decades of the nineteenth century.[2] Full-length ballet had been performed onstage in England beginning in the 1750s and gained traction in the 1780s, building to the height of its popularity in the 1820s and 1830s, when London truly saw a golden age of ballet, including the rise of the celebrity ballerina. The period during which Jane Austen was attending the theaters, therefore, was one of increasing popular interest in ballet and saw its evolution into a professional art form.[3]

Most information about Jane Austen's experience with stage dance can be found in the margins of theater history. As critics such as Penny Gay and Paula Byrne have demonstrated, in addition to participating in home theatricals, the Austens were a theater-going family, and Jane took advantage of the available theater offerings in Bath, Southampton, and London during her visits and residences there. For the Austens, an evening at the theater would have included several forms of entertainment in addition to the main performance. The ballets that were performed in these early nineteenth-century theatrical venues would have combined dance with pantomime in staging movement-based narratives for the audience and often appeared on the playbills that advertised the evening's entertainment. For instance, an advertisement for *The Birth-Day*, which Austen saw during a visit to Bath in June 1799, indicates that the program included two three-act plays, a melodrama featuring music, speaking, and pantomime, and a "Fancy Dance, incidental to the piece" in the second act.[4] The dance pieces that accompanied stage dramas and comedies during the late eighteenth and early nineteenth centuries raised stage dance's popularity during this period. Sometimes, the dance would even share the headline, as in an 1803 advertisement for *Lovers' Vows*, which Jane Austen certainly read and likely saw sometime during her residence in Bath from 1801 to 1806, as the play to be performed at the Theatre Royal in Bath seventeen times during this period.[5] Along with *Lovers' Vows*, the evening's entertainment included *Le grand ballet de Cerceaux*, composed by Bath-based "Professor of French Dancing" Monsieur Mingaud, and starring his pupil Miss Loder.[6] This ballet was likely a one-act piece, appearing on the program after *Lovers' Vows* and before the Scots pastoral opera the *Gentle Shepherd*.

In addition to appearing in conjunction with drama or comedy, dance also appeared on stage at variety theaters, such as Astley's, which were the forerunners of Victorian music halls. Originally conceived as an equestrian theater, Astley's also obtained a license for music and dancing. Thus, an evening at Astley's might include short plays alongside farce, pantomime, music, dancing, and various other forms of stage entertainment. The theater-loving Austens patronized both the minor theaters and the patent theaters, and Jane Austen mentions an anticipated visit to Astley's in a 1796 letter to Cassandra: "We are to be at Astley's to night, which I am glad of."[7] Austen likely visited Astley's on later trips to London as well, and she imagines the theater as the London meeting place for Harriet Smith and Robert Martin in *Emma*. Although Austen's letters do not contain evidence of her seeing a full-length ballet, it is likely that she may have done so. The London theaters frequented by the Austens, such as Covent Garden, Lyceum, and Drury Lane, all produced full-length ballets during the 1780s and 1790s, when Austen was visiting London. In addition, given the excitement around the brilliant postwar ballet season of 1815, which saw the return of popular French dancers to England (including Auguste Vestris and his son Armande) and the increasing presence of dance commentary and reviews in periodicals, Austen would likely have encountered full-length ballets on the page, if not on the stage.

The popularity of ballet grew at the turn of the nineteenth century, and this period also saw the transition to a narrative form of dance—*ballet d'action*—that told stories and developed characters through movement. French-born dancing master Jean Georges Noverre (1727–1810) is generally credited with founding the narrative ballet, which departed from the established choreographical tradition dominated by symmetry and symbolism and for which dance was necessarily accompanied by speaking or pantomime that conveyed the story. Called "the Shakespeare of the dance" by David Garrick, Noverre worked in London in the 1750s and reconceived dance as an independent art form in his 1760 treatise *Letters on Dance and Ballet*. This work was one of the earliest attempts at comprehensive dance scholarship. According to dance historian Dorion Weickmann, Noverre "systematically defined the body in relation to plot and action.... [D]ance and mime melted into one dramatic plot that would be conveyed through gestures, steps and figures," moving away from dance combined with spoken word and singing to just dance.[8] Indeed, Noverre even suggests that dance is superior to language in some cases, writing in the *Letters*: "There is a degree of expression to which words cannot attain or rather there are passions for which no words exist. Then dancing allied with action triumphs. A step, a gesture, a movement, and an attitude express what no words can say."[9] For Noverre, dancing transcends speech, conveying its own meaning clearly and effectively. Indeed, Noverre argues that a ballet should be narrative; it "should be divided into scenes and acts, and each scene should possess, like the act, a beginning, central portion and conclusion; that is to say, its introduction, plot and climax."[10] Such ideas were controversial, as Noverre attempted to move stage dance away from the tradition of masque and pantomime upon which it had relied for storytelling and suggested that narrative could be expressed effectively through pure dance. In the introduction to the second edition of the *Letters*, he acknowledged that his unorthodox ideas "aroused the indignation of nearly all the dancers of Europe, and especially those attached to the *Opéra* at Paris."[11] Despite objections from some of Noverre's peers, his *ballet d'action* certainly inspired fellow artists, dramatists, and writers at the end of the eighteenth century and ultimately changed the course of ballet as an art form.

Jane Austen herself was clearly attuned to the narrative power of dance, and although stage dancing does not appear in her novels, the cultural recognition of the interchange between stage and social dance allows her to infuse her scenes of social dance with important elements of stage dance that carry beyond the ballroom. In addition, the development of character through physicality in the novels parallels the ways in which physical dancing bodies were used to develop character in the *ballet d'action*. Austen uses dance scenes at significant moments in her novels as opportunities for bringing characters into contact, revealing hidden attractions, and exploring the function (and sometimes transgression) of social and personal boundaries. The awkward dancing of Mr. Collins, provocative back-and-forth between Elizabeth and Darcy, coming-out of Fanny Price, rescue of the partnerless Harriet Smith by Mr. Knightley, and comparison of a country dance to a marriage by Henry Tilney are just some of the rich moments that take place in Austen's ballrooms. Although literary critics have productively studied these scenes in the context of writings on dance and social dance practices from the period, I suggest that incorporating ballet/stage dance into these conversations can be fruitful not only for understanding the significance of dance in her novels but also for comprehending more fully how shifting concepts of physicality and spectatorship transformed the spirit of the age.[12]

As noted above, the narrative elements of ballet and stage dance were becoming more prominent during the period that Austen was attending the theater and seeing dance. The heroes and heroines of ballet were also undergoing a transition during the late eighteenth and early nineteenth centuries. With the rise of narrative ballets and the simultaneous emergence of Romanticism, audiences demanded characters who were defined less by static poses and more by human passions. In the wake of the Revolution in France, cultural ideologies were shifting, and individuality was emerging as a guiding principle. Stage performances reflected this change, placing increased attention on character and narrative over mere spectacle. As dance historian Selma Jeanne Cohen writes, "Whereas earlier periods had been content to see dances alternated with portions of merely cadenced mime, the new era applauded [Jules] Perrot's innovative productions, which integrated dancing and dramatic action."[13] Stage dance offered a space in which bodies could tell stories and express characterization while underscoring the importance of the spectacle/spectator relationship. Reading *Pride and Prejudice*, then, in relation to stage dance calls attention not only to the narrative power of bodies but also to the interpretive power of the reader/spectator. Moreover, the cultural moment in which Austen was writing was one of transition in ballet with regard to narrative and character; thus, spectators were beginning to understand dance as something to be interpreted through a narrative lens. In *Pride and Prejudice*, Austen engages with dance and the body to allow Darcy and Elizabeth to emerge as a new kind of hero and heroine, moving away from the eighteenth-century Enlightenment traditions into the Romantic.

The ballroom is a place of spectacle and spectatorship in *Pride and Prejudice*, and this is established from the very first Meryton ball, which takes place in the third chapter of the novel. Although the type of dancing found on the stage and in the ballroom differed, the ballroom still retained elements of a staged performance. Very little was left to chance, and both the host and the guests understood that a ball was a carefully choreographed evening of entertainment. Dance manuals offered advice to hostesses regarding arrangements for the room, invitations, music, dinner, introductions, dancing, and dress.[14] Indeed, one might argue that the delineation of social behaviors and ballroom preparations was as complex as the delineation of the steps for country dances and quadrilles.

At the Meryton ball, the introduction of Darcy and Bingley to the assembled company and to the reader is framed in terms of their ballroom performance. We learn that Mr. Bingley "danced every dance," whereas Mr. Darcy "danced only once with Mrs. Hurst and once with Miss Bingley, declined being introduced to any other lady, and spent the rest of the evening in walking about the room, speaking occasionally to one of his own party" (P&P, 11).¹⁵ In addition to establishing the general agreeableness of the gentlemen and their propensity for romance because, as the narrator reminds us, "to be fond of dancing was a certain step towards falling in love" (9), the initial dance also establishes the respective roles of Bingley and Darcy. Bingley is both a participant and a performer, fully engaged in the scene, while Darcy is an observer, more comfortable on the fringes of the room.

As an observer, Darcy is particularly attentive to the actions of Jane and Bingley. At the Netherfield ball, which follows the Meryton ball, "his eyes were directed with a very serious expression towards Bingley and Jane, who were dancing together" (P&P, 104), and he later translates this reading to Elizabeth in his letter: "It was not till the evening of the dance at Netherfield that I had any apprehension of his feeling a serious attachment. . From that moment I observed my friend's behavior attentively; and I could then perceive that his partiality for Miss Bennet was beyond what I had ever witnessed in him" (219). Darcy mentions this observation in building his excuse regarding his attempts to separate Bingley and Jane—he objects to the Bennet family, and his observations have led him to doubt Jane's attachment to his friend. In addition to creating unnecessary strife for Jane Bennet, then, this episode also reminds the reader that Darcy is frequently so caught up in the role of spectator/observer that he fails to see the limitations imposed by his overly confident spectatorship on his own self-understanding.

His confusion over his role as spectator emerges as he turns from watching Jane and Bingley and drawing conclusions about their relationship, to his own increasingly obsessive watching of Elizabeth. The more he looks at her, the more he wants to look at her. In their initial interaction, when he rejects her as a dance partner, Darcy "looked for a moment at Elizabeth, till catching her eye, he withdrew his own" (P&P, 12). This brief glance and even briefer moment of eye contact leads Darcy to dismiss Elizabeth. Yet he quickly begins to reconsider, and the first volume of the novel is filled with examples of his increasing attachment to her, relayed through the gaze:

> Occupied by Mr. Bingley's attractions to her sister, Elizabeth was far from suspecting that she was herself becoming an object of some interest in the eyes of his friend. Mr. Darcy had at first scarcely allowed her to be pretty; he

had looked at her without admiration at the ball; and when they next met, he had looked at her only to criticise. But no sooner had he made it clear to himself and his friends that she had hardly a good feature in her face, than he began to find it was rendered uncommonly intelligent by the beautiful expression of her dark eyes. To this discovery succeeded some others equally mortifying. Though he had detected with a critical eye more than one failure of perfect symmetry of her form, he was forced to acknowledge her figure to be light and pleasing; and in spite of his asserting that her manners were not those of the fashionable world, he was caught by their easy playfulness. Of this she was perfectly unaware. (25–26)

This paragraph is worth quoting at length because Austen's details take us into Darcy's mind and allow us to see Elizabeth through his eyes. He struggles as a spectator, trying to reconcile the evidence of his eyes with his inclinations and beliefs.[16] The articulation of Elizabeth's shortcomings both to himself and to his friends underscores Darcy's internal struggle as he continually backtracks: convinced she is unattractive, he begins to appreciate the beautiful expression of her eyes; convinced her figure is faulty, he is forced to acknowledge that it is pleasing. These discoveries are "mortifying" to Darcy not only because he is beginning to find himself attracted to Elizabeth but also because they force him to confront his role as a spectator and acknowledge that his confident habit of reading individuals and scenes may need to be adjusted. We see this contradiction at work when Sir William presses him to agree that "dancing is one of the first refinements of polished society," to which Darcy infamously replies, "Every savage can dance" (28).[17] His internal rhetorical maneuvering is prompted by the same "mood of self-denial" that, for Peter Knox-Shaw, leads Darcy to decline the opportunity to dance with Elizabeth at the Lucases' party. Dancing, like other social relations, is situational, and although Darcy can dance quite well, he is unwilling to dance in this situation because, Knox-Shaw adds, he is "determined to avoid entanglement in what he primly considers to be inappropriate company."[18] Thus, he must choose between his desire to observe Elizabeth as a spectator and his desire to engage her as a partner.

Similar moments of watching Elizabeth occur throughout the novel as Darcy wages an internal battle between heart and head, between his desire to gaze at Elizabeth and his need to police his own gaze. Critics and audiences of ballet during the late eighteenth and early nineteenth centuries were encountering a similar struggle in which their expectations for dance no longer fit what was on the stage before them. As dance historian Dorion Weickmann writes, during this period ballet saw a move toward "the imitation and illustration of human passions and sentiments," engaging audiences through plot and character.[19] Thus, audience members expecting what Noverre dismissed as the "symmetrical and formal figures" of an earlier generation were now encountering dances that "speak with fire and energy."[20] Detached delight in formal spectacle alone was giving way to a more passionate engagement in the emotional sparks communicated through the dancers' bodies.

Along with the changes in the structure of dance and move toward the *ballet d'action*, dance critics in the late eighteenth and early nineteenth centuries were also confronted with a new kind of female beauty onstage. As the ballerina began her rise to the celebrity status she would achieve in the 1820s and 1830s, her somewhat formal and stilted movements were replaced with a more natural carriage and bearing designed to reflect natural human emotion. This change in the subject and nature of ballet was in keeping with the rising "Romantic" spirit of the age that privileged the natural world and humanity's connection to nature over contrived scenarios and artifice. The ballerina's ability to inhabit that world—accentuated by her rise onto pointe and into the air in ballets such as *Le sylphide*—was seen as a mark of her beauty and artistry, and audience members had to shift their focus to appreciate this new kind of performance.

Austen's Elizabeth Bennet requires her spectators to rethink their critical frameworks as would performers in the new narrative forms of stage dance. Darcy's internal monologue, quoted above, suggests that even within the most scripted of social situations—a ballroom—Elizabeth is outside the norm, but this aspect of her character is truly highlighted when she moves outside such situations. The infamous "muddy walk" Elizabeth undertakes in her determination to visit her sister at Netherfield firmly establishes her as a new kind of performer. The action is physically rigorous—she moves "at a quick pace, jumping over stiles and springing over puddles with impatient activity" (*P&P*, 36). Elizabeth betrays a dancer's athleticism here—she is not merely walking and posing but is leaping and jumping and working up a sweat as she does so. She is on the forefront of a change in women's athleticism on the stage; as Molly Engelhardt explains, during most of the eighteenth century, women's roles in ballet "were less physically demanding, and the jumping and turning were left exclusively to the men," but this began to change as the century turned.[21] Elizabeth's appearance in the Netherfield breakfast parlor occasions yet another moment of internal conflict for Darcy. He is "divided between admiration of the brilliancy which exercise had given to her complexion, and doubt as to the occasion's justifying her coming so far alone" (*P&P*, 36). In the context of stage dance, it is also easy to see that Darcy is aroused by Elizabeth's appearance. Just as spectators would ogle the legs of ballerinas through their diaphanous skirts, so Darcy might catch a glimpse of Elizabeth's legs beneath her dirty petticoat. Following this spectacle, it is understandable that Darcy barely notices Caroline Bingley's attempt to draw his attention by simply walking around the room. Although she is "elegant" and "walked well," her attempts feel old-fashioned and stale in comparison to Elizabeth's high-energy performances (61). As Erin Smith points out, during this scene, "Miss Bingley's cultivated physicality comes across as calculating and artificial."[22] In contrast, for Darcy, Elizabeth is the fantasy ballerina, able to transcend the boundaries of the physical body by eschewing the earthbound concerns of propriety or gravity.

Darcy's preference for the role of observer over performer may reflect his disinclination to expose himself to public commentary and review. Indeed, after the Meryton ball, Mrs. Bennet gushes that "Mr. Bingley . . . danced with her [Jane] twice," using this as evidence of his partiality for her eldest daughter (*P&P*, 13). For once, she is not overreading the situation. The device of using the ballroom as a space to publicly portray one's preferences is employed not only in *Pride and Prejudice* but also in Austen's other novels and in historical ballroom situations. Indeed, the matter of dancing as a public expression of preference was so familiar that dance manuals warned against it, lest an attachment be made public that was not fully formed or finalized. This context helps to explain Elizabeth's strong reaction against dancing with Mr. Collins, which she describes as "dances of mortification." Austen writes, "Mr. Collins, awkward and solemn, apologising instead of attending, and often moving wrong without being aware of it, gave her all the shame and misery which a disagreeable partner for a couple of dances can give" (101). The strong language here signals more than the unpleasant experience of having Mr. Collins step on her toes; it reflects the unwanted attention Collins's awkwardness attracts to his public choice of partner. Ballroom spectators are likely to be drawing conclusions about the relationship between Elizabeth and Mr. Collins based on their dance. It was precisely for this reason—wishing to avoid undue significance to a choice of partner—that led Mr. Darcy to reject Elizabeth as a partner. His claim that she was "not handsome enough to tempt *me*" masked a disinclination to put himself on display at all, lest it start the gossip mills churning about a potential connection between himself and a young lady who has been "slighted by other men" (12). It is, therefore, additionally surprising to Elizabeth when Darcy seeks her out as a partner at the Netherfield ball. Elizabeth finds herself "amazed at the dignity to which she was arrived in being allowed to stand opposite to Mr. Darcy, and reading in her neighbours' looks their equal amazement in beholding it" (102). Although Austen certainly deploys some of her trademark wryness here, this moment marks Darcy's reversal of perspective on Elizabeth and announces his preference for her to the gathered company.

Although Darcy may generally prefer to be a ballroom observer, torn between attraction and judgment, he is not a static observer. During the Meryton ball, he does not simply sit and observe but is in constant motion, "walking about the room" (*P&P*, 11). Indeed, as the novel demonstrates, walking is Darcy's preferred state, and it is when he is trapped and unable to move that his character appears the most problematic. For instance, when Darcy and Elizabeth dance together at Netherfield, he chafes against the scripted nature of ballroom conversation (which readers of Austen, of course, will remember Henry Tilney lampooning in *Northanger Abbey*). Elizabeth, however, will not indulge Darcy. She says, "It is *your* turn to say something now, Mr. Darcy—*I* talked about the dance, and *you* ought to make some kind of remark on the size of the room or the number of couples." Darcy placates her and then asks, "Do you talk by rule then, while you are dancing?" (102). This exchange reflects not only the social expectation in which partners will converse during the dance but also links the physical and the verbal. The italicization in Elizabeth's opening parry *your/I/you* demonstrates the back-and-forth of couples in a country dance, coming together and moving apart as dictated by the patterns of the dance. The "rule" then is not just the social prescription that calls for interaction but also the literal rule of the figure and the spacing each dancer is required to maintain as she or he moves through the figures of the dance. Indeed, dance masters were often quite strict and prescriptive about this spacing, as errors would throw off the symmetry and pattern of the performance (and also lead to collisions with one's neighbor). Although Darcy is physically active in this moment, the ballroom is still a confining space—it is not one in which he can move or speak freely.

Austen carries over this reading of bodies into the first proposal Darcy makes to Elizabeth. This scene takes place within the confines of the Collinses' home, and the narrator notes that Darcy sits, stands, leans, and paces, interjecting these descriptors into the dialogue to allow the reader to share in Darcy's physical restlessness, which is evident from his first entry into the room: "He sat down for a few moments, and then getting up walked about the room. . . . After a silence of several minutes he came towards her in an agitated manner, and thus began" (*P&P*, 211). Elizabeth is unable to read this agitated Darcy—her "astonishment was beyond expression"—and he is unable to perform a staid detachment but instead falls prey to his passions. This is intensified during the dialogue that follows, in which Austen shows Darcy's failed attempts at performance. Some of the descriptors that she applies during the scene include: "He was struggling for the appearance of composure" (212), "he changed colour" (213), loses his "tranquil tone" (214), and his "astonishment" is "obvious" (215). Austen clearly suggests that this is a man who finds the literal and metaphorical constraints of most social interactions to be suffocating and who, despite his attempt to maintain a composed demeanor, gives way to Romantic/romantic emotion. Despite himself, when he must move from the role of observer to performer, he is less composed courtier and more Childe Harold. Unfortunately, Darcy does not yet have a frame of reference for this newly emerging Romantic hero or his active female counterpart, and the first proposal is something of a disaster. Of course, as the novel progresses, Elizabeth begins to watch Darcy, too, culminating in her encounter with his portrait at Pemberley, and Darcy becomes more comfortable with his role as performer and counterpart to Elizabeth. Pride and prejudice are overcome, and the lovers move together toward their happy ending.

Although Austen's novels have been widely adapted for stage and screen, dance-based adaptations of Austen are limited. In 2008, Chicago's Joffrey Ballet staged a new piece by choreographer Edwaard Liang titled *Age of Innocence*. The ballet, Liang explains, was inspired by his general interest in "women's roles in the 19th-century" and, more specifically, the work of Jane Austen. Interviewer Catherine L. Tully writes, "Imagining a ballroom long ago, full of expectation and uncertainty, where no one had any more than a few moments and a few whispers to find love, Liang began to reflect on what it would be like to live that way, with only those kinds of choices."[23] Prior to the Ballet Met's 2016 performance of the piece, Liang, now the company's artistic director, noted that the depiction of gender roles in Austen—specifically with regard to marriage—resonated with him. He explained that his parents were in an arranged marriage, so he found himself connecting to the depictions of courtship and marriage in the novels. *Age of Innocence* is not a narrative-based adaptation of Austen, but it is an example of how Austen's themes and characters have inspired broader explorations of gender and identity through dance.

Canadian company Ballet Fantastique did produce a direct adaptation of *Pride and Prejudice* in 2013. This version, subtitled "a Parisian jazz ballet," is set in a 1920s Paris nightclub. In this adaptation, the Bennet sisters (Frenchified to "Bennette") perform intricately entwined steps, reminiscent of the cygnets in *Swan Lake*, and Mr. Wickham crosses the stage in grand leaps and tours, steps that match both his overt masculinity and braggadocio. This adaptation appears to have been successful and has been restaged multiple times by the company, most recently in Portland's Hult Center in fall of 2016, where Gwen Curran of the *Register Guard* hailed it as "truly fantastic."[24]

In April 2017, the American Repertory Ballet (ARB) and Princeton Symphony Orchestra performed a new ballet version of *Pride and Prejudice* choreographed by Douglas Martin, who served as a principal dancer with both the Joffrey Ballet and the ARB before becoming the director of the latter company. Unlike the adaptation by *Ballet Fantastique*, this was a traditional period-based work, and Martin even incorporated elements of historical dances, such as the minuet and country dance. Jane Austen scholar Claudia Johnson was interviewed about the production for the *Princetonian* and noted the appropriateness of the medium of ballet for telling the story of *Pride and Prejudice*: "In some ways it might be even more effective than the movies themselves because the dances are in large [part] to convey that emotional intensity through the bodies instead of through some mangled script. . . . [W]atching these characters in motion makes you realize how Austen really worked all of these characters out visually. Even though she's working in a verbal medium, she's imagining the characters in movement."[25] Austen's skill at using dance to telegraph emotional intensity accounts for the ease with which her novels have been adapted into contemporary dance forms. The complexity of the characters was certainly a challenge for Martin, who, in an interview for *Hollywood Soapbox*, discusses the challenge of showing the emotional development of the characters, particularly Elizabeth and Darcy, over the course of the piece.[26] The ballet was well reviewed, although critics were divided about Martin's decision to preserve rather than streamline Austen's complex plot. Writing for the review blog *Critical Dance*, Jerry Hochman objects to the minute attention to details of plot and inclusion of "characters that, for the ballet's purposes, don't need to be there."[27] However, Robert Johnson, writing for NJArts.net, argues that the ballet more than lives up to its storytelling responsibilities: without the minute detail and "in the absence of program notes, any duffers who have not read the novel will flounder helplessly. Never mind that the performers act convincingly and have been rehearsed to perfection."[28]

Ballet also inspired young adult author Jessica Evans's 2014 novel *The Muse: A Pride and Prejudice Variation*, which sets Austen's characters in a contemporary ballet company. In this version, Elizabeth is an aspiring young member of the *corps de ballet*, Darcy a superstar choreographer, Lady Catherine a patron of the arts, Wickham a disgraced former member of the company, and Caroline a diva prima ballerina. Evans's novel dispenses with many of the *Pride and Prejudice* plots. The Bennet parents are absent, and the number of sisters is reduced to two: Elizabeth and Jane. Wickham appears only as a foil for Darcy without the extended complication of his relationship with Lydia and threat to the family. Likewise, Lady Catherine and Mr. Collins appear only briefly. Limiting the focus to the relationships among Elizabeth, Jane, Darcy, Caroline, and Bingley allows Evans to explore the group dynamic further and imagine this fivesome (occasionally supplemented with Louisa) as a social group. Evans seems to have the most fun with Caroline Bingley's character, imagining how the competitive world of professional ballet would suit Caroline's desire to be the center of attention and tendencies to degrade other women. There are also a number of allusions that will resonate with readers of Austen: Darcy has a ginger cat named "Austin" and lives in the "Pemberley building" in New York City, and the ballet company's annual fundraiser is known as the "Netherfield Gala."

With regard to adapting Austen for ballet, Evans draws a light, if consistent, thread throughout the novel, in which she shows that ballerinas are subject to many of the same stereotypes and limitations as nineteenth-century women. Determined not to be simply a "bunhead," Elizabeth takes classes in Afro-Caribbean dance and even performs in a summer festival. She is also taking college courses online, having left school after a year to dance with a company overseas. For Elizabeth, education helps her find her individual artistic voice, and, as Darcy eventually recognizes, individuality in members of the *corps de ballet* is something to be valued rather than something to be discouraged for the sake of uniformity. This is the same battle Noverre was fighting when he, too, argued for individuality in the *corps*, writing, "Make your *corps de ballet* dance, but, when it does so, let each member of it express an emotion or contribute to form a picture."[29] Caroline Bingley, in contrast, does not understand the point of individuality in the *corps* or college for dancers: "College really isn't the place for serious professional ballet dancers. Why waste the best years of your career reading stuffy, old books?"[30] She assures the group, however, that she does read because "Everyone should read, including dancers," to which Elizabeth responds, "There's nothing worse than a dumb ballerina."[31] Caroline's line about reading echoes her assertion in *Pride and Prejudice*, "I declare after all there is no enjoyment like reading!" (60), which is similarly ironic because it comes during a moment when Caroline has not been reading at all but instead pretending to read in the hope of catching Darcy's attention. Throughout the novel, Evans's Elizabeth tries to counter the stereotypes about ballerinas, and this ultimately causes Darcy to identify her as his muse and leads to their happy ending.

Just as *ballet d'action* increasingly used physicality and beauty to engage spectators, so, too, does Darcy learn the rules of physical and social engagement. During one of the strained evenings at Rosings Park, Elizabeth, Darcy, and Colonel Fitzwilliam discuss Darcy's inability (or unwillingness) to ingratiate himself in social situations. Elizabeth recalls the Meryton ball where Darcy chose to remain an observer rather than seek introductions and participate in the dancing. Darcy claims that he lacks the "talent" for such interactions, but Elizabeth, seated at the pianoforte at the time and acknowledging her own lack of virtuosity, points out that such talents can be developed with practice. Darcy replies in agreement and concludes, "We neither of us perform to strangers" (*P&P*, 197). This is a telling commentary on performance because Darcy is suggesting that both he and Elizabeth resist the social expectations (interaction for him, accomplishments for her) that might be expected based on their class and gender. The word "strangers" is also important here, however, because Darcy seems to be suggesting that while he and Elizabeth are unwilling to perform for strangers, they are willing to perform for friends. He recognizes their mutual preference for observation over unreflective participation. Perhaps like his creator, he comes to understand more fully the role of the spectator in understanding and interpreting performance. In addition, he signals a kinship with Elizabeth, noting that they both might resist certain social expectations but that they are nonetheless readable by those who are kindred spirits. The moment is significant because, for the first time, Darcy acknowledges not just shared feeling with Elizabeth but shared participation in a select community that includes her.

Ballet audiences, too, needed to learn to interpret how physicality could express character and narrative in *ballet d'action*. As Noverre wrote, ballet should be comprised of a scene/act format that follows a clear narrative structure. This familiar format would enable audiences to follow the plot of the ballet more easily. Similarly, Austen borrows from shifting trends within stage and social dance in using the physicality of her characters to dramatize emotion. Employing language, phrasing, and images that evoke dance, Austen intensifies her characterization and the relationship between characters while also playing on her readers' emerging ability to read physicality onstage and in the ballroom. For Elizabeth, Darcy, Austen, and her interpreters, then, perhaps the most important factor in being an effective performer is finding the right audience.

Notes

1. Theresa Jill Buckland, *Society Dancing: Fashionable Bodies in England, 1870–1920* (New York: Palgrave, 2011), 13.

2. See Judith Chazin-Bennahum, *The Lure of Perfection: Fashion and Ballet 1780–1830* (New York: Routledge, 2005).

3. For detailed discussion of ballet's popularity during the early nineteenth century and the emergence of the celebrity ballerina, see Ivor Guest, *The Romantic Ballet in England* (Middleton, CT: Wesleyan University Press, 1972).

4. Paula Byrne, *Jane Austen and the Theatre* (London: Hambledon and London, 2002), 37.

5. Byrne, *Jane Austen and the Theatre*, 150.

6. Miss Loder is Ann Matilda Loder (1786–1848), elder sister of Bath-based master violinist and teacher John David Loder (1788–1846), whose 1803 performance in the ballet accompanying *Lovers' Vows* was her first performance in Bath, her stage career having begun earlier that year in Bristol (see Nicholas Temperley, ed., *Musicians of Bath and Beyond: Edward Loder [1809–1865] and His Family* [Suffolk, UK: Boydell, 2016], 94).

7. *Jane Austen's Letters*, ed. Deirdre Le Faye, 4th ed. (Oxford: Oxford University Press, 2011), 5.

8. Dorion Weickmann, "Choreography and Narrative: The *ballet d'action* of the Eighteenth Century," in *The Cambridge Companion to Ballet*, ed. Marion Kant (Cambridge: Cambridge University Press, 2007), 53–64, 59.

9. Jean Georges Noverre, *Letters on Dancing and Ballets*, trans. Cyril W. Beaumont (Alton, UK: Dance Books, 2004), 4.

10. Noverre, *Letters on Dancing and Ballets*, 22.

11. Noverre, *Letters on Dancing and Ballets*, 1.

12. Recent critical work on dance in Austen's novels includes Molly Engelhardt, *Dancing out of Line: Ballrooms, Ballets, and Mobility in Victorian Fiction and Culture* (Athens: Ohio University Press, 2009); Susannah Fullerton, *A Dance with Jane Austen: How a Novelist and Her Characters Went to the Ball* (London: Frances Lincoln, 2012); Nancy M. Lee-Riffe, "The Role of Country Dance in the Fiction of Jane Austen," *Women's Writing* 5 (1998): 103–12; Maria Marcsek-Fuchs, *Dance and British Literature: An Intermedial Encounter* (London: Rodopi, 2015); Nora Foster Stovel, "An Invitation to Dance and a Proposal of Marriage: Jane Austen's *Emma* and Two Film Adaptations," *Persuasions Online* 28 (2007); Allison Thompson, "The Felicities of Rapid Motion: Jane Austen in the Ballroom," *Persuasions Online* 21 (2000); and Cheryl A. Wilson, *Literature and Dance in Nineteenth-Century Britain: Jane Austen to the New Woman* (Cambridge: Cambridge University Press, 2009).

13. Selma Jeanne Cohen, "The English Critic and the Romantic Ballet," *Theatre Survey* 1, no. 17 (1976): 82–91, 89.

14. Additional discussion of dance manuals and their function during the nineteenth century appears in Wilson, *Literature and Dance*.

15. Jane Austen, *Pride and Prejudice*, ed. Pat Rogers (Cambridge: Cambridge University Press, 2006). All subsequent references to this text appear as in-text citations.

16. Feminist dance critic Ann Daly discusses how film theory—specifically Laura Mulvey's writings on the "male gaze"—has influenced feminist analyses of dance, shifting "the object of analysis . . . from just the image itself, in isolation, to the entire *process* of representation, which also encompasses the spectator and her/his process of interpretation" (Daly, "Unlimited Partnership: Dance and Feminist Analysis," *Dance Research Journal* 23, no. 1 [1991]: 2–5, 4).

17. Additional discussion of this scene appears in Allison Thompson, "Dancing at St. James," *Persuasions On-Line* 33, no. 1 (2012); and Nora Foster Stovel, "'Every Savage Can Dance': Choreographing Courtship," *Persuasions* 23 (2003): 29–49.

18. Peter Knox-Shaw, *Jane Austen and the Enlightenment* (Cambridge: Cambridge University Press, 2009), 87.

19. Weickmann, *Choreography*, 57.

20. Noverre, *Letters on Dancing*, 13.

21. Engelhardt, *Dancing*, 33.

22. Erin Smith, "Miss Bingley's Walk: Jane Austen and the Aesthetics of Movement," in *Jane Austen and the Arts*, ed. Natasha Duquette and Elisabeth Lenckos (Bethlehem, PA: Lehigh University Press, 2014), 37–45, 37.

23. Catherine L. Tully, "The Choreography of Understanding: Edwaard Liang's 'Age of Innocence' at the Joffrey," April 26, 2012, *Joffrey Ballet News Archive*, www.joffrey.org/news/choreography-understanding-edwaard-liang%E2%80%99s-%E2%80%9Cage-innocence%E2%80%9D-joffrey-0.

24. Gwen Curran, "Ballet Fantastique's 'Pride and Prejudice' Truly Fantastic," review of Ballet Fantastique's *Pride and Prejudice: A Parisian Jazz Ballet*, *Register-Guard*, October 16, 2016, http://projects.registerguard.com/rg/entertainment/arts/34856721-60/ballet-fantastiques-1920s-take-on-pride-and-prejudice-shines-excites.html.csp.

25. Johnson qtd. in Danielle Hoffman, "American Repertory Ballet's *Pride and Prejudice*," review of American Repertory Company's *Pride and Prejudice*, Princeton, NJ, *Daily Princetonian*, April 19, 2017, www.dailyprincetonian.com/article/2017/04/american-repertory-ballet-pride-and-prejudice.

26. John Soltes, "Interview: American Repertory Ballet Stages New Ballet Based on 'Pride and Prejudice,'" *Hollywood Soapbox*, www.hollywoodsoapbox.com/?p=17211.

27. Jerry Hochman, "American Repertory Ballet: *Pride and Prejudice*," review of American Repertory Company's *Pride and Prejudice*, Princeton, NJ, *Critical Dance*, April 21, 2017, http://criticaldance.org/first_impression/american-repertory-ballet-pride-and-prejudice-2/.

28. Robert Johnson, "Elizabeth and Darcy Dance as 'Pride and Prejudice' Debuts as a Ballet," review of American Repertory Company's *Pride and Prejudice*, Princeton, NJ, NJArts.net, April 23, 2017, www.njarts.net/dance/elizabeth-darcy-dance-pride-prejudice-debuts-ballet/.

29. Noverre, *Letters on Dancing*, 30.

30. Jessica Evans, *The Muse: A Pride and Prejudice Variation* (Oysterville, WA: Meryton, 2014), 57.

31. Evans, *The Muse*, 58.

Jane Austen, Marginalia, and Book Culture

MARILYN FRANCUS

Jane Austen was an avid reader of books, and much of our knowledge of Austen's literary opinions has come from her correspondence or from her characterizations of reading in her novels. Recently Austen's marginalia have garnered attention as another means to document her literary taste and values, largely thanks to Peter Sabor's inclusion of the marginalia in the Cambridge edition of Austen's *Juvenilia*. Even a glance at Austen's marginalia shows that Austen was a highly engaged reader, prodding, challenging, and laughing at writers as she wrote back to them from the blank spaces on the page. The marginal comments in the books read by this remarkably playful artist and by members of her family help us see more clearly how reading fed family dynamics, and how family dynamics took artistic forms recorded in the margins of books.

While Austen's marginalia provide evidence of her reading and opinions, they also reveal her understanding of the material status and use of books in her society. For Austen, books were not pristine private objects for personal consumption, nor sumptuous objects for display, nor disposable objects. Rather, books circulated as part of a cultural conversation in which Austen was a full participant: Austen read books, talked about books, wrote in books, borrowed books, and gave books as gifts. While this is not news, I want to suggest that this book sensibility was characteristic of her family. There is significant data about the literariness of the Austens, which can be seen not only in the family's participation in theatricals and charades but also in their publications, which ranged from her brother James's periodical, the *Loiterer*, to the novels of her nieces Anna Lefroy and Catherine Hubback, and the memoir of Austen by her nephew James Edward Austen-Leigh.[1] But the extent to which the Austens engaged with books—reading, sharing, and writing in books—seems to be less charted territory. It is worth remembering that Reverend George Austen had a collection of more than five hundred books, which was fairly impressive for a not particularly affluent country clergyman.² While his collection no longer exists, Edward Austen Knight's extensive collection at Godmersham (now housed at Chawton House) includes many annotated volumes demonstrating the habits of reading that were part of the family legacy.³ The Austens were irrepressible readers and annotators, invested in book culture—much like their famous relative, who may have anticipated her readers engaging with her novels in these ways as well. I would like to comment on the bookishness of the Austens, first by looking at the copy of *Elegant Extracts* that Austen gave to her niece Anna in 1801, and then by turning to some of the annotated texts in Edward Austen Knight's collection at Chawton House.⁴ In doing so, I hope to provide evidence of their book behaviors and to tease out some of the challenges and implications of Austen family book culture.

In 1800 the Austens decided to retire, leave Steventon, and move to Bath. Jane was not happy with this decision, but more pertinently for my purposes, the move to Bath involved disposing of books.⁵ Jane gave her niece Anna two books in 1801, presumably before the move to Bath that spring—and one of those books was *Elegant Extracts* (fig. 7). The inscription on the inside cover reveals the provenance of the text and its status as a family heirloom: Anna's full name (Jane Anna Eliz[abe]th Austen) and the date of the gift (1801) in Austen's handwriting, followed by the phrase "the gift of her Aunt Jane" is written in pencil with a decided upward tilt by young Anna. Underneath appears the name of Anna Jemima Lefroy, Anna Austen Lefroy's first child, who was born in 1815.⁶ According to Peter Sabor, this copy of *Elegant Extracts* stayed in the Lefroy family until the 1980s, when it was presented to the Jane Austen Memorial Trust; the book is currently on display in Jane Austen's House Museum in Chawton.⁷ There is no publication date on this copy of *Elegant Extracts*. It is possible that Austen's copy was a first edition, which was published in September 1782; the second edition of *Elegant Extracts* was published in 1784, and all the other editions I have found have dates on the title page.⁸ If Austen received *Elegant Extracts* not long after it was published, she would have been approximately seven years old, since she was born in December 1775. To give this text to Anna in spring 1801, when Anna was turning eight, would have been appropriate.

Elegant Extracts was a popular text that reached its ninth edition in 1808, and it spawned a series of related texts: *Elegant Extracts in Poetry* (1789); *Elegant Epistles* (1790); *The Prose Epitome, or Elegant Extracts Abridged* (1791); *The Poetical Epitome, or Extracts, Elegant, Instructive, Entertaining, abridged from the larger volume* (1791).⁹ The Knight Collection includes the 1791 and 1803 editions of *Elegant Extracts*, and the 1801 edition of *Elegant*

Fig. 7. Jane Austen's inscription of frontispiece and title page of Vicesimus Knox, *Elegant Extracts* (London, ca. 1782–83). (Author's photograph, with permission of Jane Austen's House Museum, Chawton)

Extracts of Poetry. Like all books given as gifts, this volume carries the hope that the recipient will read it and the implication that the contents of the book are deemed valuable by the donor, or considered by the donor to be valuable for the recipient. But this copy of *Elegant Extracts* carries a particular weight: Austen's marginalia guided Anna toward specific political positions, and this gift text helped indoctrinate Anna into the family's book culture.

For Austen scholars, *Elegant Extracts* holds general interest because Robert Martin reads it in *Emma*, and Emma copies "Kitty, a fair but frozen maid" from it.[10] But this copy is of particular interest for the annotations by Austen on the entries for Mary, Queen of Scots, and Queen Elizabeth I, excerpted from William Robertson's *History of Scotland* (second edition, 1759) and David Hume's *The History of England* (1763) respectively (J, 352). Austen's marginalia are cognate with her "History of England" ("By a partial, prejudiced & ignorant Historian"): she's a partisan of the Stuarts.[11] Her comments at the end of the entries make this evident. Robertson's concluding comment about Mary, Queen of Scots—"No man, says Brantome, ever beheld her person without admiration and love, or will read her history without sorrow"—elicits the following response from Austen: "No one *ought*, but I fear Mr. Brantome has too favourable an opinion of Human Nature if he makes no exception" (fig. 8). Austen's devotion to Mary, Queen of Scots is matched by her disdain for Elizabeth

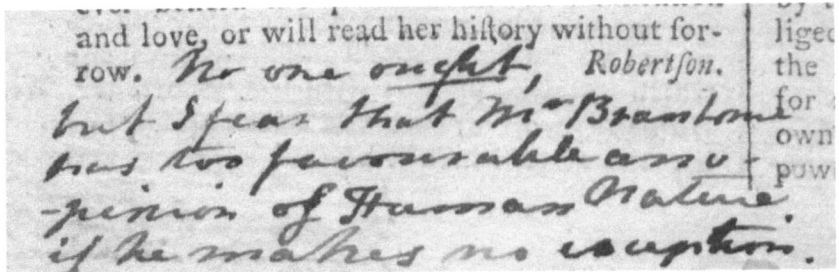

Fig. 8. Jane Austen's marginalia in "The Character of Mary Queen of Scots," excerpted from Robertson's *History of Scotland*, in Vicesimus Knox, *Elegant Extracts* (London, ca. 1782–83). (Author's photograph, with permission of Jane Austen's House Museum, Chawton)

I. Hume summarizes the queen's life: "We may find it difficult to reconcile our fancy to her as a wife or a mistress; but her qualities as a sovereign, though with some considerable exceptions, are the object of undisputed applause and approbation." To which Austen retorts: "A lie—an entire lie from beginning to end" (fig. 9). Austen's comments grapple with the ways that history is written and read. Hume is not being uncritical of Elizabeth I; the phrase "though with some considerable exceptions" suggests that he recognizes that there is much to balance the laudatory conclusion that Elizabeth I was "the object of undisputed applause and approbation." But Austen does not see Hume's assessment as an effort toward fairness, or perhaps she does not want to see it as such. By dismissing Hume's work as false ("a lie"), Austen plays the role of resistant reader: not only does she refute the text because it does not represent her political position, but she also flattens Hume's text into a caricature, by refusing to acknowledge the possibility of truth or nuance in it. Austen signals a different resistance in her concluding comment on Robertson, for while she is less vehement, she remains skeptical—in this instance, of Brantome, who trusts that a reader's response will align with his own.[12]

Austen's readerly resistance differs greatly from the reading habits of her characters: Catherine Morland's uncritical reading, Marianne Dashwood's infatuated reading, and Emma Woodhouse's incomplete reading all tend to defer to the author. But Austen's readerly resistance also has a physical manifestation, as she refuses to stay in the margins. Austen's final comment on Robertson starts at the end of the excerpt and works its way into the margin at the bottom of the page, but her concluding comment on Hume begins at

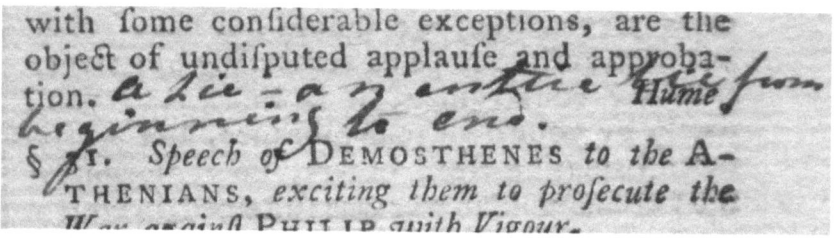

Fig. 9. Jane Austen's marginalia in "The Character of Queen Elizabeth," excerpted from David Hume's *History of England*, in Vicesimus Knox, *Elegant Extracts* (London, ca. 1782–83). (Author's photograph, with permission of Jane Austen's House Museum, Chawton)

the end of his text, in the middle of the column—she is not writing in the margin at all. Rather, Austen does not hesitate to grapple with an author in the text itself; she invades the text, as can be seen in her earlier comments on the excerpt from Robertson (fig. 10). Many of Austen's remarks here—"no"; "yes"; "another lie"; "a third"; "She was not attached to him"—are embedded in the text. While Austen uses the margins for some comments ("No"; "A lie"; "They do"), she does not confine herself to that space.[13]

In addition to these annotations, there is an ink *X* in the right-hand margin marking the excerpt entitled "The Necessity of forming religious principles at an early age" from Hugh Blair's *Sermons*. There are ink *X*s for other entries from Blair's *Sermons* as well: "The Happiness and Dignity of Manhood depend on the Conduct of youthful age," "Piety to God the Foundation of Good Morals," and "Sincerity and Truth recommended." Many other entries have pencil *X*s. In fact, of the 591 entries that compose *Elegant Extracts*, 84 have some sort of marking.[14] There are also pencil markings in the table of contents, all of which highlight entries that involve writing; these marked entries are primarily excerpts from Henry Felton's *Dissertation on Reading the Classics, and Forming a Just Style* and James Harris's *Miscellanies*. (Curiously, the entries on Mary, Queen of Scots, and Elizabeth I are not marked in the table of contents.) Not all of the marked entries in the table of contents have markings in the corresponding passages in the text, but the majority of them do. That the pencil markings focus on the writing sections of *Elegant Extracts* suggests that someone is looking to learn the conventions of style and authorship in the period. Given that the full title of *Elegant Extracts* emphasizes that it is "for the Improvement of Scholars at Classical & other Schools in the Art of Speaking, in Reading, Thinking, and Composing," the pencil markings writing with equal ease and dignity. Sudden, however, and violent in all her attachments; ~No.~ because her heart was warm and unsuspicious. Impatient of contradiction, because she had been accustomed from her infancy to be treated as a queen. No stranger, on some occasions, to dissimulation ~Yes~ which in that perfidious court where she received her education, was reckoned among the necessary arts of government. Not insensible to flattery, or unconscious of that pleasure, with which almost every woman beholds the influence of her own beauty. Formed with the qualities that we love, not with the talents that we admire; ~a lie~ she was an agreeable woman rather than an illustrious queen. The vivacity of her spirit, not sufficiently tempered with sound judgment, and the warmth of her heart, which was not at all times under the restraint of discretion, betrayed her both into errors and into crimes. ~another lie~ To say that she was always unfortunate, will not account for that long and almost uninterrupted succession of calamities which befel her; we must likewise add, that she was often imprudent. Her passion for Darnly was rash, youthful, and excessive. And though the sudden transition to the opposite extreme, was the natural effect of her ill-requited love, and of his ingratitude, insolence, and brutality; yet neither these, nor Bothwell's artful address and important services, can justify her attachment ~the hardened attacked to him~ to that nobleman. Even the manners of the age, licentious as they were, are no apology for this unhappy passion; nor can they induce us to look on that tragical and infamous scene which followed upon it with less abhorrence. ~They~ Humanity will draw a veil over this part of her character which it cannot approve; and ~It more than approves, it admires~ may

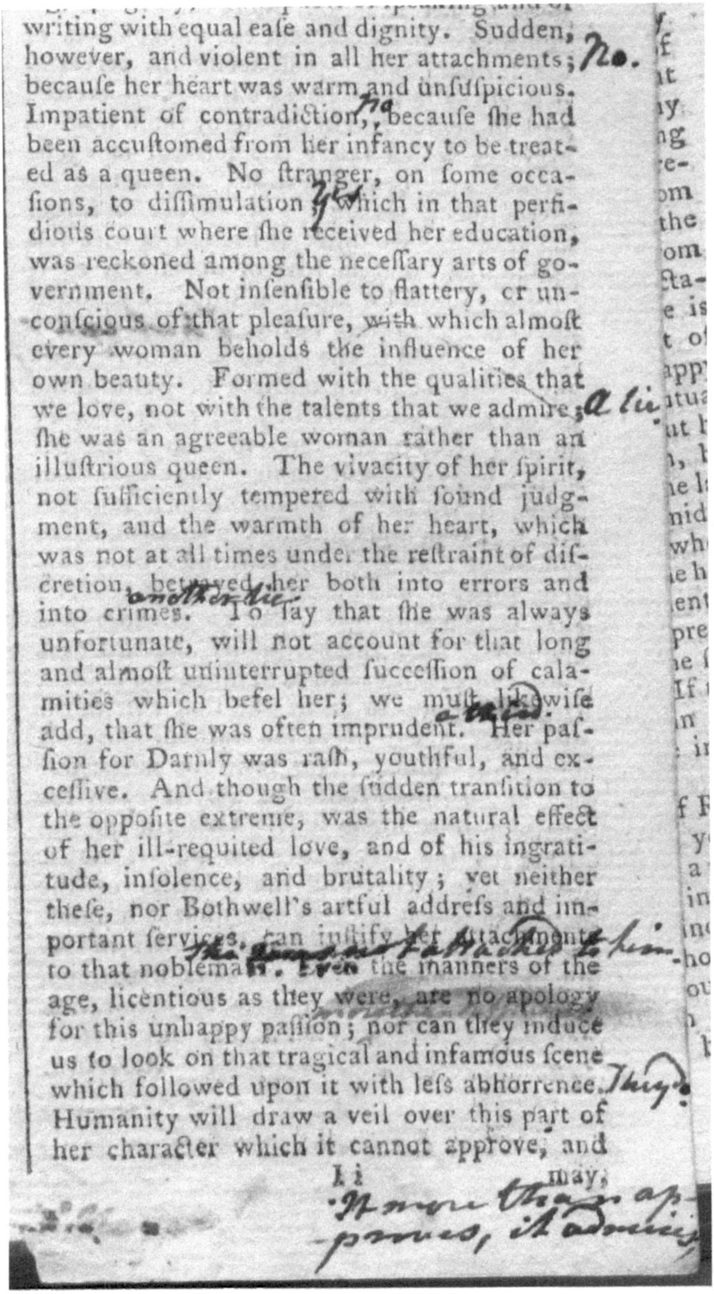

Fig. 10. Jane Austen's marginalia in "The Character of Mary Queen of Scots," excerpted from Robertson's *History of Scotland*, in Vicesimus Knox, *Elegant Extracts* (London, ca. 1782–83). (Author's photograph, with permission of Jane Austen's House Museum, Chawton)

suggest that this copy of *Elegant Extracts* was used for those purposes.¹⁵ Most of the literature in *Elegant Extracts* is classical or canonical, and mastery of the literary canon is the first step toward writing oneself into a tradition or to appropriate the canon for new literary purposes. Similarly, to become a writer, it is necessary to know the literary rules—the conventions of literary styles, forms, and images—before one can bend or break them. *Elegant Extracts* serves as a literary rule book and, given its popularity, a guide to contemporary literary conventions and expectations.¹⁶

While the annotations of Robertson and Hume have been identified as in Austen's hand, it is not possible to identify the maker of Xs and vertical lines in a text with certainty. However, the ownership of the text suggests some possibilities:

(1) That Austen wrote the pencil Xs and pencil vertical lines, *and* the ink comments. She may have had this volume in her possession for a while—particularly if Austen owned it soon after publication—and it is possible that Austen wrote in it in pencil and pen over time, as she was thinking about writing, literary form, and style. If so, then there may be more work to be done on Austen in light of the works of Felton, Harris, and Blair.

(2) That Austen wrote the comments in ink before she gave the book to Anna, to teach her the family preference for the Stuarts, and to proffer some moral guidance since the few ink Xs are all for passages to Blair's *Sermons*.¹⁷ The ink marginalia are not signaled by marks in the table of contents, but that may have been a tease—a game for Anna to find her Aunt Jane's comments inside. (And Austen was fond of playing games with her nieces and nephews.) If Austen wrote the ink comments, then it is possible that Anna wrote the pencil markings and pencil comments, since some of those comments refer to Todd's Johnson's *Dictionary*, which was published in 1818, after Austen's death (J, 353). If so, then Anna was using *Elegant Extracts* extensively, and hopefully as her aunt wished.

(3) There is a third possibility: that Anna Jemima (1815–1855), Anna's daughter, wrote some or all of the pencil markings and comments. Anna gave her daughter the text from her beloved aunt, possibly looking to inscribe her daughter into a literary tradition.

While it is possible that someone beyond Anna Jemima's generation could have written in *Elegant Extracts*, it seems unlikely. As the nineteenth century progressed and Austen's legacy became more powerful, the artifacts of her life became more valuable and less likely to be tampered with.

Austen's relationship with her niece Anna is particularly fertile ground for the analysis of the Austen family's engagements with book culture, for there is evidence that Austen both encouraged Anna to engage with literature and provided opportunities for her to do so. Anna was born on April 15, 1793, and Austen dedicated part of volume 1 of her juvenilia to her in June 2, 1793, declaring:

> Though you are at this period not many degrees removed from Infancy, Yet trusting that you will in time be older, and that through the care of your excellent Parents, You will one day or another be able to read written hand, I dedicate to You the following Miscellanious Morsels, convinced that if you seriously attend to them, You will derive from them very important Instructions, with regard to your Conduct in Life.---If such my hopes should hereafter be realized, never shall I regret the Days and Nights that have been spent in composing these Treatises for your Benefit. (J, 90)

The miscellaneous morsels, all comic and satiric, include "A fragment, written to inculcate virtue," "A beautiful description of the different effects of sensibility on different minds," and "The generous curate, a moral tale setting forth the Advantages of being Generous and a Curate." Thus Anna, the second-eldest of the Austen grandchildren, was written into the family's bibliophilia at the age of two months. Anna writes of hearing *Pride and Prejudice* being read as Austen was composing it, between October 1796 and August 1797; Anna would have been three or four years old. She also provides evidence of Austen's habit of telling stories to her nieces and nephews.[18] The impulse to engage the next generation in literature may also be reflected by the Grandison manuscript, a theatrical adaptation of Samuel Richardson's final novel, which appears to be a collaborative effort between Austen and Anna, circa 1800.[19] Austen gave Anna books as gifts—for Anna received Austen's copy of Ann Murry's *Mentoria* in 1801 as well.[20] And Austen maintained a correspondence with Anna—and her half siblings James Edward and Caroline—about their novels.[21] All of these behaviors suggest that Austen was looking to inspire the next generation of Austens in bibliophilia and literary geekiness.

The marginalia in Austen's *Elegant Extracts* highlight some characteristics of her family's book culture. First, one reads actively, not passively; reading provides a platform for response, resistance, and exchange.[22] Reading instigates writing. And reading with a pen or pencil in hand (or at hand) seemingly focuses the mind. A reader should get into the text: a reader need not settle for commenting in the margins but may write in between the lines.²³ There is no sacred space in a book. While this writing is derivative—in the sense that annotation and marginalia rely on someone else's text to exist—it can be vibrant. While marginalia can be for oneself (at the moment, or for later rereading), they can be written for others—or at least, a writer of marginalia ought to expect that their comments and marks will be shared with other readers, as texts continually circulate.²⁴ Marginalia can serve as a code about patterns of reading (think of those *X*s and lines), signaling the ways that readers dip into texts, and revealing what draws and sustains attention, and what does not.

But while marginalia can make evident patterns of reading and thinking, deducing the import of specific marginalia can be complicated: multiple people may have access to the same text; an individual's handwriting is not consistent over time; annotators may not initial or date their marginalia. We know that Austen wrote the ink marginalia in *Elegant Extracts*, but we do not know who wrote the ink *X*s, the pencil marks, or, with any certainty, the pencil comments. It can be difficult to discern who is responding to a text, even if one can discern how they are responding.²⁵

Many characteristics of the marginalia in *Elegant Extracts* appear in other books owned by the Austens, which suggests that the Austens as a family were invested in marginalia. By making this claim, I am putting pressure on Katie Halsey's claim that "The Austens, in fact, extremely rarely wrote in their books."²⁶ These next examples all come from the collection of Edward Austen Knight, whose library at Godmersham was accessible to many people: not only Edward, his wife, Elizabeth, and their eleven children but the many Austen relatives who visited, including Jane and Cassandra; Francis and his children; and Charles with his children. Consequently, determining who engaged with a particular text is a difficult proposition. While the owner of a book is most likely to be the annotator, given the circulation of books among the Austens, the authorship of annotations is not necessarily clear.²⁷ It was recently discovered that Francis Austen's daughter Mary Jane graffitied her name on a painting of Chawton House, so it is possible that some of the nieces and nephews even felt empowered to write in their uncle's or cousins' books.²⁸

Someone scribbled "Boo" in large cursive letters into the 1801 edition of *Elegant Extracts of Poetry*, a two-volume set that is inscribed on the inside cover, "Edward Austen 1806." Presumably the owner is Edward Austen Knight's second child and eldest son, Edward (1794–1879), who would have

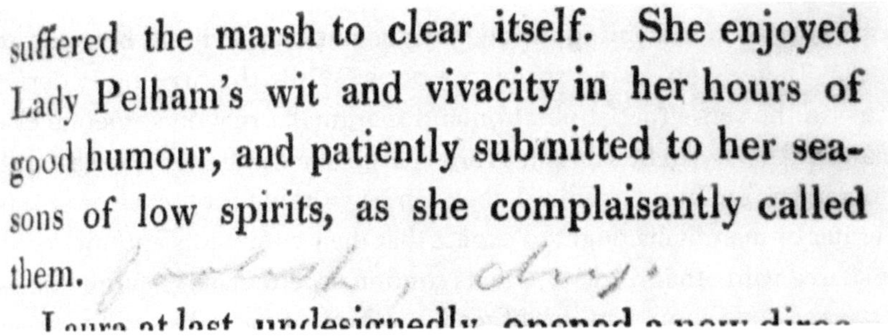

> suffered the marsh to clear itself. She enjoyed Lady Pelham's wit and vivacity in her hours of good humour, and patiently submitted to her seasons of low spirits, as she complaisantly called them. *foolish, dry*

Fig. 11. Annotation—"foolish, dry"—inscribed in Mary Brunton, *Self-Control* (Edinburgh, 1811). (Knight Family Collection, on deposit at Chawton House, Chawton)

been about twelve years old when he received the book in 1806.[29] The poem next to the "Boo" is Alexander Pope's *Epistle to Bathurst* (1733) in volume 1. Why this poem elicited a "Boo" seems to be a mystery. A bored reader? Someone writing to surprise another reader? Someone not impressed with Pope's poem? But this volume also has other annotations: the word "Kent" sandwiched between the columns of Pope's *Epistle to a Lady* and his *Epistle to Bathurst*; a capital *K* written next to Pope's *Epistle to Burlington*; and ink parentheses around a passage from Edward Young's "Night Thoughts."[30] The "Kent" presumably is a reference to the county where Godmersham is located; the capital *K* looks as if it were made by a young person practicing their handwriting with a flourish. The parentheses around the passage from Young perhaps point to a reader who found these lines particularly important or beautiful. The annotations here raise questions similar to those in *Elegant Extracts*: Why the variations in the capital *K*s? Why use pencil and pen? Is this evidence of one annotator or more? Are these annotations meaningful, in drawing attention to the poems of Pope and Young, or not? There is other evidence of usage in these two volumes (including ink spots, turned-down pages, a passage cut out), which suggests that like Austen's *Elegant Extracts*, these two volumes of *Elegant Extracts of Poetry* were dipped into but probably not read cover to cover.

If the annotations in *Elegant Extracts of Poetry* suggest that books can be a space for playful invasion, then the words "foolish, dry" in volume 2 of Mary Brunton's 1811 novel *Self-Control* suggest that textual spaces are also for criticism and commentary (fig. 11). This is the third edition, published in three volumes in 1811 in Edinburgh. As in Austen's *Elegant Extracts*, the comments are in the middle of the page, not in the margin. Austen read Brunton's novel, but I cannot confirm that this is her handwriting.[31] Austen commented on *Self-Control* in her correspondence: "I am looking over Self Control again, & my opinion is confirmed of its' being an excellently meant, elegantly-written Work, without anything of Nature or Probability in it. I declare I do not know whether Laura's passage down the American River, is not the most natural, possible, every-day thing she ever does" (*Letters*, 244). The pencil comment "foolish, dry," like the inscribed "stupid" at the end of a paragraph about "easy hospitality" (2:230), seem to be consonant with Austen's opinion of the novel. Whether the phrase "pleasing seriousness," which is underlined in pencil, is also part of the critique is anyone's guess.[32] Marginalia can also signal the reader's psychological state, much as Austen's *Elegant Extracts* marginalia signaled her indignation, irony, and attitude. The words "thank God" are written in the margin next to "time is short" in a copy of the ninth edition of Hannah More's 1809 novel *Coelebs in Search of a Wife*. Usually annotators do not write on the inside margin (it is difficult to do so), and it is possible that this annotator did not want that comment to be seen. But the underlining and the line on the left margin suggest that this passage, with its commentary on patience in the face of adversity—and a Christian faith in the world to come—was important to the annotator. Another text that suggests that a reader was struggling, and experiencing depression if not despair, is found in Frances Burney D'Arblay's novel *The Wanderer* (1814) in which a passage was cut out (fig. 12). The eliminated passage is part of a letter from Albert Harleigh to Elinor Joddrel, in which he tries to convince her not to commit suicide because he has rejected her advances. It is possible that the reader wanted to keep this passage as a source of comfort, or thought that it was particularly well written or inspiring, or wanted to prevent others from reading it.

These are just some of the marginalia that have been discovered in the Knight Collection at Chawton House Library; much more work remains to be done.[33] Based on these examples, it seems evident that the Austens were engaged readers who did not hesitate to enter books (and occasionally mangle them) to serve a variety of purposes. Katie Halsey remarks that "Austen's own novels frequently display a similar awareness of the part books play in denoting character. Time and again, characters reveal themselves through their responses to literature."[34] I agree, and I would suggest that it is not only what characters choose to read but how they read—not only in Halsey's sense of how characters interpret literature but how they

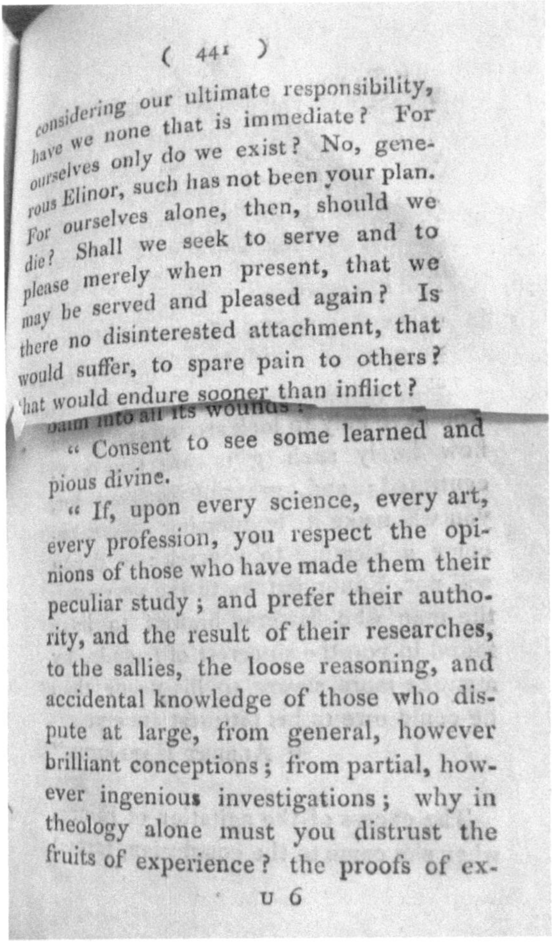

> (441)
>
> considering our ultimate responsibility, have we none that is immediate? For ourselves only do we exist? No, generous Elinor, such has not been your plan. For ourselves alone, then, should we die? Shall we seek to serve and to please merely when present, that we may be served and pleased again? Is there no disinterested attachment, that would suffer, to spare pain to others? that would endure sooner than inflict? balm into all its wounds :
>
> " Consent to see some learned and pious divine.
>
> " If, upon every science, every art, every profession, you respect the opinions of those who have made them their peculiar study; and prefer their authority, and the result of their researches, to the sallies, the loose reasoning, and accidental knowledge of those who dispute at large, from general, however brilliant conceptions; from partial, however ingenious investigations; why in theology alone must you distrust the fruits of experience? the proofs of ex-
>
> U 6

Fig. 12. Remnant of cut page in Frances Burney D'Arblay, *The Wanderer* (London, 1814). (Knight Family Collection, on deposit at Chawton House, Chawton)

interact with books as physical objects. When Becky Sharp throws her copy of Johnson's *Dictionary* out of the carriage in Thackeray's novel *Vanity Fair* (1848), her character and her feelings about her education become clear. When the Austens write, underline, mark, cut, and give books, their relationship to literary culture—the ways they engaged with books, used books, and participated in literary culture—starts coming into focus. The traces of readers in the Knight Collection suggest that Jane Austen was far from alone in her marginalia, and that in fact, her intense engagement with books was a family trait.

Notes

1. Anna Austen Lefroy's published works include a novel, *Mary Hamilton* (1833), and the children's books *The Winter's Tale* (1841) and *Springtide* (1842); Anna wrote (but did not complete) a continuation of *Sanditon*. Catherine Anne Austen (later Hubback) published *The Younger Sister* (a completion of *The Watsons*) and nine other novels (see Deirdre Le Faye, *Jane Austen: A Family Record* [Cambridge: Cambridge University Press, 2004], 268). James Edward Austen wrote an unpublished continuation of *Evelyn* and wrote (but did not complete) a continuation of *Catherine*. For family theatricals, see Le Faye, *Family Record*, 46, 49–50, 53; for evidence of family charades, see Jane Austen, *Charades &c. Written a Hundred Years Ago by Jane Austen and Her Family* (1895; London: Spottiswoode, 1972).

2. For the number of volumes in George Austen's library, see *Jane Austen's Letters*, ed. Deirdre Le Faye, 4th ed. (Oxford: Oxford University Press, 2011), 77. All references to Austen's letters are to this edition and will be supplied parenthetically in the text. Katie Halsey suggests that Austen and her siblings had unusual access to her father's library: "George Austen's library was small, but all of his books were available to his children, and, uncommonly in the period, their choice of reading does not seem to have been censored" (Halsey, *Jane Austen and Her Readers, 1786–1945* [London: Anthem, 2013], 19). I disagree with Halsey's assessment of the size of Reverend Austen's library, but her comment about access is cognate with my argument regarding the Austen family's interest in literariness.

3. For a general description of the Knight Collection at Chawton House Library, see Alice Villaseñor, "Edward Austen Knight's Godmersham Library and Jane Austen's *Emma*," *Persuasions* 29 (2007): 79–87. As she notes: "Close to twelve hundred titles are listed in the [1818 Godmersham Park Library] catalogue, the majority of which would have been in the library at Godmersham during Jane Austen's visits. Approximately one-third of the titles listed in the catalogue are represented in the current Knight Collection" (80). Halsey provides further details: "The Godmersham Library Catalogue records the books held in the collection at the time, including details of the edition, (place and date of publication), and where it was located in the room at Godmersham. Careful research in the Knight collection suggests that it still contains some of the actual copies of books read by Austen, including Mary Brunton's *Self-Control* (2nd ed., Edinburgh, 1811), Frances Burney's *The Wanderer* (London, 1814), Gay's *Fables* (London, 1746), Barretti's *Italian Library* (London, 1757), Blair's *Sermons* (London, 1801), Gisborne's *An Enquiry into the Duties of the Female Sex* (London, 1797), Hannah More's *Coelebs in Search of a Wife* (9th ed., London, 1809), Hester Chapone's *Letters on the Improvement of the Mind* (London, 1773), Madame de Genlis's *Adele et Theodore* (various editions), Vicesimus Knox's *Elegant Extracts* (London, 1801), Walter Scott's *Marmion* (6th ed., Edinburgh 1810), Maria Edgeworth's *Patronage* (London, 1814), Voltaire's *History of the King of Sweden* (London, 1732) and about twenty others" (Halsey, *Jane Austen and Her Readers*, 218n1). For more information about the Godmersham Park books and the Knight Collection, see also Gillian Dow, "Jane Austen's Reading and the Eighteenth-Century Woman Writer," *Sensibilities* 39 (2009): 69–88.

4. I would like to thank the Jane Austen Society of North America, whose International Visitor Program enabled the research presented in this essay. I would also like to thank Gillian Dow and Darren Bevin at Chawton House Library and Mary Guyatt and Isabel Snowden at Jane Austen's House Museum for their assistance and support.

5. Robin Vick prints the text of the April 20, 1801, advertisement of the Steventon Parsonage sale of goods posted in the *Reading Mercury*, which mentions two hundred volumes of books. As Vick notes, "'Volumes' may here mean complete works (consisting of two or more individual books), for Jane wrote on 14 January 1801: 'My father has got above 500 volumes to dispose of;—I want James to take them at a venture at half a guinea a volume.' Alternatively, it could mean that James Austen, who succeeded his father at the parsonage, did in fact agree to buy three hundred of the five hundred volumes" (Vick, "The Sale at Steventon Parsonage," *Jane Austen Society Report* [1993]: 296). Olivia Murphy hypothesizes that Austen's books were "eventually sent to Austen's brother Edward Knight's estate at Godmersham Park, where it maintained a degree of separateness from the larger Godmersham library" (Murphy, *Jane Austen and the Reader: The Artist as Critic* [Basingstoke, UK: Palgrave Macmillan, 2013], 177). She bases her claim on an addendum to the library catalogue after 1835. The data she presents are suggestive but not conclusive. She concludes, "At this time it seems unlikely that we will ever know for certain what books Austen possessed during her lifetime, and what became of them" (182).

6. Peter Sabor suggests that "Anna Jemima Lefroy" was written by Anna Jemima as an adult, but it may be possible that this is Anna Austen Lefroy's adult handwriting, inscribing the book for her daughter as her aunt did for her (see Jane Austen, *Juvenilia*, ed. Peter Sabor [Cambridge: Cambridge University Press, 2006], particularly appendix C, "Marginalia in Vicesimus Knox's *Elegant Extracts . . in Prose*," 352–55; all references to *Juvenilia* are to this edition).

7. Austen, *Juvenilia*, ed. Sabor, 352.

8. *The Oxford Dictionary of National Biography*'s entry for Vicesimus Knox states the publication year of *Elegant Extracts* as 1783, but I have found an advertisement that suggests that *Elegant Extracts* was published in September 1782; see *St. James Chronicle*. The *Whitehall Evening Post* advertised the publication of *Elegant Extracts* in its issue of January 2–4, 1783.

9. See WorldCat and the *Oxford Dictionary of National Biography* entry for Vicesimus Knox.

10. See Jane Austen, *Emma*, ed. Richard Cronin and Dorothy McMillan (Cambridge: Cambridge University Press, 2005), 28, 84. See also Susan Allen Ford, "'Not What You Would Think Anything Of': Robert Martin and Harriet Smith," *Persuasions* 38 (2016): 137–54.

11. Misty Krueger also recognizes the alignment of the marginalia and Austen's "History of England" and argues that Austen's marginalia serve as a type of prewriting for her "History" (see Krueger, "From Marginalia to Juvenilia: Jane Austen's Vindication of the Stuarts," *Eighteenth Century* 56, no. 2 [2015]: 243–59).

12. H. J. Jackson argues that marginalia is a sign of resistant reading in *Marginalia: Readers Writing Books* (New Haven, CT: Yale University Press, 2002): "Theorists, in fact, maintain that the experience of reading always involves an element of contest or struggle, and an oscillation between surrender and resistance, identification and detachment. Marginalia lend support to this view" (85–86). He also reads marginalia as an indication of author-reader rivalry: "Annotation combines—synthesizes, I should say—the functions of reading and writing. This fact in itself heightens the natural tension between author and reader by making the reader a rival of the author, under conditions that give the reader considerable power. The author has the first word, but the annotator has the last" (90).

13. The frequency of Austen's marginalia here exemplifies Jackson's point that "there is an obvious correlation between the level of interest and absorption in the reader and the length of the reader's notes. Some particularly intense readers respond sentence by sentence and even point by point, especially when they disagree with the author" (*Marginalia*, 30).

14. There are thirty-three marked entries in book 1 (entitled "Moral and Religious"); thirty-seven in book 2 ("Classical and Historical"); four in book 3 ("Orations and Characters"); and ten in book 4 ("Narrative, Dialogues, Letters, Sentences, with Other Miscellaneous Pieces").

15. H. J. Jackson discusses habits of annotation by schoolchildren and students, and the encouragement they received to annotate texts (Jackson, *Marginalia*, 21–22, 48).

16. In addition to the marginalia and markings noted, there is a marginal comment in pencil that defines "antithesis." On the inside back cover, a reading list with definitions of "antistrophe" and "strophe" appears. The reading list is suggestive of the way one reads, particularly the ways a reader dips into a compendium. The list does not include Mary, Queen of Scots or Elizabeth I, perhaps because entries on these figures have already been read. Instead, the list features entries on Columbus, Charles V, Francis I, and Martin Luther, suggesting a different historical interest than Austen's. All the items on the reading list have pencil markings on their entries in the text.

17. Evidently Austen was consistent in advocating her Stuart allegiances to her nieces and nephews, as Caroline Austen remarks in "My Aunt Jane Austen: A Memoir (1867)," in *A Memoir of Jane Austen and Other Family Recollections*, ed. Kathryn Sutherland (Oxford: Oxford University Press, 2008): "Of her historical opinions I *am* able to record *thus* much—that she was a most loyal adherent of Charles the 1st, and that she always encouraged my youthful beleif [sic] in Mary Stuart's perfect innocence of all the crimes with which History has charged her memory" (173).

18. "I have been told that one of her earliest Novels (Pride & Prejudice) was read aloud (in M. S. of course) in the Parsonage at Dean, whilst I was in the room, & not expected to listen—Listen however I did, with so much interest, & with so much talk afterwards about 'Jane & Elizabeth' that it was resolved, for prudence sake, to read no more of the story aloud in my hearing" (Anna Lefroy, "Recollections of Aunt Jane," in *A Memoir of Jane Austen*, ed. Sutherland, 157–58).

19. Brian Southam discusses the issues of attribution in his introduction to *Jane Austen's "Sir Charles Grandison"* (Oxford: Clarendon, 1981), including the family tradition that the play was written by Anna and transcribed by Austen (4–5), the case for Austen's authorship (8–10), and the possibility of collaboration between the two (10–11). Given the dating of the manuscript (circa 1800), it seems unlikely that seven-year-old Anna would have mastered Richardson's *Grandison*, and at this point in time, Austen had largely outgrown the satiric, snarky tone of the juvenilia that the "Grandison" manuscript still manifests. I suspect that the "Grandison" manuscript was a game for Austen and Anna, at once invoking the miniature plays in Austen's juvenilia and teaching Anna the basics of stagecraft and playwriting. Notably, the manuscript includes pencil markings (including a few edits) by a hand that does not appear to be Austen's and that may have been Anna's.

20. *Mentoria* was a popular didactic text; according to WorldCat, a twelfth edition appeared in 1823. In a series of twelve dialogues, Mentoria teaches Lady Mary and Lady

Louisa about morality and ethics, along with grammar, history, geography, and science. This copy of *Mentoria* is of interest because of the annotations on the title page, and the inside front cover. The title page has Anna's full name and the date, and another hand has written "from her Aunt Jane." There are also two stanzas of a poem, numbered 2 and 5, written in pencil upside down. The rest of the poem is on the inside cover (with the stanzas numbered 1, 3, and 4), also upside down. The poem has some words crossed out and some words added on top of lines, which suggests that this is a work in progress. The inside cover also includes Austen's youthful signature, crossed out, and the date "June 24th, 1785." The editors of the Cambridge edition of Austen's works write that the poem is "in a hand similar to Austen" but that "it is impossible to verify" ("Attributed Poems," 577). Deirdre Le Faye seems more confident that this poem is by Austen, but she is puzzled by the occasion for the poem, wondering if it was written for Cassandra, in the aftermath of the death of Cassandra's fiancée, Tom Fowle, in 1797 (Le Faye, "New Marginalia in Jane Austen's Books," *Book Collector* 49, no. 2 [2000]: 222–26).

21. Austen's correspondence provides evidence that she read and advised Anna, James Edward, and Caroline Austen about their novels; see her letters to Anna (*Letters*, 279–81, 286–90, 296–97), Caroline (*Letters*, 300, 340), and James Edward (*Letters*, 337; see also 333, 339–40, 349). In her memoir of Austen, Caroline wrote: "As I grew older, she would talk to me more seriously of my reading, and of my amusements—I had taken early to writing verses and stories, and I am sorry to think *how* I troubled her with reading them. She was very kind about it, and always had some praise to bestow but at last she warned me against spending too much time upon them—She said—how well I recollect it! that she *knew* writing stories was a great amusement, and *she* thought a harmless one—tho' many people, she was aware, thought otherwise—but that at *my* age it would be bad for me to be much taken up with my own compositions—Later still—it was after she got to Winchester, she sent me a message to this effect—That if I would take her advice, I should cease writing till I was 16, and that she had herself often wished she had *read* more, and written *less*, in the corresponding years of her own life" (Caroline Austen, "My Aunt Jane," in *Memoir of Jane Austen*, by Austen-Leigh, ed. Sutherland, 174).

22. Murphy claims that "it is through her critical reading that Austen produced her creative contribution to the novel." Her argument is cognate to my own, for as she analyzes Austen's novels in light of her reading, Murphy identifies literary commentary, allusion, and critique in Austen—much like the response, resistance, and exchange that I contend are evident in the marginalia (see Murphy, *Jane Austen and the Reader*, 29).

23. See Jackson, *Marginalia*, for the typical locations for annotations: the top margins for headings; the bottom margins for footnotes; the side margins for commentary; the end of chapters; the flyleaf; the back of the book (27–28, 36–37).

24. Jackson argues that "to the evidence of novels, diaries, letters, and contemporary prints we may now add that of eighteenth-century marginalia, which would not have the personal and critical qualities that distinguish this period from earlier ones but for the generally social character of reading itself. Writers of marginalia at this time usually worked with an audience in mind, not a nebulous scholarly community merely, but known individuals in their own social circles" (*Marginalia*, 67).

25. Jackson notes that "one of the great dividers of kinds is the medium used: are the notes in pencil, or in ink? In one color, or more than one? Are they by one hand only, or

by more than one? If there are two annotators, what appears to be the relations between them—does the later annotator ignore the first, or is she or he drawn to passages the other has marked? If they are by one hand, are they the product of one reading, or more than one? Do repeat readers return to their own notes, and comment on them? Are all sections of the book evenly marked? Are the notes dated? Are they signed or initialed? Are they in the same language as the text? Is the annotation roughly contemporary with the text, or not? And in all these cases, *why so*? (*Marginalia*, 42–43).

26. Halsey, "Jane Austen and Her Readers," 18.

27. For evidence of book circulation within the Austen family, see the Knight Family Collection copy of Goldsmith's *Vicar of Wakefield*. The inside front cover has two names: "E. Austen August 23 1804" crossed out and replaced with "William Austen."

28. See Sarah Parry, "'Give My Love to Mary Jane': The Story behind the Austen Graffiti," *Female Spectator (Chawton House)* 1, no. 3 (2015): 4–5, which contains the observation that "On close examination of a corner of the painting of Chawton House by Mellichamp (ca. 1740), one can just make out the scribbled words 'Mary Jane Austen 1819'" (4).

29. Austen's brother Edward (1767–1838) officially took the name Knight in 1812 (Le Faye, *Family Record*, 192). It is possible that this copy of *Elegant Extracts of Poetry* was his since he still was Edward Austen in 1806, but it seems likely that the text would have been purchased for a twelve-year-old rather than a thirty-nine-year-old. Francis Austen also had a son named Edward, but he was born in 1820, so the book could not be his.

30. The text from Young's *Night Thoughts* (Night Seventh, The Infidel Reclaimed, Part 2) is as follows:

> Heaven is all love; all joy in giving joy:
> It never had created, but to bless:
> And shall it, then, strike off the list of life,
> A being bless'd, or worthy so to be?
> Heaven starts at an annihilating God.

31. Murphy records similar ambivalence regarding the identity of the annotator: "The word 'stupid' is in a hand similar to Austen's, but 'foolish' and the illegible word that follows it do not resemble Austen's customarily neat script" (*Jane Austen and the Reader*, 211n8). See also Murphy's comments on Brunton's *Self-Control* as one of the novels that provides examples of particular literary conventions that Austen modifies and critiques (36, 75, 107–8, 118).

32. Under the last paragraph of chapter 23, the word "Good" appears, with small underline (2:237). This volume also has some corrections—the word "in" inserted in the phrase "that, spite of herself" (2192), and there is a similar correction in volume 3, as the pencil insertion of "in" in the phrase "But, spite of Laura's efforts . . ." (3:48).

33. My initial foray into the Knight Family Collection also found some drawings and pages turned down in Goldsmith's *Vicar of Wakefield*, a few markings and signs of pages turned down in Marianne Knight's copy of Edgeworth's *Patronage*, and multiple pencil markings in Blair's *Sermons*.

34. Halsey, "Jane Austen and Her Readers," 25.

Gender and Things in Austen and Pope

BARBARA M. BENEDICT

Things were a source of both delight and derision in the works of two of the most important authors of their day: Alexander Pope (1688–1744), who witnessed the birth of the long eighteenth century, and Jane Austen (1775–1817), who witnessed its end. For both writers, things were and were not objects—more than mere physical or material items, things were also vehicles of fashion, idea, identity. Whereas Pope wielded enormous influence during his own time, Austen's influence grew over time. Each speaks satirically and in the perfect idiom of their period: the elegant, public poetry of moral and social engagement, and the ironic, free indirect discourse of the Romantic novel. This essay concentrates on Austen's careful reading of Pope and on her use of luxurious and ordinary objects and their consumption to reflect meaning, morality, and identity.

Pope and Austen share a host of values and skills: moderation, decorum, a respect for social duty, a hatred of hypocrisy, ostentation, and affectation, and the skillful deployment of irony, to name just a few. Both reflect the historical specificity of their times. Pope's influence on Austen is clear. Like any cultivated reader in the eighteenth century and Regency, Austen was familiar with Pope's works. Indeed, Willoughby's snipping of Marianne's hair in *Sense and Sensibility* serves as an obvious allusion to Pope's *The Rape of the Lock*.[1] In 1967, Frank W. Bradbrook argued that Austen's "attitude toward the greatest of the poets of the Augustan age is one of detachment," but he also noted that "she owed much to him for her general ideas about self-love, reason, the passions, the predominant passions, instinct, happiness, the characters of men and women, the use of riches, and the various kinds of stupidity to be found in society."[2] More recently, George Justice observes Austen's "rethink[ing] . . . the pervasiveness of print in her culture."[3] Austen also borrows Pope's use of antithesis, symmetrical structure and balanced rhetoric, succinct sketches of character types, and themes. Her portrait of the miserly Mrs. Norris in *Mansfield Park,* for example, who triumphantly bears home a cream cheese begged from the housekeeper at Sotherton, echoes that of Old

Cotta, a character in Pope's *Moral Essays*, whose fortune and intelligence cannot save him from a pointless passion for saving, and whose neglected house repels laughter and love as does Mrs. Norris's cottage. And like Pope, Austen values the median between "mad Good-nature and mean Self-love" exemplified by Pope's portraits of Lord Bathurst and the Man of Ross, a median located somewhere between Willoughby's thoughtless gift of a horse to Marianne, and Fanny Dashwood's grasping denial of justice, charity, duty—and money—to her husband's stepmother and her daughters.[4]

The period from the start of the eighteenth century to the Regency saw an enthusiastically commercializing urban citizenry whose engagement with material culture was undergoing a radical change.[5] Overseas trade and technological innovations were providing a wealth of exotic commodities and fashionable items that appeared everywhere, from enticing displays in shop windows to detailed literary descriptions of furnished interiors.[6] As Maxine Berg remarks, endorsing Neil McKendrick's argument in his seminal book *The Birth of a Consumer Society*, "the eighteenth century is the defining moment in the history of consumer culture in the West," thanks both to this influx of goods and to the "spirit of emulation" that characterized the age. These forces, she adds, produced "a shared language of commerce, luxury, and products."[7] Commodities, particularly luxury items, came to mark not only people's economic standing but also their gentility, refinement, and sophistication.[8] Their power to embody social and intellectual values led writers and thinkers during the long eighteenth century to ask how to represent, evaluate, humanize, and moralize the changing relationship of people to things.

In addition, the emulative—or imitative—and competitive attitude that commodities promoted itself presented a challenge to traditional hierarchies of class and value that had been based on genealogy, personal relationships, social role, and social standing.[9] This challenge is especially complex because of the twin nature of many material items as both utilitarian objects and symbolically resonant components of a person's physical, social, emotional, and imaginative space. On the one hand, many of the new commodities are merely objects, defined by utility. On the other hand, as "things," to use Bill Brown's formulation, these items, like most of the luxury items of earlier historical periods, hold affective, symbolic, even mystical power.[10] They are both material items and embodiments of ideas and feelings.[11]

In Austen's work, books, to take one category of objects, often exhibit this power to define characters' refinement and desires in a world where reading is itself commodified.[12] Books are both individually precious to characters and tokens of social status and identity, and they often carry stereotypically gendered associations. Catherine Morland defines herself as "a heroine" by the ill-understood extracts from her poetic miscellany in *Northanger Abbey*; her reading threatens to turn her into a literary commodity.[13] Moreover, Pope himself appears commodified in Austen's works: Marianne Dashwood vets Willoughby by ensuring that he admires "Pope no more than is proper" as evidence of his sympathy for feminized, sentimental values.[14] In *Mansfield Park*, Fanny Price needs books to survive Portsmouth with her Mansfield-cultivated identity intact, an identity shaped by her male cousin and clergyman-in-training Edmund; her success in subscribing to a circulating library enables her to escape being subsumed by the Prices. In *Persuasion*, Captain Harville's modest library defines his equally modest intellectual and class range, while Romantic poetry, hopelessly fetishized, has swallowed the identity of Captain Benwick, who uses it to woo Anne and then Louisa in *Persuasion*. Less sympathetically, Sir Edward Denham in *Sanditon* fancies himself a Byronic seducer. For her part, Caroline Bingley in *Pride and Prejudice* poses as a devoted reader, declaring that "there is no enjoyment like reading," as part of her failed strategy for winning Darcy's approbation—and a place within Pemberley.[15] Austen uses characters' attitudes to books to reveal their moral and mental natures. Books often measure both education and depth of character: one need only compare lonely Fanny Price's longing for books with shallow Harriet Smith's. The former seeks intellectual engagement; the latter is content with the frivolous entertainment books provide as part of a flirting game with Robert Martin.

In the early eighteenth century, books were often subjects of scatological jokes, wherein their paper appears more important than the ideas they contain. As Pope writes in "Verses to be prefix'd before Bernard Lintot's New Miscellany," "*Lintot*'s [books] for gen'ral Use are fit; / For some Folks read, but all Folks sh—" (lines 29–30). Pope treats books as a symptom of the battle between men and things—a battle that itself symbolizes the struggle for dominance over culture. Austen likewise sees literature as not merely ideational but bathetically material. As Justice points out, Austen's work reflects Pope's mixture of "the stuff of art and the detritus of culture."[16] But Austen also uses books-as-things more particularly to explore the dangers of commodified gender. She expresses this trope when in *Sanditon* she depicts Charlotte Heywood joining Miss Whitney "with all her glossy curls and smart trinkets" to enter Mrs. Whitby's circulating library, itself a site that offers books together with other expensive commodities:

The library, of course, afforded every thing; all the useless things in the world that could not be done without, & among many pretty temptations, and with so much good will for Mr. Parker to encourage expenditure, Charlotte began to feel that she must check herself . . . and that it would not do for her to be spending all her money the very first evening. She took up a book; it happened to be a volume of *Camilla*. She had not Camilla's youth, and had no intention of having her distress,—so she turned from the drawers of rings and brooches, repressed farther solicitation and paid for what she bought.[17]

Charlotte here exhibits the virtues and hazards offered by material culture: her consumption of the intellectual commodity of Frances Burney's novel allows her to escape the false delights of self-enhancing, feminine material items.

As symbols of class and sophistication, books become objects of competition, especially in *Pride and Prejudice*. Caroline Bingley sneers that "'Miss Eliza Bennet . . . despises cards," adding that "she is a great reader and has no pleasure in anything else" (40). Her condescension identifies books as tokens of Elizabeth's intellectual detachment from the desperate female world of husband-hunting; for Caroline, books become signs of gender-betrayal, a bluestocking imitation of a male practice. This implication explains Elizabeth's protest: stung by the charge of unsociability and resistant to being categorized by the consumption of a commodity, she declares, "I deserve neither such praise nor such censure . . . I am *not* a great reader, and I have pleasure in many things" (41). This echoes Austen's own comment to her sister: "You distress me cruelly by your request about Books; I cannot think of any to bring with me, nor have I any idea of our wanting them. I come to you to be talked to, not to read or hear reading."[18] Ironically, Elizabeth's pedantic sister Mary and her satirical father Mr. Bennet are both great readers, but their identities have been subsumed by books—Mary's lesser powers are drowned by her reading and her extracts from books. The contrast between Elizabeth and Caroline also echoes that between Henry Tilney, who boasts of reading novels, and the boorish John Thorpe, who dismisses them: the former is proud of his pleasure in female entertainments (including muslin and the delights of Bath) and able to deploy his knowledge of them in conversation; the latter is eager to assert his masculinity by rejecting them.

Darcy's library at Pemberley serves similarly to define him. When Caroline Bingley sycophantically praises it, Darcy replies, "It ought to be good . . . it has been the work of many generations," and declares that he adds to it because he "cannot comprehend the neglect of a family library in such days as these" (*P&P*, 41). His social position and lineage are realized by the material contents of his library. Indeed, this consideration leads Caroline to attempt to imitate him by immersing herself in a book "which she had only chosen because it was the second volume of his," a humorous depiction of her actual disregard for the items she pretends to admire (60). Alexander Pope also comments frequently on books' ambiguous status as material and ideational items, symbols of class aspiration and competition, taste, and refinement. In his *Epistle to Burlington*, for example, he mocks the arriviste who buys "Rare monkish Manuscripts for Hearne alone, / And Books for Mead, and Butterflies for Sloane," wasting his wealth on objects he knows are precious to virtuosi like Sir Hans Sloane but represent only power and status to him (lines 9–10). By contrast, Robert Martin's reading from Vicesimus Knox's *Elegant Extracts* reflects the disciplined effort that stirs Mr. Knightley's admiration as he watches Martin labor to educate and elevate himself and his family.

However indebted Austen was to Pope, she implicitly criticized Pope's outdated formal style and his privileged self-confidence as a member of an elite, male, homosocial circle. Writing in 1813 to Cassandra, disappointed at the cancellation of her journey, she quotes ironically from Pope's *Essay on Man*: "Whatever is, is best," adding, "There has been one infallible Pope in the world"—a poke at both Pope's Olympian cultural standing and his Catholicism (*Letters*, 256). In *Northanger Abbey*, the narrator sneers at banal miscellanies that feature "some dozen lines of Milton, Pope, and Prior, with a paper from the Spectator and a chapter from Sterne" in favor of the fresher, female-friendly genre of the novel (31). In *Persuasion* (1818), Pope's lines are both cited and inverted in an exchange between Anne Elliot and her hypocritical cousin Mr. William Elliot over the merits of the vapid Dalrymples. When he contends that the Dalrymples offer "good company," she redefines his term "good": "My idea of good company, Mr. Elliot, is the company of clever, well-informed people, who have a great deal of conversation; that is what I call good company." His response reflects his Popean education: "'You are mistaken,' said he gently, 'that is not good company. That is the best. Good company requires only birth, education and manners, and with regard to education is not very nice. Birth and good manners are essential; but a little learning is by no means a dangerous thing in good company, on the contrary, it will do very well.'"[19] Mr. Elliot's use of the line from Pope's *Essay on Criticism* (1711) that "*A little Learning* is a dan'grous Thing" authorizes his definition of "good" as equivalent to high social rank and accompanying elite "manners." Anne supplants this understanding to define "good" in

Persuasion as high intellectual ability and social generosity (215). Although Anne succeeds best at expressing Popean values, Austen's irony also invites consideration of Mr. Elliot's shrewd articulation of the intruding realities of the frivolous, commercializing, socially ambitious Regency world.

Indeed, Austen echoes the Augustan ambivalence toward revered classical predecessors in her direct quotations of and allusions to Pope's verse. This results in the depiction of Pope as alternately admired and mocked, a revered cultural giant who is just a little bit dated. Much of this attitude is entangled in Austen's complex view of the commodification of literature. As a reliable, irreproachable cultural reference, Pope himself becomes a commodity, and a somewhat stale one at that, in Austen's contemporary cultural cabinet of upper-class education. In *Northanger Abbey* (1818), Austen's heroine Catherine Morland absorbs Pope's dictum from his "Elegy to an Unfortunate Lady" (1717) "to censure those who 'bear about the mockery of woe.'" Austen's ironic echo of Pope, however, distances her novel from Pope's stylized lament for the suicide of a seduced and abandoned woman. In her hands, the allusion underscores the difference between the male poet's privileged sentimental sympathy and the danger such sentimental attitudes toward sexual passion presented to women, evidenced by the lady's tragic fate (*NA*, 8, 31). Again, the narrator's sneer at cribs containing "some dozen lines of Milton, Pope, and Prior, with a paper from the Spectator and a chapter from Sterne" indicts "the improbable circumstances, unnatural characters . . . topics of conversation" and coarse language of the previous century.[20] Pope appears merely a token of a fashionable education, opposed to contemporary novels that more adequately reflect women's lives. In these instances, Austen represents Pope's verse as exemplifying an outdated mentality insufficient for addressing the complexities of female reality.

Yet if Pope hovers throughout Austen's novels as an influential male poet, whose style and attitudes she intentionally rewrites, the two writers nevertheless share criticism of a consumer culture that threatens to narrow and even corrupt self-understanding. Pope himself cultivated a luxurious if miniature estate at Twickenham, even as he possessed very few things and only "modest" furniture, but his poetry brims with specific descriptions and inventories of the popular commodities of his day—most famously in the depiction of Belinda's dressing table in *The Rape of the Lock*, which holds "the various Off'rings of the World" (line 130). While objects on her dressing table appear marvelous, the "bodies chang'd to various Forms by Spleen" into objects later in the poem represent the perverse consumer-lust that overtakes more natural forms of desire (line 4:48). These staggering, wailing human commodity-forms—the human Tea-pot and the crying "Bottels"—dramatize the reduction of person to thing and underscore the threat things pose to human integrity (line 4:54). Despite his posture of rising above the profit-grubbing crowd, Pope was known both for his parsimony and for his desire for opulence.[21] Similarly, though he despised vulgar display and mercenary greed, he paid close enough attention to his own profits to project the illusion of independence from the print and financial marketplaces. His attitude toward things, and the relationship of things to people, is ambivalent and complex.

Jane Austen's attitude is also complex. Like Pope, Austen actually owned relatively few objects and is correspondingly restrained in her descriptions of things, but for this very reason, they hold great symbolic meaning in her novels. Recently, Paula Byrne has shown how important the objects that occupy domestic space were to Jane Austen, from clothes and paintings to cards, letters, and bathing machines.[22] Elsewhere I have written about Austen's use of jewels, but it is worth noting here that such precious material items serve in her fiction as metaphors for important relationships and values.[23] In the works of both authors, things bear directly on social relationships and reveal moral character.

Austen often explores the way sentimental values transform the value of things in a materialistic world. Notably, in *Sense and Sensibility*, Edward Ferrars teases Marianne Dashwood's acute sensitivity by claiming that she "would buy up every copy" of her favorite authors "to prevent their falling into unworthy hands" (107). Just as Fanny Price cites William Cowper's "The Task," "Ye fallen avenues, once more I mourn your fate unmerited," to respond to Mr. Rushworth's tree-cutting fervor, so, too, does Marianne define herself by her poetic consumption (66). In *Mansfield Park*, Fanny Price's sister Susan reveres a silver knife for its sentimental value. Bequeathed to her by her sister Mary on her deathbed and coveted by her sister Betsey, the knife appears unique, and Fanny regards it as a reification of "duty, honour and tenderness" (446). Betsey, however, fails to read the knife's sentimental value; for her, it is only a possession, and when Fanny buys another knife to prevent her sisters' squabbling, the new knife proves superior to Betsey because of "its newness" (459). Silver was one of the most coveted luxurious materials in the period, newly used by ingenious manufacturers for a variety of domestic items, including tea ware.[24] The silver knife serves here as a hermeneutically rich symbol: for Betsey, it is merely a signal of class aspiration, a replaceable token of popular luxury; for Susan, it is a unique remembrance of her dead sister's affection. The knife exposes both Betsey's greed and Susan's affectionate—if pathetic—desire to commodify a memory of a beloved sister. Although the squabble over the knife is sharply comic and satirizes the sentimental values represented by mementoes and embodied by contemporary fiction, it is also a poignant reminder of the competing values things hold for consumers. Investing personal significance in things helps them escape the monetary valuations of the cultural world. Despite their mass production, neither Susan's silver knife nor Harriet's Tunbridge-ware box can be replicated, at least not for their sentimental owners.[25] By contrast, Betsey's pride in her own silver knife demonstrates how things as possessions in a novelty-mad, commodifying world merely testify to ownership.

Several mementoes in Austen's work demonstrate the sentimental fallacy of personalizing things. The miniature that Marianne Dashwood wears around her neck turns out to be not, as Margaret suspects, a portrait of Willoughby but instead a portrait of the Dashwoods' grand-uncle. Margaret's mistake underscores the fungibility of apparently unique items. More pathetically, Harriet Smith's pathetic collection of remnants of her infatuation with Mr. Elton serve in *Emma* as a material testament to her delusions:

> "Cannot you guess what this parcel holds?" said she, with a conscious look. . . . Within abundance of silver paper was a pretty little Tunbridge-ware box, which Harriet opened: it was well lined with the softest cotton; but, excepting the cotton, Emma saw only a small piece of court plaister.
>
> "Now," said Harriet, "you *must* recollect."[26]

Harriet has preserved a valueless item—a remnant of the plaister from which Mr. Elton cut a piece to bandage his finger—as a relic of his body, placing it on cotton and significantly encasing it not only in expensive silver paper but in a tourist trinket. Tunbridge-ware items, like Battersea boxes, were commercially produced, small vessels made from inlaid wood, sometimes decorated with scenes from Tunbridge Wells, and sold as holiday souvenirs of the resort. Here, Harriet's possession highlights the complementarity between her sentimentality and mass-produced memories, both manipulated by a cynical market. The remnant of the plaster that Mr. Elton applied to his finger at Emma's suggestion testifies ironically to women's role as nurse and home-healer in this world of commodified feeling. Harriet's box also contains a leadless pencil stub once held by Mr. Elton. This item again parodies sentimental artifacts since its utility as a writing instrument vanishes into its meaning as Eltoniana, a sentimental relic of Elton, with the further innuendo of impotence.

A number of things in Austen's works hold sexual connotations. Harriet's box, like the cabinet holding a laundry list that Catherine Morland locks in her attempt to open, suggests female enclosure, and both hold worthless items. By contrast, Robert Ferrars's richly jeweled case for his toothpick signals masculine overcompensation. Scissors appear frequently as instruments of sexual destruction: like Pope's Baron, Willoughby uses them to cut Marianne's lock, kisses the lock, folds "it up in a piece of white paper," and puts it "into his pocket-book" (S&S, 71). The pressing of hair and flowers between the pages of favorite volumes or other receptacles that could be carried on the body was a sentimental custom, but here it hints at Willoughby's desire to possess Marianne sexually, even to carry her off. The same object thus signals both Willoughby's aggressive male sexuality and the hazards of Marianne's sensibility. Similarly, when Edward arrives to explain Lucy's marriage to Robert and propose to Elinor, he takes up "a pair of scissars that lay there . . . spoiling both them and their sheath by cutting the latter to pieces as he spoke," the mutual spoliation symbolizing the severance of his burdensome relationship with Lucy and the possibility of his new relationship with Elinor (407). While purportedly instruments of women's work, these scissors hold traditional sexual associations that underscore the dangers posed to women by both domestic life and sexual activity.[27]

The prevalence of scissors in women's "work" throughout Austen's novels hints at the rich revelation of female character offered by such work. This work includes such accomplishments as screen-painting, netting, crocheting, embroidery, and making clothes, and may serve to reveal moral strength, to protect women in uncomfortable circumstances by providing an occupation, or, less benignly, to advertise feminine virtue. Georgiana Darcy, for example, drafts designs for a decorative tablecloth in *Pride and Prejudice*, and her skill testifies to her refinement. Such items function as both material "accomplishments" and indices of character and morals. Though Georgiana is admirable, other characters expose less admirable character through their work. The Bertram sisters, for example, make "artificial flowers" and "[waste] gold paper," producing useless creations (*MP*, 16). Their luxury and wanton spoilage of the fashionable, precious commodity demonstrates their own moral spoilage (*MP*, 16). Lydia Bennet, too, plans to "pull . . . to pieces" the ugly bonnet she bought with the money intended to treat her sisters to lunch, symbolizing her dangerous disregard for propriety (*P&P*, 242). Lady Bertram's "long piece of needlework, of little use and no beauty," provides the merest pretense of work to justify her languor as she sits "nicely dressed on a sofa," while her commands to Fanny to continue to "tack on my patterns" for applique embroidery or patchwork on cloth indicates her selfish laziness and disposal of more substantive work to others (*MP*, 22, 28). More positively, women's work screens embarrassment or discomfort: when Elinor summons the courage to ask after Lucy, whom she believes to be Edward's wife, she takes up "some work from the table" to appear poised. Similarly, her gift for screen-painting represents her shielding of her own feelings from prying observation.

As examples of both female production and consumption, these items illustrate the key role of gender in the social life of things.[28] Writers, particularly moralists and religious commentators, typically characterize women and dandyish bachelors stigmatized as effeminate and thoughtless consumers of fashion, dazzled by new things and awash in a reprehensible love of luxury. In contrast, normative men's consumption often demonstrates taste.[29] Both Pope and Austen probe the reification of stereotypical notions of femininity into trivial luxuries. Indeed, when male characters flaunt things gendered as female, they appear effeminate: Austen's Robert Ferrars, fussily selecting "the ivory, the gold, and the pearls" for his toothpick-case, for example, or Edward Ferrars, unwillingly ensnared by Lucy's hair ring (*S&S*, 251). Similarly, when Pope's Sporus wishes to mock his apparent romantic rival and satirical detractor Lord Hervey, he characterizes him as the unmanly, even nonhuman, Sporus, "that Thing of Silk . . . this Bug with gilded wings, / This painted Child of Dirt that stinks and stings," whose costume and makeup indicate his ambiguous sexuality (*Epistle to Dr. Arbuthnot*, lines 305, 309–10).

Similarly, Austen's depiction of Lady Bertram's addiction to comfort and luxury as rendering her emotionally and intellectually numb owes something to Pope's antifeminist satire and particularly to his depiction of the prudent spotless Chloe in *To a Lady: Of the Characters of Women*. Lady Bertram shares Chloe's appetite for luxury, and correspondingly both women "want[] a Heart":

> She speaks, behaves, and acts just as she ought;
> But never, never reach'd one gen'rous Thought.
> Virtue she finds too painful an endeavor.
> Content to dwell in Decencies for ever.
> So very reasonable, so unmov'd,
> As never yet to love, or to be lov'd.
> She, while her Lover pants upon her breast,
> Can mark the figures on an Indian chest;
> And when she sees her Friend in deep despair,

Barbara M. Benedict

> Observes how much a Chintz exceeds Mohair.
> . . . .
> Of all her Dears she never slander'd one,
> But cares not if a thousand are undone.
> Would Chloe know if you're alive or dead?
> She bids her Footman put it in her head. (lines 161–70; 175–78)

Lady Bertram too remains placidly indifferent and torpidly proper through most of *Mansfield Park*, even as her children violate moral values. She is only mildly shocked out of this torpor by one daughter's adultery, another daughter's elopement, and her eldest son's dangerous illness. Things rather than people interest both characters: Lady Bertram values her sofa, roses, and pug. Indeed, she treats Fanny affectionately as a thing belonging to her manor-house. When Pope concludes his epistle by praising Martha Blount, to whom it is addressed, for remaining "Mistress of herself, tho' China fall," and contrasts the value for "Dross" with hers for "Sense, Good-humour, and a Poet," he seals the identification of derogated, fashionable femininity with materiality (*Epistle to a Lady*, lines 269, 291, 292). Martha Blount's virtues also resemble those of the Cowper-loving, self-disciplined, and humble Fanny, albeit Fanny is a more complex figure. By setting the *Epistle to a Lady* in a painting gallery that registers the importance of paintings in elite culture, Pope depicts women as objects of male acquisition: indeed, Belinda in *The Rape of the Lock* herself becomes a commodity, just as the Baron becomes indistinguishable from the material artifacts associated with his conquests.[30] The threat of sexual conquest similarly endangers many Austen heroines, but Austen rewrites the narrative so that her heroines become more self-aware of their culture's interest in commodifying and possessing their lives.

Paintings, miniatures, and sketches appear in both authors' lives and work in a similarly ambiguous way. While both writers represent scenes and people uniquely and sentimentally important to the possessor, both scenes and people also serve as commodities. Maynard Mack records that Pope acquired fifty-six portraits, mostly of his friends, many of whom he named in his will as gifts, thus celebrating not merely the subject but the personal relationship the portraits represent.[31] In turn, Austen's "close-knit" family "cherished their profiles and miniatures, the equivalent of framed photographs of loved ones in a modern home."[32] Fanny Price herself possesses a collection of "profiles" that commemorate those she loves; discarded by others, these items are treasured by Fanny for their sentimental value alone (*MP*, 178). The gallery of family portraits at Pemberley, through which the housekeeper escorts Elizabeth while commenting on their subjects' personalities, likewise functions both to reveal Darcy's true nature and cultural power, thereby transforming Elizabeth's understanding of him. The paintings function much as the furniture, which provides evidence of "his taste... neither gaudy nor uselessly fine; with... real elegance," "suitable to the fortune of their proprietor" (*P&P*, 272).

Austen's women do not merely possess things: they repeatedly risk becoming them. When collaborators in an oppressive patriarchy rather than heroines, they commodify both themselves and other women. This appears most clearly in the way clothes both represent women's complicity in their objectification in the social world, and condition the way others, both women and men, judge them. Perhaps the most classic example lies in *Pride and Prejudice*, when, upon Elizabeth Bennet's arrival at Netherfield to see the ailing Jane, Mr. Bingley's sister comments disparagingly on her appearance, particularly her muddied petticoat. Louisa Hurst remarks, "I shall never forget her appearance this morning. She really looked almost wild," and Caroline chimes in, "Her hair so untidy, so blowsy!" Louisa adds, "Yes, and her petticoat. I hope you saw her petticoat, six inches deep in mud, I am absolutely certain; and the gown which had been let down to hide it, not doing its office" (*P&P*, 39). By reducing Elizabeth to a savage, "wild" creature because her clothes are in disarray, the sisters deliberately erase her personality. Her loving motive in attending Jane and her lack of vanity or pride in walking, because the carriage was unavailable, vanish beneath her appearance. Women also treat other women as things: Lady Catherine de Bourgh regards her daughter Anne as a coin in her game of power. In *Sanditon*, Charlotte Heywood describes Clara Brereton as a fiction: "Charlotte could see in her only the most perfect representation of whatever heroine might be most beautiful and bewitching, in all the numerous volumes they had left behind on Mr. Whitby's shelves.—Perhaps it might be partly owing to her having just issued from a circulating library" (*LM*, 168–69). Charlotte punningly identifies the freshly beheld character as a literary object or a new library "issue." Perhaps worst of all, women sometimes equate themselves with their clothes. In *Northanger Abbey*, Mrs. Allen's fear for the durability of her latest muslin reveals her superficiality. She is all dress without substance, consumed by fashion. Like Pope's Ariel, who sees no difference between staining honor or a new brocade, Mrs. Allen values equally her own worth and the quality of her gowns.

Men, too, are subject to being objectified and played as tools or fools. In *Sense and Sensibility*, Robert Ferrars rakes the Dashwood sisters over with a commodifying glance, but he is the one whom the scheming, money-hungry Lucy Steele collects as a richer replacement for her reluctant fiancé, Edward. In *To Bathurst*, Sir Balaam's daughter "flaunts a Viscount's tawdry wife; / She bears a Coronet and P-x for life" (lines 391–92). Austen does not go so far, but her portraits of women who have manipulated men into making the bad bargain of marrying for money include Miss Grey, the heiress for whom the rakish Willoughby abandons Marianne, to his lasting regret, and who dictated the cruel letter he sends Marianne returning both her lock of hair and her letters. In *Persuasion*, the fortune-hunting Mrs. Clay, daughter of Sir Walter Elliot's lawyer Mr. Shepherd, abandons her plan of seducing the baronet and succumbs to the manipulative powers of Mr. William Elliot, but we are told that however much her "affections had overpowered her interest. . . . She has abilities . . . and it is now a doubtful point whether his cunning, or hers, may finally carry the day; whether, after preventing her from being the wife of Sir Walter, he may not be wheedled and caressed at last into making her the wife of Sir William" (273). Like Pope, Austen often blames the corruption of sexual relationships on a lust for gold that makes humans view one another as puppets in a mercenary game.

Both authors represent decadent men as collectors of women. Pope often portrays women as luxurious commodities that exemplify the misuse of wealth and mad excess of meaningless desire. Among the visible goods in the *Epistle to Bathurst* that gold can buy are "Fair Coursers, Vases, and alluring Dames" (line 58). Pope lists "another's Wife" as equivalent to the pleasures of an opulent table, supplied unjustly by the toil of the starving (line 28). Such descriptions evoke Austen's characterizations of the collectors of sexual trophies, seducers such as Willoughby in *Sense and Sensibility*. In *Mansfield Park*, Henry Crawford sets traps for Fanny Price, Julia Bertram, and, successfully, Maria Bertram. Wickham, too, in *Pride and Prejudice* attempts to accumulate victims of seduction, in or outside marriage: Georgiana Darcy, Elizabeth Bennet, Miss King, Lydia. Henry Crawford's uncle and role model Admiral Crawford installs a mistress and behaves boorishly, reveling in "*Rears* and *Vices*" (*MP*, 71). He may owe a debt to Pope's Uxorio, who "Bear[s] home six Whores" and makes "his Lady weep" (*Epistle to Bathurst*, line 60).

Just as women must arrive at a proper understanding of the relation of objects, so, too, must they understand their relation to money. Lord David Cecil once commented that in the world of Austen's novels, it is wicked to marry for money but stupid to marry without it. Edward Copeland similarly observes that "would-be consumers, over-consumers, and wise consumers" and consumption in general constitute key tropes in Austen's oeuvre.[33] Whereas Pope's society identified judicious luxurious consumption with taste and refinement, in Austen's world, consumption offered a challenge to the Shaftesburian equation of virtue and taste.[34] Lavish expenditure might indicate self-indulgence and prodigality, but in the early eighteenth century, the thoughtful purchase of items of *virtu* designated the fashionable sophisticate, whose natural impulses correlate to the appreciation of beauty and goodness. For Regency women with fewer means and fewer choices, luxuries represent the misdirection of natural impulse into consumption and display in place of the social values of charity and decorum.

Both writers aspired to a class slightly above them: Pope, as the Catholic son of a linen draper, climbed the class ladder to become intimate with nobility as a literary lion, while Austen, as a member of the lesser gentry, the child of a clergyman with a fair income, sank down to its lower rungs upon her father's death. Both authors, consequently, paid close attention to the intellectual and material accomplishments and accouterments of the upper classes, and both joined the chorus of many of their contemporaries in condemning opulence. For Pope, too much money entailed crass ostentation, and the right "Use of Riches" constitutes his subject in the last two *Moral Epistles*. Both of these depict luxurious objects of fashion as the symptoms of spineless emulation, degraded social ambition, and wasted value. In both, such objects elicit actions that consume the identity of their supposed owners. For example, the money-saving efforts of the miserly "Vultur Hopkins," famed according to Pope's *Epistle to Bathurst* for using his will to redirect his vast fortune of £300,000 away from his legal heir to the second generation so that it could accumulate interest, ultimately transform him into an object:

> When Hopkins dies, a thousand lights attend
> The wretch, who living sav'd a candle's end:
> Should'ring God's alter a vile image stands,
> Belies his features, nay extends his hands;
> That live-long wig which Gorgon's self might own
> Eternal buckle takes in Parian stone.
> Behold what blessings Wealth to life can lend!
> And see, what comfort it affords our end. (lines 291–98)

Hopkins is metamorphosed into a bloated bust. The marble replaces the person, as the ambition for immortality devolves from spiritual desire to self-objectification.

Nonetheless, both authors recognize that there is a correct, appropriate approach to material items and to the union of art with nature. Pope's argument in the *Epistle to Burlington* depicts material items as a moral touchstone: they testify to a character's "taste," "good sense," and relationship to "Nature, even in works of mere Luxury and Elegance" (586). This meditation on the proper "Use of Riches" thus suggests that well-chosen things may improve spiritual or emotional life by surrounding one with beauty and elegance. For Pope, this is, however, a male prerogative and privilege: whereas women in *To a Lady* are defined by their passions and represented as objects, both Bathurst and Burlington suggest that men can define themselves by their things. Despite this gendered difference, Austen echoes several of Pope's ideas about beauty. As many critics have noted, Pope's emphasis on harmonizing art and nature, particularly through his tropes of "Architecture and Gardening," informs Austen's depiction of Darcy's estate Pemberley in *Pride and Prejudice*. Elizabeth admires Darcy's graceful improvement of nature "without any artificial appearance," which results in "natural beauty . . . so little counteracted by an awkward taste" (271). This estate serves to guarantee Darcy's fundamentally good nature and character, as Wickham's "extravagance and general profligacy" demonstrate his immorality (228). Copeland shrewdly observes that, in *Pride and Prejudice*, "Pemberley exists as a consumer token in Austen's novels . . . in a much deeper game of desire."[35] In *Northanger Abbey*, too, the Tilneys' appreciation of the picturesque proves their tastefulness. At the same time, in both instances Austen teases her heroines for faddishness and for imbuing things—even things as large as an estate—with moral force. When Catherine Morland "voluntarily reject[s] the whole city of Bath, as unworthy to make part of a landscape," she exhibits a youthful sycophantic emulation and desire to please rather than natural taste (*NA*, 113). More alert to irony, Elizabeth Bennet exclaims, "What are men to rocks and mountains?" (*P&P*, 174). Posing as a naïve Romantic, for whom nature supersedes humanity, Elizabeth also suggests the absurdity of such a stance. Nonetheless, both authors find the proper use of things to be their power to enhance social and moral relations.

For both writers, however, investing identities into things also poses the danger of loss of self in ostentatious and vulgar display. For Austen's women, the things that seem to hold the power to declare—even upgrade—status appear on the body. Jewels and clothes are intimately connected to the female body and threaten to commodify it. Dress often seems to overtake women in Austen's work too: the clothes wear the woman rather than the reverse. In *The Watsons*, for example, "Mrs. Edwards's satin gown swept along the clean floor of the ball-room, to the fireplace at the upper end" (*LM*, 94). Isabella Thorpe daydreams of "a brilliant exhibition of hoop rings on her finger," rings that render her "the admiration of every acquaintance at Fullerton [and] the . . . envy of every valued old friend" (*NA*, 125, 124). Her daydream subsumes her identity into a metonymy of high social position. Likewise, Mrs. Elton, in *Emma*, boasts that her status as a married (and moneyed) woman demands she wear "lace and pearls" and "finery," and she meditates on adding trimming to her "white and silver poplin" (316, 327). In the ugly scene in *Mansfield Park* in which Mary Crawford manipulates Fanny into accepting the "prettily worked," elaborate gold chain given to her by her brother Henry to put around her "lovely throat," the thing works as a surrogate for the halter of marriage, serving to entangle Fanny in an unwanted obligation to Henry (300). Not that Austen holds a Puritanical view of material culture: she mentions in a letter to Cassandra on May 24, 1813, from London that, "I have bought your Locket, but was obliged to give 18s for it—which must be rather more than you intended; it is neat & plain, set in gold" (*Letters*, 221). Yet she measures self-possession by her characters' resistance to equating themselves with the metonymic glamor of things.

For Pope's men, the threat to gendered identity that love of things offers lies in their power to sap or usurp individual potency, sexual or social. In "To Burlington," the arriviste Timon, like Sir Balaam, is swallowed by the things he acquires in order to impress his would-be friends. He buys enormous statues and builds a vast estate: "To compass this, his building is a Town, / His Pond an Ocean, his Parterre a Down," and not one but "*two* Cupids squirt" from a fountain (lines 105–6, 111, emphasis mine). This magnificence overshadows him, shrinking him to insignificance instead of swelling him to grandeur: "Who but must laugh, the Master when he sees, / A puny insect, shiv'ring at a breeze!" (lines 107–8). Pope's Timon, named for the proverbial profligate who thought to buy his friends with lavish gifts but who, when he loses his wealth, ends deserted and alone, amasses all the fashionable works of *virtu* to impress more astute virtuosi; the result is that his power vanishes into the towering things around him. This portrait brings to mind General Tilney in *Northanger Abbey*, who constructs an extensive greenhouse to grow rarities like pineapples, considers purchasing a fresh set of Wedgewood china every two years, and marches the supposed heiress Catherine through his estate in a transparent aim to impress her. Ironically, his avarice and pride convince her that he is a murderer. Timon similarly expands his gardens to "purchase" applause: "His Gardens next your admiration call" (*Epistle to Burlington*, line 4:113). Mr. Rushworth in *Mansfield Park* also values himself upon his estate, seeking to expand the avenues of Sotherton to achieve a fashionable impressiveness that he hopes will enhance his appeal in the eyes of Maria Bertram and others. In contrast to Timon and such men, who indulge in extravagance and are thereby weakened into impotence, Pope represents the Man of Ross as charitable, rational, and loved with a mere £500 a year, and attributes his own moral compass to his modest upbringing. Austen's female exemplar for such grounded attitudes is the level-headed Elinor Dashwood, who similarly articulates her balanced attitude toward money by rating £1,000 a year as "wealth," whereas Marianne dubs £1,800–£2,000 a mere competence (*S&S*, 105–6).

Things hold richly ambiguous significance for both authors. For Pope, the many objects of an increasingly commercialized and commercializing material culture present both a fund of metaphor and meaning, and also a threat to traditional moral valuations. His poetry mocks men who objectify either themselves or others, even as it acknowledges the role played by things in the artful display of taste. Despite frequently exulting over things' tactical, visual, and imaginative richness, Pope remains worried about the ambiguous power that owning things can confer. Almost a century later, Austen absorbs Pope's concern with things' power to upset moral order. Her characters struggle, sometimes unsuccessfully, to escape being subsumed by the world of objects, especially when they invest sentimental value in things, seek emotional significance in objects, or evaluate self-worth through ownership of dresses, rings, hunting dogs, or carriages. Austen makes clear that relationships, not things, lift women into full humanity. If she uses things more sparely and subtly than Pope, she nevertheless uses them, as does Pope, to contrast the cruelties and crassness of a mercantile society with the rich interior life of her characters. The works of these authors show how deeply the multiplying material objects of an increasingly commercialized society were perceived as encroaching on human self-definition throughout the long eighteenth century.

Notes

1. See also Catherine Bustow, "Unlocking the Rape: An Analysis of Austen's Use of Pope's Symbolism in Sense and Sensibility," *Persuasions* 20 (1998): 31–37.

2. Frank W. Bradbrook, *Jane Austen and Her Predecessors* (Cambridge: Cambridge University Press, 1967), 75–76.

3. George Justice, "Sanditon and the Book," in *A Companion to Jane Austen*, ed. Claudia L. Johnson and Clara Tuite (Oxford: Wiley-Blackwell, 2009), 154.

4. Alexander Pope, *Epistle III: To Bathurst*, in *The Poems of Alexander Pope*, ed. John Butt (New Haven, CT: Yale University Press, 1966), 228. All subsequent citations of Pope's poetry refer to this edition; line numbers or, where necessary, page numbers are provided parenthetically in the text.

5. Neil McKendrick, John Brewer, and J. H. Plumb, *The Birth of a Consumer Society: The Commercialization of Eighteenth-Century England* (Bloomington: Indiana University Press, 1982). See also *Consumption and the World of Goods*, ed. John Brewer and Roy Porter (London: Routledge, 1993); and *The Consumption of Culture*, ed. Ann Bermingham and John Brewer (London: Routledge, 1995).

6. See Cynthia Sundberg Wall, *The Prose of Things: Transformations of Description in the Eighteenth Century* (Chicago: University of Chicago Press, 2002).

7. Maxine Berg, *Luxury and Pleasure in Eighteenth-Century Britain* (Oxford: Oxford University Press, 2005), 9, 5.

8. Berg, *Luxury and Pleasure in Eighteenth-Century Britain*, 6. Berg cites John Styles, "Georgian Britain 1714–1837," in *Design and the Decorative Arts: Britain 1500–1900*, ed. Michael Snodin and Styles (London: Victoria and Albert Publications, 2001), 184.

9. For an account of how cultural fables developed around the material realities of the increasingly urban culture of eighteenth-century England, see Laura Brown, *Fables of Modernity: Literature and Culture in the English Eighteenth Century* (Ithaca, NY: Cornell University Press, 1985).

10. Bill Brown, "Thing Theory," *Critical Inquiry* 28, no. 1 (2001): 1–22.

11. For critical discussions of the role of things in eighteenth-century literature, see *The Secret Life of Things*, ed. Mark Blackwell (Lewisburg, PA: Bucknell University Press, 2006); Lynn Festa, *Figures of Empire in Eighteenth-Century Britain and France* (Baltimore, MD: Johns Hopkins University Press, 2006); Jonathan Lamb, *The Things Things Say* (Princeton, NJ: Princeton University Press, 2011); Jonathan Kramnick, *Actions and Objects from Hobbes to Richardson* (Stanford, CA: Stanford University Press, 2010); and Sean Silver, *The Mind Is a Collection: Case Studies in Eighteenth-Century Thought* (Philadelphia: University of Pennsylvania Press, 2015).

12. Barbara M. Benedict, "Jane Austen and the Culture of Circulating Libraries," in *Revising Women: Eighteenth-Century "Women's Fiction" and Social Engagement*, ed. Paula R. Backscheider (Baltimore, MD: Johns Hopkins University Press, 2000), 147–99.

13. Jane Austen, *Northanger Abbey*, ed. Barbara M. Benedict and Deirdre Le Faye (Cambridge: Cambridge University Press, 2006), 7. All references to this text are to this edition and will be provided parenthetically in the text.

14. Jane Austen, *Sense and Sensibility*, The Cambridge Edition of the Works of Jane Austen, ed. Edward Copeland (Cambridge: Cambridge University Press, 2006), 57. All references to this text are to this edition and will be provided parenthetically in the text.

15. Jane Austen, *Pride and Prejudice*, The Cambridge Edition of the Works of Jane Austen, ed. Pat Rogers (Cambridge: Cambridge University Press, 2006), 60. All references to this text are to this edition and will be provided parenthetically in the text.

16. Justice, "Sanditon and the Book," 154.

17. Jane Austen, "Sanditon," in *Later Manuscripts*, ed. Janet Todd and Linda Bree (Cambridge: Cambridge University Press, 2008), 167. All references to this text are to this edition and will be provided parenthetically in the text.

18. *Jane Austen's Letters*, ed. Deirdre Le Faye, 4th ed. (Oxford: Oxford University Press, 2011), 61. All subsequent references to Austen's letters are to this edition and will be provided parenthetically in the text.

19. Jane Austen, *Persuasion*, The Cambridge Edition of the Works of Jane Austen, ed. Janet Todd and Antje Blank (Cambridge: Cambridge University Press, 2006), 162–63. All references to this text are to this edition and will be provided parenthetically in the text.

20. Barbara Benedict, *Making the Modern Reader: Cultural Mediation in Early Modern Literary Anthologies* (Toronto: University of Toronto Press, 1997), 215.

21. Catherine Ingrassia, "Money," in *The Cambridge Companion to Alexander Pope*, ed. Pat Rogers (Cambridge: Cambridge University Press, 2007), 175, 185. See also Maynard Mack, *The Garden and the City: Retirement and Politics in the Later Poetry of Pope, 1731–1743* (Toronto: University of Toronto Press, 1989).

22. Paula Byrne, *The Real Jane Austen: A Life in Small Things* (New York: HarperCollins, 2013).

23. Barbara M. Benedict, "Jewels, Bonds and the Body: Material Culture in Shakespeare and Austen," in *Interconnections between Shakespeare and Austen*, ed. Marina Cano and Rosa Garcia-Periago, forthcoming. Byrne notes that Dr. Cooper gave Austen's elder sister Cassandra a "'ring representing a sprig of diamonds, with one emerald' and Jane was given a headband, which she wore to balls" (*Real Jane Austen*, 23). See also Deirdre Le Faye, *Jane Austen: A Family Record* (Cambridge: Cambridge University Press, 2003), 49, which presents a variant wording of the quotation.

24. Helen Clifford, "Silverwares," in *Design and the Decorative Arts: Britain 1500–1900*, by Michael Snodin and John Styles (London: V&A, 2001), 305–6; Maxine Berg, *Luxury and Pleasure*, 163. See also Maxine Berg, *The Age of Manufactures: Industry, Innovation and Work in Britain 1700–1820* (London: Fontana, 1985).

25. Deidre Lynch, "Personal Effects and Sentimental Fiction," *ECF* 12, nos. 2–3 (January–April, 2000): 345–68. See *Subject and Object in Renaissance Culture*, ed. Margreta de Grazia, Maureen Quilligan, and Peter Stallybrass (Cambridge: Cambridge University Press, 1996).

26. Jane Austen, *Emma*, The Cambridge Edition of the Works of Jane Austen, ed. Richard Cronin and Dorothy McMillan (Cambridge: Cambridge University Press, 2005), 366. All references to this text are to this edition and will be provided parenthetically in the text.

27. Aaron Santesso, "William Hogarth and the Tradition of Sexual Scissors," *SEL, 1500–1900* 39, no. 3 (summer, 1999): 499–521. My thanks to Anna Battigelli for pointing out the role of scissors in *Sense and Sensibility*.

28. See *The Social Life of Things: Commodities in Cultural Perspective*, ed. Arjun Appadurai (Cambridge: Cambridge University Press, 1986).

29. John Styles and Amanda Vickery, introduction to *Gender, Taste, and Material Culture in Britain and North America, 1700–1830*, ed. Styles and Vickery (New Haven, CT: Yale University Press, 2006), 1–5.

30. Kate Scarth, "It-Narratives, Thing Theory, and 'Trivial Things': Sophie Gee's *The Scandal of the Season* and *The Rape of the Lock*," in *Pope's "Rape of the Lock" 300 Years On*, ed. Don Nichols (Toronto: University of Toronto Press, 2015), 151–66.

31. Mack, "Appendix B: "Inventory of Pope's Goods," in *The Garden and the City*, 244–58.

32. Byrne, *The Real Jane Austen*, 9–10.

33. Edward Copeland, "Money," in *The Cambridge Companion to Jane Austen*, ed. Copeland and Juliet McMaster (Cambridge: Cambridge University Press, 2001), 132.

34. Elsie B. Michael, *The Vulgar Question of Money: Heiresses, Materialism and the Novel of Manners from Jane Austen to Henry James* (Baltimore, MD: Johns Hopkins University Press, 2011), 6.

35. Copeland, "Money," 131.

"A Very Pretty Amber Cross"
Material Sources of Elegance in *Mansfield Park*

NATASHA DUQUETTE

In forming definitions of beauty and harmony we often move from the concrete and visible toward the abstract and theoretical rather than vice versa. Such must have been the case for Jane Austen. The details and textures of her novels reflect her empirical observation of objects she held in her own hands. In *Mansfield Park*, specifically, the amber-colored cross given to Fanny Price by her brother William, paired with Edmund Bertram's gift of a plain chain, suggest an Austenian ethical aesthetic of simplicity, strength, and purpose. Austen's narrator sets this aesthetic of moral beauty, characterized by simplicity and utility, in contrast to the extravagant baroque tastes displayed by some of the wealthiest characters. The decadence of artificial elegance and excess is countered by the thoughtfully simple elegance of the small amber cross.

Jane Austen's Topaz Cross

Jane Austen herself was given a topaz cross by her younger brother Second Lieutenant Charles Austen, who purchased two topaz crosses in May 1801 for his sisters Cassandra and Jane. He purchased the crosses after receiving thirty pounds in prize money for his role in the capture of the French privateer *Le Scipio* as a second lieutenant on board the British ship *Endymion*. In her biography *The Real Jane Austen: A Life in Small Things*, Paula Byrne writes: "The crosses are not identical: one is in the traditional crucifix shape, the other with the symmetry of a saltire. We do not know which one went to Cassandra and which to Jane."[1] However, Carrie Wright, in a *Persuasions* article published one year after Byrne's book, claims, "Jane's is the Greek style cross."[2] Though there is some ambiguity regarding which cross was actually Jane Austen's, we do know that Austen treated the gift with what Byrne terms her "characteristic irony."[3] Austen wrote of Charles, in a letter to Cassandra on May 27, 1801: "He has been buying Gold chains & Topaze

Crosses for us;—he must be well scolded . . . I shall write again by this post to thank & reproach him.—We shall be unbearably fine."[4] Behind her irony, one senses Austen's true delight in her gift from her younger brother.

In his book *Jane Austen and the Navy*, Brian Southam portrays Charles Austen as the darling of the family, noting that whenever his name appears in Jane Austen's correspondence, she "writes of him with tenderness and solicitude."[5] Sheila Johnson Kindred also remarks on the close bond between Charles and Jane Austen, explaining, "She proudly followed his career from its beginning—the initial three-year period of study at the Academy, a further three years at sea as a midshipman, and his subsequent promotion to service as a lieutenant."[6] Byrne suggests that their brother and sister love was infused by a shared Christian faith: "The fact that Charles chose crosses rather than lockets is significant, alluding as it does to his sisters' deep Christian faith as well as marking their delight in fashion."[7] She is thus aligned with Laura Mooneyham White's emphasis in *Jane Austen's Anglicanism* on the Austen family's faith. In the narrative of her novel *Mansfield Park*, Jane Austen depicts a shared familial faith when William Price gives his older sister Fanny the gift of a cross. This amber cross's religious significance in the narrative is undeniable, and shortly after receiving it Fanny engages in "fervent" prayer.[8]

Fanny Price's Amber Cross

The strong parallels between the fictional William Price and the real Charles Austen have been duly noted by critics such as Southam and Byrne, among others. One explicit tie to the history of Charles Austen's gift is the fact that in *Mansfield Park* there is a ship named Endymion stationed at Portsmouth harbor, an oblique reference to the ship Charles was serving on when he gained the money used to purchase the crosses for his sisters. In reality, Charles Austen's naval career took him to the Mediterranean and to Bermuda, and in *Mansfield Park* Austen's narrator explains how William Price has "been in the Mediterranean—in the West Indies—in the Mediterranean again" and has "been often taken on shore by the favour of his Captain" (275). In the course of *Mansfield Park*'s narrative, William Price slowly rises through the lower ranks of British naval officers, from midshipman to lieutenant, partially aided by Henry Crawford's connection to Admiral Crawford. When Fanny first speaks to Henry of her brother's role aboard a ship called the *Antwerp* she displays a remarkable intensity, and as the narrator notes, she is "elevated beyond the common timidity of her mind by the flow of her love for William" (271). The language of elevation or loftiness imparts a sublime quality to Fanny's love for her brother. This elevation of discourse is akin to what Edmund Bertram earlier describes as Fanny's "enthusiasm" when she utters her short but intense meditation on the "wickedness" and "sorrow" of humanity and the "sublimity of Nature" (132) as she gazes out at a starry sky.

Once William returns from his seven years at sea and visits Fanny at Mansfield, the usually reserved Fanny finds a discursive freedom in conversing with her brother, in what the narrator depicts as "unchecked, equal, fearless" (*MP*, 273) self-expression. He, in turn, voices his "desire" (293) to see Fanny dance to his uncle, Sir Thomas Bertram. Perhaps this desire to see Fanny elevated into the ranks of those who dance at a Mansfield Park ball is behind William's gift to his sister of a "very pretty amber cross" (295). Coming from his naval background, William would be aware of the significance carried by medallions and other ornaments adorning a naval uniform. Motivating his gift of the amber cross may be his desire to lift up the lowly Fanny by bequeathing dignity and honor to his sister. This is a very different kind of motive than that of Henry Crawford, who through duplicity sends Fanny a gold necklace on which to hang her amber cross, as part of his plan to make her fall in love with him. As he puts it crassly, "I cannot be satisfied without Fanny Price, without making a small hole in Fanny Price's heart" (267). Henry's gift of the gold necklace is manipulative and driven by his egoistic longing to make a conquest of Fanny, to capture her as an object, whereas William's gift of the cross signifies his hope for Fanny's elevation, his faith in God's providential care for Fanny, and his own love for his sister.

Interestingly, Austen represents the ornate gold necklace Henry has chosen for Fanny as too large to accommodate the ring of her amber cross. Thankfully, Edmund Bertram also provides her with a piece of jewelry on which to hang her cross, and Edmund's gift is more straightforward, more suitable, and more aesthetically appealing to Fanny than the overly ornate and intricate necklace snuck into her hands by Henry via his sister Mary. When Edmund himself presents his gift directly to Fanny, it is "a plain gold chain perfectly simple and neat," which causes her to exclaim, "Oh! this is beautiful, indeed!" (*MP*, 304). She responds with a spontaneous and positive aesthetic judgment of approbation. Elaine Bander's essay in this volume presents Fanny Price as "artless," since she is not an accomplished artist herself, yet Fanny does emerge as an aesthetic theorist in the narrative. Edmund is in alignment with Fanny's aesthetic judgments by keeping in mind "the simplicity of [her] taste" (303) when he selected the chain, which causes her

"A Very Pretty Amber Cross"

to respond, "It will exactly suit my cross" (304). The emphasis on simplicity here is significant. In his 1759 *Philosophical Enquiry into the Origin of Our Ideas of the Sublime and the Beautiful*, Edmund Burke had argued for the aesthetic power of "perfect simplicity."[9] Burke makes this comment in a section on architecture, but Austen applies the same concept of the aesthetic merit of simplicity to Edmund Bertram's gold chain.

Edmund Price observes Fanny articulate her aesthetic preference for natural simplicity and thus reveals his own ability to see Fanny as a thinking and perceiving woman with a taste of her own. This is opposed to Henry, who imposes his own decadent taste on Fanny via the baroque-sounding necklace he has somewhat forced upon her. Brian Southam notes:

> Jane Austen sets poetic justice to work. The necklace proves too large for the ring of the cross; so, instead, Fanny uses a chain offered by Edmund; and, worn together, all three—the cross, suspended from the chain, and the necklace on its own—become the adversative emblems of true love and false friendship. . Charles Austen, and other members of the family, would be delighted at such a notable working-up of the topaze crosses and gold chains sent to Jane and Cassandra in 1801: his gift of jewellery now answered with a gift of literature.[10]

Interestingly, in a novel within which the heroine reflects philosophically on the nature of human memory, Austen's narrator applies the word "memorial" to both the amber cross and the simple gold chain, noting how, for Fanny, they are "memorials of the two most beloved of her heart . . . dearest tokens so formed for each other by everything real and imaginary" (*MP*, 314). With the idea of the cross as a memorial that appeals to empiricism and imagination, to the mind and the heart, Austen reminds us of how the shape of a cross has functioned as a memorial for centuries within the international history of Christianity.

This particular amber cross, in the narrative of *Mansfield Park*, has come from Sicily, acquired during one of Williams's side trips ashore with his captain while sailing in the Mediterranean. Crafted in Sicily, it is no doubt a Catholic cross, or at least a cross made by the hands of a Catholic artisan, which has made its way, via international trade and naval routes, into the center of an English novel depicting the Anglican ordination of Edmund Bertram. Of course, Austen is paying tribute to the amber-*colored* cross, actually crafted from the mineral topaz, given to her by her own brother Charles, but still, she has intentionally added the detail of her fictional cross's Sicilian origin. Austen allows her readers to imagine her fictional cross as truly made of actual amber, congealed and fossilized tree sap, rather than simply being constructed out of topaz which happens to be amber-colored, like the historical crosses given to Jane and Cassandra by their brother Charles. In the fictional world of *Mansfield Park*, the amber medium and Sicilian craftsmanship bring an air of international cosmopolitanism and Catholic sensibility to Fanny's cross. Due to the material history of ancient amber trade routes, originating in Scandinavian forests and flowing south through the Mediterranean,[11] amber jewelry is still much more prevalent in countries such as Latvia, Poland, and Italy than it is in England. In his 2017 monograph *Jane Austen and the Reformation*, Roger E. Moore presents Fanny's amber cross as a metonym for Catholicism, writing, "The cross of course declares Fanny's Christian faith, but it also testifies to a specifically Catholic form of Christianity; it is from Sicily, deep in the heart of Catholic Europe. Fanny reveres the buildings and rituals of England's Catholic past, and the cross's Sicilian origin subtly solidifies her association with Catholicism."[12] In Catholic tradition broadly, the image of the cross (and especially a crucifix) has served, over and over again, in multitudinous mediums, to memorialize the painful death of Jesus Christ.

Historically, a cross signifies intense suffering, and it is a quite suitable emblem for Fanny Price, a young woman who does suffer much during the course of *Mansfield Park*, so much that critic Sarah Emsley has identified Fanny's story as a tragedy which concludes with a comic ending only in its very last chapters. Emsley traces how "in the language and action of *Mansfield Park* [Austen is] making a tragedy, whether it is of the new or old type."[13] Direct references to the "pain" of Fanny Price appear over thirty times in *Mansfield Park*. Coming from a disadvantaged background, Fanny "must take . . . pains" (22) with her education. She is pained, emotionally and physically, when Edmund takes his quiet mare away from her in order that Mary Crawford may ride it. The pain of a headache afflicts Fanny after she has been made to cut roses and run errands in the glare of the hot sun. During her years at Mansfield Park, she experiences "the pains of tyranny, of ridicule, and neglect" (178). Austen's narrator hints that, due to Fanny's impoverished and highly dysfunctional family of origin, she has experienced significant emotional pain long before her initial arrival on the doorstep of Mansfield Park at the age of ten. As readers, we receive hints that both she and her brother William have endured trials together as the children of an underemployed, alcoholic father who is prone to violence. When Fanny is later embraced by her father, for example, she is "sadly pained by his language and his smell of spirits" (440). Fanny and William share the intense bonds of affection often felt by children who have grown up sheltering each other from the corrosive behavior and speech of an alcoholic parent. To return to the amber cross, when William Price gives it as a gift to his sister Fanny, it carries the weight of their strong and loving bond created through the shared suffering of their childhood home.

Spiritually as well as aesthetically, then, the amber cross shines out amid the darkness of *Mansfield Park* as a beautiful emblem of brotherly love forged in the crucible of suffering. William and Fanny are not passive victims, and they are able to courageously transfigure their difficult childhood experiences into what the narrator terms "heroism." When William visits at Mansfield Park, Henry Crawford is actually abashed by what he terms "the glory of heroism" at sea, the "usefulness," "exertion," and "endurance" that make Henry self-conscious about his own "shameful" "selfish indulgence" and lack of clear vocation (*MP*, 275). After William gives Fanny her amber cross, Fanny is able to exert "all the heroism of principle" (307), when she witnesses Edmund's growing infatuation with Mary Crawford. Specifically, she finds the courage to pray rather than be consumed with jealousy. The narrator explains: "Could she believe Miss Crawford to deserve him, it would be—Oh, how different it would be—how far more tolerable! But he was deceived in her: he gave her merits which she had not; her faults were what they had ever been, but he saw them no longer. Till she had shed many tears over this deception, Fanny could not subdue her agitation; and the dejection which followed could only be relieved by the influence of fervent prayers for his happiness" (307). Fanny is the only heroine explicitly described as praying in a Jane Austen novel. And, not only does she pray, but she fervently prays for the happiness of someone who is paining her through his blindness and lack of discernment. She prays for Edmund's happiness regardless of whom he ultimately chooses to marry, and Austen cleverly invites us to imagine her prayers being answered when Edmund marries Fanny herself at the very conclusion of the narrative. Fanny's uttering of these prayers occurs almost immediately after she receives the amber cross from William, near the center or crux of Austen's narrative. This moment is a turning point for Fanny. After praying, Fanny displays the "heroism of principle," and her character increasingly strengthens through the rest of the novel, evidenced by her ability to defy her uncle Sir Thomas Bertram when he tries to coerce her into marrying Henry Crawford. Emsley goes so far as to argue that "the tragic action of the novel centers on Fanny Price's prolonged temptation to marry Henry."[14] Ultimately, Fanny resists this temptation through her growing ethical and spiritual fortitude. Elaine Bander has labeled this quality Fanny's "true heroism."[15]

This dauntless heroism of Fanny's, evidence of increasing inner strength, is akin to the naval heroism of William and appears to have been amplified through his gift of the amber cross. In *Mansfield Park*, this small amber cross symbolizes the beauty of love, endurance, faith, and devotion, as well as resistance to temptation. It elevates Fanny not only socially at the ball but also spiritually through her prayers and ethically through her growing courage to stand her ground. Wearing her amber cross, Fanny grows into a woman of strength and elegance.

The Question of Elegance in Mansfield Park

Elegance is a complicated aesthetic category for Jane Austen, however. In *Mansfield Park*, specifically, Austen takes the concept of elegance and turns it about, examining it from multiple angles. Her careful examination of this aesthetic term tests various definitions of what it meant to be an elegant woman in Georgian England. For example, Fanny Price's cousins Maria and Julia Bertram, daughters of her wealthy uncle Sir Thomas Bertram, are introduced into the narrative of *Mansfield Park* as "elegant, agreeable girls" (52). The terms are highly ironic here, as Maria and Julia's selfish superficiality quickly becomes manifest in their belittling of their cousin Fanny. As postcolonial critic Edward Said has convincingly shown, the material elegance of Mansfield Park, and the Bertram family who inhabit this country estate, is implicated with the labor of oppressed slaves in the West Indies. Though British involvement in the slave trade became illegal in 1807, British citizens continued to illegally participate in the slave trade, and the British navy was deployed to catch ships engaged in illicit human trafficking. Deployed in the West Indies, Charles Austen himself likely served in this manner, apprehending slave traders on behalf of the British. Although the slave trade was abolished, slavery itself remained legal in the British West Indies well into the 1820s and early 1830s, as testified to by slave narratives such as *The History of Mary Prince*, published in 1831. It was not until 1833 that slavery was completely outlawed in the British West Indies. Therefore, when Jane Austen published *Mansfield Park* in 1814, her readers would have understood Sir Thomas's economic interests in Antigua, an island in the British West Indies, as complicit in the practices of slavery.

Edward Said has essentially accused Austen of not being a vocal enough critic of the continuing practice of slavery in the British West Indies during her lifetime.[16] However, we know Austen read and admired antislavery writers such as the poet William Cowper and essayist Thomas Clarkson, and she expressed fondness for a brother, Charles Austen, who patrolled the waters off the Americas during a period when one of the British navy's primary tasks was to capture slave ships. In *Jane Austen in the Context of Abolition*, Gabrielle White focuses on Fanny Price's courageous question about the slave trade, which she poses to Sir Thomas after he has returned home to Mansfield Park from a trip to Antigua. Another critic, the narratologist Susan Fraiman, argues that "had Said placed Sir Thomas Bertram . . . in line with the deficient fathers who run unrelentingly from *Northanger Abbey* through *Persuasion*, he might perhaps have paused before assuming that Austen legitimates the master of Mansfield Park."[17] Indeed, what the narrator terms Sir Thomas's "government" (*MP*, 229) of Mansfield Park certainly brings order and a degree of surface elegance to his home and children, but it also brings "gloom" (229). The reader cannot help interpreting what Fanny initially perceives as his "absolute power" (326) over her as an extension of the autocratic slave owner's will. The order of Mansfield Park is maintained through powerful control, and the elegant lifestyle of Julia, Maria, and the brother Tom Bertram is at least partially supported through an ethically troubling socioeconomic system. This makes "elegance" a complex term for Austen, especially in this novel. As Vivasvan Soni has written in his preface to *Jane Austen and the Arts*, "Austen herself undoubtedly retains a certain complicated commitment to the values of elegance, propriety, harmony, and a neoclassical aesthetics more generally, but to the extent that she does, she also recognizes that . . . [r]ules can lead us astray."[18] Rules can also attempt to control and repress at Mansfield Park.

As she does with the idea of sensibility, Austen implies that elegance can appear in false or distorted, even deforming, modes. She resists an overly didactic or simplistic approach either for or against elegance through her use of subtle irony. Against Said, Rajeswari Rajan defends Jane Austen's place as a *satirical critic* of social normativity, pointing to the "effects of irony" in *Mansfield Park,* a novel which is after all a complex yet harmonious and elegant structure in its own right.[19] Ana-Karina Schneider writes of this novel that "although published only one year after *Pride and Prejudice, Mansfield Park* (written between February 1811 and the summer of 1813) is more mature in both tone and purport than any of her earlier works: fashioned in a style of flawless versatility and consistent elegance, it is serious and moralising without losing its ironic critical edge."[20] Schneider associates *Mansfield Park*'s elegant form with maturity of tone and a moral irony that allows for ambiguity. Austen resists didacticism by balancing tragic notes with textual harmony and a satirical edge sustained to the end.

Austen certainly satirizes false notions of "elegance" based solely in prideful social constructions of superior class or rank, beginning with the labeling of the vapid Julia and Maria Bertram as "elegant." To help define the term in historical context, one element to consider is dress or fashion. The only full-length portrait we definitely know to be a portrayal of Jane Austen herself, a watercolor painted by her sister Cassandra in 1804, suggests she preferred a mode of dress that balanced modesty with subtle detail, sense and comfort, and a certain flare. Her surviving letters to her sister Cassandra, after all, reveal that the young Jane Austen was somewhat of a bonnet enthusiast. The practical elegance of Austen's early nineteenth-century dress in what has been termed the "Bonnet Portrait" contrasts with the extravagance of the fashions in France leading up to the French Revolution. Mid-eighteenth-century French portraits include elaborate hats, for example, which could be crowned by tropical fruit or artificial birds' nests, and the omnipresence of lapdogs, such as Marie Antoinette's papillon, whom she supposedly carried with her to the guillotine in 1793. In *Mansfield Park*, Lady Bertram's pug is a fashionable French affectation, which Austen repeatedly deploys to satirical purpose. Women artists and writers of the late eighteenth and early nineteenth centuries often resisted the artificial excesses in fashion and opted for a simpler elegance, as in a self-portrait by Angelica Kauffmann (fig. 13). The soft folds and empire waist of Kauffmann's dress would have been more comfortable for her hours spent sitting at an easel and painting. We can compare Kauffmann's seated portrait with Austen's and note both women have chosen simple, two-tone, flowing fabric, though Austen's dress, as well as her pose, creates greater modesty and privacy, with her chest, neck, and arms fully covered, and her face turned away. Regardless, the simplicity of each woman's dress suggests resistance to extravagant (or even ridiculous) excess in fashion.

Austen knew the satire of fashionable excess in the work of eighteenth-century poets such as Alexander Pope. Pope's critique of luxury for luxury's sake may have been another source for her view of elegance, including her at times ironic approach to it. In 1735, Pope wrote a commentary on his *Epistle to Burlington*, wherein he explains how his poem satirizes "the vanity of expense in people of wealth and quality. The abuse of the word taste, verse 13. That the first principle and foundation, in this as in everything else, is good sense, verse 40. The chief proof of it is to follow nature even in works of mere luxury and elegance. Instanced in architecture and

Fig. 13. Angelica Kauffmann, *Self-Portrait*, 1787, oil on canvas. (Uffizi Gallery, Florence)

gardening, where all must be adapted to the genius and use of the place, and the beauties not forced into it, but resulting from it, verse 50."[21] The poem moves from an aesthetic discussion of good and bad taste in landscape design and architecture to a description of "Timon's Villa" as an exemplar of bad taste and wasteful excess, before concluding with a vision of a possible future when landowners will steward wealth with both taste and purpose in ways that enable communities to flourish. Within his poem, Pope argues that good sense is "the gift of Heav'n,"[22] which we ignore to our detriment, "a light, which in yourself you must perceive."[23] Above all, he believes that landscape and architectural design need guidance by sense and by nature in order to succeed, adding "let Nature never be forgot."[24]

"Decency," or privacy, is key to Pope's sense of elegance. In reference to landscape, he writes:

> Let not each beauty ev'rywhere be spied,
> Where half the skill is decently to hide.
> He gains all points who decently confounds,
> Surprises, varies, and conceals the bounds.[25]

Toward the end of his poem, Pope envisions a possible future age not guided by vanity but sense, when land will be used responsibly for agriculture; aesthetics will be subordinated to purpose; and tenants will be well cared for by their Lord. Pope presents this vision in order to contrast it with the extravagant waste at Timon's Villa.

In *Mansfield Park*, Jane Austen similarly considers how notions of elegance, false or true, may be perpetuated by people of means via two young male characters: Mr. Rushworth and Henry Crawford. When Fanny Price visits the estate of Sotherton, which Mr. Rushworth is to inherit, she is with Maria Bertram, now engaged to Rushworth. After the young women and their party are greeted by the Rushworths, "it was first necessary to eat, and the doors were thrown open to admit them through one or two intermediate rooms into the appointed dining-parlour, where a collation was prepared with abundance and elegance. Much was said, and much was ate, and all went well. The particular object of the day was then considered. How would Mr. Crawford like, in what manner would he choose, to take a survey of the grounds?" (*MP*, 98). Sotherton is initially presented to visitors as a fashionably elegant estate to be more admired than enjoyed, not unlike "Timon's Villa" in Alexander Pope's poem. Austen's Rushworth parallels Pope's Timon with his strong desire to display his wealth with lavish food and to take visitors on tours of the landscape surrounding his country house. Like Mr. Rushworth, Henry Crawford is also a single man with money to spend who tries to convey his knowledge of elegance. He reflects on the idea of Fanny dancing and claims, in a conversation with William Price, "I have had the pleasure of seeing your sister dance, Mr. Price . . and will engage to answer every inquiry which you can make on the subject, to your entire satisfaction. But I believe (seeing Fanny look distressed) it must be at some other time. There is *one* person in company who does not like to have Miss Price spoken of" (291). The narrator wryly remarks, "True enough, he had once seen Fanny dance; and it was equally true that he would now have answered for her gliding about with quiet, light elegance, and in admirable time, but in fact he could not for the life of him recall what her dancing had been, and rather took it for granted that she had been present than remembered anything about her" (291–92). Though apparently imaginary, Henry's idea of Fanny's subtle, light elegance is apt, as it corresponds with the simple elegance of her small Sicilian amber cross.

Fanny's actual increase in real elegance becomes clear in chapter 28 of *Mansfield Park* when she appears, ready for her first formal ball, wearing her amber cross. The astute narrator notes: "Her uncle and both her aunts were in the drawing-room when Fanny went down. To the former she was an interesting object, and he saw with pleasure the general elegance of her appearance, and her being in remarkably good looks. The neatness and propriety of her dress was all that he would allow himself to commend in her presence, but upon her leaving the room again soon afterwards, he spoke of her beauty with very decided praise" (316). Lady Bertram mistakenly thinks Fanny looks well because the servant Chapman has been sent to dress her. And, Mrs. Norris, Fanny's other aunt, cries out, "she has good reason to look well with all her advantages: brought up in this family as she has been, with all the benefit of her cousins' manners before her" (316). Mrs. Norris wrongly believes Fanny has acquired her elegant appearance by watching and imitating her cousins Julia and Maria Bertram. Her cross is not mentioned by anyone at this point, but we know she is wearing it.

When Fanny's increased elegance eventually attracts the attentions of Henry Crawford, she resists her uncle's pressure to marry Henry and as a result is exiled from Mansfield Park. While banished temporarily to her rough, chaotic, and impoverished birth family in their lodgings at Portsmouth, Fanny Price yearns for what she remembers as the elegant order of her adoptive family and their country house estate. Nestled in the fresh green landscape of Northamptonshire, on its surface, Mansfield Park is characterized by what Fanny recalls nostalgically as a peaceful serenity in contrast with the discord of Portsmouth. In Portsmouth, the tensions and disagreements disturbing Fanny's family of origin are fueled by the heavy drinking of her birth father, Lieutenant Price, and the sibling rivalries of her sisters Susan and little Betsey. Betsey, by contrast perceives Fanny as a "fine new sister" (*MP*, 438). This reference to Fanny's "fineness" resonates with Jane Austen's statement in her letter to her sister Cassandra that they will be "unbearably fine" wearing their amber crosses. In *Mansfield Park*, immediately after Betsey's statement, Mr. Price bursts on the scene, and his loud swearing and violent, abrupt actions stand in direct contrast to such fineness. He enters his home shouting an "oath" and forcefully kicking "away his son's portmanteau, and his daughter's band-box in the passage" (438). In Fanny's bandbox may be some of the treasures from her East Room, to which Peter Sabor has drawn attention in his essay for this collection, including the small sketch of the *Antwerp* sent to her from the Mediterranean,[26] and perhaps also her amber cross. Not only has Mr. Price not provided adequately for his children, but he also adds insult to injury by physically harming what small possessions they have been able to acquire when he kicks their traveling gear aside.

The tumult at Portsmouth makes Fanny miss the elegance and propriety of Mansfield Park. The narrator describes her inner state at length:

> The elegance, propriety, regularity, harmony—and perhaps, above all, the peace and tranquility of Mansfield, were brought to her remembrance every hour of the day, by the prevalence of everything opposite to them *here*.
>
> The living in incessant noise was to a frame and temper, delicate and nervous like Fanny's, an evil which no superadded elegance or harmony could have entirely atoned for. It was the greatest misery of all. At Mansfield, no sounds of contention, no raised voice, no abrupt bursts, no tread of violence was ever heard; all proceeded in a regular course of cheerful orderliness; everybody had their due importance. (*MP*, 453)

Through free indirect discourse, the narrator takes on Fanny's consciousness, and Mansfield Park is idealized via the filter of her very human and fallible atmospheric memories. Fanny misses the physical elegance of Mansfield Park, which she associates with regularity and order, editing out how this order is maintained by Sir Thomas's wielding of "absolute power" and control. She appears to be forgetting how the silence of Sir Thomas's household has resulted from a repression that forces desires and opinions underground and beyond control. One of the most striking examples of this tension occurs when her question about the slave trade is met with "dead silence" (231). Fanny's subjective memory of *all* proceeding with cheerful orderliness at Mansfield Park directly contradicts her earlier experiences of painful socialization into what the narrator had termed the "gloom" of its elegant order.

Any mention of Mansfield Park's elegance is abruptly dropped when Sir Thomas's daughter, the married Maria Rushworth, commits adultery with Henry Crawford, to the horror of both Fanny Price and Sir Thomas Bertram. At this point, Sir Thomas realizes he has raised his daughters to be elegant and agreeable on the surface, but with no sense of an inner moral compass to guide their actions in the world:

> He saw how ill he had judged . . . clearly saw that he had but increased the evil, by teaching them to repress their spirits in his presence, so as to make their real disposition unknown to him. . . . Here had been grievous mismanagement; but, bad as it was, he gradually grew to feel that it had not been the most direful mistake in his plan of education. Something must have been wanting *within*, or time would have worn away much of its ill effect. He feared that principle, active principle, had been wanting, that they had never been properly taught to govern their inclinations and

tempers, by that sense of duty which can alone suffice. They had been instructed theoretically in their religion, but never required to bring it into daily practice. To be distinguished for elegance and accomplishments—the authorised object of their youth—could have had no useful influence that way, no moral effect on the mind. (*MP*, 535–36)

With his strict government of the external words and actions in his home, Sir Thomas has taught Maria and Julia Bertram to govern, or control, their outward speech and etiquette in his presence, so they may be admired for their surface elegance. However, he now realizes this was but an external façade of obedience maintained in his presence but with no correspondent inner moral conviction. The Bertram sisters exactly lack what the narrator terms Fanny Price's "heroism of principle" (307), which is strengthened by her prayer after she receives the amber cross. The spiritual or theological point Austen is making here becomes even clearer when Sir Thomas laments how his accomplished daughters have a theoretical knowledge of religious concepts but no ability to wisely apply them to everyday decisions.

This epiphany is a turning point in Sir Thomas's own character development, which occurs toward the very end of the novel and gives the reader hope for his further growth. Throughout his concern for his son Tom's grave illness and his shock at his daughter Maria's adultery, Sir Thomas Bertram reflects on his past mistakes. During these difficult and unstable times Fanny Price is a steady and edifying presence, a sort of rock within the shifting sands of the Bertram family dynamic. But, as readers, we are still left with an unresolved question. Why has Sir Thomas Bertram's parenting and educating of his own children at home led to "elegant and agreeable" daughters without moral discernment? Part of the problem may lie in societal pressures for daughters of the aristocracy to acquire learning and accomplishments, ranging from theological knowledge to piano playing, for the purpose of display alone, in order to marry a wealthy partner of the highest possible rank.

Approximately thirty years before the publication of Austen's *Mansfield Park*, the philosopher Mary Wollstonecraft warned that the socializing of women to appear superficially attractive and amiable would cause them to sacrifice the sterner virtues of duty. In her *Vindication of the Rights of Men* (1790), Wollstonecraft argues against Edmund Burke's definition of feminine beauty in terms of coquettish and yielding weakness and softness. She cautions how women who conform to this model of beauty risk becoming amoral creatures, hesitant to sacrifice their amiability to "the force of those exalted qualities, fortitude, justice, wisdom, and truth."[27] In her *Vindication of the Rights of Woman* (1792), Wollstonecraft likewise critiques male "despotism that kills *virtue* and genius in the bud."[28] She argues: "Women are everywhere in this deplorable state; for, in order to preserve their innocence, as ignorance is courteously termed, truth is hidden from them, and they are made to assume an artificial character before their faculties have acquired any strength. Taught from their infancy that beauty is woman's sceptre, the mind shapes itself to the body, and, roaming round its gilt cage, only seeks to adore its prison."[29] Here again is the idea of young girls, through their (mis)education, being discouraged from the pursuit of both virtue and truth in order to maintain a beautiful, or elegant, appearance. Later, Wollstonecraft extends her metaphor of the gilded bird cage by describing wealthy married women thus: "Confined then in cages like the feathered race, they have nothing to do but to plume themselves, and stalk with mock majesty from perch to perch."[30] Within *Mansfield Park*'s narrative, during the touring of Sotherton, Maria Bertram compares herself to a starling in a cage, a domesticated bird who cannot escape its prison. This is, of course, a direct allusion to the starling in Laurence Sterne's *Sentimental Journey* (1768), but it may also be a veiled reference to Wollstonecraft's powerful figurative imagery of elegant yet entrapped aristocratic young women, like beautiful birds in gilded cages. The possible Wollstonecraft connection lends Maria's statement poignancy and could create a degree of readerly sympathy for her, despite her later transgression. Her action partly arises from the mode of her education and socialization, as Sir Thomas Bertram himself remorsefully acknowledges.

Sir Thomas Bertram's eldest son, Tom Bertram, also falls into a pattern of unhealthy excess, transgression, and dissipation, which ultimately threatens his life. Indeed, instability and lack of integrity pervade both male and female "elegance" at Mansfield Park. Austen sets true elegance in tension with false elegance throughout her novel, using various situations to draw the contrast. Philosopher and antislavery activist Mary Anne Schimmelpenninck likewise differentiated between a truly graceful elegance and its distortion or corruption in her *Theory on the Classification of Beauty and Deformity, and Their Correspondence with Physiognomic Expression, Exemplified in Various Works of Art, and Natural Objects* (1815). In this treatise, Schimmelpenninck divides beauty into three "genera"—the sublime (subdivided into two species: "the horrible" and "the contemplative"), the sentimental, and the sprightly. Each of these aesthetic categories can be twisted or deformed into grotesque antitypes. She explains, "The distinguishing characteristic of the sentimental is elegance," and she associates such elegance with "grace,"[31] as well as "lightness."[32] For Schimmelpenninck, however, when such elegance increases in relaxation and inactivity and diminishes in sensibility, it morphs into "British sensuality," "Luxurious indolence," and "self-indulgence."[33] In her "Chart No. 2—Deformities," she suggests that human beings caught in this deformation of elegance are sluggishly imperceptive, governed by sloth, and "destitute of fixed principle."[34] These are indeed characteristics notable in Lady Bertram and her children. There is a reason Fanny Price reads Samuel Johnson's satirical journal the *Idler* while coping with her years at Mansfield Park. Perhaps the very idleness and lack of struggle in the young Bertrams' early lives, and the resultant general languor of Mansfield Park, has contributed to their atrophied sense of principle.

Before his epiphany regarding his errors in raising his own children, Sir Thomas Bertram boasts about the elegance of plantation owners' luxurious lifestyles in Antigua. During the same conversation within which Henry Crawford imagines Fanny Price dancing with "light elegance," the narrator observes Sir Thomas "by no means displeased," becoming deeply "engaged in describing the balls of Antigua" (*MP*, 292). The extravagant abundance of such Antiguan balls in the British Caribbean was supported by the labor of African slaves. So-called "house slaves" would have been present at Antiguan balls, working hard to support their master's appearance of elegance. In creating the character of Sir Thomas Bertram, Austen had available to her the known travel patterns of absentee slave-owning British fathers who were away from home for years at a time while attending to their economic interests in the West Indies. One such father is depicted in Johann Zoffany's group portrait *The Family of Sir William Young*, painted in the 1760s (fig. 14). Sir William Young was a British man with economic interests in the Caribbean who was away from his family for eight years between 1764 and 1773. The Jamaican historian Lennox Honychurch notes, "Sir William ensured that the finer trappings of the British aristocracy were transported across the Atlantic and planted upon rain-drenched volcanic islands amidst the bland brutishness of a colonizing plantocracy."[35] Honychurch's word "brutishness" is striking, as it echoes Schimmelpenninck's characterization of a deformed elegance marked by not only excessive luxury but also "brutal carelessness."[36] What is striking in the portrait of Sir William Young's family is the general indolence and lack of activity. The cello at the center could signify an elegant accomplishment, but the cello is not being played. And the letter in the lap of the young woman on the right could signify literacy, but the couple leaning over the letter are more interested in each other than the

Fig. 14. Johann Zoffany, *The Family of Sir William Young*, 1767–69, oil on canvas. (Walker Gallery, Liverpool)

text. The one vigorously active person in this painted scene is the African man on the left, who literally supports the youngest boy in the family, as he lifts him onto a horse's back. In French style, a lapdog lounges at Lady Young's feet. The reader of Austen can discern a societal pattern for Pug and Lady Bertram in Austen's *Mansfield Park*.

In *Mansfield Park*, Jane Austen shows us that elegance, like sensibility, is not a good in and of itself. We should not strive to be so elegant and smooth that we gloss over what Fanny calls "wickedness" and "sorrow" (132) in the world. There exists an artificial elegance aligned with deceit and what Mary Anne Schimmelpenninck called the "British sensuality" of the deformed sentimental. Austen allows for elegance, however, in right proportion. A poised elegance was adopted by free black and mulatto women in the Caribbean and England as an expression of self-worth, intelligence, and dignity, for example. Fanny Price, too, marginalized as she is for the majority of Austen's narrative in *Mansfield Park*, is able to adopt a degree of simple elegance through her amber cross, light dancing, and even her careful choosing of edifying books from the Portsmouth circulating library. In the end, Fanny emerges as a quietly elegant woman of wisdom and strength, sensibility and sense, with not only taste but also a mindful moral discernment of her own.

Notes

1. Paula Byrne, *The Real Jane Austen: A Life in Small Things* (New York: Harper Perennial, 2014), 237.
2. Carrie Wright, "'Unbearably Fine': The Socio-Political Powers of Jewelry in Jane Austen's World," *Persuasions Online* 36, no. 1 (2015), www.jasna.org/persuasions/on-line/vol36no1/wright.html.
3. Byrne, *The Real Jane Austen*, 238.
4. Jane Austen, "To Cassandra Austen," in *Jane Austen's Letters*, ed. Deirdre Le Faye, 4th ed. (Oxford: Oxford University Press, 1997), 95.
5. Brian Southam, *Jane Austen and the Navy* (London: Hambledon Continuum, 2003), 14. For further detail on Jane Austen's sensitive younger brother Charles and his career in the navy, see also Natasha Duquette, "The Sensibility of Captain Benwick in Literary and Historical Context," in *Jane Austen and Masculinity,* ed. Michael Kramp et al. (Lewisburg, PA: Bucknell University Press, 2018), 103–5.
6. Sheila Johnson Kindred, *Jane Austen's Transatlantic Sister: The Life and Letters of Fanny Palmer Austen* (Montreal: McGill-Queen's University Press, 2017), 14.
7. Byrne, *The Real Jane Austen*, 238.
8. Jane Austen, *Mansfield Park*, ed. John Wiltshire (Cambridge: Cambridge University Press, 2005), 307. Subsequent references are to this edition and will be provided parenthetically throughout the text.
9. Edmund Burke, *A Philosophical Enquiry into Our Ideas of the Sublime and the Beautiful* (London: Routledge, 1958), 142.
10. Southam, *Jane Austen and the Navy*, 195
11. See Arnolds Spekke's *The Ancient Amber Routes and the Geographical Discovery of the Eastern Baltic* (Stockholm: M. Goppers, 1967), 17–18. Among the classical writers Spekke cites as describing the circulation of amber are Homer, Herodotus, Pytheas, and Didorus of Sicily.
12. Roger E. Moore, *Jane Austen and the Reformation* (New York: Routledge, 2017), 128.
13. Sarah Emsley, "The Tragic Action of *Mansfield Park*," in *Approaches to Teaching Austen's "Mansfield Park*," ed. Marcia McClintock Folsom and John Wiltshire (New York: Modern Language Association, 2014), 170.
14. Emsley, "Tragic Action," 170.
15. See Elaine Bander, "Jane Austen's 'Artless' Heroines: Catherine Morland and Fanny Price," in this volume.
16. Edward W. Said, *Culture and Imperialism* (New York: Vintage, 1994), 55.
17. Susan Fraiman, "Jane Austen and Edward Said: Gender, Culture, and Imperialism," *Critical Inquiry* 21, no. 4 (1995): 808.
18. Vivasvan Soni, "A Critique of Aesthetic Judgment," preface to *Jane Austen and the Arts: Elegance, Propriety, and Harmony*, ed. Natasha Duquette and Elisabeth Lenckos (Bethlehem, PA: Lehigh University Press, 2013), xi.
19. Rajeswari Rajan, "Austen in the World: Postcolonial Mappings," in *The Postcolonial Jane Austen*, ed. You-Me Park and Rajeswari Sunder Rajan (New York: Routledge, 2000), 8.

20. Ana-Karina Schneider, "Mansfield Park," in *The Literary Encyclopedia*, www.litencyc.com, first published January 9, 2008.

21. Alexander Pope, "Argument" prefacing *Epistle 4. To Richard Boyle, Earl of Burlington*, in *The Broadview Anthology of British Literature: The Restoration and the Eighteenth Century*, ed. Joseph Black et al. (Peterborough, NH: Broadview, 2015), 597.

22. Pope, *Epistle 4. To Richard Boyle, Earl of Burlington*, line 43.

23. Pope, *Epistle 4. To Richard Boyle, Earl of Burlington*, line 45.

24. Pope, *Epistle 4. To Richard Boyle, Earl of Burlington*, line 50.

25. Pope, *Epistle 4. To Richard Boyle, Earl of Burlington*, lines 53–56.

26. Peter Sabor, "Portraiture as Misrepresentation in the Novels and Early Writings of Jane Austen," in this volume.

27. Mary Wollstonecraft, *Works*, ed. Janet Todd and Marilyn Butler (London: William Pickering and Chatto, 1989), 5:45.

28. Mary Wollstonecraft, *A Vindication of the Rights of Woman*, ed. Deirdre Shauna Lynch (New York: Norton, 2009), 48.

29. Wollstonecraft, *A Vindication of the Rights of Woman*, 48.

30. Wollstonecraft, *A Vindication of the Rights of Woman*, 60.

31. Mary Anne Schimmelpenninck, *Theory on the Classification of Beauty and Deformity* (London: John and Arthur Arch, 1815), 285.

32. Schimmelpenninck, *Theory on the Classification of Beauty and Deformity*, 244.

33. See the large, fold-out chart at the back of Schimmelpenninck's *Theory on the Classification of Beauty and Deformity*.

34. Schimmelpenninck, *Theory on the Classification of Beauty and Deformity*, 47.

35. Lennox Honychurch, *Negre Mawon: The Fighting Maroons of Dominica* (Dominica: Island Heritage Initiatives, 2014), 65.

36. Schimmelpenninck, *Theory on the Classification of Beauty and Deformity*, 47.

Religious Views
English Abbeys in Austen's *Northanger Abbey* and *Emma*

TONYA J. MOUTRAY

In the old schoolroom at Mansfield Park, an ideal haven for self-reflection and solitude, Fanny Price has set up "three transparencies . . . where Tintern Abbey held its station between a cave in Italy, and a moonlight lake in Cumberland."[1] Though the print of Tintern Abbey calls to mind the politico-religious trauma of the English Reformation and the dissolution of the monasteries in the sixteenth century, these sharp historical edges are neatly framed in Fanny's arrangement by picturesque images of the natural world at home and abroad. By the late eighteenth century, English abbeys, significant sites whose historical and physical integrity was at stake, were fundamental to the concept of the English "picturesque" as developed by the artist William Gilpin (1724–1804). Gilpin's travel writings reveal both his fascination with medieval religious ruins and his dismay at the structural and aesthetic violations that abbeys had endured at the hands of private owners. He considered them a feature of English landscape that must remain untouched in order to remain "natural." Recent criticism has positioned Austen's writings on medieval-era architecture within the changing and increasingly Catholic milieu of the Romantic period, or explored her use of Catholic architecture solely within a gothic framework. What has not been fully investigated are the ways that Gilpin's travel writings on monastic ruins provided Austen with an aesthetic and discursive model for her depictions of English abbeys in *Northanger Abbey* (1817) and *Emma* (1815).[2]

English abbeys in various stages of decay were the subject of a fraught debate when Austen composed and published her fictions. Gilpin's writings positioned abbey ruins as national sites of natural and aesthetic significance. However, rather than shoring them up to delay deterioration, his writings promoted the natural decay of ruins, seeing them as an extension of nature. Ruins' picturesque appeal impacted garden design, where they might create a visual tableau that reminded spectators of Britain's progress from the so-called Dark Ages to the Enlightenment. Lingering anti-Jacobite sentiment had inspired the installment of *faux* gothic ruins on some landowners' properties, signaling their political progressiveness. By the 1790s, preservationists decried "improvements" to medieval architecture and compared such tampering with the religious devastations and democratizing impulses of the French Revolution.[3]

English abbeys were a reminder of not only Penal-era religious displacements but also contemporary and foreign ones: In 1792 the anti-Catholic efforts of the new French government had resulted in the dismantling of its monasteries and convents; the closure of English convents in France and Belgium followed soon after. By 1809, nineteen houses of English nuns, as well as some French and Belgian religious, had migrated to Britain seeking safe asylum and settled across the country with little possibility of returning to the Continent.[4] Though Austen refers only once to "emigrants" (in *Sense and Sensibility*), leaving Catholic refugees and their place in Britain to be imagined, the abbey-turned-estate is a central trope in both *Northanger Abbey* and *Emma*. By emphasizing the preservation of former abbeys, and their significance to English picturesque landscape, Austen largely evades the stickiness of Catholic or Protestant polemic.

Austen's depictions of Northanger Abbey and Donwell Abbey are steeped in the tradition of the picturesque, though her treatments of these two abbeys point in different directions. In *Northanger Abbey*, Catherine's "gothic" experience at the Tilney estate is not merely a quixotic misreading of the environment but a reminder of past terrors and a harbinger of future fears. General Tilney's aggressive modernization of medieval space has nearly emptied the estate of its Catholic features and history. The narrator's satiric tone, which persists through the novel's "happy ending," in which Catherine succumbs to Henry Tilney's rational authority, can be read ironically, validating Catherine's earlier intuition that the Tilney household is one of dark secrets. The novel's generic and structural ironies preclude a definitive answer to Henry's question to Catherine: "Could [atrocities] be perpetrated without being known, in a country like this . . where every man is surrounded by a neighbourhood of voluntary spies, and where roads and newspapers lay every thing open?" (*NA*, 203).

In contrast, Donwell Abbey's story is not one of monastic hauntings or untold crimes but of structural and aesthetic integrity. In sync with its natural environment, the Donwell estate is described through Emma's consciousness as "English verdure, English culture, English comfort, seen under a sun bright, without being oppressive" (*E*, 391). The fictional Donwell remains isolated from contemporary politics or the Catholic refugee migration, which were very real phenomena during Austen's lifetime. This past and present Catholic context is left outside of the frame of this novel altogether. To better understand the ways in which Austen's images of abbeys took their cue from Gilpin and elided significant Catholic content, it is important to review the emergence of the picturesque as an aesthetic concept and to flesh out Gilpin's treatment of English abbeys in his travel writings.

William Gilpin and Monastic Ruins: Man versus Nature

In Henry Austen's 1817 "Biographical Notice," which prefaces *Northanger Abbey*, we are told that "[Austen] was a warm and judicious admirer of landscape, both in nature and on canvas. At a very early age she was enamoured of Gilpin on the Picturesque; and she seldom changed her opinions either on books or men."[5] Austen frequently integrates Gilpin's methods and theories of the picturesque into her novels. *Sense and Sensibility* (1811), likely the earliest of her fictions to be drafted, is replete with Gilpinesque descriptions of landscapes, such as Edward Ferrars's satiric references to picturesque principles. *Pride and Prejudice* (1813) contains perhaps the most well-known picturesque description in Austen's oeuvre: the view of Pemberley as seen through Lizzie's eyes.[6] Before looking more closely at Gilpin's ideas about monastic ruins, it is important to clarify the concept of the picturesque as he defined it, as it animates Austen's writings.

The term "picturesque," developed by the art theorists William Gilpin, Richard Payne Knight, and Uvedale Price, extended Edmund Burke's binary categories of the sublime and the beautiful, as outlined in his *Philosophical Inquiry into the Origins of Our Ideas of the Beautiful and the Sublime* (1757). Burke's two categories—beautiful and sublime—contrast in many ways, including the run of the line, texture, size and proportion, mood, and symmetry. While beautiful views showcased even lines, smoothness, smallness, symmetry, and pleasing arrangement, sublime prospects contained irregularity, roughness, largeness, and a mix of chaotic elements in nature and architecture. Though there are variations in terminology and definitions among art theorists, Gilpin's picturesque combined "various" and "contrary" elements, some beautiful, some sublime.[7] Gilpin pointed to roughness or ruggedness as a primary feature of the picturesque line, distinct from the smooth lines of the beautiful. In addition, landscapes could not be picturesque without a proper prospect or view from which the artist might assess the effect of contrasting lights and shadows, and the position of the structural elements themselves. In an early definition, Gilpin described the picturesque as "uniting in one whole a variety of parts" and producing "that peculiar kind of beauty, which is agreeable in a picture."[8]

Gilpin considered ruins from the medieval period, including towers, castles, and abbeys, to be the most picturesque artifacts in England, though scholars have not fully appreciated this fascination with abbeys.[9] "These are the richest legacies of art. They are consecrated by time; and almost deserve the veneration we pay to the works of nature itself," he wrote in 1792.[10] In his 1772 tour of Cumberland and Westmoreland, Gilpin describes the deteriorating situation of English abbeys in late eighteenth-century Britain: "Abbeys formerly abounded so much in England, that a delicious valley could scarcely be found, in which one of them was not stationed. The very sites of many of these ancient edifices are now obliterated by the plough; yet still so many elegant ruins of this kind are left; that they may be called, not only one of the peculiar features of the English landscape; but may be ranked also among one of its most picturesque beauties."[11] Austen's playful remark in "The History of England" (1791) that Henry VIII's dissolution of monasteries has been of "infinite use to the landscape of England in general" echoes this passage from Gilpin.[12] Gilpin toured multiple monastic ruins across England and Wales, including Fountains Abbey, Lewes Priory, Battle Abbey, Tintern Abbey, Forde Abbey, Netley Abbey, and the monastery at Glastonbury. In *Observations on the River Wye, and Several Parts of South Wales, &c. Relative Chiefly to Picturesque Beauty; Made in the Summer of the Year 1770* (1882), Gilpin relates that his contemporaries painted and drew abbeys and other medieval-era ruins to give "consequence to the scene."[13] In fact, the picturesque provided artists with a means of integrating Catholic architecture into a national landscape, while, as Dale Townshend puts it, "consigning history to a place beyond or outside of the frame, with the ruin itself becoming as a broken architectural form emptied of all historical content."[14]

Three central themes emerge in Gilpin's musings on religious ruins. The first is the negative impact of improvements upon the ruins' aesthetic appeal, structural integrity, and historical accuracy. As he asserts in his discussion of Lewes Priory in East Sussex, "Whenever we see a ruin in the hands of improvement, we may be almost sure of seeing it deformed."[15] Secondly, abbeys, Gilpin elsewhere muses, "being naturalized to the soil, might indeed, without much impropriety, be classed among its natural beauties." In contrast to contemporary foreign monasteries, which are "less adapted to landscape" due to their ongoing "popery," English abbeys have metamorphosed into nature itself.[16] The safety of a ruin reformed by time and integrated into nature allows Gilpin to express sentimentality about a Catholic England where monasticism flourished.[17] His artistic methods reform Catholic ruins further: his 1782 aquatints of Tintern Abbey, seen in figures 15 and 16, minimize specific gothic features and reduce the scale of the abbey itself; through this sleight of hand, the images reinforce a focus on the English picturesque rather than medieval Catholicism. Finally, though he decries improvements to abbeys, Gilpin imagines physically manipulating the ruins of Tintern Abbey to further their picturesque appeal, even as he affirms the sacrilege of such an act.[18] His views are, at times, contradictory.

So-called improvements to abbey ruins—one of the central issues at stake in Austen's *Northanger Abbey*—are a key concern in Gilpin's travel writings. For example, during his 1770 tour of Cumberland and Westmoreland, Gilpin lamented the improvements introduced by William Aislabie, who had purchased Fountains Abbey in 1768 to serve as an extended formal garden to Studley Royal, Aislabie's adjacent estate. A cleared prospect from Studley Royal to the ruins of Fountains, and a manufactured hilly prospect for viewing them, work that was completed by the architect Colen Campbell, was trendsetting among estate owners and political in purpose. As Sarah Thompson explains, Fountains Abbey, a "symbol of the power of Catholicism[,] was transformed into a garden curiosity."[19] Gilpin disliked Aislabie's approach: "Busy hands were let loose upon it," he exclaims, employing a trope of physical violence by a male hand that Gilpin frequently uses. Gilpin's ire is also directed at the owner's determination to restore fallen fragments to their original places (creating an "awkward patchwork") and to "decorate" and "ornament" the space—two anathemas for Gilpin—in newfangled ways: the former monk's garden has been converted to a "trim *parterre*" with flowering shrubs, statues of Anne Boleyn, and classical, "heathen" figures. These "monstrous absurdities" interrupt the ruin's natural progression toward decay: "How unnatural, in a place, evidently forlorn and deserted by man, are the *recent* marks of human industry!—Besides, every sentiment, which the scene suggests, is destroyed. Instead of that soothing melancholy, on which the mind feeds in contemplating the ruins of time; a sort of jargon is excited by these heterogeneous mixtures."[20] The combining of new and old, past and present, is reduced to a speaking and writing error ("jargon"), suggesting that anachronistic and supposedly restorative improvements denigrate the worth or quality of the ruin's aesthetic appeal, which is itself dependent upon chronological accuracy. Gilpin expresses similar views when touring Forde Abbey, where "old parts and new are blended together, to the mutual disgrace of both"—the cloister had become

Fig. 15. William Gilpin, *Tintern Abbey I*, from *Observations on the River Wye* (London, 1782), aquatint. (HathiTrust)

a greenhouse, and "Indian paper" was now on gothic walls.[21] Battle Abbey, which Gilpin visited in 1774, is "all transposition," a fully modernized residence, like Austen's Northanger Abbey. Likewise, at Lewes Priory in East Sussex, Gilpin exclaims that "some busy hand" has attempted to decorate the space.[22]

Vulnerable to the machinations of human self-interest, monastic structures were subject to seismic shifts in identity and ownership (Catholic vs. Protestant, private vs. public, man-made vs. natural). Gilpin concludes his musings on Fountains Abbey by figuring monastic ruins as nature itself: "A Ruin is a sacred thing. Rooted for ages in the soil; assimilated to it; and become, as it were, a part of it; we consider it as a work of nature, rather than of art."[23] Ultimately, the ruin is sacralized by means of its ecological value rather than its religious history, foregrounding the significance of the structure to English landscape. As David S. Miall explains, though Gilpin's "aesthetic was unstable," his interest in "ecologic integrity" positions him as a proto-environmentalist and a forerunner of the Romantic movement.[24]

The epitome of the abbey-turned-nature was at Tintern, and the three sequential views as he moves from outside of the ruin to its close-up interiors, which Gilpin describes from his tour in 1770, reveal the colonization of the ruin by plant life: "Nature has now made it her own."[25] Gilpin's watercolors of Tintern Abbey position it next to the Wye River, but they give no indication of the kind of natural invasion that he describes in his prose, where ivy

Religious Views

Fig. 16. William Gilpin, *Tintern Abbey II*, from *Observations on the River Wye* (London, 1782), watercolor and graphite. (HathiTrust)

is the ruin's "ornament," and lichen and moss are its "decoration," a reversal in which nature, rather than art, enhances the picturesque appeal of the structure. J. M. W. Turner's oil paintings of Tintern Abbey capture the extent to which the natural world had taken over the structure by the end of the eighteenth century.[26] Alive with nature, the abbey is a palimpsest, containing the traces of previous time periods. Here, as seen in figure 17, the confines of the ruin create a unique ecosystem—a kind of terrarium—fertile and vital—providing an ironic contrast with the celibate historical brotherhood that once inhabited the spot.

English abbeys were not only popular tourist destinations but also ample fodder for poetic and artistic renderings in the eighteenth century. The "abbey meditation poem" proliferated in the eighteenth century, originating out of a tradition of nostalgia for monasticism in Britain, the loss of monasticism's social values in society, and the beauty of its gothic architecture. Set during moonlight hours, evoking cloistered ghosts and secreted stories, these poems repeat anti-Catholic propagandist polemic and are often pervaded by a deep skepticism regarding the monastic houses' dissolution and subsequent transfer into secular hands.[27] Such poems naturalize and preserve Catholic monastic legacies, even as writers clarify their own Protestant allegiances. Gilpin identifies the sacrilegious nature of improving sacred space: "What reverence then is due to these sacred relics; which the

Fig. 17. J. M. W. Turner, *Tintern Abbey: The Crossing and Chancel, Looking towards the East Window*, ca. 1794, watercolor and graphite. (Tate Gallery, London)

rough hand of temerity, and caprice dare mangle without remorse?"[28] The ruin's fate—now as uncertain as the character of any potential proprietor—is at stake.

Alison Shell and Roger E. Moore trace this sacrilege motif throughout eighteenth-century writings on English sacred architecture, and they identify its origins in post-Reformation fears of divine repercussion for tampering with monastic structures.[29] Gilpin's visit to Leicester Abbey evokes just such anxiety: "Many a black tale might be unfolded in old houses, if walls could speak." Lost by one family to another through gaming, Leicester Abbey was then burned to prevent the transfer of the title to the new owner. Fountains Abbey's demise also began when it "fell into the hands" of the current owner.[30] In Hampshire, Netley Abbey's dilapidated state speaks to a history of sacrilege: "More of this roof might still have remained if the warnings of Heaven . . had taken effect."[31] Formerly housing a Cistercian community founded in 1239 by Henry III, Netley Abbey had been dissolved in 1536 and was conferred upon Sir William Paulet, who began a series of large-scale renovations to the space (including the demolition of the cloister walk, the south gate, and the refectory) to serve his ambitions as a politician. The estate had undergone various structural degradations by its secular owners until 1704, when the then present owner, Sir Berkeley Lucy, decided that there was more value in selling off what was left. Bad luck followed bad bargains: Lucy's contractor Walter Taylor was hired to dismantle the site but was killed when a section of the west window tracery fell on his head. It is said that Taylor had been warned in dreams to halt any further construction by a ghostly monkish figure. A pile of stones was popularly thought to have been the location of Taylor's death.[32]

Like Tintern and Fountains Abbeys, Netley attracted many eighteenth-century tourists and artists to its grounds, including Austen. It contributed both to increased domestic tourism of gothic architecture and to the national project of integrating medieval-era ruins into a Protestant narrative of historical and natural causation.[33] Alexander Pope visited in 1732 before perhaps the most flagrant act of sacrilege to the structure occurred: in 1760 Thomas Dummer moved the north transept to decorate his own estate, Cranbury Park, located near Winchester. Thomas Gray, who toured Netley in 1764, was highly entranced by the ruin and its haunted history.[34] Other tales, one of a trapped nun, were also associated with the site, perhaps inspiring Austen's inclusion of this motif in *Northanger Abbey*. Artists and engravers provided a visual history captured on canvas or paper of Netley's many changes. Even darker renditions than the tourist-by-night theme emerged in the nineteenth century, such as John Constable's oil painting of Netley (1833), which closed off the Abbey's interiors completely, as seen in figure 18. When the Austen family visited Netley in 1807, niece Fanny described the group's reaction: "[We] were struck dumb with admiration" at the abbey's "sublimity."[35] Though transformed into a public tourist site that Austen likely visited more than once, Netley Abbey showcased the impacts of massive renovations and structural loss. It is no wonder that it has been identified as a likely inspiration for Northanger Abbey.

A "Monstrous Absurdity": Northanger Abbey and Catholic Revelations

Netley Abbey, medieval architecture in Bath, as well as Farleigh Hungerford Castle and Hinton Priory in Somersetshire, are possible models for Austen's Northanger Abbey. That Austen was familiar with these sites has been established.[36] Catherine Morland, through whose consciousness the narrative is focalized, questions the historical erasure that Northanger Abbey has undergone by means of General Tilney and his ancestors. Reduced to its gothic

Fig. 18. John Constable, *Netley Abbey by Moonlight,* ca. 1833, watercolor and graphite on paper. (Tate Gallery, London)

facade, the abbey evokes a forgotten history, yet its exterior does not lead to deeper meanings or further knowledge. The past is cut off, a source of speculation, a story left untold. The abbey's dissolution under the reign of Henry VIII is an unalterable fact, as is the dispossession of English Catholic nuns during the Reformation whom Catherine imagines haunting its halls. As Terry F. Robinson concludes, the novel "documents the ideological tension inherent in a country with a Roman Catholic past and a Protestant-centered present, but moreover, it attests to the violence of such an ideological transition—a blatant *divorce* from or even *death* of the past in order to form a new future."[37]

While General Tilney displays no interest in the site's historical and religious foundations, Catherine is eager to explore just those elements. Before she has even arrived at Northanger, Catherine is told by Eleanor Tilney of "Northanger Abbey having been a richly-endowed convent at the time of the Reformation, of its having fallen into the hands of an ancestor of the Tilneys on its dissolution, of a large portion of the ancient building still making a part of the present dwelling although the rest was decayed" (*NA*, 144). As we know from Gilpin, an abbey that has "fallen into the hands" of an owner is usually a way to foreshadow that abbey's desecration. In fact, Northanger

Abbey has not retained its historical specificity—it is one of Gilpin's "monstrous absurdities" or "heterogeneous mixtures"—and Catherine's disappointed observations inside the estate read as Gilpinesque critique of improvements, where the abbey's post-Reformation fate is inextricably tied to private owners and their "vicious mode of reforming a ruin."[38]

Renovations inside Northanger Abbey include furniture of "modern taste," a Rumford fireplace with "plain though handsome marble, and ornaments over it of the prettiest English china," as well as stained glass replaced by clear window panes (NA, 165). Only the "ancient kitchen of the convent, rich in the massy walls and smoke of former days," has not suffered the "General's improving hand." Catherine also discovers a final and extensive violation to the actual structure of the building, something that preservationists would have railed against: "the fourth side of the quadrangle having, on account of its decaying state, been removed by the General's father.... All that was venerable ceased here.... Catherine could have raved at the hand which had swept away what must have been beyond the value of the rest" (188–89). Austen employs the trope of manual violation (typical of Gilpin), which has "swept away" the fourth side of the ancient quadrangle. The loss of this wall is analogous to the Tilney family's suppression of their own history. As Robinson asserts, Catherine wishes to recover Mrs. Tilney's story, and in so doing, identifies with revisionist historians of women's lives in her rebuke of "solemn history," in which "hardly any women at all" are documented (109, 110).[39] Though she notes the cloistral wall's "decaying state," she reflects that had it been left to nature, it would have been "beyond the value of all the rest" (189). The historical and structural integrity of the abbey is more important to Catherine than its contemporary utility, just as the recovery of the Tilney's family history is valued over more practical ends, such as seeking General Tilney's approval as a match for his son.

One of the problems with the abbey and with the Tilneys is that both point toward histories that cannot be retrieved. Another is that upon first approach Northanger Abbey fails to live up to Catherine's expectations of what a gothic building should look like: "She was actually under the abbey walls ... without feeling one awful foreboding of future misery to herself or one moment's suspicion of any past scenes of horror being acted within the solemn edifice" (NA, 165). That the abbey presents itself so inauspiciously from this vantage point frustrates the young Catherine, who desires gothic danger. However, Northanger Abbey's prospect appears in "grandeur" to Catherine upon a second viewing from the lawn during her tour of the abbey with General Tilney the following day. From this perspective,

Catherine perceives that the abbey is "rich in Gothic ornaments" which evoke "feelings of delight . . . so strong . . . she boldly burst forth in wonder and praise" (182). From this vantage point, there is a view of the past as seen in "Gothic ornaments"; from anywhere else, this view is completely occluded. Northanger Abbey is itself subject to the various views imposed upon it by the characters. Whereas General Tilney prides himself on his pragmatic re-visioning of the space, Catherine searches for evidence of its medieval inhabitants, using the genre of the gothic to determine the extent of the abbey's aesthetic appeal.

Catherine's willful imposition of a gothic horror novel upon the renovated Northanger Abbey reveals her quixotism and suggests we read the novel as pure satire. However, it is important to consider differing functions of the gothic genre in *Northanger Abbey*. Recent scholarship interrogates Austen's (or Catherine's) use of the gothic genre in the novel as a means of exposing something real about the Tilneys rather than something silly about Catherine. For example, Mary Spongberg argues that the gothic mode provides Catherine with a template for understanding her future position as another Mrs. Tilney: "Catherine is not manipulated by her reading of Gothic novels. She is validated by it. Her instincts about the General, honed first through her reading of fiction, and then through bitter experience, are retrospectively vindicated."[40] In addition, Catherine's rude expulsion from Northanger Abbey by means of General Tilney can function symbolically to reenact the removal of Catholic nuns from their abbeys during the English Reformation and the French Revolution. Once a center of hospitality, the Catholic abbey-turned-estate obliterated its own monastic history, and with it its civilizing values, as Moore argues. In this sense, once Catherine marries Henry, she "may finally be entering upon the Gothic drama she has sought throughout the novel." Or as Beatrice Battaglia states broadly of Austen's fiction, "If landscape is replaced by social setting, then Austen's novels will appear as 'economic romances' and the domestic Gothic will become visible in all its threatening reality."[41]

Austen's choice to imbue Catherine with a gothic sensibility does not clarify either the author's or the character's religious or political allegiances. As Diane Long Hoeveler argues, the well-used gothic trope of the medieval monastery was not purely anti-Catholic. The trope "could represent the seductive nostalgia of living in a pre-Reformation England while also expressing the ambivalent heritage of modernity." The gothic genre both contains and isolates Catholic residue while giving readers permission to access their Catholic fetishes. Through a process of hybridization, the Catholic elements in gothic writing may even become naturalized or domesticated.[42] Beth Kowaleski Wallace questions which gothic mode Austen is utilizing and which nun Catherine is looking for—the stock gothic figure of the female victim of the pre-Reformation religious orders or a protofeminist whose sisterhood has been dissolved? As Wallace asserts, "The nun whose ghost [Catherine] imagines would have been the victim of less melodramatic but nonetheless very real political forces."[43] However much Catherine's quest is rooted in the past, it is significant that by 1798, the year it is supposed that Austen began *Northanger Abbey*, the very real political forces of the French Revolution had been actively determining the fates of very real nuns across the Continent and Britain for nearly a decade. If she keeps looking, Catherine might just find a refugee nun seeking political asylum in one of England's many country estates. To further put into focus the ways that Austen's fictions smooth over Catholic content, it is important to clarify the ways in which Catholic refugees had changed the landscape of Britain's social and political milieu by the early nineteenth century.

Jane Austen and Catholic Refugees in Britain

We must assume that Austen, like her contemporaries, was aware of and involved in political and religious matters.[44] Austen was fifteen when the Catholic Relief Act of 1791 was passed. In 1793, while she was still at Steventon Rectory, there was a national campaign sponsored by Anglican parishes and dissenting churches to assist refugee priests, which resulted in contributions totaling around seventy thousand pounds. French priests began arriving in Britain after the September Massacres of 1792, and an estimated 1,500 of them lived in London alone; by 1800, more than five thousand priests resided in England, some four thousand of them receiving government aid.[45] Austen's contemporary Frances Burney galvanized women to donate to the cause of émigré priests in her *Brief Reflections Relative to the Emigrant French Clergy* (1793). In a letter to her father, Burney wrote in October 1792 that "it was impossible to be under the roof of an English clergyman . . without continual internal reference to the miserable contrast of the unhappy clergy of France."[46] Besides émigré priests, refugee nuns also arrived, including nineteen communities of English nuns who had been living on the Continent. Remarkably, then, when Austen writes about abbeys, it is as if she were writing in the 1770s or 1780s alongside Gilpin, not after the refugee migrations of the 1790s, and the tumultuous years of the Revolutionary Wars that followed. If Austen refers to pre-Reformation nuns in *Northanger Abbey*, she does not depict contemporary ones as did Hester Thrale Piozzi and Ann Radcliffe, who encountered them on their travels.[47] Indeed, there is a disconnect between Austen's fictions and the crisis of the Catholic refugee migration and eventual settlement of nuns in England.

How might Austen have encountered such figures? As the most visible refugee group in the 1790s, some exiled French clergy remained in Bath while Austen lived there in the early 1800s. Close to Chawton village where Austen, her sister, and mother relocated in 1805, Winchester also shared a rich history in the refugee influx. The King's House (one of the royal palaces) was repurposed in 1792 and 1793 to accommodate French emigrant priests, as many as a thousand at once, though both local concerns that the emigrants were proselytizing and the strategic need to use the King's House as a royal barracks led to the priests' gradual dispersal between 1796 and 1798.[48] Beyond priests, two houses of English nuns from Brussels (one Benedictine, the other Franciscan) sought refuge there by 1794. Discussed as they were in newspapers and popular literature, religious refugees would have been a visible reality to Austen, though her regional isolation, particularly while in Steventon and Chawton, neither provided much direct contact with these populations nor offered access to their communities. In fact, Catholic groups intentionally isolated themselves as a means of survival in a Protestant country: they were caught in the catch-22 of both performing their Catholicism to please a variety of curious patrons and disguising their religion in order to assimilate better into British society.[49] The two Catholic Relief Acts of 1788 and 1791 lifted nearly every restriction on Catholics, yet the religious orders remained subject to sixteenth-century penal codes, and religious were not officially allowed to found convents, recruit novices, or even wear their religious dress.[50]

Nevertheless, the influx of refugee religious during the French Revolution served as a reminder of the survival of English monasticism. Most communities of refugee nuns had arrived by 1795, though several more had arrived by 1809.[51] Assisted by elite Catholic families, refugee nuns settled in leased or borrowed homes located both within and outside of towns and villages, at times even occupying former religious structures. For example, the English Franciscans from Brussels stayed at Abbey House in Winchester, the former site of Nunnaminster, a well-known Benedictine community for women in the medieval period. Likewise, the English Benedictines of Dunkirk settled at the Hammersmith Convent in west London, which had been founded by Mary Ward in the seventeenth century as the Institute of the Blessed Virgin Mary and had coexisted as a secret Catholic girls' school until the 1790s.[52]

Depending upon the degree of local anti-Catholic sentiment or pro-Catholic support, local community members kept a close eye on families of nuns, patronizing them through philanthropy, attending or viewing their services, or purchasing their handiwork. Most nuns supported themselves through opening schools for Catholic children; some also turned to needlework to earn extra money, creating purses, bookmarks, and needle-books.[53]

Nuns and priests were also under the surveillance of local Anglican clergy and parish members concerned that the spread of Catholicism was imminent. In this respect, Henry Tilney's assertions about rural English nosiness could be said to have real implications for migrating religious groups. For example, local rumors of nuns' recruitment of novices in Winchester brought all nuns in Britain into the spotlight in 1800 with the proposal of the Monastic Institutions Bill by the House of Commons. The bill sought to limit the proliferation and legal rights of Catholic nuns in Britain.[54] The debates encompassed discussions of the differing positions of "foreign" versus "native" refugee nuns in Britain, and their recruitment of novices to increase their numbers. The bill did not pass, in part because of political opposition but also because there persisted an idea that refugee nuns were elderly, harmless gentlewomen, recovering from the trauma suffered at the hands of the French revolutionaries.[55]

The interplay between what Wallace terms the "ambient noise" of Catholicism during Austen's lifetime and its direct representation in her fiction is subtle indeed. Austen mentions refugees in *Sense and Sensibility* when Mrs. John Dashwood gives each of the Steele sisters a "needle-book" made by "some emigrant" (288). The ruined "Abbeyland" that Elinor and Marianne frequent, or the Northanger Abbey and Donwell Abbey estates, provide some avenues to explore Austen's monastic views further. Because Austen neither populated her imagined English abbeys with nuns or priests seeking safe asylum from the horrors of the Revolution nor provided indications of the social or political responses to refugee religious in her fiction, we must turn yet again to aesthetics to understand her views of abbeys.

A Fictional Tintern? Donwell Abbey and Catholic Erasures

In *Northanger Abbey*, General Tilney's "improving hand" has obliterated the structure's Catholic origins, signaling a violation of former sacred space and revealing a tyrannical side to the otherwise gregarious host. In *Emma*, the narrative's silence about Donwell Abbey's pre-Reformation history whitewashes any negative elements of its sixteenth-century dissolution and shifts the reader's perspective into the present. Although it is the epitome of picturesque description, the Donwell Abbey episode does not occur until the third volume, perhaps a device that mirrors the heroine's delayed realization that Robert Martin is a natural choice for Harriet Smith and that Mr. Knightley is just such a choice for Emma herself. In fact, a second Woodhouse-Knightley marriage all but ensures that the "notch" from Donwell—Hartfield Hall—will soon be owned again by the same family, and hence medieval-era estates will be restored under one owner (*E*, 147).[56]

Unlike Catherine, who is disappointed that Northanger Abbey does not scream medieval Catholicism, Emma is highly satisfied with her view of Donwell Abbey:

> She felt all the honest pride and complacency which her alliance with the present and future proprietor could fairly warrant, as she viewed the respectable size and style of the building, its suitable, becoming characteristic situation, low and sheltered—its ample gardens stretching down to meadows washed by a stream, of which the Abbey, with all the old neglect of prospect, had scarcely a sight—and its abundance of timber in rows and avenues, which neither fashion nor extravagance had rooted up.—The house was larger than Hartfield, and totally unlike it, covering a good deal of ground, rambling and irregular, with many comfortable and one or two handsome rooms.—It was just what it ought to be, and it looked like what it was. (*E*, 388–89)

Donwell, then, looks like an abbey, something that Northanger Abbey has lost, and connects back to the theme of trusting appearances with which Emma contends in her relationships with Frank Churchill, Jane Fairfax, and Mr. Elton. In terms of the abbey, the question here is understanding what Emma thinks abbeys "ought to be": her depiction does not indicate the extent to which the abbey's pre-Reformation details have been preserved, nor does it outline the various components of the former monastic building (chapel, dormitories, refectory, and so forth). Unlike Catherine Morland, who surveyed Northanger Abbey as a tourist of gothic architecture, Emma views Donwell as family property, which functions on both aesthetic and practical levels. The abbey-turned-estate has undergone minimal renovations necessary to the comfort of the family and has not suffered any structural changes. What Emma points to is the way that the abbey exists in picturesque accordance with the landscape, significantly noting that its structure, as well as the woods that surround it, have been left intact. Emma eschews gothic conventions of medieval interiors haunted by ghostly monks

Religious Views

and nuns and views the estate through Gilpin's eyes, assigning an aesthetic value to Donwell that points to similar descriptive protocols employed by Gilpin in his treatment of Tintern Abbey, both in terms of narrative details and artistic methods. Both Austen and Gilpin exclude any disruptive historical content from their images of the abbeys, suggesting that they can be seen anew without reference to contemporary politics.

Gilpin toured Tintern Abbey in 1770, and his playfully simplistic watercolors of the site revamped how viewers saw the ruin; his descriptive prose reframed ruins as natural sites whose Catholic past poses no threat. Gilpin's 1782 aquatints of the abbey, almost entirely mute the Catholic features of the building, domesticating the otherness of Catholicism, as is demonstrated in figures 15 and 16. Most fascinating is the fact that in the 1800 edition of his *Observations on the River Wye*, the Catholic exterior becomes even less visible, and the building loses even more of its medieval specificity as seen in figures 19 and 20. As Paul Smethurst discusses, the picturesque presupposes an "unmediated way of seeing nature," yet its imposition of limits and frames, and avoidance of disruptive political content, "reproduce[s] the power structure whereby one class . . assert[s] their authority on the landscape."[57]

If Gilpin's aquatints provide a progressively muted sense of Tintern Abbey's (or England's) Catholic origins, his narrative description of the site in *Observations on the River Wye* outlines a picturesque framework that shares much in common with Emma's view of Donwell Abbey:

> The abbey, intended for meditation, is hid in the sequestered vale. . Such is the situation of *Tintern-abbey*. It occupies a gentle eminence in the middle of a circular valley, beautifully screened on all sides by woody hills, through which the river winds its course; and the hills . . leave no room for inclement blasts to enter. A more pleasing retreat could not easily be found. The woods and glades intermixed; the winding of the river; the variety of the ground; the splendid ruin, contrasted with the objects of nature; and the elegant line formed by the summits of the hills, which include the whole, make all together a very enchanting piece of scenery.[58]

Like Donwell Abbey, Tintern is what it looks like and what it ought to be. It has not been "improved" and conforms to picturesque principles. Both the real Tintern Abbey and the fictional Donwell Abbey are positioned in the middle of a valley, next to a river, surrounded by hills, and with ample woods that provide protection for the structure. It may be coincidence that from Tintern the River Wye cannot be viewed (according to Gilpin), and

Fig. 19. William Gilpin, *Tintern Abbey I*, from *Observations on the River Wye* (London, 1800), aquatint. (HathiTrust)

from the river next to Donwell Abbey the abbey is out of sight (according to Emma/Austen).

Austen's homage to Gilpin continues after Emma joins the rest of the party to view the adjacent properties and landscapes. The group, headed by the indomitable Mrs. Elton, takes a walking path that terminates at two *faux* Palladian pillars. The narrator comments on the "Disputable" taste of such follies, in line with Gilpin's repugnance for anachronistic landscape effects. Yet, "the view which closed it [was] extremely pretty" (*E*, 391):

> The considerable slope, at nearly the foot of which the Abbey stood, gradually acquired a steeper form beyond its grounds; and at half a mile distant was a bank of considerable abruptness and grandeur, well clothed with wood;—and at the bottom of this bank, favourably placed and sheltered, rose the Abbey-Mill Farm, with meadows in front, and the river making a close and handsome curve around it.
>
> It was a sweet view—sweet to the eye and the mind. English verdure, English culture, English comfort, seen under a sun bright, without being oppressive. (391)

This scene of Abbey-Mill Farm integrates similar elements found in Gilpin's description of the picturesque Tintern Abbey (its shielded position in a valley, protection by woods, and "enchanting scenery"). The picturesque

Fig. 20. William Gilpin, *Tintern Abbey II*, from *Observations on the River Wye* (London, 1800), aquatint. (HathiTrust)

scene also makes possible Emma's "corrected perception" of Robert Martin as a suitable partner for Harriet.[59] The scene functions to refigure supposed danger into nature itself. This notion also extends into the conservative social paradigm that the novel foregrounds. As Wallace argues, "in this neo-feudal fantasy *noblesse oblige* 'naturally' prevails." Or, as Moore phrases it, the "social and economic functions of the old monastery continue to be 'done well.'"[60] Critics have argued that the final lines of the scene, "English verdure, English culture, English comfort," align landscape with "national feeling."[61] If this is the case, then Austen's—or Emma's—"national feeling" is also connected to a preservationist ethos in which medieval architecture performs a significant aesthetic and emergent nationalist function for tourists, estate owners, and artists. This focus emphasizes "continuity and tradition,"[62] while also obscuring from view English abbeys' connections to refugee Catholics or English Catholic histories.

Though she integrated English abbeys into her fiction, Austen did not engage more fully in the contemporary questions regarding Catholic refugees, such as where they would settle, how they would survive, or how villages like the fictional Highbury might integrate actual emigrating or returning religious into the social and economic fabric of English country life. *Northanger Abbey* interrogates the negative historical and artistic impacts of altering religious structures for the sake of utility, a position that aligns Catherine as a political conservative in response to the General's radical refashionings. Catherine's questions point back in time to the dismantling of religious institutions in the sixteenth century, though the past remains inaccessible and outside of the narrative's frame. Like Gilpin's images of Tintern Abbey, which soften harsh gothic details and make even a ruined abbey look comforting, Donwell Abbey naturalizes Catholic otherness through its overt aesthetic alignment with the picturesque. Though both reader and Austen know that Donwell Abbey does not really represent the "real England" that Emma projects,[63] its depiction conforms to picturesque protocols that reify a homogeneous view of a rural England far away from the political turmoil that had changed the religious landscape of the country in both the sixteenth century and in Austen's lifetime.

Notes

1. Jane Austen, *Mansfield Park*, ed. John Wiltshire (Cambridge: Cambridge University Press, 2013), 178–79. All subsequent references are to this edition and will be provided parenthetically in the text.

2. Jane Austen, *Emma*, ed. Richard Cronin and Dorothy McMillan (Cambridge: Cambridge University Press, 2005); Austen, *Northanger Abbey*, ed. Barbara M. Benedict and Deirdre Le Faye (Cambridge: Cambridge University Press, 2006). Subsequent references are to these editions and will be provided parenthetically within the text. For Austen and abbeys, see Roger E. Moore, *Jane Austen and the Reformation: Remembering the Sacred Landscape* (Farnham, UK: Ashgate, 2016); Natasha Duquette, "'The Grandeur of the Abbey': Exploring Gothic Architecture in Novels by Helen Maria Williams, Ann Radcliffe, and Jane Austen," *Persuasions: The Jane Austen Journal Online* 31, no. 1 (2010); Mary Spongberg, "History, Fiction, and Anachronism: Northanger Abbey, the Tudor 'Past' and the 'Gothic' Present," *Textual Practice* 26, no. 4 (2012): 631–48; and Beth Kowaleski Wallace, "'Penance and Mortification For ever': Jane Austen and the Ambient Noise of Catholicism," *Tulsa Studies in Women's Literature* 31, nos. 1/2 (2012): 159–80.

3. For more on garden design and the role of ruins, see Sarah Thompson, "Recycling Ruins: The Critical Reception of John Aislabie's Work at Fountains Abbey and the Changing Function of the Gothic," *Third Text* 25, no. 6 (November 2011): 675–86. For the political implications of gothic sham ruins, see David Stewart, "Political Ruins: Gothic Sham Ruins and the '45," *Journal of the Society of Architectural Historians* 55, no. 4 (1996): 400–411. For preservationists' response to improvements, see Dale Townshend, "Improvement and Repair: Architecture, Romance, and the Politics of the Gothic," *Literature Compass* 8, no. 10 (2011): 712–38.

4. Carmen M. Mangion, *Contested Identities: Catholic Women Religious in Nineteenth-Century England and Wales* (New York: Manchester University Press, 2008), 35.

Religious Views

5. Henry Austen, "Biographical Notice of the Author," in *The Novels of Jane Austen*, ed. R. W. Chapman, 3rd ed. (Oxford: Oxford University Press, 1934–1966), 5:7.

6. For discussions of Austen's use of the picturesque, see Alice Davenport, "An Adaptable Aesthetic: Eighteenth-Century Landscape, Ann Radcliffe, and Jane Austen," in *Jane Austen and the Arts: Elegance, Propriety, and Harmony*, ed. Natasha Duquette and Elisabeth Lenckos (Bethlehem, PA: Lehigh University Press, 2014), 105–6; Rosemarie Bodenheimer, "Looking at the Landscape in Jane Austen," *Studies in English Literature 1500–1900* 21 (1981): 607–9. Duquette and Lenckos tackle the scholarly heritage of equating Pemberley and Donwell Abbey to the value or worth of the owner. See their introduction to *Jane Austen and the Arts*, xxxv. For a discussion of Henry Tilney's lecture on the picturesque, see Terry F. Robinson, "'A Mere Skeleton of History': Reading Relics in Jane Austen's *Northanger Abbey*," *European Romantic Review* 17, no. 2 (2006): 220.

7. For further discussion of these variations and the distinctions made by Price, Uvedale, and Gilpin, see Davenport, "Adaptable Aesthetic," 99–101.

8. William Gilpin, *Three Essays: "On Picturesque Beauty," "On Picturesque Travel," and "On Sketching Landscape": To Which Is Added a Poem, "On Landscape Painting"* (London, R. Blamire, 1794), 19; Gilpin, *An Essay on Prints*, 3rd ed. (London, G. Scott, 1781), xii.

9. For example, David S. Miall spends one paragraph referencing Gilpin's naturalization of the ruins of Tintern Abbey in "Representing the Picturesque: William Gilpin and the Laws of Nature," *Interdisciplinary Studies in Literature and the Environment* 12, no. 2 (summer 2005): 82–83. Though Thompson's analysis is confined to Fountains Abbey, she argues that Gilpin was interested in the affective response that ruins provoked rather than in their authenticity or historical significance (see Thompson, "Recycling Ruins," 680).

10. Gilpin, *Three Essays*, 46.

11. Gilpin, *Observations, Relative Chiefly to Picturesque Beauty, Made in the Year 1772, On Several Parts of England, Particularly the Mountains and Lakes of Cumberland and Westmoreland*, 3rd ed. (London, 1792), 1:18. Hereafter, this work is referred to as *Cumberland and Westmoreland*.

12. Jane Austen, *The History of England*, in *Juvenilia*, ed. Peter Sabor (Cambridge: Cambridge University Press, 2006), 181. Subsequent references are to this edition and will be provided in the text.

13. William Gilpin, *Observations on the River Wye, and Several Parts of South Wales, &c. Relative Chiefly to Picturesque Beauty: Made in the Summer of the Year 1770*, 4th ed. (London: 1800), 26.

14. Dale Townshend, "Ruins, Romance and the Rise of Gothic Tourism: The Case of Netley Abbey, 1750–1830," *Eighteenth-Century Studies* 37, no. 3 (2014): 378.

15. Gilpin, *Observations on the Coasts of Hampshire, Sussex, and Kent: Relative Chiefly to Picturesque Beauty: Made in the Summer of the Year 1774* (London, 1804), 46.

16. Gilpin, *Cumberland and Westmoreland*, 13, 14. As Moore comments, "Gilpin's travel books introduced readers to a range of intellectual positions concerning the Dissolution" (30).

17. While Gilpin's criticisms of Catholic religious life are scant, some anti-Catholic bias is expressed in his comments about Glastonbury Abbey: "These houses were the great nurseries of superstition, bigotry, and ignorance . . we are led to acquiesce in the

fate of these great foundations, and view their ruins, not only with a picturesque eye, but with moral and religious satisfaction" (Gilpin, *Observations on the Western Parts of England, Relative Chiefly to Picturesque Beauty: To Which Are Added, a Few Remarks on the Picturesque Beauties of the Isle of Wight* [London, 1798], 138–39). On the other hand, when viewing Tintern Abbey, Gilpin writes, "It is easy to conceive, a man of warm imagination, in monkish times, might have been allured by such a scene to become an inhabitant of it" (Gilpin, *Observations on the River Wye*, 32).

18. In *Observations on the River Wye*, Gilpin states of Tintern Abbey: "Though the parts are beautiful, the whole is ill-shaped . . a number of gabel-ends hurt the eye with their regularity, and disgust it by the vulgarity of their shape. A mallet judiciously used (but who durst use it?) might be of service in fracturing some of them; particularly those of the cross isles, which are both disagreeable in themselves, and confound the perspective" (49).

19. Thompson, "Recycling Ruins," 685.

20. Gilpin, *Cumberland and Westmoreland*, 2:179, 2:182.

21. Gilpin, *Observations on the Western Parts*, 276, 277. Moore considers Gilpin's concerns about Forde Abbey to be artistic rather than political, and places Austen in line with the political criticism of William Cobbett rather than Gilpin (Moore, *Jane Austen and the Reformation*, 87–89).

22. Gilpin, *Observations on the Coasts of Hampshire*, 45.

23. Gilpin, *Cumberland and Westmoreland*, 2:183.

24. Miall, "Representing the Picturesque," 76, 82–83.

25. Gilpin, *Observations on the River Wye*, 50.

26. Gilpin, *Observations on the River Wye*, 33. Duquette asserts that both Gilpin and Turner "naturalize" Tintern Abbey's ruins in their art (see Duquette, "The Grandeur of the Abbey").

27. Moore, *Jane Austen and the Reformation*, 26–27. For more on the broader tradition of "vernacular ruin poetry," see Anne Janowitz, *England's Ruins: Poetic Purpose and the National Landscape* (Cambridge: Basil Blackwell, 1990), 54–91.

28. Gilpin, *Cumberland and Westmoreland*, 2:184.

29. Moore, *Jane Austen and the Reformation*, 21–24. Alison Shell, *Oral Culture and Catholicism in Early Modern England* (Cambridge: Cambridge University Press, 2007).

30. Gilpin, *Cumberland and Westmoreland*, 2:243, 2:179.

31. Gilpin, *Observations on the Western Parts*, 1:350.

32. A. Hamilton Thompson, *Netley Abbey* (London: Her Majesty's Stationery Office, 1953), 4–22.

33. Townshend, "Ruins, Romance and the Rise of Gothic Tourism," 378; Deborah Kennedy, "The Ruined Abbey in the Eighteenth Century," *Philological Quarterly* 80, no. 4 (2001): 506–7.

34. Edmund Gosse, *Gray* (London: Macmillan, 1902), 168.

35. As qtd. in Claire Tomalin, *Jane Austen: A Life* (New York: Random House, 1997), 203.

36. For connections between Northanger Abbey and Farleigh Hungerford Castle or Hinton Priory, see Janine Barchas, *Matters of Fact in Jane Austen: History, Location, and Celebrity* (Baltimore, MD: John Hopkins University Press, 2012), 96–111. For connections

between Austen's fiction and Netley Abbey and Bath, see Moore, *Jane Austen and the Reformation*, 79–83 and 97–104.

37. Robinson, "Mere Skeleton," 224.

38. Gilpin, *Cumberland and Westmoreland*, 2:183, 2:182; Gilpin, *Observations on the Coasts of Hampshire*, 51 (where he describes Battle Abbey). See also Bodenheimer, "Looking at the Landscape," 605.

39. Robinson, "Mere Skeleton," 222.

40. Spongberg, "History, Fiction, and Anachronism," 643.

41. Moore, *Jane Austen and the Reformation*, 97. Beatrice Battaglia, "'Italian Lights on English Walls': Jane Austen and the Picturesque," in *Re-Drawing Austen: Picturesque Travels in Austenland*, ed. Battaglia and Diego Saglia (Napoli: Liguori Editore, 2004), 34.

42. Diane Long Hoeveler, *The Gothic Ideology: Religious Hysteria and Anti-Catholicism in British Popular Fiction 1780–1880* (Cardiff: University of Wales Press, 2014), 216.

43. Wallace, "Penance and Mortification," 168–69.

44. For more on Austen's religious underpinnings and fictional depictions of Anglican theology, see Laura Mooneyham-White, *Jane Austen's Anglicanism* (Farnham, UK: Ashgate, 2011). Mooneyham-White asserts that Austen considered England's pre-Reformation past as a "permanent but essentially non-historical foundation of religious principle and faith. The adult Austen was not a crypto-Catholic of any sort, but her *History of England* shows a juvenile enthusiasm for this Catholicism of the past" (117). Michael Wheeler positions Austen in line with her father's moderate Anglicanism in contrast to more evangelical forms of Protestantism. He does not address Catholic influences or the impact of migrating Catholic refugees, referring to native Catholics as a "minority [that] kept a low profile in English society" (Wheeler, "Religion," in *Jane Austen in Context*, ed. Janet Todd [Cambridge: Cambridge University Press, 2005], 406–14).

45. Dominic Aiden Bellenger, *The French Exiled Clergy* (Bath, UK: Downside Abbey, 1986), 3–4; Kirsty Carpenter, *Refugees of the French Revolution: Émigrés in London, 1789–1802* (New York: St Martin's, 1999), 44–47.

46. Frances Burney, *Diary and Letters of Madame D'Arblay*, ed. Charlotte Barrett (Cambridge: Cambridge University Press, 2013), 5:285.

47. Hester Thrale Piozzi and Ann Radcliffe, for example, describe multiple communities of women religious encountered in their travels abroad; Radcliffe even witnessed nuns in transit as refugees (see Tonya J. Moutray, *Refugee Nuns, the French Revolution, and British Literature and Culture* [New York: Routledge, 2016]; Ann Radcliffe, *A Journey Made in the Summer of 1794, through Holland and the Western Frontier of Germany, with a Return down the Rhine: to Which Are Added Observations during a Tour to the Lakes of Lancashire, Westmoreland, and Cumberland*, 2nd ed, 2 vols. [London: G. G. and J. Robinson, 1795]; and Hester Thrale Piozzi, *Mrs Thrale's French Journal, 1775, The French Journals of Mrs Thrale and Doctor Johnson*, ed. Moses Tyson and Henry Guppy [Manchester: Manchester University Press, 1932]).

48. Moore, *Jane Austen and the Reformation*, 31–32; Dominic Aidan Bellenger, "The Brussels Nuns at Winchester 1794–1857," English Benedictine Congregation History Commission Symposium (1999), 3, www.monlib.org.uk/papers/ebch/1999bellenger.pdf; Bellenger, *French Exiled Clergy*, 73–79.

49. Bellenger, *French Exiled Clergy*, 14–20.

50. For more on the Catholic Relief Acts, see Michael Tomko, *British Romanticism and the Catholic Question: Religion, History and National Identity, 1778–1829* (New York: Palgrave Macmillan, 2010), 16–22.

51. English communities and arrival dates are as follows: English Augustinians of Bruges (1794), English Augustinians of Louvain (1794), English Benedictines of Brussels (1794), Benedictines of Ghent (1794), Carmelites of Antwerp (1794), Carmelites of Lierre (1794), Dominicans of Brussels (1794), Franciscans of Brussels (1794), Sepulchrines of Liège (1794), Poor Clares of Liège (1794), Poor Clares of Dunkirk (1795), Poor Clares of Gravelines (1795), Poor Clares of Rouen (1795), Benedictines of Paris (1795), Benedictines of Cambrai (1795), Benedictines of Dunkirk (1795), Carmelites of Hoogstraten (1795), Poor Clares of Aire (1799), Conceptionists/Blue Nuns (1800), Bridgettines of Lisbon (1809). Four known French groups also migrated to England (Bernardines of Douai, Salesians of Cambrai, Benedictines of Montargis, and the Hospitalières of Cambrai). In addition, unaccounted for individuals and groups of nuns also sought refuge in England (*Who Were the Nuns? A Prosopographical Study of the English Convents in Exile 1600–1800*, Queen Mary University of London and the Arts and Humanities Research Council, http://wwtn.history.qmul.ac.uk/).

52. Bellenger, "Brussels Nuns," 1; *A History of the Benedictine Nuns of Dunkirk: Now at St Scholastica's Abbey, Teignmouth, Devon*, ed. by the Community (London: Burns and Oates, 1958), 131–32.

53. Wallace, "Penance and Mortification," 160. For example, see Margaret J. Mason, "The Blue Nuns in Norwich: 1800–1805," *Recusant History* 24 (1998): 101. Austen, *Sense and Sensibility* (Cambridge: Cambridge University Press, 2006).

54. Bellenger, "Brussels Nuns," 1–7; Bernard Ward, *The Dawn of the Catholic Revival in England, 1791–1803* (London: Longmans, Green, 1909), 2:202–4, 206.

55. See my discussion of this bill in *Refugee Nuns, The French Revolution, and British Literature and Culture* (New York: Routledge, 2016), 117–18, 148–52.

56. Douglas Murray suggests that Donwell Abbey's separation from Hartfield Hall reveals the "ruptures of history." I argue that Austen's focus is on the restoration of the two by means of the comic plot (Murray, "Donwell Abbey and Box Hill: Purity and Danger in Jane Austen's *Emma*," *Review of English Studies*, n.s., 66, no. 277 [2015]: 961n21).

57. Paul Smethurst, *Travel Writing and the Natural World, 1768–1840* (London: Palgrave Macmillan, 2012), 146.

58. Gilpin, *Observations on the River Wye*, 48–49.

59. Bodenheimer, "Looking at the Landscape," 612.

60. Wallace, "Penance and Mortification," 174; Moore, *Jane Austen and the Reformation*, 106.

61. For an excellent summary of these arguments, see Murray, "Donwell Abbey," 955–56. Murray argues that we must see these scenes as Emma's, not Austen's, reflections.

62. Nigel Everett, *The Tory View of Landscape* (New Haven, CT: Yale University Press, 1994), 1.

63. Everett, *The Tory View of Landscape*, 194.

Intimate Portraiture and the Accomplished Woman Artist in Emma

JULIETTE WELLS

"No great variety of faces for you," observes Emma Woodhouse to Harriet Smith and Mr. Elton, when opening her portfolio of drawings in chapter 6 of Austen's *Emma*. "I had only my own family to study from."[1] If it had been spoken by another, this remark about the narrow range of one's artistic subjects might seem self-pitying. Emma's tone, however, is matter-of-fact. Though she may seem to the reader to be trapped in Highbury by her devotion to her querulous father, she never thinks of herself as confined or deprived. Indeed, by the standards of the day, Emma's filial dedication is arguably her greatest virtue.

To this virtue Emma's portfolio vividly attests. It contains portraits of those closest to her, including blood relations (father, sister, nephews, and niece); a relation by marriage (her sister's husband); and the woman to whom Emma is most deeply attached, her former governess. By embarking on a portrait of Harriet, Emma pays her young protégée the profound—and perhaps ill-judged—compliment of admitting her to this inner circle, in spite of Harriet's unknown parentage. Of course, Emma's avowed aim is to deepen Mr. Elton's supposed interest in Harriet. Inwardly, Emma also looks forward to exercising her own skills in the visual arts.

Like music-making, in which Emma competes for attention with the much more gifted and proficient Jane Fairfax, drawing was considered a core feminine accomplishment in Austen's era, amid controversy regarding the purpose, limits, and morality of gentlewomen's education in the arts.[2] Austen most thoroughly establishes the centrality of drawing to conventional notions of accomplishment in *Pride and Prejudice*: Caroline Bingley lists "music, singing, drawing, dancing and the modern languages" as essential accomplishments, and Lady Catherine de Bourgh judges it "very strange" that none of the Bennet sisters draw.[3] Noteworthy too is that Elizabeth Bennet finds the drawings in "crayons" (pastels) done by the impeccably accomplished Georgiana Darcy to be more appealing than the "many good paintings" on display in the picture gallery at Pemberley (277, 276). That drawing as well as music-making can spark rivalry among women comes across plainly in *Sense and Sensibility*, when Marianne Dashwood warmly defends her sister Elinor's painted screens over the reportedly virtuosic landscapes of Miss Morton.[4]

The "taking" of likenesses in particular was thought to be a suitable activity for women, since affective ties could be strengthened both through the production of a portrait and also by its subsequent possession, which was especially valuable in the era before photography.[5] Indeed, Cassandra Austen's much-discussed portraits of Jane are just such likenesses by a female family member, undertaken without any intent of serving as public records of an author.[6] Only in *Emma* does Austen examine this special case of feminine accomplishment in the visual arts: one woman's portrait of another. Elsewhere, when Austen explores characters' emotional reactions to viewing portraits, the likenesses are exclusively of men: the miniature of Edward Ferrars, which Lucy Steele furtively shares with the inwardly agonized Elinor Dashwood in *Sense and Sensibility*; the full-sized portrait of Fitzwilliam Darcy at Pemberley, which evokes a strong response from Elizabeth Bennet, much more so than the miniature of Wickham she also sees there; and the miniature of Captain Benwick in *Persuasion*, the sentiment-laden circulation of which Peter Sabor analyzes extensively in his essay in this volume. As Sabor notes, Austen specifies that the portrait of Benwick was made by "a clever young German artist at the Cape";[7] by implication, the other portraits mentioned by Austen are likewise the work of professionals. All, moreover, are finished objects. *Emma* is unique in Austen's oeuvre in depicting the entire process of a portrait's creation, from conception to (domestic) exhibition.

In a time when women had limited access to professional artistic realms, fictional representations of accomplishments enabled women novelists to explore, discreetly, questions of artistry and ambition.[8] This Austen certainly does in the portrait episode of *Emma*, by showing the pleasure Emma takes in casting herself in the role of artist, even as other characters—Mr. Elton most prominently—insist on viewing her in familiar, nonthreatening terms as an accomplished woman. The complex power dynamics and currents of desire that Austen delineates in this episode are best illuminated by the theory of the "portrait contract" developed by Marcia Pointon in her influential study of British portraiture, *Hanging the Head*.[9] Relevant, too, is the category of the "intimate portrait" elaborated by Stephen Lloyd and Kim Sloan, which pertains explicitly to Emma's artwork and, more broadly, to

Intimate Portraiture and the Accomplished Woman Artist

Austen's art as a novelist.[10] Before introducing these art-historical concepts and bringing them to bear on *Emma*, it is necessary to consider ekphrasis, the rhetorical technique of describing in words a visual object, which Austen deploys when conveying to the reader both the contents of Emma's portfolio and her completed likeness of Harriet.

An opportunity for ekphrasis arises in a novel each time an artwork is contemplated, undertaken, reviewed by its creator, or shown to another. An author's use of ekphrasis in every case depends on, and also affects, the narrative context in which the artwork is discussed. Ekphrasis does not, in other words, take place in isolation, or in reference only to a rhetorical or theoretical tradition, as critics often consider it.[11] Rather, what an author or narrator "shows"—and doesn't show—the reader when one character portrays another or looks at a likeness created by a fellow character makes possible implications and revelations on multiple narrative levels. Indeed, portraits share with narratives the capacity to encode, displace, and disclose desire. As exposed through ekphrasis, these desires may take the shape of longings for one or more of the following: love, social power in various forms, artistic satisfaction, and moral improvement.

As Nanette Thrush has argued, attention to the operation of ekphrasis in novels "refocus[es] attention on how artists and their production are represented in fictional literature, rather than how writers are influenced by art."[12] In the case of women novelists, such analysis redresses two significant gaps in scholarship on ekphrasis, of gender and genre. Murray Krieger, for example, presents ekphrasis as wielded by Homer and revisited by poets from Dante to William Carlos Williams.[13] W. J. T. Mitchell suggests that gender may be deserving of notice, though he cautions that it "is not the unique key to the workings of ekphrasis, but only one among many figures of difference that energize the dialectic of the imagetext." Mitchell asserts, too, that portraiture is worth investigating as a special case of ekphrasis: "the otherness of the ekphrastic image," he argues, "is not just defined by the subject matter of the visual representation, but also by the kind of visual representation it is," with the result that each form of object represented "carries its own peculiar sort of textuality into the heart of the visual image."[14]

As an art historian, Marcia Pointon is concerned with analyzing paintings, not ekphrastic descriptions. Yet her treatment of portraits as embedded in "ritual" and "narratives" renders her insights especially applicable to portraits that are created, and beheld, within novels.[15] How a portrait is presented for viewing, Pointon contends, decisively affects its perceived consequence: "the ordering of imagery in particular spaces and settings," she observes of historic houses, "produces meanings specific to those times and places. . . . It is thus not only what is possessed that is significant but where and how it is made visible."[16] When assessing the significance of an ekphrastic rendering of a portrait, too, we must attend fully to the narrative circumstances, including who gives voice to the description (narrator or character) and who, in addition to the reader, takes on the role of viewer.[17]

Moreover, according to Pointon, we must take into account the power relationships evident or implicit among the various parties concerned in the production and viewing of a portrait: the artist, subject, and viewer, who collectively comprise what she calls the portrait contract. When all three parties in the portrait contract are male, each directs attention to the other two, a balanced power dynamic that Pointon represents with a triangular schema. When the gender of the subject changes from male to female, Pointon argues, the power relations among the three parties shift decisively: the (male) viewer and the (male) artist now both direct attention to the female sitter, but not to each other.[18] "In eighteenth century society taste was a male prerogative," claims Pointon. "Therefore the notional viewer in any theoretical model must be masculine."[19] Pointon further asserts that the status accorded to a completed portrait depends upon both the gender and age of its subject: "portraiture of women and children is one of the disciplines where representation, linking theory and practice, establishes the analogous relationship that equates femininity and childhood."[20]

The portrait contract in *Emma* differs from those delineated by Pointon for the obvious reason that Austen's fictional artist is female. Pointon's terminology points us to another crucial distinction: since Emma is an amateur, no actual (in the sense of financial) *contract* determines her portrait's creation or ownership. In the absence of a commissioner, we must consider who in *Emma* initiates the portrait, and why. In the absence of a purchaser, we must examine the implications of other forms of exchange depicted by Austen, whether successful or only attempted.

Pointon calls attention, too, to what is at stake in determinations of a portrait's "likeness." Invoking research by psychologists on recognition, she contends that "'likeness' is that which enables the viewer to match a representation with a given human subject. But this is never an isolated activity; such processes of reading are culturally determined."[21] To adapt this argument to the novel, when any party to a portrait contract makes a judgment on the degree of likeness achieved by the portrait, this judgment has the capacity to reflect or reveal that character's perceptions about the desires aroused by or encoded in the portrait. In particular, determinations of likeness made by a character taking the role of viewer often depend more on that character's attraction to the subject—and, in some cases, to the artist—than on any qualities in the portrait per se. When the artist character herself praises or disdains the level of likeness she has achieved, this assessment involves, in addition to any avowed or hidden attraction, her own artistic aspirations and her sense that she has fulfilled them or fallen short.

Unlike the formal oil portraits to which Pointon's theories directly apply, Emma's likeness of Harriet is a work on paper: an "intimate portrait," in the evocative term by which Stephen Lloyd and Kim Sloan designate drawings and miniatures intended to be viewed chiefly or exclusively by those to whom the subject is known, and in private rather than public spaces.[22] Lloyd and Sloan acknowledge that such portraits are "'intimate' in multiple senses of the word," an idea on which John Leighton and Neil MacGregor elaborate: "Behind the scenes, in domestic spaces such as sitting rooms, studies and bedrooms, smaller portraits on paper and ivory were at the heart of a more private conversation."[23] In just such domestic spaces, too, were novels typically read and set—and, indeed, written.

Austen herself characterized her artistic scope and subject matter in terms of an intimate miniature, in her much-quoted formulation, "the little bit (two Inches wide) of Ivory on which I work with so fine a Brush, as produces little effect after much labour."[24] Her brother Henry Austen developed the metaphor in his 1833 "Memoir of Miss Austen," in which, as in his 1818 "Biographical Notice," he presented her as faultlessly ladylike in spite of her authorship:

> With regard to her genius, we must adventure a few remarks. She herself compares her productions to a little bit of ivory two inches wide, worked upon with a brush so fine, that little effect is produced after much labour. It is so: her portraits are perfect likenesses, admirably finished, many of them gems, but it is all miniature painting; and, satisfied with being inimitable in one line, she never essayed canvass and oils; never tried her hand at a majestic daub.[25]

The conventional categories of feminine accomplishment and professional male artistry serve Henry's purpose well here. Rather than attempting large-scale ("majestic") compositions or employing masculine media ("canvas and oils"), his sister chose to confine herself to small-scale works, rendered in the novelistic equivalent of watercolor. In so doing, she created realistic portraits that strike readers as being "perfect likenesses." Only in being "inimitable" in that mode did she distinguish herself.

Yet, as Sloan points out, intimate portraits were created by professional and amateur artists alike, and from the same motives. "Artists would wish for portraits of their loved ones," she explains, "for many of the same reasons as any of their clients—to remind themselves of distant relatives, to capture a particular stage in their lives, to present as a gift, to commemorate an occasion or record a new fashion."[26] For professional artists, however, depicting friends and family members was, in Sloan's words, "an art of leisure and pleasure . . . quite separate from the business of painting portraits or drawing them on commission."[27] The rigid roles of artist, subject, and viewer in Pointon's portrait contract must, then, be reenvisioned for intimate portraits. With "leisure and pleasure" governing the artist's work, and with friendship or love connecting those present, the creation of an intimate portrait was highly personal.

In other respects, however, intimate portraits invite analysis much as does any artwork. Lloyd and Sloan advise approaching these portraits "as physical objects as well as symbolic ones, [by] asking how and why they were made, commissioned, whether for pleasure or as gifts, where they were kept and hung or worn—displayed, encased or bejeweled."[28] Such questions serve well to guide a reappraisal of the portrait episode in *Emma*.

As presented by the narrator, Emma's idea for a likeness of Harriet seems a mere whim: "a sudden wish . . to have Harriet's picture" (*E*, 44). Though Emma acknowledges no deeper inspiration, Austen has laid considerable groundwork for this apparent impulse in earlier chapters, as well as in the conversation between Emma and Mr. Elton in chapter 6 that directly precedes the "sudden wish."

During Harriet's first visit to Hartfield, in chapter 3, the narrator makes clear that Harriet possesses considerable visual appeal, both in general and to Emma especially: "She was a very pretty girl, and her beauty happened to be of a sort which Emma particularly admired. She was short, plump and fair, with a fine bloom, blue eyes, light hair, regular features, and a look of great sweetness" (*E*, 22). For a novelist as sparing with physical description as is Austen, such a list of attributes constitutes a veritable blazon—minus metaphors, of course. By contrast, Austen portrays the appearance of her eponymous heroine in much more abstract terms. According to the narrator, Emma is "handsome" (1), and Mr. Knightley, encouraged by the partial Mrs. Weston, "confess[es]" that he has "seldom seen a face or a figure more pleasing . . . than her's" (39). In reply, Mrs. Weston rhapsodizes about Emma's appearance, but she offers few specifics to help the reader visualize her: "Such an eye!—the true hazel eye!—and so brilliant! regular features, open countenance, with a complexion! oh! what a bloom of full health, and such a pretty height and size; such a firm and upright figure" (39). Mrs. Weston's words convey an ideal of beauty rather than an individual—an effect to which she indirectly admits by summing Emma up as "the complete picture of grown-up health. She is loveliness itself" (39). Mrs. Weston's unabashed celebration of the beauty of Emma's face and body is an important reminder, too, that in Austen's world one woman can gaze upon another with appreciation rather than desire.

In chapter 6, the "gallant" Mr. Elton, as the narrator calls him (*E*, 44), subliminally plants the suggestion for a portrait, as he praises Emma for having "given Miss Smith all that she required" in terms of manners. "You have made her graceful and easy," he effuses. "She was a beautiful creature when she came to you, but in my opinion, the attractions you have added are infinitely superior to what she received from nature. . . . Skilful has been the hand" (43–44). Mr. Elton's flattery casts Emma, figuratively, as the artist who has touched up Harriet. "Great has been the pleasure, I am sure," Emma politely replies (44). And before long—on "another day," but only a few lines later in the text—Emma's subconscious mind prompts her to take on the artist's role literally, and enjoy the artist's particular pleasure.

According to the narrator, Emma's initial wish is to "*have* Harriet's picture" (44, emphasis added) rather than to create it. Emma's effort to persuade Mr. Elton, too, begins by invoking terms of ownership and purchase: "What an exquisite possession a good picture of her would be!" Emma exclaims to him; "I would give any money for it" (44). Money is no object to Miss Woodhouse, of course, and a commissioned portrait would certainly allow Mr. Elton to admire Harriet, both during the work's preparation and when it was complete. Even if a professional portraitist were available in Highbury, however, such a transaction would not satisfy the artistic desires that have welled up in Emma. As she continues, "I almost long to attempt her likeness myself. You do not know it I dare say, but two or three years ago I had a great passion for taking likenesses, and attempted several of my friends, and was thought to have a tolerable eye in general. But from one cause or another, I gave it up in disgust. But really, I could almost venture, if Harriet would sit to me. It would be such a delight to have her picture!" (45). Emma's explanation that she gave up drawing "in disgust" accords with Mr. Knightley's judgment to Mrs. Weston, apropos of Emma's ambitious reading lists, that she "will never submit to any thing requiring industry and patience, and a subjection of the fancy to the understanding" (37). By returning to her discarded pastime, Emma is challenging herself to see a project through.[29]

Mr. Elton hears only that the woman he admires is ready to show off her accomplishments to him. "Let me entreat you, Miss Woodhouse," he replies, "to exercise so charming a talent in favour of your friend" (*E*, 44). As befits a suitor, he has noticed her prior work and is ready to compliment the "landscapes and flowers" on display at Hartfield as well as the "inimitable figure-pieces" in Mrs. Weston's drawing room (44, 45).[30] Oblivious as ever to Mr. Elton's signals, Emma bristles at what she sees as his presumption, thinking to herself: "What has all that to do with taking likenesses? You know nothing of drawing. Don't pretend to be in raptures about mine. Keep your raptures for Harriet's face" (45). Out loud, she only thanks him for his "kind encouragement" and, again emphasizing her own artistry, mentions the difficulty of rendering Harriet's "delicate" features, especially her eye and mouth (6).

Austen establishes, then, a complex portrait contract in which each party misconstrues the other's intentions and desires. Emma believes herself to be an altruistic matchmaker and an artist taking pleasure in exercising her skill and her eye. Mr. Elton understands Emma in purely conventional terms, as an accomplished woman who aims to charm. Passive Harriet so craves Emma's approbation that she has managed to deny even to herself that she still loves Robert Martin.

Emma's enjoyment of the artist's role is evident even before she picks up her pencil. She insists that Harriet and Mr. Elton survey her portfolio of her previous intimate portraits "that they might decide together on the best size for Harriet" (*E*, 45), much as a commissioner might look through samples of a portraitist's work in the studio. Via ekphrasis, readers "see" the portfolio's contents twice, as described first by the narrator and then by Emma herself. Each view is a partial one and conveys as much or more about the heroine's character and attitudes as about the artworks themselves.

The narrator surveys the contents of Emma's portfolio in terms of media and format but offers no sustained account of any particular artwork. Instead, the narrator takes the range of Emma's efforts as evidence that she has fallen short of what she is capable of, both artistically and morally: "Her many beginnings were displayed. Miniatures, half-lengths, whole-lengths, pencil, crayon, and water-colours had been all tried in turn .. but steadiness had always been wanting; and in nothing had she approached the degree of excellence which she would have been glad to command, and ought not to have failed of. She was not much deceived as to her own skill either as an artist or a musician, but she was not unwilling to have others deceived, or sorry to know her reputation for accomplishment often higher than it deserved" (*E*, 45–46). The stern phrase "ought not to have failed of" echoes Mr. Knightley's earlier assessment that Emma has not done justice to her talents. In being "not unwilling to have others deceived," too, Emma shows insufficient integrity. She is all too tempted by the uncritical praise heaped on her portfolio by Harriet and Mr. Elton: "They were both in extasies. A likeness pleases every body; and Miss Woodhouse's performances must be capital" (46).

The narrator does acknowledge that the works indicate Emma's talent: "There was merit in every drawing—in the least finished, perhaps the most; her style was spirited" (46). The narrator's insistence on general description, however, frustrates readers' desire to envision the individual pieces in Emma's portfolio. Which *is* the "least finished," in which the most merit can be discerned? Is it a miniature or a full-length, a pencil drawing or a watercolor? What is its subject?

These questions are not answered by the extended monologue in which Emma herself presents the portfolio. She does, however, offer more detail about certain individual pieces and the circumstances of their creation and reception. Unlike the narrator, who comments on "merit" and "style," Emma expresses her estimation of the works solely by assessing, often deprecatingly, each one's degree of likeness. She complains that impatient sitters like her father and Isabella resulted in poor likenesses; perhaps tellingly, she makes no remark on the likeness of her portraits of her most cooperative sitter, Mrs. Weston. Emma claims satisfaction only in the "strong" likeness of her portrait of her baby nephew George (*E*, 47).[31]

Emma's lengthy account of the final drawing in her portfolio underscores what is at stake when those beyond the artist herself assess the quality of likeness. Austen highlights the importance of this particular drawing by breaking into Emma's monologue to provide a more direct, if brief, glimpse of the work: it is "a pretty sketch of a gentleman in small size, whole-length" (*E*, 47). Emma considers this drawing of Mr. John Knightley, her brother-in-law and most reluctant sitter, to be her "best," erring only in being "too flattering," which she explains is "a fault on the right side" (47). Because her sister Isabella offered the "cold approbation" of considering the portrait only "a little like," however, Emma refused to finish it (47). "Altogether it was more than I could bear," she explains, "to have it apologized over as an unfavourable likeness, to every morning visitor in Brunswick-square" (47), John and Isabella's London house. In other words, had Emma completed the portrait, she would have been obliged—in thanks to John for the "great favour" of sitting for it (47)—to give it to him and Isabella, who would then have been obliged to hang it in their drawing room. The layers of obligation and friction among artist, subject, and viewer in this particular portrait contract indicate just how fraught the production and reception of an amateur artwork can be. Moreover, this fracas casts new light on Emma's decision to abandon her art, or, as she puts it here, to "forswear ever drawing anybody again" (47). Emma's decision not to persevere in the face of family tension is neither the "disgust" (44) to which she referred earlier nor the lack of "steadiness" (46) for which the narrator blamed her.[32]

Though Emma tells Harriet and Mr. Elton, as I have noted, that she has had "no great variety of faces . . only my own family to study from" (*E*, 46), in fact one family member is conspicuously missing from her portfolio: Mr. (George) Knightley. At issue is Mr. Knightley and Emma's insistence, at this stage of the narrative, on viewing each other as siblings rather than potential romantic partners. For a young woman to paint a portrait of an unmarried man would, in the context of domestic art, invite supposition as to the nature of her interest in him, supposition that Austen must avoid for the sake of the plot. On Mr. Knightley's side, too, Austen carefully offsets expressions of regard, as when he follows his observation to Mrs. Weston about Emma's "pleasing" face and figure, in chapter 5, by stating, "But I am a partial old friend" (39).

Rather than any unacknowledged affection for Mr. Knightley, what comes to the fore in the portrait episode is Emma's desire for control, which she expresses not only through matchmaking but also by refusing to consider marriage herself.[33] Characteristically, it is she who makes all the decisions concerning the portrait of Harriet, deciding upon "a whole-length in water-colours, like Mr. John Knightley's" (*E*, 48). Recalling her experience with that work, however, Emma is determined to better manage this new portrait's reception. Rather than giving the completed piece to the sitter (Harriet), or even the viewer (Mr. Elton), it is "destined, if she could please herself, to hold a very honourable station over the mantel-piece" at Hartfield (48).[34] *This* intimate portrait will be finished, framed, and displayed to all, Emma intends, as a "standing memorial of the beauty of one, the skill of the other, and the friendship of both; with as many other agreeable associations as Mr. Elton's very promising attachment was likely to add" (49).

Emma does finish the portrait, and it is subsequently "elegantly framed" in London, courtesy of Mr. Elton, and hung "over the mantelpiece of the common sitting-room" (*E*, 73).[35] In other crucial respects, however, she fails to dictate either the work's production or reception as she hoped. During the sittings, docile Harriet performs according to plan: "smiling and blushing, and afraid of not keeping her attitude and countenance, [she] presented a very sweet mixture of youthful expression to the steady eyes of the artist" (48). That final phrase represents the narrator's most approving acknowledgment of Emma's endeavor: her attention, previously so haphazard, is now "steady," and she merits—if only briefly—the designation of "artist." As Emma has anticipated, too, she enjoys the process of painting Harriet very much: she finds the first day's sitting "altogether very satisfactory," and "the whole progress of the picture . . . was rapid and happy" (48, 49).

Yet Emma's artistic concentration is continually interrupted by the overzealous Mr. Elton. Instead of taking the opportunity, which Emma has contrived for him, to "gaze and gaze again without offence" at Harriet (*E*, 48), he hovers around Emma, "fidgetting behind her and watching every touch" (48).[36] Moreover, he is so ready with his praise that he hardly waits for the painting to be created: "his admiration," remarks the narrator dryly, "made him discern a likeness almost before it was possible" (48). Emma's emphasis on likeness when describing the contents of her portfolio has evidently alerted Mr. Elton to the desirability of praising this element. Privately, however, she—like a professional portraitist—is not aiming for absolute accuracy. In keeping with her overall goal of enhancing Harriet's charms, Emma "meant to throw in a little improvement to the figure, to give a little more height, and considerably more elegance" (48).

Emma's persistence in misinterpreting Mr. Elton's very pointed attention to her would strain belief were it not for her strong dual investment in matchmaking and in her own role as artist. In her eyes, she is the initiator and creator in this portrait contract, as well as the artwork's eventual owner; Harriet is the subject; and Mr. Elton is the viewer. Mr. Elton, by contrast, perceives no portrait contract, because he perceives no artist, only a beautiful, wealthy, accomplished woman who has arranged an utterly conventional occasion that allows him to admire and flatter her. Of course, by far the greatest artistry evident in the episode is that of Austen herself, as she delineates the complex social dynamics at play in the production of an intimate portrait. Nowhere else in her novels, moreover, does she take such advantage of the possibilities for misunderstanding that result from unaligned views of artistry versus accomplishment.

Austen capitalizes, too, on the narrative potential of the portrait's unveiling to its wider domestic audience. Rather than allowing Emma to stage a scene in which the completed work is displayed for comment, Austen has the sittings give way without pause to a scene of observation and critique. Moreover, as Antonia Losano has pointed out, the narrator offers neither a full ekphrastic description nor an evaluation of the completed portrait.[37] Instead, characters' discussions of the picture call attention to specific elements, as Emma did when narrating her portfolio. In each case, these comments—like Mr. Elton's—reveal at least as much about those characters' regard for Emma as about their estimation of the work. Mr. Woodhouse, for instance, proclaims the portrait "very pretty. . Just as your drawings always are, my dear" (*E*, 50), though he frets about Harriet's being portrayed outdoors "with only a little shawl over her shoulders" (50).

Not surprisingly, likeness is the key point of contention among the viewers. Mr. Elton gushes that he "never saw such a likeness" (*E*, 50), but he has no coherent language for discussing either the figure or the backdrop: "the tree is touched with such inimitable spirit!" he burbles.[38] Supportive Mrs. Weston observes that Emma "has given her friend the only beauty she wanted . . Miss Smith has not those eye-brows and eye-lashes. It is the fault of her face that she has them not" (49). Since Emma's intentions for "improvement" all pertained to Harriet's "figure" (48), it is unclear whether the beautifications that Mrs. Weston notices were accidental or purposeful. Mr. Knightley's sole contribution is a comment on the boost Emma has given to her subject's height: "'You have made her too tall, Emma,' said Mr. Knightley. Emma knew that she had, but would not own it, and Mr. Elton warmly added, 'Oh, no! certainly not too tall; not in the least too tall'" (49). Here in a nutshell is the dynamic between Mr. Knightley and Emma at this stage of the novel, with his truth-telling followed by her quiet recognition and self-protective lack of response.

Whether Emma herself is satisfied with the finished portrait, or with her success at meeting her challenge to herself to complete it, Austen never reveals. "Every body who saw it was pleased" (49), states the narrator blandly, in a sentence that confirms the earlier observation that a "likeness pleases every body" (46). But does "every body" include Emma? Or, for that matter, Mr. Knightley, her most stringent moral critic?

Nor does Austen specify the eventual fate of her heroine's artwork. No sooner has the portrait been hung, at the beginning of chapter 9, than Emma and Harriet move on to collaborate on their book of riddles, an activity with no artistic overtones.[39] The lasting purpose Emma imagined for the likeness—a "standing memorial" (49) to friendship and courtship—begins to disappear once she belatedly recognizes Mr. Elton's true intentions, when he drunkenly proposes in the carriage in chapter 15 and ceases to exist entirely upon the revelation of Harriet's actual parentage and her marriage to Robert Martin. It is inconceivable that Emma would leave a picture of her former protégée hanging at Hartfield in perpetuity, to serve as a reminder of her own delusion and (inadvertent) cruelty. But the picture merits no further mention once its immediate narrative function has been fulfilled.

Emma's artistic eye, skill, and gratification ultimately matter less to Austen than does the development of the clear moral vision with which Emma can see her own faults and delusions, as well as of the resolution with which she can remedy them. The portrait episode is but the first of many in *Emma* in which Austen tests, and gradually builds, her heroine's self-awareness. While real, the artistry Emma exercises in her likeness of Harriet is fleeting, neither threatening nor expanding notions of feminine accomplishment. The characters' roles in this portrait contract prove temporary, too, reconfigured first by Mr. Elton's proposal to Emma and her rejection of him, and subsequently by the dwindling of her friendship with Harriet. Mr. Knightley, the man missing from Emma's portfolio, moves to the center of her life. From him, Emma finally learns to "own" (49) both internally and out loud her flights of fancy and failures of vision; to recognize and to prefer honest and accurate representations; and to understand fully the role she occupies in the world, with all its privileges and responsibilities. And the conventional roles of wifehood and motherhood await to occupy Emma's powers of creation.

Notes

I am grateful to Anna Battigelli for her encouragement and astute comments, and to all the participants in the 2017 "Jane Austen & the Arts" conference for their enthusiastic questions and suggestions. Thanks, too, to Jill Ehnenn, whose work on women writers and ekphrasis provided the initial inspiration for developing these ideas.

1. Jane Austen, *Emma*, ed. Richard Cronin and Dorothy Macmillan (Cambridge: Cambridge University Press, 2005), 46. All subsequent citations are to this edition and will be provided parenthetically in the text.

2. Drawing as a feminine accomplishment has been most fully examined by the art historian Ann Bermingham, in *Learning to Draw: Studies in the Cultural History of a Polite and Useful Art* (New Haven, CT: Yale University Press, 2000). In "'In Music She Had Always Used to Feel Alone in the World': Jane Austen, Solitude, and the Artistic Woman," *Persuasions* 26 (2004): 98–110, I offer an overview of the accomplishments controversy and show how both Austen and her heroines find solace and self-expression in artistic pursuits. For another summary of the accomplishments debate, plus attention to the ways in which historic women exercised autonomy and creativity via conventional

accomplishments, see Amanda Vickery, *Behind Closed Doors: At Home in Georgian England* (New Haven, CT: Yale University Press, 2009), chap. 9. Noël Riley, too, stresses the creativity of women in a wide variety of artistic pursuits in *The Accomplished Lady: A History of Genteel Pursuits c. 1660–1860* (Huddersfield, UK: Oblong, 2017). Amateur drawing was widely practiced by men as well (see Kim Sloan, *"A Noble Art": Amateur Artists and Drawing Masters c. 1600–1800* [London: British Museum Press, 2000]). Sloan notes that "the ratio of males to females" in her catalogue is "to the best of our knowledge, fairly accurate, in spite of the traditional vague perception that most amateurs were women" (8).

3. Jane Austen, *Pride and Prejudice*, ed. Pat Rogers (Cambridge: Cambridge University Press, 2004), 43, 186. All subsequent citations are to this edition and will be provided parenthetically in the text.

4. Jane Austen, *Sense and Sensibility*, ed. Edward Copeland (Cambridge: Cambridge University Press, 2006), 267–68.

5. For an overview of the role of portraiture in women's amateur and professional art practice in this period, see Antonia Losano, "A Great Passion for Taking Likenesses: The Woman Painter in *Emma*," *Persuasions* 27 (2005): 185–93. On Austen's engagement with the ideology of accomplishments in *Emma*, see also Kelly M. McDonald, "'A Reputation for Accomplishment': Marianne Dashwood and Emma Woodhouse as Artistic Performers," in *Jane Austen and the Arts: Elegance, Propriety, and Harmony*, ed. Natasha Duquette and Elizabeth Lenckos (Bethlehem, PA: Lehigh University Press, 2013), 21–36. McDonald's primary focus is on Emma's accomplishments in music, a topic also addressed by Kathryn L. Libin's essay "Daily Practice, Musical Accomplishment, and the Example of Jane Austen," in *Jane Austen and the Arts*, ed. Duquette and Lenckos, 3–20.

6. For an experiment in viewing Cassandra's sketches of Jane in conjunction with formal public portraits, see Jeff Nigro, "The Sister Artist: Cassandra Austen's Portraits of Jane Austen in Art Historical Context," in *Jane Austen and the Arts*, ed. Duquette and Lenckos, 47–64. On the range of surviving portraits of Austen, see Margaret Kirkham, "Portraits," in *Jane Austen in Context*, ed. Janet Todd (Cambridge: Cambridge University Press, 2005), 68–79; and Susan Owens, "A Life in Portraits," in *Jane Austen: Writer in the World*, ed. Kathryn Sutherland (Oxford: Bodleian Library, 2017), 165–85.

7. Jane Austen, *Persuasion*, ed. Janet Todd and Antje Blank (Cambridge: Cambridge University Press, 2006), 252.

8. See Juliette Wells, "In Music" and also "'Some of Your Accomplishments Are Not Ordinary': The Limits of Artistry in *Jane Eyre*," in *The Brontës in the World of the Arts*, ed. Sandra Hagan and Wells, 67–80 (Aldershot, UK: Ashgate, 2008), which examines the significance of Jane's display of her portfolio of visionary drawings to Rochester as well as of her self-abnegating creation of portraits of herself and Blanche Ingram. For broader arguments concerning Austen's quiet and not-so-quiet subversion, see Jill Heydt-Stevenson, *Austen's Unbecoming Conjunctions: Subversive Laughter, Embodied History* (New York: Palgrave Macmillan, 2005); and Helena Kelly, *Jane Austen, the Secret Radical* (New York: Knopf, 2017).

9. Marcia Pointon, *Hanging the Head: Portraiture and Social Formation in Eighteenth-Century England* (New Haven, CT: Yale University Press, 1993).

10. Stephen Lloyd and Kim Sloan, *The Intimate Portrait: Drawings, Miniatures and Pastels from Ramsay to Lawrence* (Edinburgh and London: National Galleries of Scotland/British Museum, 2008).

11. Much recent theoretical work on ekphrasis is concerned with reconsidering the boundaries of the field, either by recasting working definitions of the term itself or by returning to classical discussions of ekphrasis, enargeia, and related concepts. These efforts are particularly evident in Valerie Robillard and Els Jongeneel, eds., *Pictures into Words: Theoretical and Descriptive Approaches to Ekphrasis* (Amsterdam: Vu University Press, 1998).

12. Nanette Thrush, "A Picture's Worth a Thousand Lies: Portraits in Victorian Literature," in *Auto-Poetica: Representations of the Creative Process in Nineteenth-Century British and American Fiction*, ed. Darby Lewes (Lanham, MD: Lexington, 2006), 196.

13. Murray Krieger, *Ekphrasis: The Illusion of the Natural Sign* (Baltimore, MD: Johns Hopkins University Press, 1992).

14. W. J. T. Mitchell, *Picture Theory: Essays on Verbal and Visual Representation* (Chicago: University of Chicago Press, 1994), 181.

15. Pointon, *Hanging the Head*, 1.

16. Pointon, *Hanging the Head*, 13.

17. On the involvement of readerly desire in ekphrasis, see Ellen J. Esrock, *The Reader's Eye: Visual Imaging as Reader Response* (Baltimore, MD: Johns Hopkins University Press, 1994), 143, 183.

18. Pointon, *Hanging the Head*, 188.

19. Pointon, *Hanging the Head*, 258n39. Pointon's later book, *Strategies for Showing: Women, Possession, and Representation in English Visual Culture 1665–1800* (Oxford: Oxford University Press, 1997) focuses entirely on women as possessors and subjects of art and artifacts.

20. Pointon, *Hanging the Head*, 184.

21. Pointon, *Hanging the Head*, 81. Joe Bray has explored the implications of likeness in *Emma* in light of Pointon's theories in *The Portrait in Fiction of the Romantic Period* (New York: Routledge, 2016), chap. 4.

22. Indeed, the faces captured in the portraits chosen by Lloyd and Sloan for their exhibition and catalogue are arrestingly individual and realistic. Like Austen, who famously sought likenesses of Elizabeth Darcy and other characters from *Pride and Prejudice* when visiting public exhibitions in 1813, we may be tempted to look for faces that resemble our conceptions of her characters (Jane Austen to Cassandra Austen, May 24, 1813, *Jane Austen's Letters*, ed. Deirdre Le Faye, 4th ed. [Oxford: Oxford University Press, 2011], 220). Subsequent references refer to this edition. For a recent effort to connect Austen's characters with portrait images of the period, as opposed to faces of actors in adaptations, see John Sutherland and Amanda Vickery's much-publicized study "The Real Mr Darcy—A Dramatic Re-appraisal," which, along with a newly created portrait of Darcy by a twenty-first-century artist, was commissioned by a UK television channel (*Drama*, February 9, 2017, drama.uktv.co.uk/pride-and-prejudice/article/real-mr-darcy-dramatic-re-appraisal/).

23. Lloyd and Sloan, *Intimate Portrait*, 9; John Leighton and Neil MacGregor, foreword to *Intimate Portrait*, by Lloyd and Sloan, 7.

24. Jane Austen to James Edward Austen, 16–17 December 1816, *Jane Austen's Letters*, ed. Deirdre Le Faye, 4th ed. (Oxford: Oxford University Press, 2012), 337. I discuss the "little bit … of Ivory" comment in light of Austen's views on her authorship in Juliette Wells, introduction to *Persuasion*, by Jane Austen (New York: Penguin Classics, 2017), xviii.

25. Henry Austen, "Memoir of Miss Austen" (1833), in J. E. Austen-Leigh, *A Memoir of Jane Austen and Other Family Recollections*, ed. Kathryn Sutherland (Oxford: Oxford University Press, 2008), 151. On Henry's authorship of the "Biographical Notice," see Juliette Wells, "A Note on Henry Austen's Authorship of the 'Biographical Notice,'" *Persuasions On-Line* 38.1 (2017), n.pag.

26. Kim Sloan, "Portraits of Artists' Families and Friends," in *Intimate Portrait*, by Lloyd and Sloan, 123.

27. Kim Sloan, "Drawing for Business or Drawing for Pleasure? The Place of Portraits on Paper," in *Intimate Portrait*, by Lloyd and Sloan, 31.

28. Lloyd and Sloan, *Intimate Portrait*, 9.

29. Michelle Ruggaber Dougherty argues that Emma's motivation stems not from creativity per se but from related impulses "to separate herself from others," and to "mediate between her desire for importance and her reluctance to marry" (Dougherty, "Creativity and Social Power in Jane Austen's *Emma*," in *Auto-Poetica*, ed. Lewes, 103, 106). Losano notes the unconventionality of the social superior painting her inferior and argues that, in Emma's hands, portraiture is a "radically imperial" project (Losano, "A Great Passion," 187, 188).

30. The *Oxford English Dictionary* credits Austen with being the originator of the term "figure-piece" ("figure, n.," OED Online, June 2017, Oxford University Press, www.oed.com.goucher.idm.oclc.org/view/Entry/70079?redirectedFrom=figure-pieces).

31. As Dougherty points out, however, Emma prides herself on her rendering not of the baby's face but of "the cockade on the baby's hat and the corner of the sofa on which he is sleeping—both inanimate objects" (Dougherty, "Creativity and Social Power," 105).

32. Cronin and McMillan gloss "disgust" as "dissatisfaction," but the usual meaning of "disgust" also seems applicable to Emma's reactions to her sister's criticism (Austen, *Emma*, 545n2).

33. For an extensive consideration of this refusal, and the role of Emma's creativity in relation to it, see Dougherty, "Creativity and Social Power."

34. Losano calls attention to the unconventionality of Emma's intentions regarding the eventual disposal of the portrait: "under normal circumstances," she contends, Harriet would own it, and the "honourable station" for which Emma intends it, "according to traditions of the period, should be reserved for portraits of illustrious ancestors, or perhaps an original work by a contemporary artist or a landscape sketch by the lady of the house" (Losano, "'A Great Passion,'" 187, 188).

35. Cronin and McMillan explain that the common sitting room was open to guests, not only family (Austen, *Emma*, 548n1).

36. For a reading of this scene's focus on the artist rather than the art object in light of contemporary aesthetics, see Losano, "A Great Passion."

37. Losano, "A Great Passion," 191.

38. Cronin and McMillan point out Elton's ignorant mimicry of "the language of the connoisseur" (Austen, *Emma*, 545n8).

39. In *Reading Austen in America*, I note that the book of riddles is the "closest that Austen's 'imaginist' heroine Emma ever comes to actual authorship" (Juliette Wells, *Reading Austen in America* [New York: Bloomsbury Academic, 2017], 96).

"Is She Musical?"

Players and Nonplayers in Austen's Fiction

LINDA ZIONKOWSKI AND MIRIAM HART

When Mary Crawford in *Mansfield Park* fears that the man she loves will be attracted to the daughters in the home where he is visiting, her anxieties focus on her prospective rivals' good looks and musical talents alike: "There is a beauty in every family.—It is a regular thing. Two play on the piano-forte, and one on the harp—and all sing—or would sing if they were taught—or sing all the better for not being taught—or something like it."[1] Mary refers to music as a common feminine charm because in Jane Austen's culture, the ability to play and sing had become a "regular thing." Throughout the eighteenth century, genteel young women—or those wanting to appear genteel—learned music routinely, with instruction on the harp, keyboard instruments, and (to a lesser extent) the guitar becoming an integral part of a polite education. The time spent on vocal and instrumental lessons both displayed women's proper use of the leisure they were given and showcased their family's financial ability to cultivate their improvement, yet all of this talent was intended only for home consumption. Since, as Richard Leppert notes, "a well-bred woman who took music seriously constituted a threat to social boundaries," practicing and playing had to remain decorative activities in keeping with the precepts of domestic ideology.[2]

Conduct literature of the period policed these boundaries diligently, but even women who played and sang at home found themselves the objects of criticism and concern. Writing in 1773, Hester Chapone approved of music as an "innocent amusement" to make young women desirable companions; however, she also warned readers not to take pride in their skills. Since a "private person" lacks the time to become truly proficient, women should not fool themselves over the quality of their playing and singing: "Your own partial family are perhaps the only persons who would not much rather be entertained by the performance of a professor than by yours."[3] Catherine Macaulay's *Letters on Education* (1790) offers an even harsher assessment of music's value to young women. While agreeing with Chapone that music can be an "elegant and innocent amusement," she argues that the "frivolous task of modulating air into sound" is unworthy of the effort it takes to master the craft. Worse yet, the sensuality of music troubled Macaulay: she warns that playing and singing make women into "objects of sense" for men's pleasure and "contribute to encrease imbecility" if these activities take time away from more intellectual pursuits, like reading.[4] Finally, both Maria Edgeworth in *Practical Education* (1798) and Hannah More in *Coelebs in Search of a Wife* (1804) caution against music's use as a "means of attracting temporary admiration."[5] In the words of More's ideal bachelor, "The excellence of musical performance is a decorated screen, behind which all defects in domestic knowledge, in taste, judgment, and literature, and the talents which make an elegant companion are creditably concealed." Despite having a "correct ear," More's heroine—the modest, well-educated Lucilla Stanley—neither sings nor plays.[6]

As her own devotion to music reveals, Austen did not share these anxieties. At the age of twelve—when she first started writing—she began lessons on the piano with William Chard, assistant organist of Winchester Cathedral; at twenty-one she still continued under Chard's tuition, even though most women completed their instruction much earlier. Throughout her life, Austen always owned or rented a piano, even when her family lived in lodgings, and she played every morning that she could, rising early to practice rather than using the time and the solitude to write; as Robert Wallace remarks, "The fact that she instead played her pianoforte suggests that the music she played must have meant something to her."[7] The music in Austen's collection of seventeen songbooks (some of them hand-copied and hand-stitched) offered a cultural heritage of favorite pieces and a means of instructing future generations of musicians; ranging from simple ballads to concertos requiring advanced technical skill, the selections gave Austen a chance to test and expand her artistry and to be alone doing something she enjoyed. To Austen, the hours that women spent practicing and transcribing music were not time wasted, for proficiency at the keyboard demanded the same physical and mental discipline—the same dedication and attention—required for the composition of her novels; as she famously told her sister Cassandra, "an artist cannot do anything slovenly."[8] Significantly, it is Austen's ignorant, vacuous Mr. Collins who echoes conduct book descriptions of music as a "very innocent diversion."[9]

Yet playing and singing in Austen's fiction are by no means simple pleasures. Rather, her novels squarely confront cultural anxieties regarding the purpose and value of women's music by focusing on how the absence or misuse of musical instruction affects characters' development. In these narratives, women who view music as a mere accomplishment to catch a husband are quickly dismissed as vain, self-deluded, and insipid: these include Lady Middleton of *Sense and Sensibility* and Augusta Elton of *Emma*, both of whom consider themselves "doatingly fond of music,"[10] but permanently and happily close their pianos after marriage. By contrast, Austen turns attention to characters who have the intelligence for and access to musical training but either decide not to pursue it, do not give it sustained attention, or misemploy the knowledge they have gained. In all of these instances, the novels suggest how such attitudes toward playing and singing reflect limitations in the characters themselves, as well as their blindness to their own inadequacies. Rather than preserving female modesty and simplicity, women's decision not to play or not to commit themselves to music too seriously is a cause for concern in Austen's narratives, for it signals their choice of a life less devoted to introspection, self-development, and influence upon the listeners who heard them.[11]

"She Learnt a Year, and Could Not Bear It"

Austen's juvenilia offers a sustained attack on conventions of female conduct that her culture endorsed, and particularly on the fiction that reproduced these norms. Some of these texts mock the concept of sensibility, featuring heroines who die of love or grief in comic circumstances, while others challenge the belief in female passivity by having their heroines engage in murder and theft as a matter of course. The vogue for female accomplishments, including music, also became a target of the juvenilia's satire. In *Catharine, or the Bower*, the vain Camilla Stanley embodies all that is wrong with the practice of educating young women for genteel marriages: "Those Years which ought to have been spent in the attainment of useful knowledge and Mental Improvement, had been all bestowed in learning Drawing, Italian and Music, more especially the latter," which results in "an Understanding unimproved by reading and a Mind totally devoid either of Taste or Judgement."[12] Yet apart from this rather common critique of the accomplished woman, the juvenilia also reveals Austen's love of song, and her love of satirizing song, especially in literature written for her family. *Volume the First* contains "Frederic and Elfrida, a novel," dedicated to her friend Martha Lloyd, a fellow musician with whom Austen shared musical manuscripts. The story of first cousins in love—full of fainting fits, a suicide, and a passionate friendship—includes two one-stanza songs. Prefaced by a parody of pastoral conventions ("In this Grove they had scarcely remained above 9 hours, when they were suddenly agreably surprized by hearing a most delightfull voice"), the lyrics of the first are pure doggerel:

> That Damon was in love with me
> I once thought and beleiv'd
> But now that he is not I see
> I fear I was deceiv'd. (J, 5)

Some pages later, Austen again parodies the pastoral—and the practice of young ladies' singing—by introducing a dialect word to expose the artificial contrivance of songs and singers alike in contemporary fiction:

> When Corydon went to the fair
> He bought a red ribbon for Bess,
> With which she encircled her hair
> And made herself look very fess (11)

"Henry and Eliza" also features a singing heroine, one who "with a conscious knowledge of her own Excellence" has been "turned out of doors" (39, 38) by her adoptive parents for stealing a £50 banknote. In these texts, music as an accomplishment appears a clichéd expression of female worth that Austen found ripe for ridicule.

By the time that Austen composed "Lesley Castle" (1792)—an unfinished burlesque of an epistolary novel—she was nearly seventeen and had stopped writing lyrics. Like her previous work, this novel examines her heroines' education and behavior, juxtaposing the widely diverging characters of two sisters, Charlotte and Eloisa Lutterell. Charlotte is the domestic mother's favorite, while Eloisa is the intellectual father's, and their preferences reflect the mentoring they have received. Yet only Charlotte's activities are satirized. Blind to the cultural hierarchy elevating mental over manual labor, she unconsciously exposes her own deficiencies: "Never to be sure were there two more different Dispositions in the World. We both loved Reading. *She* preferred Histories, and *I* Receipts. She loved drawing Pictures, and I drawing Pullets. No one could sing a better Song than She, and no one make a better Pye than I.... We have for many years entered into an agreement always to admire each other's works; I never fail listening to *her* Music, and she is as constant in eating *my* pies" (J, 164–65). Despite Charlotte's pride in her accomplishments, the narrative makes it clear that cooking is a less esteemed skill than music.

Dissension begins when Eloisa's playing and singing attract a suitor, and Charlotte perceives (and resents) the attention given to her sister's talents:

> My Scheme was to treat her as she treated me, and tho' she might even draw my own Picture or play Malbrook (which is the only tune I ever really liked) not to say so much as "Thank you Eloisa"; tho' I had for many years constantly hollowed whenever she played, *Bravo, Bravissimo, Encora, Da Capro, allegretto, con espressioné,* and *Poco presto* with many other such outlandish words, all of them as Eloisa told me expressive of my Admiration; and so indeed I suppose they are, as I see some of them in every Page of every Music-book, being the Sentiments I imagine of the Composer. (165–66)

Austen's familiarity with musical language and musical reception—one does not applaud a dance tune, one does not shout tempos or instructions at a player—sharpens the satire and suggests that the nonmusical sister has, in spite of her domestic abilities, received an inferior education and become an inferior person. Although the juvenilia, composed of experimental pieces and fragments, does not outline a consistent plan for young women's instruction, in her early work Austen begins to draw distinctions between the types of activities that prove valuable to women and those that do not.

Completed seven years after *Lesley Castle,* the more mature *Northanger Abbey* features a distinctly nonmusical heroine in Catherine Morland: while Catherine is far less an object of satire than Charlotte Lutterell, *Northanger Abbey* suggests that her naiveté and immaturity have their roots in her dislike of anything involving disciplined intellectual application—including music and reading. Catherine is an "outdoor" heroine: her physicality is emphasized in her description, since she is "fond of all boys' plays," including cricket, base-ball, horseback riding, rolling down the hill, and being "noisy and wild" in the spirit of childish joy.[13] With no love for learning—"she shirked her lessons .. whenever she could" (*NA,* 6)—Catherine especially detests instruction on the piano, which began when she was eight: "She learnt a year, and could not bear it" (6). Unwilling to persevere with a clearly reluctant child, Mrs. Morland gives in and allows her daughter to stop ("The day which dismissed the music-master was one of the happiest of Catherine's life" [6]). While Catherine has potential for growth—"she could listen to other people's performance with very little fatigue" (8)—her education is stunted and incomplete, leaving her to begin her experiences in Bath "ignorant and uninformed" (10).

Although she seems a refreshing contrast to the accomplished woman, the "artless, guileless" (*NA,* 212) Catherine remains fairly simple throughout the narrative, lacking the introspection and emotional intelligence that a more disciplined education—including time at the piano—might have brought her. Her immaturity enables Isabella Thorpe to manipulate her into a friendship founded upon "dress, balls, flirtations, and quizzes" (25) fairly easily, for Catherine admires Isabella's supposedly superior knowledge of the world: Catherine cannot perceive that Isabella uses their intimacy as a means to attract James Morland or that Isabella ultimately intends to jilt James in favor of the richer, more eligible Frederick Tilney. Catherine also fails to recognize the clumsy signs of feigned affection that John Thorpe bestows upon her, even though Isabella claims that "his attentions were such as a child must have noticed" (146). Like a child, Catherine is intuitive—she knows that John is insincere and senses General Tilney's capacity for cruel behavior—but still relies upon the far more sophisticated Henry Tilney to help her investigate her feelings and reflect upon her experiences. At the end of the novel, Catherine begins to assert her own opinions, even venturing to believe that Henry himself might possess "some slight imperfection" (206) of character, but her development is far less substantial than that of Austen's other heroines, all of whom approach education in general and music in particular with a more complex perspective.

"You Have Delighted Us Long Enough"

Unlike Catherine Morland, who is thrilled when her music lessons end, Mary Bennet in *Pride and Prejudice* devotes herself to the piano. Spending her days "deep in the study of thorough bass and human nature" (67), Mary resembles those musical young women whom conduct books censure for mistaking their powers of pleasing: her hours at the keyboard and in the library are apparently misspent, for she learns nothing that renders her more useful to the household or in company. *Pride and Prejudice* makes the reason for Mary's efforts pathetically clear: as the only plain girl in a family of attractive sisters, she tries to compensate for her deficiencies and distinguish herself, "work[ing] hard for knowledge and accomplishments" (27) and jumping at the opportunity to display them. Predictably, though, Mary's attempts to employ music for this purpose fail: her vanity blinds her to her deficiencies, and she tries too hard to gain approval and attention. Elizabeth, less concerned about her own improvement, plays with an "easy and unaffected" style, while Mary, with a "pedantic air and conceited manner" (27), brings only derision upon herself. At the Netherfield ball, Mr. Bennet puts an end to Mary's drawn-out performance with a sarcastic comment mocking her lack of talent—"You have delighted us long enough" (113)—but the damage is done. Knowing that her sister has taxed the patience of the audience, "Elizabeth was in agonies" (112); Mary's playing and singing, which were supposed to highlight the refined education of the Bennet girls, instead expose the family's lack of taste and manners and thereby threaten their genteel status.

In contrast to Mary, Elizabeth seems to follow conduct book advice in not thinking highly of her talent, yet Austen clearly links her playing to her pride. Although she is attractive, Elizabeth's breezy, almost careless musical style reveals her limitations: early in the novel, she remains quite satisfied with her own knowledge, judgments, and abilities and tries to redirect attention away from her performance at the keyboard, where she knows herself weak. In the only two instances in the novel where Elizabeth plays, she speaks first, modestly preparing Darcy, both times her intended audience, for an unimpressive performance. When Charlotte Lucas insists that she perform during her family's party, Elizabeth responds verbally, then musically, with her characteristically sarcastic charm: "If my vanity had taken a musical turn, you would have been invaluable, but as it is, I would really rather not sit down before those who must be in the habit of hearing the very best performers" (P&P, 27). Later in the novel, before playing for the company at Rosings, Elizabeth again denies being proficient because she "would not take the trouble of practising" (197). Socially, Elizabeth employs her musical skills well, responding with seeming grace to requests to perform, and her style distinguishes itself as the most non-exhibiting, and therefore the most genuine, of any female player in the novel: as Sarah Webster Goodwin notes, "Elizabeth Bennet ultimately refuses... forms of self-marketing, and in Austen's text more power accrues to her because of her refusal."[14] Yet Elizabeth's speeches excusing her mediocrity at the piano in fact reveal where her real vanity lies: her snappy repartee, like her lively but restricted playing ability, shows her decision to be smart rather than wise, to be an "easy" player rather than a serious one, and her attitude toward music reflects her general complacency. In fact, Darcy's observation about his friend Bingley may apply to Elizabeth as well: "Nothing is more deceitful... than the appearance of humility. It is often only carelessness of opinion, and sometimes an indirect boast" (P&P, 53). While Elizabeth initially prides herself on playing adequately without having practiced much and claims that she "'knows exactly what to think'" (96) of people's motives and behavior even after a slight acquaintance, her subsequent experience in discovering Darcy's true character awakens her to her own overconfidence: she learns that superficial performances, or playing and talking with "ease," do not always indicate excellence, and she comes to recognize the benefit she could receive from more informed, practiced application of her talents.[15]

Far wealthier than the Bennet sisters, Emma Woodhouse faces no pressure to showcase her accomplishments, but her attitude toward music nonetheless reveals the boundaries of her self-awareness. An heiress with £30,000, Emma is "first in consequence" (*E*, 5) in the village of Highbury, and as Claudia Johnson notes, she "possesses and enjoys power, without bothering to demur about it."[16] Emma, however, is forced to acknowledge a threat to her power through music: after having heard the performance of Jane Fairfax—an orphan trained to earn her living as a governess—Emma "did unfeignedly and unequivocally regret the inferiority of her own playing and singing. She did most heartily grieve over the idleness of her childhood—and sat down and practised vigorously an hour and a half" (249). Because her status has required little in the way of a thorough education and self-discipline, Emma attains insight only through outside influences, and the admiration that Jane receives, particularly from an acute, attentive listener like Mr. Knightley, forces Emma to evaluate her own playing honestly; as she confesses to her protégée Harriet Smith, "my playing is just good enough to be praised, but Jane Fairfax's is much beyond it."

Although Emma's unashamed enjoyment and exercise of her authority transgresses the norm of male dominance, Emma herself unwittingly satirizes her agency by making few distinctions among the pursuits available to her as a single woman—and thus devaluing them all: "If I draw less, I shall read more; if I give up music, I shall take to carpet-work" (*E*, 92). As Richard Leppert notes, cultural representations of women's accomplishments as deliberately nonproductive justified the distinctions between men's and women's labor: "The trivialization of women's activities, to men and women alike, was essential to maintaining a status quo based on gender hierarchy."[17] Austen links Emma's complicity in this process to her immaturity. Emma dabbles in painting, drawing, matchmaking, and playing the piano, but her neglect of her own education and her decision to avoid serious commitment in her life appear most visibly in her relation to music: she does no more than wish she played as well as Jane Fairfax and makes no serious attempt to improve. Emma's being bested at the piano prefigures a later, pivotal development in character: when Emma perceives Harriet threatening her romantically, as Jane did musically, she quickly becomes self-aware and expressive. Just as she "heartily grieves" over her inferiority as a musician, her realization of her love for Knightley renders her mortified over the "blindness of her own head and heart" (*E*, 448). While Emma's privilege impedes her ability to be truly accomplished—unlike Jane, she has no need to nurture her talent—the fear of losing Knightley's affection shakes Emma out of her complacency and allows her to develop both her compassion for her less advantaged neighbors and her consciousness of the "difference of woman's destiny" (417), a difference rooted in accidental circumstances rather than personal merit or depth of talent.

In *Persuasion*, Louisa and Henrietta Musgrove resemble Emma in their carelessness toward music, a lack of seriousness satirized by Austen's pairing of instruments and furniture: arriving home from boarding school, the sisters give their parents' old-fashioned parlor "the proper air of confusion by a grand piano forte and a harp, flower-stands and little tables placed in every direction."[18] Aesthetic charm clearly means more to them than actual talent, for although the "usual stock of accomplishments" (43) the sisters obtain at school includes playing the piano and the harp, Austen never reveals which sister plays which instrument; the narrative only states that their parents' "fond partiality" for their music obscures the fact that Anne Elliot "played a great deal better than either" (50) of the Musgrove girls. Like Austen's own niece Anna Lefroy, the girls view their instruments primarily as decorative household items, and like Anna, they might have been better off spending their family's money on sheets and towels.[19]

Anne's musical talent—which indicates her "elegant and cultivated mind" (*P*, 43), or the level of her intelligence and maturity—clearly surpasses that of the Musgrove sisters. Yet Louisa and Henrietta appear no more than silly, using the harp to divert their mother's "large fat sighings" (73) over the death of her troublesome son and quickly turning the grand piano over to Anne's use. By contrast, in *Mansfield Park*, the harp seems the seductive device that conduct book writers feared, for it makes Mary Crawford the willing object of sexual attention. Mary's degree of musicianship and choice of instrument, though, illustrate the complexity and contradictions of her character: from the moment her harp arrives at the Mansfield parsonage, the narrative represents her as both an engaging young lady happy to please the small family parties for whom she plays, and a woman well aware of the attractive power of her instrument: "The harp arrived, and rather added to her beauty, wit, and good humour, for she played with the greatest obligingness, with an expression and taste which were peculiarly becoming, and there was something clever to be said at the close of every air. Edmund was at the parsonage every day to be indulged with his favourite instrument" (76). Played almost exclusively by women in Austen's time, the harp was highly popular but also highly problematic, with complex cultural resonances: as

Jeffrey Nigro notes, this "fashionable drawing room instrument *par excellence*" was associated with diverse players, including French aristocrats such as Marie Antoinette and Celtic bards such as Ossian.[20] Yet even for the most discerning listeners, the instrument's visual impact could easily overwhelm its aural effect. While harpists were the first female musicians to perform with orchestras, Johann Friedrich Reichardt's review of Caroline Longhi's concert performance in Vienna (1809) still reveals a greater focus on her body than on her music: "She played very well, and what is more, looked very well, because she understood how to show off a beautiful figure to its greatest advantage, especially at the harp, where she managed to place herself and deport herself in so many varied and yet still graceful positions that we received a good view of her entire beautiful figure from all sides."[21]

Mansfield Park demonstrates Austen's awareness of the player as spectacle in its description of Mary at her harp: "A young woman, pretty, lively, with a harp as elegant as herself; and both placed near a window, cut down to the ground, and opening on a little lawn, surrounded by shrubs in the rich foliage of summer, was enough to catch any man's heart" (76). As Juliette Wells observes, this passage focuses on the harp's elegance rather than its sound: "Mary is merely 'with' the harp, 'placed' near the window—this is the language of posing, not of actively playing."[22] Moreover, unlike Anne Elliot's elegance, which arises from her moral and intellectual refinement, Mary Crawford's elegance does not surpass that of her instrument—they are equal in degree, and both the woman and the harp function as objects of display, privileging the performer over the performance. The physical posture the harp demands emphasizes display as well: at the piano, women keep their arms close to their sides, but the harp requires them to lift and expose their arms, while parting their legs to accommodate the instrument. By detailing Mary's appearance at the harp, Austen highlights the erotic influence of this scene upon the viewer. As Richard Leppert claims, music's embodiment in the performer makes it an "activity subject to the gaze"—a form of interaction between musician and audience that is "supercharged with sexuality," anxiety, and the possibility of pleasure.[23] Edmund Bertram's indulgence in the repetition of this pleasure—he returns every day to the parsonage to hear Mary—reveals the degree to which he is indeed caught: "Without studying the business .. or knowing what he was about" (*MP*, 76), Edmund falls in love with her beauty and playing alike.

Mary gives no reason to doubt that she herself "dearly love[s] music" (*MP*, 69), yet her choice of instrument suggests that she adheres to a set of values different from those associated with playing the piano, preferring superficial attractiveness to internal depth of character, just as the harp's plucked strings produce a lighter sound distinct from the piano's deeper resonances. Although the harp shares with the piano harmonic possibilities—they both allow for chordal accompaniment to the melody—Austen uses the word "harmony" ironically in the novel, calling attention to the distinction between the elusive musical ideal and the Mansfield world of sexualized artistic performances, imprudent marriages, inept parents, and flagrant adulterers. When Mary first plays for Edmund, the narrator reports that "it was all in harmony," for the music and the venue both arouse his "tenderness and sentiment" (76), feelings of attachment and romance that he eagerly projects onto the scene.[24] Mary herself uses the phrase "the most delicious harmony" (481) to describe what she believes is the growing love between Fanny and Henry Crawford, even though Fanny feels no affection for him and openly objects that she finds his courtship painful. The illusion of harmony which the characters try to maintain finally breaks when Mary downplays the adulterous affair between Henry and Maria Rushworth as a reparable folly, or "*etourderie*" (506), rather than a sin. By making Mary Crawford an excellent musician, one who has practiced hard and mastered her craft, Austen heightens the contrast between surface and depth, charm and morality: the ultimate failure of Mary's performance solidifies the connection between her "faults of principle" (528) and the instrument she chooses to play.

"She Does Not Want to Learn"

Given their culture's ambivalence toward women's playing and singing, it is not surprising that some of Austen's more reflective heroines choose to have no involvement with music. Although the novels' female musicians do not all play for the same reasons nor with the same degree of talent, the nonmusicians share distinct traits that they reveal, in part, through their decision to exclude knowledge of music from their lives. Yet unlike Hannah More's Lucilla Stanley, who understands music perfectly without ever playing a note, Austen's characters receive no praise for this decision; rather, by refusing an opportunity to learn music, they reveal their emotional and psychological limitations and deny their need for self-awareness and self-expression. Despite their differences in class backgrounds and family lives, Elinor Dashwood in *Sense and Sensibility* and Fanny Price in *Mansfield Park* both demonstrate the consequences of rejecting music as a constitutive part of their education.

"Is She Musical?"

While her younger sister Marianne is devoted to her piano (and even the youngest, Margaret, is learning to play), Elinor is not musical and instead prefers drawing and painting screens—an activity that Darcy had criticized as trivial in *Pride and Prejudice*. According to Sally B. Palmer, screens in Austen's fictional households "were more purely decorative than functional"; whether stationary or hand-held, screens—made of paper or cloth stretched over a wooden frame and usually painted with landscape or wildlife scenes—primarily "served as art objects and props" for the display of women's talents.[25] Elinor's screens certainly showcase her artistry, which her sister Marianne loyally points out, but metaphorically they have a deeper significance: they suggest both her social role as an intermediary who deflects the emotional heat of uncomfortable encounters and situations, and her belief that propriety must supersede passion. The psychological cost of Elinor's screening reveals the dangers of refusing self-expression, including the expressive activity of musical performance.

Those who read *Sense and Sensibility* as a tale of caution—with Marianne, the musician, being chastised for her indulgence in her own feelings—usually commend Elinor for her "more rational accomplishment," since drawing requires "balance, proportion, and perspective."[26] As the oldest daughter of an impulsive, emotive mother, Elinor at the age of nineteen finds herself acting as "counsellor" to her parent: she "possessed a strength of understanding, and coolness of judgment" (*S&S*, 7) that enable her to guide Mrs. Dashwood away from "imprudence," particularly in regard to the family's precarious finances. Like her mother, Marianne is "eager in every thing" and "every thing but prudent" (7), and the weight of navigating both women through uneasy, unstable social situations never leaves Elinor's shoulders. Along with handling incidents that might give pain to her family—her sister-in-law's callous behavior, the intrusive conduct of neighbors, and even her own disappointment in love—she protects them from the results of their own unguarded conduct: "to screen Marianne from particularity" (100), Elinor prevents her racing down the road toward a horseman she mistakes for her lover Willoughby and later tries "to screen her from the observation of others" (202) when Marianne, snubbed by Willoughby, falls to pieces at a ball. In such episodes, Elinor's function as a screen appears both necessary and admirable, and her self-command contrasts favorably with her sister's emotional excess, as figured in Marianne's "alternately singing and crying" (96) at the piano after Willoughby's departure from Barton Cottage.[27]

Yet although Elinor's choice not to play music seems to reflect her self-containment and selflessness as opposed to Marianne's self-absorption at the keyboard, it also reveals her reluctance to influence the tone of a social gathering and to articulate, communicate, and assert her own desires. In an evening party at the Middletons, Marianne freely speaks her opinions and refuses to do what she finds distasteful: she turns down a request to play cards and begins to play the piano instead, avoiding the "insipidity of the meeting" (S&S, 164) by turning to her music, which she enjoys. Elinor, by contrast, asks to be excused from the card table in order to assist Lucy Steele in constructing a filigree basket for Lady Middleton's spoiled little daughter, and Lucy uses the opportunity afforded by the piano's "noise" to torment Elinor, who is her rival for Edward Ferrars's affection. As Lucy expects, Elinor's self-command enables her to keep the secret of Lucy's engagement to Edward, but the cost of acting as a screen is high: having chosen to conceal her pain from her mother and sister, Elinor suffers alone and soon finds that her false confidences with Lucy are "dangerous to herself" (173), as evidenced by the physical effects of their concealment. "Mortified, shocked, [and] confounded" (155) at Lucy's revelations, Elinor displays on her body the trauma of repressing her feelings: with "civil triumph" (274), Lucy remarks that she looks ill, knowing well that she herself has caused Elinor's pain. Predictably, when Edward finally reveals that Lucy has deserted him to marry his brother Robert, Elinor's reaction is explosive: "She almost ran out of the room, and as soon as the door was closed, burst into tears of joy, which at first she thought would never cease" (408). Elinor still keeps a screen—in this case, a door—between herself and others, remaining staunch in hiding her emotional life behind her sense of decorum, yet her sense of relief suggests the enormous pressure she endured for having—unlike Marianne—"no . . . pleasure in music" (286), no outlet for communication, and no form of refuge from the constant, often painful demands of her social world.

As Claudia Johnson remarks of the sisters in *Sense and Sensibility*, "what is at stake finally is not propriety, but survival" in a culture that severely limits women's power to direct and determine their own lives.[28] Music provides Marianne with a means of survival: her playing articulates her identity and draws to her the man—Colonel Brandon—who listens appreciatively to the depth of feeling and sensuality she conveys. Elinor's screen-making, by comparison, offers a strategy for self-preservation that requires suppression rather than assertion of her character to the point at which even her own mother unwittingly "had been unjust, inattentive, . . . almost unkind" (S&S, 403) in mistaking Elinor's quietude for contentment. By "turning away her eyes from the grand pianoforte" (283), Elinor displays her difference from her often fervidly self-involved sister, but this difference does not imply superiority: the novel suggests that in turning away from the possibility of self-expression, Elinor dangerously rejects the chance to be heard, listened to, and understood by others.

Like Elinor, *Mansfield Park*'s Fanny Price lives in a family of female musicians but neither plays nor sings herself. From her arrival at the estate as a dependent niece—a ten-year-old child taken into the Bertram household as an object of benevolence—Fanny's lack of interest in music distinguishes her from her cousins Maria and Julia, both of whom play the piano and sing. The sisters consider Fanny "odd" and "stupid" for not wanting instruction in music or drawing, but their Aunt Norris declares "it is not at all necessary that she should be as accomplished" (*MP*, 21) as her cousins, since a difference in the talents they possess will properly emphasize the difference in their social classes and marital prospects. Dullness, however, is not the cause of Fanny's disregard for learning music; rather, because she "thought too lowly of her own claims" (23) to attention, Fanny does not seek opportunities for displaying her abilities, particularly to people who do not encourage or value her. Her subordinate role in the Bertram family lies somewhere between the servants' quarters and the drawing room: even after a decade of Fanny's residence at Mansfield, her cousin Edmund cannot break his family's "habit of employing her" (171) as an errand-girl—a position that Fanny happily occupies, provided she can be "suffered to sit silent and unattended to" (260). Internalizing Aunt Norris's dictum that she "must be the lowest and last" (258) in all company has made Fanny a "creepmouse," almost too anxious to speak aloud before others, let alone sing and play; given her status in the household, musical performance and the self-assertion it entails would be for Fanny an instance of unimaginable impertinence and audacity.

Fanny's background, then, complicates readings of the novel that stress her moral objections to female accomplishments and her moral superiority to her cousins, who criticize her for not wanting to follow their pattern of education: her choice of silence arises less from principle than from an ingrained habit of self-protection. Grounded in her fear of ridicule and embarrassment, Fanny's tendency to shrink from notice—to avoid expressing herself, even to members of her household—determines that she "could not possibly have been a musician."[29] For Fanny, who constantly expects "some very grave reproof, or at least the coldest expression of indifference" (*MP*, 291) from her adoptive family, social interactions of the most casual sort can produce anxiety, even distress: she prefers solitary reading to learning an instrument and stargazing with Edmund to joining the group of singers around the piano. Attracted by the music and the enjoyment it promises—the sound of the piano, the mingled voices, and the sight of Mary's figure as she sings—Edmund leaves Fanny sighing "alone at the window" (133), refusing to become part of the group and missed by no one.

By turning her back to the piano, Fanny shows her anxiety toward sociability and sensuality alike; her own conception of harmony is entirely unmusical, and Austen's use of the word consistently proves ironic, as when Fanny vainly tries to turn Edmund's attention from Mary toward the night sky ("Here's harmony!" [*MP*, 132]) or when, from the distance of her father's house at Portsmouth, Fanny recalls the "elegance, propriety, regularity, harmony" (453) of Mansfield Park, the scene of her repeated humiliations. The conclusion of *Mansfield Park* continues this note of irony. Although Fanny and not Mary finally ends up sharing with Edmund "the home of affection and comfort" (547), the harmony of their household appears subdued, somber, and distinctly unmusical—an equivocal kind of happiness for a novelist who clearly valued the community that women created as they played and sang at home.

While *Mansfield Park* makes it clear that not all women, even talented ones, acquire self-discipline and self-awareness through their hours of practicing, Austen's fiction suggests that those who turn from music—who refuse the opportunities it offers for pleasure, agency, and self-expression—restrict their own possibilities for growth, just as Fanny adjusts the boundaries of her emotional and intellectual world to the "view and patronage" (548) of the Mansfield estate. In representing women who do not take music seriously, misemploy their abilities, or lack any involvement with music, Austen challenges domestic ideology's trivialization of female musical education and performance: whereas (in Catherine Macaulay's phrase) the "lighter accomplishments"[30]—painting tables, covering screens, netting purses—are the objects of Austen's satire, her characters' attitude toward music is critical in revealing their sense of their own identity and their relations to others. While Mary Crawford's anxious query—"Are they musical?" (*MP*, 334)—is intended to assess her possible competitors for Edmund's attention, in Austen's fiction, the question is far more probing: whether women play, what they play, and how well they play indicate not only their degree of talent but, more importantly, their knowledge of themselves and their place in the world.

"Is She Musical?"

Notes

1. Jane Austen, *Mansfield Park*, ed. John Wiltshire (Cambridge: Cambridge University Press, 2005), 335. Subsequent references are to this edition.

2. Richard Leppert, *The Sight of Sound: Music, Representation, and the History of the Body* (Berkeley: University of California Press, 1993), 70. In its description of music's significance to the extended Austen family, David Selwyn's *Jane Austen and Leisure* (London: Hambledon, 1999) recounts this dismissive view of domestic singing and playing.

3. Hester Chapone, *Letters on the Improvement of the Mind*, 2 vols. (London, 1773), 2:117–18. Jane Girdham offers an insightful overview of responses to women's domestic music in "Music for Young Ladies: Growing up with Music in the Late Eighteenth Century," paper presented at the American Society for Eighteenth-Century Studies Conference, Minneapolis, MN, April 2017.

4. Catherine Macaulay, *Letters on Education* (London, 1790), 62–63.

5. Maria Edgeworth, *Practical Education*, 2 vols. (London, 1798), 2:531.

6. Hannah More, *Coelebs in Search of a Wife*, introd. Mary Waldron (Bristol: Thoemmes, 1995), 111, 64.

7. Robert K. Wallace, *Jane Austen and Mozart: Classical Equilibrium in Fiction and Music* (Athens: University of Georgia Press, 1983), 252.

8. Jane Austen to Cassandra Austen, November 17–18, 1798, *Jane Austen's Letters*, ed. Deirdre Le Faye, 4th ed. (Oxford: Oxford University Press, 2011), 21. Kathryn L. Libin describes the impressive collection of handwritten and printed music owned by women of the Austen family as evidence of their commitment to "serious keyboard study," in "Daily Practice, Musical Accomplishment, and the Example of Jane Austen," in *Jane Austen and the Arts: Elegance, Propriety, and Harmony*, ed. Natasha Duquette and Elisabeth Lenckos (Bethlehem, PA: Lehigh University Press, 2014), 11.

9. Jane Austen, *Pride and Prejudice*, ed. Pat Rogers (Cambridge: Cambridge University Press, 2006), 113. Subsequent references are to this edition and will be provided parenthetically in the text.

10. Jane Austen, *Emma*, ed. Richard Cronin and Dorothy McMillan (Cambridge: Cambridge University Press, 2005), 298. Subsequent references are to this edition and will be provided parenthetically in the text.

11. The insights Austen gained from her own musical training are borne out by research in neuroscience: brain imaging of musicians and nonmusicians suggests that years of dedicated practice "can leave a lasting impression on the nervous system of individuals" by enhancing memory, concentration, and the reception of sensory impressions (S. Ausim Azizi, "Brain to Music to Brain!," *Neuroscience Letters* 459 [2009]: 1–2). Active listeners, or those who understand music, experience similar neurological effects. Moreover, the soundscape of a particular culture—its native language and music—"leaves an imprint on our minds" that enables us to interpret and find pleasure in certain acoustical effects; in this way, women's playing and singing at home could shape the intellect and sensibility of their households (Aniruddh D. Patel, *Music, Language, and the Brain* [Oxford: Oxford University Press, 2008], 9).

12. Jane Austen, *Juvenilia*, ed. Peter Sabor (Cambridge: Cambridge University Press, 2006), 248. Subsequent references are to this edition and will be provided parenthetically in the text.

13. Jane Austen, *Northanger Abbey*, ed. Barbara M. Benedict and Deirdre Le Faye (Cambridge: Cambridge University Press, 2006), 5–6. Subsequent references are to this edition and will be provided parenthetically in the text.

14. Sarah Webster Goodwin, "Wordsworth and Romantic Voice: The Poet's Song and the Prostitute's Cry," in *Embodied Voices: Representing Female Vocality in Western Culture*, ed. Leslie C. Dunn and Nancy A. Jones (Cambridge: Cambridge University Press, 1994), 68. Gerry Smyth agrees that "Lizzy's deficiency as a musician bespeaks her proficiency as a woman," since music does not distract her from pursuing romantic and sexual fulfillment (*Music in Contemporary British Fiction: Listening to the Novel* [Basingstoke, UK: Palgrave, 2008], 64–65). However, this praise for Elizabeth overlooks the connection between her effortless, charming playing and her often glib judgments upon others.

15. Juliette Wells notes that Austen's fiction deflects concerns that a commitment to mastery might render players unfit for domestic life, in "'In Music She Had Always Used to Feel Alone in the World': Jane Austen, Solitude, and the Artistic Woman," *Persuasions* 26 (2004): 98–110. Since the novels do not represent her heroines practicing hard at their instruments, the "dedication and ambition [required to play well] are invisible" (105), and thus unthreatening. Gillen D'Arcy Wood continues this argument in *Romanticism and Music Culture in Britain, 1770–1840: Virtue and Virtuosity* (Cambridge: Cambridge University Press, 2010): although Regency culture often viewed technical virtuosity as mechanical and uninspired, in Austen's novels, serious attention to playing and singing signifies her heroines' emotional and psychological depth, for "the discourse of self-expression" (159) that accompanied Romantic styles of music linked proficiency to women's possession of a rich interior life. Similarly, Ruth Perry claims that in "making music the visible sign of Jane Fairfax's cultivation, sensitivity and highly wrought consciousness," Austen supports the transition in music's status from an artisanal skill or accomplishment to an art form signifying "largeness of soul" ("Music," in *The Cambridge Companion to "Emma,"* ed. Peter Sabor [Cambridge: Cambridge University Press, 2015], 140).

16. Claudia Johnson, *Jane Austen: Women, Politics, and the Novel* (Chicago: University of Chicago Press, 1988), 125.

17. Leppert, *Sight of Sound*, 70.

18. Jane Austen, *Persuasion*, ed. Janet Todd and Antje Blank (Cambridge: Cambridge University Press, 2006), 43. Subsequent references are to this edition and will be provided parenthetically in the text.

19. Because she respected and admired women who were truly attentive to music, Austen criticized the newly married Anna's purchase of a piano to furnish her home: writing to Fanny Knight—a niece who practiced and played diligently—Austen proclaimed herself "rather sorry to hear that [Anna] *is* to have an Instrument; it seems throwing money away," for "as to her playing, it never can be anything" (November 30, 1814, *Letters*, 297).

20. Jeffrey A. Nigro, "'Favourable to Tenderness and Sentiment': The Many Meanings of Mary Crawford's Harp," *Persuasions On-Line* 35, no. 1 (Winter 2014), www.jasna.org/

persuasions/on-line/vol35no1/nigro.html. As Nigro explains, technical developments in constructing the harp, the proliferation of music composed for the instrument, and the popularity of operas featuring female harpists who accompanied their playing with song made Austen's era "the Golden Age of the harp."

21. Qtd. in Nancy B. Reich, "European Composers and Musicians, ca. 1800–1890," in *Women and Music: A History*, ed. Karin Pendle, 2nd ed. (Bloomington: Indiana University Press, 2001), 169.

22. Juliette Wells, "A Harpist Arrives at Mansfield Park: Music and the Moral Ambiguity of Mary Crawford," *Persuasions* 28 (2006): 105.

23. Leppert, *Sight of Sound*, 64.

24. Nigro describes Mary's harp as an analogue to Mary herself: "a multivalent, open-ended symbol" upon which listeners like Edmund and Fanny project their fears and hopes.

25. Sally B. Palmer, "Screens and Screening in *Sense and Sensibility*," *Persuasions* 33 (2011): 154.

26. Kathryn L. Libin, "Lifting the Heart to Rapture: Harmony, Nature, and the Unmusical Fanny Price," *Persuasions* 28 (2006): 141.

27. Kelly M. McDonald maintains that through the juxtaposition of Marianne and Elinor, Austen reveals a "reliance on theatrical operatic conventions" (27), particularly those of Mozart's *opera buffa*, *Così fan tutte*. "'A Reputation for Accomplishment': Marianne Dashwood and Emma Woodhouse as Artistic Performers," in *Jane Austen and the Arts*, ed. Duquette and Lenckos, 21–36.

28. Johnson, *Jane Austen*, 50.

29. Libin, "Lifting the Heart," 147. Libin argues that Fanny's attraction to nature and her aesthetic preference for the sublime make her the "moral mainspring of Mansfield Park" (146), for Fanny rejects the merely attractive arts (such as music) in favor of experiences that offer transcendence. Yet as a "parlour" musician herself who spent hours transcribing and playing country dances, marches, and ballads, Austen treasured domestic music and the sense of fellowship it created. For a longer discussion of Austen's relation to the musical culture of her time, see Linda Zionkowski and Miriam Hart, "'Aunt Jane Began Her Day with Music': Austen and the Female Amateur," *Persuasions* 37 (2015): 165–85.

30. Macaulay, *Letters on Education*, 62.

What Jane Saw—in Henrietta Street

JOCELYN HARRIS

Jane Austen eagerly sought out exhibitions of high art, but I shall argue that she was equally intrigued by the low art of caricature. Satirical street art enhanced the pleasures of perambulation, and Austen was just as energetic as Elizabeth Bennet. On April 20, 1811, she speaks of a "good dose of Walking & Coaching" around London, and on May 24, 1813, she found it "very pleasant" to be "Driving about" in Henry Austen's open carriage.[1] On March 5, 1814, even though getting out was "impossible" on a "nasty day" of "nothing but Thickness & Sleet," she went the following day to the theater and to church—most likely St. Paul's, Covent Garden, next to Henry's home in Henrietta Street. On March 7, she reported that she and her niece Fanny Knight had been into "the Park, yesterday & drove about & were very much entertained." She probably meant Hyde Park, the place to see and be seen, for she jokes that though they saw three people known to Fanny, "*I* could not produce a single acquaintance." The next day, snow prevented their plan to "have walked out early to near Shops, & had the Carriage for the more distant." They still went "out, as far as Coventry S^t—; Edwd escorted us there & back to Newtons, where he left us, & I brought Fanny safe home." It was "snowing the whole time. We have given up all idea of the Carriage." She meant Newton's the linen-draper at 14 Leicester Square on Coventry Street (*Letters*, 557), quite close to Covent Garden, but the snow would have deterred all but determined walkers. And yet they loitered, for Austen exclaimed about "a great many pretty Caps in the Windows of Cranbourn Alley!"—a tiny street off Leicester Square.

A *flâneuse* of her time, she was "out great part [*sic*] of the morning too, shopping & seeing the Indian Jugglers" at 87 Pall Mall, even in "cruel weather," on March 9, 1814 (*Letters*, 272). She took "some delightful Drives in the Curricle" on September 2, 1814, and was "very busy all yesterday," she reported on November 26, 1815, "from ½ past 11 to 4 in the Streets, working almost entirely for other people, driving from Place to Place," and "encountering the miseries of Grafton House," meaning the drapers Wilding & Kent on the corner of Grafton Street and 164 New Bond Street (608). Like

Admiral Croft staring "in earnest contemplation of some print" in a window in Bath, for he "can never get by this shop without stopping,"[2] Austen could not have missed the lampoons so prominently displayed in London streets. I shall discuss her response to high art, indicate where she could have seen satiric prints, explain why caricatures might have appealed to her, suggest what information she could have transferred into her novels, and show how the methodology, humor, and vulgarity of caricatures entered into her own style.

So how did Austen respond to high art? On April 20, 1811, Jane and the Henry Austens visited Count d'Antraigues, scholar, friend to Rousseau and Voltaire, royalist propagandist against Napoleon, spy, forger, and double agent (*Letters*, 514). On April 25, 1811, Austen called him "a Man of great Information & Taste."[3] Henry was delighted with the "fine Paintings," but Jane, unlike the Count with his elitist "Taste,"[4] preferred "a Miniature of Philip 5. of Spain, Louis 14.s Grandson, which exactly suited *my* capacity." Here Austen sounds like Catherine Morland, for while the Tilneys are "viewing the country with the eyes of persons accustomed to drawing" and "all the eagerness of real taste," Catherine knows "nothing of drawing—nothing of taste:—and she listened to them with an attention which brought her little profit, for they talked in phrases which conveyed scarcely any idea to her." Like the Count, perhaps, Henry lectures her on the picturesque until "fearful of wearying her with too much wisdom at once."[5]

As Lance Bertelsen observes, Austen implied an "absolute equivalency" between portraits and their real-life subjects,[6] writing on September 15, 1796, "At Nackington we met Lady Sondes' picture over the Mantlepeice [sic] in the Dining room, and the pictures of her three Children in an Antiroom, besides Mr Scott, Miss Fletcher, Mr Toke, Mr J. Toke, and the Archdeacon Lynch." She was disappointed to discover on September 18, 1796, that her "*first veiw* [sic]" of the real Miss Pearson bore "no great resemblance" to "the opinion I had formed of her" from her portrait. An equivalency between portraits and subjects appears in *Sanditon*, where, as Peter Sabor explains, a whole-length portrait of Lady Denham's second husband, Sir Harry, overshadows a miniature of her first: "Poor Mr Hollis!—It was impossible not to feel him hardly used; to be obliged to stand back in his own House & see the best place by the fire constantly occupied by Sir Harry Denham."[7]

Austen admired the "characteristical" portraits for which Shakespeare and Samuel Richardson were especially praised. In 1796, she may have attended John Boydell's exhibition, where life-sized canvases brought Shakespeare's characters vividly to life.[8] Like her two literary heroes, Austen was as fascinated by evil characters as virtuous ones, writing about Don Juan on September 16, 1813, "I have seen nobody on the stage who has been a more interesting Character than that compound of Cruelty & Lust." As she confessed on March 23, 1817, "pictures of perfection as you know make me sick & wicked." Like Austen, Elizabeth Bennet finds "the estimable" Mr. Bingley easy to comprehend but declares that "intricate characters" are "the *most* amusing."[9] I suggest that the *im*perfect characters of low art amused and interested Austen more than the perfect ones of high art.[10]

In *Pride and Prejudice*, Elizabeth Bennet ignores the "many good paintings" at Pemberley, knowing "nothing of the art," and turns instead to drawings by Miss Darcy, "whose subjects were usually more interesting, and also more intelligible." Walking on "in quest of the only face whose features would be known to her," she is "arrested" by the "striking resemblance of Mr. Darcy." Choosing a spot where she "fixed his eyes upon herself," and judging its "warmth" of regard as true to the "original," she animates the portrait into life (276, 277).

Four months after the novel appeared, Austen did the same. "Disappointed" on May 24, 1813 that "there was nothing like Mrs D." at either the Reynolds retrospective or an exhibition at the Society of Painters in Oil and Water Colours in Spring Gardens (*Letters*, 424n3), she explained the absence of the portrait by writing that "Mr D. prizes any Picture of her too much to like it should be exposed to the public eye.—I can imagine he w^d have that sort [of] feeling—that mixture of Love, Pride & Delicacy." Mrs. Darcy, she thought, would be "in Yellow." That was the signature color of actress Dorothy Jordan, who may have inspired Elizabeth Bennet.[11] Similarly at the Spring Gardens, Austen was very well pleased to find "a small portrait of Mrs Bingley, excessively like her . . exactly herself, size, shaped face, features & sweetness; there never was a greater likeness." The fact that she was "dressed in a white gown, with green ornaments," said Austen, "convinces me of what I always supposed, that green was a favourite colour with her." Here she identified Jane Bingley as a woman she already knew—Mrs. Georgina Quentin, "professed spanker" and mistress to the prince regent.[12]

Thus it seems that Austen, rather than admiring art for art's sake, sought out interesting and amusing material for her fiction. On April 18, 1811, she "had some amusement" from the exhibition at Bullock's Liverpool Museum at 22 Piccadilly, and confessed about a show at the British Gallery, 52 Pall Mall, "My preference for Men & Women, always inclines me to attend more to the company than the sight" (*Letters*, 411nn1–2). On May 24, 1813, she wrote similarly of the Royal Academy's Great Exhibition at Somerset House and Sir Joshua Reynolds's blockbuster retrospective of 1813, "I had great amusement among the Pictures" (222).[13]

In *Emma*, Austen mocks the idealizing tendency of high art when the heroine admits that her likeness of her brother-in-law is "only too handsome—too flattering."[14] Nevertheless, to make Mr. Elton fall for Harriet Smith, she means to throw in "a little improvement to the figure, to give a little more height, and considerably more elegance." Gallant Mr. Elton declares that he "never saw such a likeness," but as Mrs. Weston observes, Harriet "has not those eye-brows and eye-lashes. It is the fault of her face that she has them not." Mr. Knightley says tersely, "You have made her too tall, Emma" (48–49).

Even when Austen viewed Benjamin West's celebrated history paintings, she praised only his ability to reveal character. In 1811, he had received three thousand guineas for *Christ Healing the Sick*, and on September 2, 1814, she reported to Martha Lloyd, "I have seen West's famous Painting [*Christ Rejected by the Elders*], & prefer it to anything of the kind I ever saw before. I do not know that it *is* reckoned superior to his 'Healing in the Temple,' but it has gratified *me* much more, & and indeed is the first representation of our Saviour which ever at all contented me." She wanted "to have You & Cassandra see it," as though what mattered to her was West's capture of Christ's character as she imagined it, not his celebrity, skill, or financial rewards. Caricaturists, on their more realistic and profane level, captured character even more starkly.

In London, dubbed by Vic Gatrell the City of Laughter,[15] Austen would have seen the low art of caricatures everywhere she went. The artistic establishment disdained caricatures, for as Francis Grose the antiquary wrote in 1788, "The art of drawing Caricaturas is generally considered as a dangerous acquisition, tending rather to make the possessor feared than esteemed." Satirical painting, "like poetry of the same denomination, may be most efficaciously employed in the cause of virtue and decorum, by holding up to public notice many offenders against both." He meant those who, "though they contemptuously defy all serious reproof, tremble at the thoughts of seeing their vices or follies attacked by the keen shafts of ridicule."[16]

In 1815, Mary Russell Mitford's friend responded to Austen with fear as well as esteem, saying that she had "stiffened into the most perpendicular, precise, taciturn piece of 'single blessedness' that ever existed." Until *Pride and Prejudice* "showed what a precious gem was hidden in that unbending case, she was no more regarded in society than a poker or a fire screen or any other thin, upright piece of wood or iron that fills its corner in peace and quiet." After the publication of the novel, however, the case was very different, she said, for Austen was "still a poker but a poker of whom every one is afraid." This "silent observation from such an observer is rather formidable," for "a wit, a delineator of character, who does not talk, is terrific indeed!" Austen's friend Charlotte-Maria Beckford also recalled her "keen sense of humour," which "oozed out very much in Mr. Bennett's Style." Austen, she said, was "somewhat stiff & cold to Strangers," for she "used to sit at Table at Dinner-parties without uttering much probably gathering matter for her charming novels."[17]

I suggest, then, that Austen valued a portrait, whatever its genre or size, not for its aesthetic status but for what it told her about the character of the sitter. In the young Jane's "History of England," Cassandra drew caricatures that matched her sister's sharp, satiric texts; in Austen's juvenilia, the character sketches are just as cartoonish; and her letters contain distortions and satires very much in the style of James Gillray: as she wrote on November 4, 1800, for instance, Mrs. Blount "appeared exactly as she did in September, with the same broad face, diamond bandeau, white shoes, pink husband, & fat neck." Austen was attracted to caricatures because unlike the idealized, mythologizing images of high art, they exaggerated individual characteristics with a relish equal to her own. They also granted her permission to mock those who were bringing her country down—the royal dukes, and all their parasitical hangers-on.

Gillray caricatured members of the royal family with astounding virulence. In *Vices Overlook'd in the New Proclamation* (1792), for example, the king and the queen, representing Avarice, clutch bags of money; the Prince of Wales, representing Drunkenness, lurches home from the bawdy house; the Duke of York, representing Gambling, throws dice; and the Duke of Clarence, representing Debauchery, fondles an adoring Dorothy Jordan. In 1802, the anonymous artist of *The Three Brothers of Gotham, a Shocking Tale and a True One, of Gothic Originals*, complains that, "When a whole People were groaning under the intolerable burthens of taxation and famine," they "lavished away their patrimony among pimps, gladiators, and harlots." In 1812, Princess Charlotte would object that the "print shops are full of *scurrilous caricatures* & infamous things relative to the Prince's conduct in different branches."[18] Like previous commentators, I believe that such visual attacks encouraged Austen to criticize the prince under the guise of John Thorpe, Tom Bertram, Frank Churchill, Sir Walter Elliot, and William Walter Elliot. Like Gillray, who warned repeatedly that the regent's extravagance was destroying the kingdom, she shows, for instance, how Sir Walter Elliot's refusal to retrench is threatening the future of Kellynch.[19]

So where could Jane Austen have seen satiric prints? In London, she often walked past print shops displaying the latest cartoons and caricatures. In 1818, a year after her death, *Johnstone's Commercial Guide and Street Directory* lists no print shops in Henrietta Street itself, but the precincts of Covent Garden, Drury Lane, and the Strand still lived up to their raffish reputations.[20] Here, as in other neighborhoods where she roamed, caricatures made up an inescapable, ubiquitous part of her visual landscape.

On a visit to London on August 23, 1796, Jane, Edward, and Frank probably stayed with their Lefroy uncle Benjamin Langlois in Cork Street, near Old Bond Street and Piccadilly.[21] By announcing to Cassandra on August 23, 1796, "Here I am once more in this Scene of Dissipation & vice, and I begin already to find my Morals corrupted," she repeats a common jest about the great city.[22] But she could also have been thinking of images displayed by Samuel William Fores. In 1783, he had set up shop at 3 Piccadilly, before moving in 1795 to number 50, near Cork Street. In the 1780s, he sold 214 titles wholesale and retail, and hired out folios of caricatures. In 1796, when Austen was staying in the neighborhood, prints by the bold and brilliant Gillray, who had worked for Fores from 1788 to 1791, could still have been on sale.[23] At nearby 41 Sackville Street, Robert Ferrars orders a toothpick case from a real jeweller, Thomas Gray, and the Dashwood sisters catch their ungenerous half brother John out shopping (*S&S*, 251–52).[24] Gillray was a spectacular draughtsman, expressing his playful but often dark, brutal, and bawdy wit in fantasies, parodies, and burlesques in prints such as *Monstrous Craws* (1787), where the Prince of Wales accuses his parents of miserliness, much as John Thorpe bursts out about "its being a d----thing to be miserly; and that if people who rolled in money could not afford things, he did not know who could" (*NA*, 87).

Also employed by Fores from 1797 to about 1815 was Charles Williams,[25] who attacked the regent's extravagance with a savagery akin to Gillray's. In *John Bull Mad with Joy! Or, the First of August 1814*, for instance, the nation's gullible representative capers with delight as the regent offers him a bill of fare for the "Grand National Jubilee." The political satires of Isaac Cruikshank, who from 1783 to 1792 produced 1,350 images for Fores and others, might still have been on view.[26] With Gillray, he proved influential in developing John Bull as the archetypal citizen, often naïve, but never fooled for long, and grumpy about the country's mismanagement by a corrupt élite. Cruikshank's lampoons of Napoleon and the royal dukes would especially have pleased the author who created the heroic sailors of *Mansfield Park* and *Persuasion*, the patriotic Mr. Martin, the emblematic Englishman George Knightley, the feckless Sir Walter Elliot, and the treacherous William Walter Elliot, that undeserving heir who mocks his uncle as the regent mocked the king, then proves as keen as he to grasp his long-delayed inheritance.

On April 18, 1811, Austen reported to Cassandra from Henry's new home at 64 Sloane Street, where she was staying to correct the proofs of *Sense and Sensibility*, that their relatives the Cookes had "called here & took me back" to Bentinck Street. She also told of walking the next day from Sloane Street to Grafton House, meaning Wilding & Kent, near 164 New Bond Street (*Letters*, 412n5). In *Sense and Sensibility*, Willoughby lodges in Bond Street, where Marianne Dashwood keeps looking for him, and he enters "many a shop to avoid your sight, as the carriage drove by" (187, 370). Elinor and Marianne stay with Mrs. Jennings in Berkeley Street (113), and in *Pride and Prejudice,* Mr. Hurst lives in Grosvenor Street (130). Austen continued on April 20, "If the Weather permits, Eliza & I walk into London this morn^g," for Knightsbridge was still a separate village.[27] As they came "Walking & Coaching" back to Henrietta Street, they probably passed Fores's shop at 50 Piccadilly once again.

Austen's last commission was to Wedgwood's showrooms in St. James's Square, and on June 6, 1811, she would write from Chawton about "the pleasure of receiving, unpacking & approving our Wedgwood ware." To get to the Square, she had to pass Hannah Humphrey's print shop at 27 St. James's Street, near Pall Mall. From 1791, Humphrey, who headed the satirical trade with Fores,[28] employed Gillray to work for her exclusively. In 1797, they moved from Old Bond Street to St. James's Street, where a French visitor wrote in 1802: "The enthusiasm is indescribable when the next drawing appears; it is a veritable madness. You have to make your way into the crowd with your fists."[29] In *Very Slippy Weather* (1808), Gillray shows the windowpanes crammed with prints, and the surging, laughing viewers.

Austen surely witnessed that striking scene, because St. James's Street, a small street off St. James's Place, was close to Cleveland Court, the site of Henry's banking premises from 1801 to 1804. She knew the area well, for Colonel Brandon lodges in St. James's Street (*S&S*, 329), and Admiral Crawford lives in nearby Hill Street (*MP*, 53). Although "stately houses" occupied the west side of St. James's, the Reverend Joseph Nightingale suspected that the "elegant shops" opposite them "appear to a stranger rather as lounging-places than resorts of trade and the busy pursuits of merchandise."

These "sinks of vice and dissipation," he fulminated, were "the bane of human happiness and domestic peace—Gaming Houses!"[30]

The warrens and courts of St. James were home to the courtesans, the demi-reps, and the "fashionable impures" who found this wealthy district so profitable, while at night, St. James's Park was a notorious haunt of prostitutes.[31] The area around St. James was therefore an appropriate home for both the adulterous Admiral Crawford and the surprisingly worldly Colonel Brandon. In his backstory, Brandon explains that he grew up with Eliza, an orphan under his father's guardianship, and one of his nearest relations. He had always loved her, but because her fortune was large and the Brandon estate much encumbered, she was married against her inclination to his older brother. Brandon and the unhappy Eliza planned to elope; he was betrayed and banished; she was seduced and divorced, then sank—like the impures—"deeper in a life of sin." Brandon found her in a sponging-house before she died, leaving a little girl he called "a distant relation; but I am well aware that I have in general been suspected of a much nearer connection with her." This second Eliza was subsequently seduced by Willoughby, whom Brandon challenged to a duel. Later, he supported her during her lying-in and removal with her child to the country (S&S, 235–36). Perhaps Austen's familiarity with this half-respectable, half-disreputable area contributed to Brandon's report from London's seamy underworld.

At Humphrey's print shop in St. James's Street, Austen could have seen Gillray's satires. From 1791, he had lodged there chastely, and in 1797, after receiving a lifetime pension from George Canning to produce propaganda for the *Anti-Jacobin Magazine*, he led ferocious attacks on the Foxites, the Prince of Wales, and Napoleon, producing some one thousand satires until his eyesight and his mind gave way in 1809.[32] In 1811, Humphrey could still have been displaying his provocative prints.[33]

Austen rarely provides physical descriptions of her characters, but one notable exception is John Thorpe, in *Northanger Abbey*. Had she seen Gillray's *Voluptuary Undergoing the Horrors of Digestion* (1792)? Like his overweight, vulgar Prince of Wales, Thorpe is a "stout young man of middling height, who, with a plain face and ungraceful form, seemed fearful of being too handsome unless he wore the dress of a groom, and too much like a gentleman unless he were easy where he ought to be civil, and impudent where he might be allowed to be easy" (*NA*, 39). Between 1808 and 1811, Humphrey also displayed George Cruickshank's grotesque lampoons on the regent's licentious, corrupt court, for instance *The Prince of Whales* (May 1812), where a huge, blubbery whale, supported by mermaids and sharks, spouts "the Dew of Favor" onto his favorite ministers. As Colleen A. Sheehan argues, Cruikshank's image may well have inspired the famous charade in *Emma* (76–78), published in 1814.[34]

By May 21, 1813, Austen was back in Sloane Street, planning to visit Henry's new home at 10 Henrietta Street. She bought material for her mother's gown and said on May 24 that Cassandra's letter had saved her "going to Remnants, & fit me for Christian's, where I bought Fanny's dimity." Glove-seller T. Remnant operated at 126 Strand, and linen-drapers Christian & Sons operated at 11 Wigmore Street (*Letters*, 424n1).[35] Lady Susan stays at number 10, where her daughter attends boarding school (*LM*, 6–7), and nearby Wimpole Street was home to Lady Henrietta Lascelles, wife to Henry Lascelles, second earl of Harewood, and beneficiary of a Yorkshire dynasty made staggeringly wealthy by the slave trade. In *Mansfield Park*, the Rushworths move to Wimpole Street, and Mary Crawford's friendship with the real Lady Lascelles compromises her character (456).[36]

Also on May 24, 1813, Austen bought her mother's fabric at Layton & Shears, a silk mercer at 11 Henrietta Street,[37] next to Henry's home, before accompanying him to the exhibition in Spring Gardens by carriage, as there had previously been a "very long & very heavy storm of hail." Spring Street, a fashionable little thoroughfare that crossed the Mall between Admiralty Arch and Trafalgar Square, was close to Robert Dighton's establishment at 12 Charing Cross. Given Austen's fascination with the theater, his prints of actors in character for John Bell's edition of Shakespeare (1775–76) and Thomas Lowndes's *New English Theatre* (1776–77) might well have attracted Austen's attention, along with William Richardson's portraits of actors and actresses (1779) and his own "enduringly funny" caricatures.[38]

On May 24, 1813, Austen attended the British Academy exhibition at Somerset House, in the Strand (*Letters*, 424n5). It was familiar ground, for the Wickhams marry in St. Clement Danes (*P&P*, 352), and the Austens bought their tea at Twining's, 216 Strand (*Letters*, 270), as she reports on March 8, 1814. That involved passing 101 Strand, where in 1797, Rudolph Ackermann had moved to what became known in 1798 as "The Repository of Arts," selling art prints and caricatures by Thomas Rowlandson.[39] In nearby Exeter Change, John Dashwood takes young Harry to view the wild beasts at Pidcock's Menagerie (*S&S*, 252).

On September 15, 1813, Austen took her nieces to have their teeth attended to by George Spence, either George III's dentist at 17 Old Bond Street, or Spence & Son of 1 Arlington Street, near Humphrey's shop in St. James's Street (*Letters*, 229). She was familiar with the area, because on June

15, 1808, she had stayed at nearby Bath Hotel, on the corner of Arlington Street and Piccadilly (130). She also walked with Edward Austen to Wilding & Kent in Grafton House, on the corner of New Bond Street, "where, by going very early, we got immediate attendance & went on very comfortably." To purchase a white silk handkerchief from John Crook, Son, and Besford, haberdashers and hosiers at 104 Pall Mall, opposite the regent's ludicrously lavish residence, Carlton House (231), they probably walked down Old and New Bond Streets, then to the Mall via St. James's Street, home to Hannah Humphrey. Perhaps they also passed Dighton's at 12 Charing Cross Road on the way back to Henrietta Street.

As planned, they returned in time for breakfast at about eleven o'clock after their long trek. "From 11 to ½ past 3 we were hard at it," she wrote on September 16, driving in the carriage to "Hans Place for 10 minutes," then to "[Isaac] Newton's in Leicester Sq^{re}"—linen-draper at number 14 (*Letters*, 232). Their next stop was Remmington, Wilson & Co., silk manufacturers at 30 Milk Street, Cheapside, beyond St. Paul's Cathedral (232). Austen knew the area well, for in *Pride and Prejudice*, the Bingley girls mock Mr. Gardiner for living "somewhere near Cheapside" (40). Mr. Darcy, says Elizabeth sarcastically, "may perhaps have *heard* of such a place as Gracechurch Street, but he would hardly think a month's ablution enough to cleanse him from its impurities, were he once to enter it" (161). To visit Gracechurch Street, Elizabeth has to travel down Cheapside, where Austen could have seen George Cruikshank's lampoons at Thomas Tegg's (no. 111), or John Johnston's (no. 101), or Johnny Fairburn's (in Blackfriars and Ludgate Hill).[40]

Cruikshank's satires for William Naunton Jones's *Scourge; or Monthly Expositor of Imposture and Folly* (1811–16) launched further lacerating attacks on the regent, his mistresses, and his ministers.[41] In the first panel of his triptych, *Gent, No Gent & Re Gent!!* (1816), the young hero stands before the rising sun; in the second, the drunken prince, applauded by a jockey and a night-watchman, sits on Mrs. Fitzherbert's lap; in the third, the alarmingly overweight regent sits in state, crowned by a miniature Chinese pagoda, illegal wife to the left, bottles to the right, and an emaciated Welsh dragon above. In *Persuasion*, Charles Musgrove would call William Walter Elliot the "rising sun" in pointed reference to the prince regent.[42] Here Cruikshank followed the political, satirical style of his father, Isaac, who, along with Gillray, developed the figure of John Bull, savaged the French and Napoleon, celebrated Britain's victories, and excoriated governmental venality committed by the Duke of York in the Clarke affair, for instance.[43] Jane Austen, with her two naval brothers, would have applauded such patriotic sentiments.

On March 5, 1814, as Austen walked the short distance to and from Henrietta Street to Drury Lane Theatre, Covent Garden (*Letters*, 434n6), she would have passed the print shop of William Holland, radical print-seller and bookseller. In 1782, he had opened his first shop in Drury Lane, and in 1786, Gillray worked for him before transferring to Fores and Humphrey.[44] Also exhibiting there was George Murgatroyd Woodward, a prolific caricaturist who specialized in crude, comic images of the sailor ashore. He produced 525 known titles for Holland, Fores, Ackermann, and Tegg.[45] Holland also published attacks on the extravagant regent by Charles Williams, and caricatures by Richard Newton, who had produced his own radical and bawdy prints from 1791 at his "Original Print Warehouse" in Brydges Street, Covent Garden, before dying young.[46] Seeing that Drury Lane Theatre stood on the northeastern corner of Brydges Street, named after Austen's mother's great-uncle and grandest relative, George, Lord Chandos,[47] she might have paid special attention to the streetscape as they walked to the theater. And on March 9, 1814, the day she went "shopping & seeing the Indian jugglers" at 87 Pall Mall, she was not far from Hannah Humphrey's in St. James's Street.

In 1811, Austen had viewed West's painting *Christ Healing the Sick* (1811) at the British Institution. Three years later, on September 2, 1814, she saw both that and its sequel, *Christ Rejected*, in special exhibitions at 125 Pall Mall, a former home of the Royal Academy.[48] As a keen observer of celebrities, she had already visited the Reynolds retrospective,[49] and here she is again, keeping up with the play. She must have known the area bordered by Piccadilly, St. James's Street, and Pall Mall extremely well, for the Institution was close to Cleveland Court, the site of Henry Austen's former banking premises from 1801 to 1804. For the next three years, he moved to 1 The Courtyard, Albany, Piccadilly, a prestigious mansion "inhabited by many of the unmarried nobility and gentry, and by officers and professional men."[50] Two friends lived nearby, Mr. Henry Sanford in apartment F.3, and Mr. Gordon in Cleveland Row (*Letters*, 606, 607). Austen visited Gordon on October 16, 1815. In 1811, Colonel Brandon has business in a stationer's shop in Pall Mall, and Edward Ferrars lodges in Pall Mall after his mother cut him off for refusing to break his engagement to Lucy Steele (*S&S*, 226, 311). All these locations were close to Humphrey's print shop in St. James's Street.

Like Gillray, Austen was playful in her humor, but she could also be as dark, cruel, and bawdy as he. Regency caricatures were often vulgar and sexually explicit, and Austen was no prude. She made knowing jokes about homosexuality in the juvenilia, and on March 23, 1817, observed of her niece Anna, who had probably miscarried, "Poor Animal, she will be worn out before she is thirty.—I am very sorry for her.—Mrs Clement too is in that way again. I am quite tired of so many Children.—Mrs Benn has a 13th" (*Letters*, 351). On February 20, 1817, she said of Mrs. Deedes having an eighteenth child, "I w^d recommend to her & Mr D. the simple regimen of separate rooms" (344), then laughed at herself for spreading "Scandal and Gossip." But like her fellow satirists, she actually delighted in scandal and gossip. For instance, on March 13, 1817, after Lord Paget had eloped with the Duke of Wellington's sister-in-law, causing great scandal, a verdict against him for £24,000, an action for criminal conversation, a duel, and two divorces, Austen remarked about the heir to the Richmond dukedom marrying his daughter: "What can be expected from a Paget, born & brought up in the centre of conjugal Infidelity & Divorces?—I will *not* be interested about Lady Caroline. I abhor all the race of Pagets" (348, 463n5).

Austen's sexual innuendoes would fit right into Regency caricatures. Lydia Bennet, after eloping with Wickham, asks for a "great slit in my worked muslin gown" to be mended (*P&P*, 321); Fanny Price cries out, "you will hurt yourself, Miss Bertram . . . you will certainly hurt yourself against those spikes—you will tear your gown—you will be in danger of slipping into the ha-ha" (*MP*, 116); Mr. Woodhouse quotes innocently from a ribald riddle (*E*, 74, 84); and Mary Crawford jokes rudely about admirals, "Of *Rears*, and *Vices*, I saw enough. Now, do not suspect me of a pun, I entreat" (*MP*, 71).[51]

As an indefatigable walker around London, Jane Austen would have encountered caricatures everywhere she went, whether in print shop windows or pasted up on walls. To judge from her own letters and fiction, she relished the comic gusto, satirical methodology, and political implications of this "low art," as well as the realism she rated over the "high art" dear to those with "taste." In all her writings, therefore, Jane Austen contributed to the golden age of Regency satire.

Notes

1. All citations of Austen's letters are cited by date and refer to Deirdre Le Faye's *Jane Austen's Letters*, 4th ed. (Oxford: Oxford University Press, 2011). References to Le Faye's editorial notes are provided parenthetically in the text.

2. Jane Austen, *Persuasion*, ed. Janet Todd and Antje Blank (Cambridge: Cambridge University Press, 2006), 183. Subsequent references are to this edition and will be provided parenthetically in the text.

3. See Colin Duckworth, *The d'Antraigues Phenomenon: The Making and Breaking of a Revolutionary Royalist Espionage Agent* (Newcastle-upon-Tyne, UK: Avero, 1986).

4. For the "high" classical taste of the Royal Academy versus the "low" art of realistic representation, see Vic Gatrell, *The First Bohemians: Life and Art in London's Golden Age* (London: Penguin, 2014), xxv–xvi; and Peter Sabor, "'Staring in Astonishment': Portraits and Prints in *Persuasion*," in *Jane Austen's Business: Her World and Her Profession*, ed. Juliet McMaster and Bruce Stovel (Basingstoke, UK: Palgrave Macmillan, 1996), 17–29.

5. Jane Austen, *Northanger Abbey*, ed. Barbara M. Benedict and Deirdre Le Faye (Cambridge: Cambridge University Press, 2006), 111–12, 113. Subsequent references are to this edition and will be provided parenthetically in the text.

6. Lance Bertelsen, "Jane Austen's Miniatures: Painting, Drawing, and the Novels," *MLQ* 45, no. 4 (1984): 350–72. I am deeply indebted to this perceptive article.

7. Jane Austen, "Sanditon," in *Later Manuscripts*, ed. Janet Todd and Linda Bree (Cambridge: Cambridge University Press, 2008), 209. All references to this text are to this edition and are provided parenthetically in the text. Peter Sabor, "Staring," 18.

8. Janine Barchas argues that when Austen stayed in Cork Street in 1796, she could have viewed Boydell's Shakespeare exhibition at the nearby British Institution, 52 Pall Mall (see "About What Jane Saw," at What Jane Saw website, www.whatjanesaw.org/).

9. Jane Austen, *Pride and Prejudice*, ed. Pat Rogers (Cambridge: Cambridge University Press, 2006), 46–47. Subsequent references are to this edition and will be provided parenthetically in the text.

10. Anita McConnell and Simon Heneage, "Gillray, James (1756–1815)," *ODNB Online* (Oxford: Oxford University Press, 2014), www.oxforddnb.com.

11. For possible connections between Mrs. Jordan and Elizabeth Bennet, see Jocelyn Harris, *Satire, Celebrity, and Politics in Jane Austen* (Lewisburg, PA: Bucknell University Press, 2017), chap. 6.

12. Harris, *Satire, Celebrity, and Politics in Jane Austen*, 233.

13. For Austen's in-jokes about artists, see Janine Barchas, "Artistic Names in Austen's Fiction: Cameo Appearances by Prominent Painters," *Persuasions* 31 (2009): 145–62. Austen's interest in Reynolds may have been personal: Charlotte and Gwendolen Mitchell reidentify Reynolds's portrait of *George Clive and his Family with an Indian Maid* (ca. 1763–65) as *Tysoe Saul Hancock, his wife Philadelphia, their daughter Elizabeth and their Indian maid Clarinda*. If Austen's cousin Elizabeth brought the painting to the London home of her new husband, Henry Austen, Jane could have been familiar with it ("Passage to India," *Times Literary Supplement*, July 18, 2017).

14. Jane Austen, *Emma*, ed. Richard Cronin and Dorothy McMillan (Cambridge: Cambridge University Press, 2005), 47. Subsequent references are to this edition and will be provided parenthetically in the text.

15. Vic Gatrell, *City of Laughter: Sex and Satire in Eighteenth-Century London* (London: Atlantic, 2006).

16. Francis Grose, *Rules for Drawing Caricaturas: with an Essay on Comic Painting*, 2nd ed. (London: Samuel Bagster, 1788), 3–4.

17. See Deirdre Le Faye, *Jane Austen: A Family Record* (Cambridge: Cambridge University Press, 2004), 221, 199; and Harris, *Satire*, 13.

18. Princess Charlotte to Miss Mercer Elphinstone, *Letters of the Princess Charlotte 1811–1817*, ed. A. Aspinall (London: Home and Van Thal, 1949), 23. See also Harris, *Satire*, 165–66.

19. See also Laurie Kaplan, "*Emma* and 'the Children of Brunswick Square,'" *Persuasions* 31 (2009): 236–47; Laurie Kaplan, "The Rushworths of Wimpole Street," *Persuasions* 33 (2011): 202–14; Douglas Murray, "Jane Austen's 'Passion for Taking Likenesses': Portraits of the Prince Regent in *Emma*," *Persuasions* 29 (2007): 132–44; Roger Sales, *Jane Austen and Representations of Regency England* (London: Routledge, 1996); Colleen A. Sheehan, "Jane Austen's 'Tribute' to the Prince Regent: A Gentleman Riddled with Difficulty," *Persuasions Online* 27, no. 1 (2006); Sheehan, "Lampooning the Prince: A Second Solution to the Second Charade in *Emma*," *Persuasions On-line* 27, no. 1 (2006); A. Marie Sprayberry, "Sex, Power, and Other People's Money: The Prince Regent and His Impact on Jane Austen's Life and Work," *Persuasions Online* 33, no. 1 (2012); and Harris, *Satire*, chap. 5.

20. *Johnstone's London Commercial Guide, and Street Directory* (London: Longman et. al., 1818), 244. The bagnios, bordellos, and dubious coffeehouses in or near Covent Garden may well have displayed prints in their windows. In 1794, shops were still being prosecuted for selling *Harris's List of Covent Garden Ladies; or, The Man of Pleasure's Kalendar* (1756–95) (see Gatrell, *Bohemians*, 46).

21. "Once more" may mean that this was not Austen's first visit to London (Barchas, *What Jane Saw*). For Lefroy, see Le Faye, *Family Record*, 47.

22. Austen's joke on September 18, 1796, that she might "inevitably fall a Sacrifice to the arts of some fat Woman who would make me drunk with Small Beer," refers to Samuel Richardson's *Clarissa*, whose virtuous heroine drinks small beer laced with drugs by the London brothel-keeper Mrs. Sinclair (see Jocelyn Harris, *Jane Austen's Art of Memory* [Cambridge: Cambridge University Press, 1989], 34; and William Hogarth, *Harlot's Progress* [1732], plate 1).

23. Gatrell, *City*, 600.

24. Louise Allen, *Walking Jane Austen's London: A Tour Guide for the Modern Traveller* (Oxford: Shire, 2013), 53.

25. Gatrell, *City*, 604.

26. Robert L. Patten, "Cruikshank, Isaac (1764–1811)," *ODNB Online*, www.oxforddnb.com/view/10.1093/ref:odnb/9780198614128.001.0001/odnb-9780198614128-e-6843; Gatrell, *City*, 599.

27. Allen, *Walking*, 4.

28. Gatrell, *City*, 600–601.

29. C. R. Ashbee, *Caricature* (London: Chapman and Hall, 1928), 47, as qtd. in McConnell and Heneage, "Gillray." In 1789, Henry Austen reported "looking at a Print Shop in Bond Street," probably Humphrey's (see Annette Upfal, "A Taste for Cruel Humour: Jane Austen's *The History of England* and James Gillray's Bawdy Caricature of Charles James Fox," in *Home and Away: The Place of the Child Writer*, ed. David Owen and Lesley Peterson [Newcastle upon Tyne: Cambridge Scholars, 2016], 217–37).

30. Joseph Nightingale, *Topographical and Historical Description of the City of London* (London: Sherwood, Neely, and Jones, 1815). See Allen, *Walking*, 47.

31. Allen, *Walking*, 73.

32. Gatrell, *City*, 600.

33. In "Cruel Humour," Upfal argues persuasively that Cassandra based her sketch of Henry VIII on Gillray's startlingly rude caricature of Fox flogging William Pitt, in *Westminster School* (1785).

34. Sheehan, "Tribute," and "Lampooning."
35. Allen, *Walking*, 84, 23.
36. For Austen's likely attitude to the slave trade, see Harris, *Satire*, chap. 7.
37. *Johnstone's Guide*, 244.
38. Timothy Clayton, "Dighton, Robert (1751–1814)," *ODNB Online*, www.oxforddnb.com/view/10.1093/ref:odnb/9780198614128.001.0001/odnb-9780198614128-e-6843; see also Gatrell, *City*, 599.
39. Gatrell, *City*, 597.
40. Gatrell, *City*, 598–99, 602, 604.
41. Patten, "Cruikshank, George (1792–1878)," *ODNB Online*.
42. See Harris, *Satire*, 195–97.
43. Patten, "Isaac Cruikshank"; Gatrell, *City*, 598.
44. Gatrell, *City*, 600–601.
45. Gatrell, *City*, 604; Simon Heneage, "Woodward, George Murgatroyd (1760?–1809)," *ODNB Online*.
46. Gatrell, *City*, 602–3.
47. Harry Benjamin Wheatley and Peter Cunningham, *London Past and Present: Its History, Associations, and Traditions*, 3 vols. (London: John Murray, 1891), 1:289–90. Brydges Street is now Catherine Street.
48. Helmut von Erffa and Allen Staley, *The Paintings of Benjamin West* (New Haven, CT: Yale University Press, 1986), 142: https://austenonly.com/2011/04/18/jane-austen-and-benjamin-west/.
49. For digital re-creations of the Boydell and Reynolds exhibitions, see Barchas, *What Jane Saw*.
50. John Feltham, *The Picture of London* (London, 1825), 345.
51. In *Austen's Unbecoming Conjunctions: Subversive Laughter, Embodied History* (New York: Palgrave Macmillan, 2005), Jillian Heydt-Stevenson identifies many more cases of possible bawdry in the novels and letters.

Bibliography

Primary Sources

"Advertisement for *Elegant Extracts*." *St. James Chronicle, or British Evening Post*, September 12, 1782.

"Advertisement for *Elegant Extracts*." *Whitehall Evening Post*, January 2–4, 1783.

Aspinall, Arthur, ed. *Letters of the Princess Charlotte 1811–1817*. London: Home and Van Thal, 1949.

Austen, Jane. *Emma*. Edited by Richard Cronin and Dorothy McMillan. Cambridge: Cambridge University Press, 2005.

———. "The History of England." 1791. Add. MS 59874. British Library.

———. *The History of England: From the Reign of Henry 4th to the Death of Charles 1st*. Edited by Deirdre Le Faye. Chapel Hill: Algonquin, 1993.

———. *Jane Austen's Letters*. Edited by Deirdre Le Faye. Oxford: Oxford University Press, 2011.

———. *Jane Austen's "The History of England" and Cassandra's Portraits*. Edited by Annette Upfal and Christine Alexander. Edmonton: Juvenilia, 1995.

———. *Juvenilia*. Edited by Peter Sabor. Cambridge: Cambridge University Press, 2006.

———. *Later Manuscripts*. Edited by Janet Todd and Linda Bree. Cambridge: Cambridge University Press, 2008.

———. *Love and Friendship and Other Youthful Writings*. Edited by Christine Alexander. London: Penguin, 2014.

———. *Mansfield Park*. Edited by John Wiltshire. Cambridge: Cambridge University Press, 2005.

———. *Northanger Abbey*. Edited by Barbara Benedict and Deirdre Le Faye. Cambridge: Cambridge University Press, 2006.

———. *Persuasion*. Edited by Janet Todd and Antje Blank. Cambridge: Cambridge University Press, 2006.

———. *Persuasion: An Annotated Edition*. Edited by Robert Morrison. Cambridge, MA: Harvard University Press, 2011.

———. *Pride and Prejudice*. Edited by Pat Rogers. Cambridge: Cambridge University Press, 2005.

———. *Sense and Sensibility*. Edited by Edward Copeland. Cambridge: Cambridge University Press, 2006.

Austen-Leigh, James Edward. *A Memoir of Jane Austen and Other Family Recollections*. Edited by Kathryn Sutherland. Oxford: Oxford University Press, 2008.

Baronetage of England: Containing Their Descent and Present State. Edited by John Debrett. London: F. C. and J. Rivington, 1815.

Bibliography

Blackstone, William. *Commentaries on the Laws of England: A Facsimile of the First Edition, 1765–1769.* 4 vols. Chicago: Chicago University Press, 2002.

Brunton, Mary. *Self-Control.* Edinburgh, 1811.

Burke, Edmund. *A Philosophical Enquiry into Our Ideas of the Sublime and the Beautiful.* London: Routledge, 1958.

———. *A Philosophical Inquiry into the Origin of Our Ideas of the Sublime and Beautiful.* London, 1767.

———. *Reflections on the Revolution in France.* London: J. Dodsley, 1790.

Burney, Frances. *Brief Reflections Relative to the Emigrant French Clergy.* London, 1793.

———. *Diaries and Letters of Madame D'Arblay.* 7 vols. Edited by Charlotte Barrett. Colburn, 1854.

———. *Early Journals and Letters of Frances Burney.* 5 vols. Edited by Lars E. Troide. Montreal: McGill-Queens Press, 1988.

———. *The Wanderer.* Edited by Margaret Anne Doody, Robert L. Mack, and Peter Sabor. Oxford: Oxford University Press, 1991.

Chapone, Hester. *Letters on the Improvement of the Mind.* 2 vols. London, 1773.

Complete Baronetage: English Baronetcies, 1611–1625 and Irish, 1618–1625. London: W. Pollard, 1900.

Cooper, Anthony Ashley, Third Earl of Shaftesbury. *Characteristics of Men, Manners, Opinions, Times.* Edited by Lawrence Klein. Cambridge: Cambridge University Press, 1999.

Dugdale, Sir William. *The Ancient Usage in Bearing of Such Ensigns of Honour as Are Commonly Call'd Arms: With a Catalogue of the Present Nobility of England.* London: Theater Dudley Davis, 1682.

Edgeworth, Maria. *Life and Letters of Maria Edgeworth.* 2 vols. London, 1894.

———. *Patronage.* London: Pandora, 1986.

———. *Practical Education.* 2 vols. London, 1798.

Feltham, John. *The Picture of London.* London, 1825.

Gilpin, William. *An Essay on Prints.* London, 1781.

———. *Observations on the Coasts of Hampshire, Sussex, and Kent: Relative Chiefly to Picturesque Beauty: Made in the Summer of the Year 1774.* London, 1774.

———. *Observations on the River Wye, and Several Parts of South Wales, &C. Relative Chiefly to Picturesque Beauty: Made in the Summer of the Year 1770.* London, 1800.

———. *Observations on the Western Parts of England, Relative Chiefly to Picturesque Beauty: To Which Are Added, a Few Remarks on the Picturesque Beauties of the Isle of Wight.* London, 1798.

———. *Observations, Relative Chiefly to Picturesque Beauty, Made in the Year 1772, on Several Parts of England, Particularly the Mountains and Lakes of Cumberland and Westmoreland.* London, 1792.

———. *Three Essays: On Picturesque Beauty, on Picturesque Travel, and on Sketching Landscape: To Which Is Added a Poem, on Landscape Painting.* London, 1794.

Gillray, James. *Vices Overlook'd in the New Proclamation.* London, 1792.

Goldsmith, Oliver. *The History of England.* 4 vols. London, 1771.

———. *The Vicar of Wakefield.* Bath, 1804.

Hall, Samuel. "An Attempt to Shew That a Taste for the Beauties of Nature and the Fine

Bibliography

Arts, Has No Influence Favourable to Morals." In *Memoirs of the Literary and Philosophical Society of Manchester*, 223–40. London, 1785.

Harris's List of Covent Garden Ladies; or, the Man of Pleasure's Kalendar. London, 1756–95.

Hogarth, William. "The Progress of a Harlot, as She Is Described in Six Prints." London, 1732.

Johnson, Samuel. *A Dictionary of the English Language.* London, 1785.

Johnstone's London Commercial Guide, and Street Directory. London: Longman, 1815.

Knight, Richard Payne. *An Analytical Inquiry into the Principles of Taste.* 2nd ed. London, 1805.

Knox, Vicesimus. *Elegant Extracts or Useful and Entertaining Pieces of Poetry.* London, 1801.

———. *Elegant Extracts or Useful and Entertaining Passages in Prose.* London: Dilly, n.d.

Le Faye, Deirdre. *Fanny Knight's Diaries: Jane Austen through Her Niece's Eyes.* Chawton: Jane Austen Society, 2000.

Macaulay, Catherine. *Letters on Education.* London, 1790.

More, Hannah. *Coelebs in Search of a Wife.* London, 1809.

———. *Coelebs in Search of a Wife.* London: Thoemmes, 1995.

———. *Strictures on the Modern System of Female Education.* 5th ed. 2 vols. London, 1799.

Murry, Ann. *Mentoria: Or, the Young Ladies Instructor.* 2nd ed. London, 1780.

Piozzi, Hester Thrale. *Mrs Thrale's French Journal, 1775, The French Journals of Mrs Thrale and Doctor Johnson.* Edited by Moses Tyson and Henry Guppy. Manchester: Manchester University Press, 1932.

Pope, Alexander. *The Twickenham Edition of the Poems of Alexander Pope.* 6 vols. New Haven, CT: Yale University Press, 1953–1964.

Radcliffe, Ann. *A Journey Made in the Summer of 1794, through Holland and the Western Frontier of Germany, with a Return down the Rhine: to Which Are Added Observations during a Tour to the Lakes of Lancashire, Westmoreland, and Cumberland,* 2nd ed., 2 vols. London: G. G. and J. Robinson, 1795.

Repton, Humphry. *Observations on the Theory and Practice of Landscape Gardening* 1803. London: Constable, 1906.

Richardson, Samuel. *Clarissa.* Edited by Angus Ross. New York: Penguin, 1985.

Schimmelpenninck, Mary Anne. *Theory on the Classification of Beauty and Deformity.* London: John and Arthur Arch, 1815.

Scott, Sir Walter. *Waverley.* Oxford: Oxford University Press, 1986.

Smith, Charlotte. *Emmeline, the Orphan of the Castle.* In *The Works of Charlotte Smith,* ed. Judith Stanton, vol. 2. London: Pickering and Chatto, 2005.

The Three Brothers of Gotham, a Shocking Tale, and a True One, of Gothic Originals. London, 1802–9.

Williams, Charles. *John Bull Mad with Joy! Or, the First of August 1814.* London, 1814.

Wollstonecraft, Mary. *Works of Mary Wollstonecraft.* Edited by Marilyn Butler and Janet Todd. Abingdon: Pickering and Chatto, 1989.

———. *A Vindication of the Rights of Women.* Edited by Deidre Shauna Lynch. New York: Norton, 2009.

William Wordsworth, *The Prelude, or Growth of a Poet's Mind.* London: Edward Moxon, 1850.

Bibliography

Secondary Sources

Adkins, Roy. *Jane Austen's England*. New York: Viking Penguin, 2013.

Allen, Louise. *Walking Jane Austen's London: A Tour Guide for the Modern Traveller*. Oxford: Shire, 2013.

Amis, Martin. "What Became of Jane Austen?" In *Jane Austen: A Collection of Critical Essays*, edited by Ian Watt, 141–45. Englewood Cliffs: Prentice-Hall, 1963.

Andrews, Malcolm. *The Search for the Picturesque: Landscape Aesthetics and Tourism in Britain, 1760–1800*. Stanford, CA: Stanford University Press, 1989.

Appadurai, Arjun. *The Social Life of Things: Commodities in Perspective*. Cambridge: Cambridge University Press, 1988.

Armstrong, Isobel. Introduction to *Pride and Prejudice*, by Jane Austen, edited by James Kinsley and Frank W. Bradbrook, vii–xxxii. Oxford: Oxford University Press, 1990.

Armstrong, Nancy. *Desire and Domestic Fiction: A Political History of the Novel*. Oxford: Oxford University Press, 1990.

Ashbee, C. R. *Caricature*. London: Chapman and Hall, 1928.

Azizi, S. Ausim. "Brain to Music to Brain!" *Neuroscience Letters* 459 (2009): 1–2.

Badiou, Alain. *Rhapsody for the Theatre*. Edited by Bruno Bosteels. London: Verso, 2013.

Bander, Elaine. "Jane Austen's Readers." Ph.D. diss., McGill University, 1980.

Barchas, Janine. "Artistic Names in Austen's Fiction: Cameo Appearances by Prominent Painters." *Persuasions* 31 (2009): 145–62.

———. *Matters of Fact in Jane Austen: History, Location, and Celebrity*. Baltimore, MD: Johns Hopkins University Press, 2012.

———. What Jane Saw. 2017. www.whatjanesaw.org/.

Barrell, John. *The Political Theory of Painting from Reynolds to Hazlitt: "The Body of the Public."* New Haven, CT: Yale University Press, 1986.

Batchelor, Jennie, and Cora Kaplan, eds. *Women and Material Culture, 1660–1830*. New York: Palgrave Macmillan, 2007.

Battaglia, Beatrice. "'Italian Lights on English Walls': Jane Austen and the Picturesque." In *Re-Drawing Austen: Picturesque Travels in Austenland*, edited by Beatrice Battaglia and Diego Saglia, 13–35. Napoli: Liguori Editore, 2004.

Battigelli, Anna, and Laura Stevens, eds. "Eighteenth-Century Women and English Catholicism." Special issue, *Tulsa Studies in Women's Literature* 31, nos. 1–2 (Spring/Fall 2012).

Bellenger, Dom Aidan. "The Brussels Nuns at Winchester." *English Benedictine Congregation History Commission Symposium* (1999): 1–7.

———. *The French Exiled Clergy*. Bath: Downside Abbey, 1986.

Benedict, Barbara M. "Jane Austen and the Culture of Circulating Libraries." In *Revising Women: Eighteenth-Century 'Women's Fiction' and Social Engagement*, edited by Paula R. Backscheider, 147–99. Baltimore, MD: Johns Hopkins University Press, 2000.

Benedictine Nuns. Congregation of Saint Scholastica. *A History of the Benedictine Nuns of Dunkirk: Now at Saint Scholastica's Abbey, Teignmouth, Devon*. London: Burns and Oates, 1958.

Berg, Maxine. *The Age of Manufactures: Industry, Innovation and Work in Britain 1700–1820*. London: Fontana, 1985.

Bibliography

———. *Luxury and Pleasure in Eighteenth-Century Britain*. Oxford: Oxford University Press, 2005.

Bermingham, Ann. *Learning to Draw: Studies in the Cultural History of a Polite and Useful Art*. New Haven, CT: Yale University Press, 2000.

Bermingham, Ann, and John Brewer. *The Consumption of Culture*. London: Routledge, 1995.

Bertelsen, Lance. "Jane Austen's Miniatures: Painting, Drawing, and the Novels." *Modern Language Quarterly: A Journal of Literary History* 45, no. 4 (1984): 350–72.

Blackwell, Mark, ed. *The Secret Life of Things: Animals, Objects, and It-Narratives in Eighteenth-Century England*. Lewisburg, PA: Bucknell University Press, 2007.

Blank, Antje. "Dress." In *Jane Austen in Context*, edited by Janet Todd, 234–51. Cambridge: Cambridge University Press, 2005.

Bodenheimer, Rosemarie. "Looking at the Landscape in Jane Austen." *Studies in English Literature, 1500–1900* 21 (1981): 605–23.

Booth, Wayne C. *The Rhetoric of Fiction*. Chicago: University of Chicago Press, 1961.

Bowden, Caroline, James Kelly, Jane Broadway, David Horne, Katharine Keats-Rohan, Michael Questier, Katrien Daemen de Gelder, and Pascal Majerus. "Who Were the Nuns? A Prosopographical Study of the English Convents in Exile, 1600–1800." http://wwtn.history.qmul.ac.uk/.

Bradbrook, Frank W. *Jane Austen and Her Predecessors*. Cambridge: Cambridge University Press, 1967.

Bradney-Smith, Adrienne. "Art and the Austen Family." *Jane Austen Society Report for 2008* (2008): 129–44.

Bray, Joe. "*Belinda*, *Emma*, and the 'Likeness' of the Portrait." *Nineteenth-Century Contexts* 33, no. 1 (2011): 1–15.

———. *The Portrait in Fiction of the Romantic Period*. London: Taylor and Francis, 2016.

Brewer, John, and Roy Porter, eds. *Consumption and the World of Goods*. London: Routledge, 1993.

Brown, Bill. "Thing Theory." *Critical Inquiry* 28, no. 1 (2001): 1–22.

Brown, James. "Jane Austen's Mental Maps." *Critical Survey* 26, no. 1 (2014): 20–41.

Brown, Laura. *Fables of Modernity: Literature and Culture in the English Eighteenth Century*. Ithaca, NY: Cornell University Press, 1985.

———. "The Ideology of Restoration Poetic Form: John Dryden." *PMLA* 97, no. 3 (1982): 395–407.

Buckland, Theresa Jill. *Society Dancing: Fashionable Bodies in England, 1870–1920*. New York: Palgrave, 2011.

Bustow, Catherine. "Unlocking the Rape: An Analysis of Austen's Use of Pope's Symbolism in *Sense and Sensibility*." *Persuasions* 20 (1998): 31–37.

Butte, George. *I Know That You Know That I Know: Narrating Subjects from Moll Flanders to Marnie*. Columbus: Ohio University Press, 2004.

Byrne, Paula. *Jane Austen and the Theatre*. London: Hambledon and London, 2002.

———. *The Real Jane Austen: A Life in Small Things*. New York: Harper-Perennial, 2013.

Carpenter, Kirsty. *Refugees of the French Revolution: Émigrés in London, 1789–1802*. New York: St. Martin's, 1999.

Chapman, R. W. *Jane Austen: Facts and Problems*. Oxford: Oxford University Press, 1948.

Bibliography

Chazin-Bennahum, Judith. *The Lure of Perfection: Fashion and Ballet 1780–1830.* New York: Routledge, 2005.

Clark, Lorrie. "Shaftesbury's Art of 'Soliloquy' in *Mansfield Park.*" *Persuasions* 24 (2002): 59–70.

———. "Transfiguring the Romantic Sublime in *Persuasion.*" In *Jane Austen's Business: Her World and Her Profession,* edited by Juliet McMaster and Bruce Stovel, 30–41. Basingstoke, UK: Palgrave Macmillan, 1996.

Clayton, Timothy. "Robert Dighton." In *Oxford Dictionary of National Biography.* Oxford: Oxford University Press, 2017.

Cochran, Peter. "Byron and Drury Lane." In *Byron at the Theatre,* edited by Cochran. Newcastle, UK: Cambridge Scholars Publishing, 2008.

Cohen, Selma Jeanne. "The English Critic and the Romantic Ballet." *Theatre Survey* 1, no. 17 (1976): 82–91.

Cohn, Dorrit. *Transparent Minds: Narrative Modes for Presenting Consciousness in Fiction.* Princeton, NJ: Princeton University Press, 1978.

Conger, Syndy McMillen. "Reading *Lovers' Vows*: Jane Austen's Reflections on English Sense and German Sensibility." *Studies in Philology* 85, no. 1 (1988): 92–113.

Conway, Alison. *Private Interests: Women, Portraiture, and the Visual Culture of the English Novel, 1709–1791.* Toronto: University of Toronto Press, 2001.

Cooke, Katherine. *Coleridge.* London: Routledge and Kegan Paul, 1979.

Copeland, Edward. "Money." In *The Cambridge Companion to Jane Austen,* edited by Copeland and Juliet McMaster, 131–48. Cambridge: Cambridge University Press, 2001.

Curran, Gwen. "Ballet Fantastique's 'Pride and Prejudice' Truly Fantastic." *Register-Guard* (2016).

Cutting-Gray, Joanne. *Woman as "Nobody" in the Novels of Fanny Burney.* Gainesville: University Press of Florida, 1992.

Daly, Ann. "Unlimited Partnership: Dance and Feminist Analysis." *Dance Research Journal* 23 (1991): 29–49.

Davenport, Alice. "An Adaptable Aesthetic: Eighteenth-Century Landscape, Ann Radcliffe, and Jane Austen." In *Jane Austen and the Arts: Elegance, Propriety, and Harmony,* edited by Natasha Duquette and Elisabeth Lenckos, 97–114. Bethlehem, PA: Lehigh University Press, 2014.

Davis, Kathryn E. *Liberty in Jane Austen's Persuasion.* Bethlehem, PA: Lehigh University Press, 2016.

Davis, Tracy C., and Ellen Donkin, eds. *Women and Playwriting in Nineteenth-Century Britain.* Cambridge: Cambridge University Press, 1999.

de Grazia, Margreta, Maureen Quilligan, and Peter Stallybrass, eds. *Subject and Object in Renaissance Culture.* Cambridge: Cambridge University Press, 1996.

Dobson, Michael. *The Making of the National Poet: Shakespeare, Adaptation, and Authorship, 1660–1769.* Oxford: Clarendon, 1992.

Donkin, Ellen. *Getting into the Act: Women Playwrights in London, 1776—1829.* London: Routledge, 1995.

Doody, Margaret Anne. *Jane Austen's Names: Riddles, Persons, Places.* Chicago: Chicago University Press, 2015.

Bibliography

———. "Jane Austen's Reading." In *The Jane Austen Handbook*, edited by J. David Grey et al., 347–63. London: Athlone, 1986.
Dow, Gillian. "Jane Austen's Reading and the Eighteenth-Century Woman Writer." *Sensibilities* 39 (2009): 69–88.
———. "Reading at Godmersham: Edward's Library and Marianne's Books." *Persuasions* 37 (2015): 152–62.
Dowell, Stephen. *History of Taxation and Taxes in England*. 4 vols. London: Longmans, Green, 1884.
Drum, Alice. "Jane Austen and the Professions." *College Literature* 36, no. 3 (2009): 92–115.
Duckworth, Alistair. *The Improvement of the Estate: A Study of Jane Austen's Novels*. Baltimore, MD: Johns Hopkins University Press, 1994.
Duckworth, Colin. *The d'Antraigues Phenomenon: The Making and Breaking of a Revolutionary Royalist Espionage Agent*. Newcastle upon Tyne: Avero, 1986.
Dunne, Leslie C., and Nancy A. Jones. *Embodied Voices: Representing Female Vocality in Western Culture*. Cambridge: Cambridge University Press, 1994.
Duquette, Natasha. "'The Grandeur of the Abbey': Exploring Gothic Architecture in Novels by Helen Maria Williams, Ann Radcliffe, and Jane Austen." *Persuasions: The Jane Austen Journal Online* 31, no. 1 (2010).
———. "The Sensibility of Captain Benwick in Literary and Historical Context." In *Jane Austen and Masculinity*, edited by Michael Kramp et al., 97–111. Lewisburg: PA: Bucknell University Press, 2018.
Duquette, Natasha, and Elisabeth Lenckos, eds. *Jane Austen and the Arts: Elegance, Propriety, and Harmony*. Bethlehem, PA: Lehigh University Press, 2014.
Dyck, Dorothy. "The Development of the Picturesque and the Knight-Price-Repton Controversy." Master's thesis, McGill University, 1991.
Edwards, Clive. "'Home Is Where the Art Is': Women, Handicrafts and Home Improvements 1750–1900." *Journal of Design History* 19, no. 1 (spring 2006): 11–21.
Ehrenpreis, Anne Henry. Introduction to *Northanger Abbey*, by Jane Austen, edited by Ehrenpreis, 7–24. Harmondsworth, UK: Penguin, 1972.
Emsley, Sarah. *Jane Austen's Philosophy of the Virtues*. New York: Palgrave Macmillan, 2005.
———. "The Tragic Action of *Mansfield Park*." In *Approaches to Teaching Austen's "Mansfield Park,"* edited by Marcia McClintock Folsom and John Wiltshire, 164–74. New York: Modern Language Association, 2014.
Engelhardt, Molly. *Dancing out of Line: Ballrooms, Ballets, and Mobility in Victorian Fiction and Culture*. Athens: Ohio University Press, 2009.
Esrock, Ellen J. *The Reader's Eye: Visual Imagining as Reader Response*. Baltimore, MD: Johns Hopkins University Press, 1994.
Evans, Jessica. *The Muse: A Pride and Prejudice Variation*. Oysterville, WA: Meryton, 2014.
Everett, Nigel. *The Tory View of Landscape*. New Haven, CT: Yale University Press, 1994.
Fennetaux, Ariane. "Female Crafts: Women and *Bricolage* in Late Georgian Britain, 1750–1820." In *Women and Things, 1750–1950: Gendered Material Strategies*, edited by Maureen Daly Goggin and Beth Fowkes Tobin, 91–108. Burlington, VT: Ashgate, 2009.

Bibliography

Festa, Lynn. *Figures of Empire in Eighteenth-Century Britain and France*. Baltimore, MD: Johns Hopkins University Press, 2006.

Ford, Susan Allen. "'Not What You Would Think Anything Of': Robert Martin and Harriet Smith." *Persuasions* 38 (2016): 137–54.

Fraiman, Susan. "Jane Austen and Edward Said: Gender, Culture, and Imperialism." *Critical Inquiry* 21, no. 4 (1995): 805–21.

Fullerton, Susannah. *A Dance with Jane Austen: How a Novelist and Her Characters Went to the Ball*. London: Frances Lincoln, 2012.

Gallagher, Catherine. *Nobody's Story: The Vanishing Acts of Women Writers in the Marketplace 1670–1920*. Berkeley: University of California Press, 1994.

Gatrell, Vic. *City of Laughter: Sex and Satire in Eighteenth-Century London*. London: Atlantic Books, 2006.

———. *The First Bohemians: Life and Art in London's Golden Age*. London: Penguin, 2014.

Gay, Penny. *Jane Austen and the Theatre*. Cambridge: Cambridge University Press, 2002.

Gevirtz, Karen Bloom. *Life after Death*. Newark: University of Delaware Press, 2005.

Gilroy, Paul. *The Black Atlantic: Modernity and Double Consciousness*. Cambridge: Cambridge University Press, 1995.

Gilson, David. "Cassandra Austen's Pictures." *Jane Austen Society Report for 1993* (1993): 17–19.

Girdham, Jane. "Music for Young Ladies: Growing up with Music in the Late Eighteenth Century." Paper presented at the Annual Meeting of the American Society for Eighteenth-Century Studies, Minneapolis, MN, March 2017.

Glickman, Sylvia, and Martha Furman Schleifer, eds. *From Convent to Concert Hall: A Guide to Women Composers*. Westport, CT: Greenwood, 2003.

Goggin, Maureen Daly, and Beth Fowkes Tobin, eds. *Women and the Material Culture of Needlework and Textiles, 1750–1950*. Burlington, VT: Ashgate, 2009.

———, eds. *Women and Things, 1750–1950: Gendered Material Strategies*. Burlington, VT: Ashgate, 2009.

Gosse, Edmund. *Gray*. London: Macmillan 1902.

Graves, David Andrews. "Computer Analysis of Word Usage in *Emma*." *Persuasions* 21 (1999): 203–11.

Greene, Donald. "The Original of Pemberley." In *The Selected Essays of Donald Greene*, edited by John L. Abbott, 301–22. Lewisburg, PA: Bucknell University Press, 2004.

Grootenboer, Hanneke. *Treasuring the Gaze: Intimate Vision in Late Eighteenth-Century Miniatures*. Chicago: Chicago University Press, 2012.

Grose, Francis. *Rules for Drawing Caricatures: With an Essay on Comic Painting*. 2nd ed. London, 1795.

Guest, Ivor. *The Romantic Ballet in England*. Middletown, CT: Wesleyan University Press, 1972.

Halperin, John. *The Life of Jane Austen*. Baltimore, MD: Johns Hopkins University Press, 1984.

Halsey, Katie. *Jane Austen and Her Readers*. London: Anthem, 2013.

Harris, Jocelyn. *Jane Austen's Art of Memory*. Cambridge: Cambridge University Press, 1989.

Bibliography

———. *A Revolution Almost beyond Expression: Jane Austen's "Persuasion."* Newark: University of Delaware Press, 2007.

———. *Satire, Celebrity, and Politics in Jane Austen.* Lewisburg, PA: Bucknell University Press, 2017.

Heneage, Simon. "George Murgatroydh Woodward." In *Oxford Dictionary of National Biography.* Oxford: Oxford University Press, 2017.

Heydt-Stevenson, Jill. *Austen's Unbecoming Conjunctions: Subversive Laughter, Embodied History.* New York: Palgrave Macmillan, 2005.

Hisamori, Kazuko. "Facing a Portrait of the 'Lover': *Frankenstein*'s Monster and the Heroines of *Sense and Sensibility* and *Pride and Prejudice*." *Persuasions On-Line* 32, no. 1 (2011).

Hochman, Jerry. "American Repertory Ballet: *Pride and Prejudice*." Review. Criticaldance.org.

Hoeveler, Diane Long. *The Gothic Ideology: Religious Hysteria and Anti-Catholicism in British Popular Fiction, 1780–1880.* Cardiff: University of Wales Press, 2014.

Hoffman, Danielle. "American Repertory Ballet's *Pride and Prejudice*." *Daily Princetonian* (2017).

Hogan, Charles Beecher. *The London Stage, 1660–1800*, Pt. 5: *1776–1800*. Carbondale: Southern Illinois University Press, 1968.

Hogarth, William. "The Progress of a Harlot, as She Is Described in Six Prints." London, 1732.

Holdsworth, Sir William. *A History of English Law.* London: Methuen, 1903.

Honan, Park. *Jane Austen: Her Life.* London: Weidenfeld and Nicolson, 1987.

Honychurch, Lennox. *Negre Mawon: The Fighting Maroons of Dominica.* Dominica: Island Heritage Initiatives, 2014.

Ingrassia, Catherine. "Money." In *The Cambridge Companion to Alexander Pope*, edited by Pat Rogers, 175–85. Cambridge: Cambridge University Press, 1989.

Jackson, H. J. *Marginalia: Readers Writing in Books.* New Haven, CT: Yale University Press, 2002.

Janowitz, Anne. *England's Ruins: Poetic Purpose and the National Landscape.* Cambridge: Cambridge University Press, 1990.

Johnson, Claudia L. *Jane Austen: Women, Politics, and the Novel.* Chicago: Chicago University Press, 1988.

Johnson, Claudia L., and Clara Tuite, eds. *A Companion to Jane Austen.* Malden, MA: Wiley-Blackwell, 2009.

Johnson, Robert. "Elizabeth and Darcy Dance as 'Pride and Prejudice' Debuts as a Ballet." NJArts.net (2017).

Johnston, Ken. *The Hidden Wordsworth: Poet, Lover, Spy.* New York: Norton, 1998.

Jones, Vivien, "Jane Austen's Domestic Realism." In *The Oxford History of the Novel in English.* Vol. 2: *English and British Fiction 1750–1820*, edited by Peter Garside and Karen O'Brien, 273–95. Oxford: Oxford University Press, 2015.

Juhasz, Suzanne. "Bonnets and Balls: Reading Jane Austen's Letters." *Centennial Review* 31, no. 1 (1987): 84–104.

Justice, George L. "Sanditon and the Book." In *A Companion to Jane Austen*, edited by Claudia L. Johnson and Clara Tuite, 153–62. Oxford: Wiley-Blackwell, 2009.

Bibliography

Kaplan, Laurie. "*Emma* and 'the Children of Brunswick Square.'" *Persuasions* 31 (2009): 236–47.

———. "The Rushworths of Wimpole Street." *Persuasions* 33 (2011): 202–14.

Kaufmann, Ruta Baublyté. *The Architecture of Space-Time in the Novels of Jane Austen*. New York: Palgrave Macmillan, 2018.

Keener, Frederick M., and Susan E. Lorsch, eds. *Eighteenth-Century Women and the Arts*. New York: Greenwood, 1988.

Kelly, Helena. *Jane Austen, the Secret Radical*. New York: Knopf, 2017.

Kennedy, Deborah. "The Ruined Abbey in the Eighteenth Century." *Philological Quarterly* 80, no. 4 (2001): 501–23.

Kerr, Sarah J. "When Computer Science Met Austen and Edgeworth." *New Perspectives: Postgraduate Symposium on the Humanities: Reflections* 1 (2017): 38–52.

Keymer, Thomas. "Rank." In *Jane Austen in Context*, edited by Janet Todd, 387–96. Cambridge: Cambridge University Press, 2005.

Kindred, Sheila Johnson. *Jane Austen's Transatlantic Sister: The Life and Letters of Fanny Palmer Austen*. Montreal: McGill-Queen's University Press, 2017.

Kirkham, Margaret. "Portraits." In *Jane Austen in Context*, edited by Janet Todd, 68–79. Cambridge: Cambridge University Press, 2005.

Kivy, Peter. *The Seventh Sense: Francis Hutcheson and Eighteenth-Century British Aesthetics*. Oxford: Clarendon, 2003.

Knox-Shaw, Peter. *Jane Austen and the Enlightenment*. Cambridge: Cambridge University Press, 2009.

Kramnick, Jonathan. *Actions and Objects from Hobbes to Richardson*. Stanford, CA: Stanford University Press, 2010.

Krieger, Murray. *Ekphrasis: The Illusion of the Natural Sign*. Baltimore, MD: Johns Hopkins University Press, 1992.

Krueger, Misty. "From Marginalia to Juvenilia: Jane Austen's Vindication of the Stuarts." *The Eighteenth Century* 56, no. 2 (2015): 243–59.

Kurnick, David. *Empty Houses: Theatrical Failure and the Novel*. Princeton, NJ: Princeton University Press, 2012.

Lamb, Jonathan. *The Things Things Say*. Princeton, NJ: Princeton University Press, 2011.

Lamont, Claire. "Domestic Architecture." In *Jane Austen in Context*, edited by Janet Todd, 225–31. Cambridge: Cambridge University Press, 2005.

Le Faye, Deirdre. "Anna Lefroy's Original Memories of Jane Austen." *Review of English Studies* 39, no. 155 (1988): 417–21.

———. *Jane Austen: A Family Record*. Cambridge: Cambridge University Press, 2003.

———. *Jane Austen: The World of Her Novels*. New York: Abrams, 2002.

———. "New Marginalia in Jane Austen's Books." *Book Collector* 49, no. 2 (2000): 222–26.

Lee-Riffe, Nancy M. "The Role of Country Dance in the Fiction of Jane Austen." *Women's Writing* 5 (1998): 103–312.

Leppert, Richard. *The Sight of Sound: Music, Representation, and the History of the Book*. Berkeley: University of California Press, 1993.

Lewes, Darby, ed. *Auto-Poetica: Representations of the Creative Process in Nineteenth-Century British and American Fiction*. Lanham, MD: Lexington, 2006.

Bibliography

Lewis, Judith S. "When a House Is Not a Home: Elite English Women and the Eighteenth-Century Country House." *Journal of British Studies* 48, no. 2 (2009): 336–63.

Libin, Kathryn L. "Daily Practice, Musical Accomplishment, and the Example of Jane Austen." In *Jane Austen and the Arts: Elegance, Propriety, and Harmony*, edited by Natasha Duquette and Elisabeth Lenckos, 1–20. Bethlehem, PA: Lehigh University, 2014.

———. "Lifting the Heart to Rapture: Harmony, Nature, and the Unmusical Fanny Price." *Persuasions* 28 (2006): 137–49.

———. "Music, Character, and Social Standing in Jane Austen's *Emma*." *Persuasions* 22 (2000): 15–30.

Lipking, Lawrence. *The Ordering of the Arts in Eighteenth-Century England*. Princeton, NJ: Princeton University Press, 1970.

Lippincott, Louise. *Selling Art in Georgian London: The Rise of Arthur Pond*. New Haven, CT: Yale University Press, 1983.

Litz, A. Walton. "The Picturesque in *Pride and Prejudice*." *Persuasions* 1 (1979): 13–24.

Lloyd, Stephen, and Kim Sloan. *The Intimate Portrait: Drawings, Miniatures and Pastels from Ramsay to Lawrence*. Edinburgh and London: National Galleries of Scotland/British Museum, 2008.

Looser, Devoney. *The Making of Jane Austen*. Baltimore, MD: Johns Hopkins University Press, 2017.

Losano, Antonia. "A Great Passion for Taking Likenesses: The Woman Painter in *Emma*." *Persuasions* 27 (2005): 185–93.

Lynch, Deidre Shauna. "Personal Effects and Sentimental Fiction." *Eighteenth-Century Fiction* 12, no. 2–3 (2000): 345–68.

———. "'Young Ladies Are Delicate Plants': Jane Austen and Greenhouse Romanticism." *ELH* 77, no. 3 (2010): 689–729.

Mack, Maynard. *The Garden and the City: Retirement and Politics in the Later Poetry of Pope, 1731–1743*. Toronto: Toronto University Press, 1989.

Mangion, Carmen. *Contested Identities: Catholic Women Religious in Nineteenth-Century England and Wales*. New York: Manchester University Press, 2008.

Marcsek-Fuchs, Maria. *Dance and British Literature: An Intermedial Encounter*. London: Rodopi, 2015.

Marsh, Honoria D. *Shades from Jane Austen*. London: Parry Jackman, 1975.

Marshall, David. *The Frame of Art: Fictions of Aesthetic Experience, 1750–1815*. Baltimore, MD: Johns Hopkins University Press, 2005.

Mason, Margaret J. "The Blue Nuns in Norwich: 1800–1805." *Recusant History* 24 (1998): 89–122.

McConnell, Anita, and Simon Heneage. "James Gillray." In *Oxford Dictionary of National Biography*. Oxford: Oxford University Press, 2016.

McKendrick, Neil, John Brewer, and J. H. Plumb. *The Birth of a Consumer Society: The Commercialization of Eighteenth-Century England*. Bloomington: Indiana University Press, 1982.

McMaster, Juliet, and Bruce Stovel, eds. *Austen's Business: Her World and Her Profession*. Basingstoke, UK: Palgrave Macmillan, 1996.

Bibliography

Mellor, Anne K. *Mothers of the Nation: Women's Political Writing in England, 1780–1830.* Bloomington: Indiana University Press, 2000.

Miall, David S. "Representing the Picturesque: William Gilpin and the Laws of Nature." *Interdisciplinary Studies in Literature and the Environment* 12, no. 2 (2005): 75–93.

Michael, Elsie B. *The Vulgar Question of Money: Heiresses, Materialism and the Novel of Manners from Jane Austen to Henry James.* Baltimore, MD: Johns Hopkins University Press, 2011.

Mingay, G. E. *English Landed Society in the Eighteenth Century.* New York: Routledge, 2013.

Miskin, Lauren. "'True Indian Muslin' and the Politics of Consumption in Jane Austen's *Northanger Abbey*." *Journal for Early Modern Cultural Studies* 15, no. 2 (spring 2015): 5–26.

Mitchell, W. J. T., ed. *Landscape and Power.* Chicago: University of Chicago Press, 1994.

———. *Picture Theory: Essays on Verbal and Visual Representation.* Chicago: University of Chicago, 1994.

Moore, Roger E. *Jane Austen and the Reformation: Remembering the Sacred Language.* Burlington, VT: Ashgate, 2016.

Moutray, Tonya. *Refugee Nuns, the French Revolution, and British Literature and Culture.* New York: Routledge, 2016.

Murphy, Olivia. *Jane Austen and the Reader: The Artist as Critic.* Basingstoke, UK: Palgrave Macmillan, 2013.

Murray, Douglas. "Donwell Abbey and Box Hill: Purity and Danger in Jane Austen's *Emma*." *Review of English Studies*, n.s., 66, no. 277 (2015): 954–70.

———. "Jane Austen's 'Passion for Taking Likenesses': Portraits of the Prince Regent in *Emma*." *Persuasions* 29 (2007): 132–44.

———. "Spectatorship in *Mansfield Park*: Looking and Overlooking." *Nineteenth-Century Literature* 52, no. 1 (1997): 1–26.

Myer, Valerie Grosvenor. *Jane Austen: Obstinate Heart.* New York: Arcade, 1997.

Nightingale, Joseph. *Topographical and Historical Description of the City of London.* London: Sherwood, Neely, and Jones, 1815.

Nigro, Jeffrey A. "'Favourable to Tenderness and Sentiment': The Many Meanings of Mary Crawford's Harp." *Persuasion On-Line* 35, no. 1 (Winter 2014).

———. "Visualizing Jane Austen and Jane Austen Visualizing." *Persuasions* 29, no. 1 (Winter 2008).

Noggle, James. *The Temporality of Taste in Eighteenth-Century British Writing.* Oxford: Oxford University Press, 2012.

Nokes, David. *Jane Austen: A Life.* New York: Farrar, Straus and Giroux, 1997.

Noverre, Jean Georges. *Letters on Dancing and Ballets.* Translated by Cyril W. Beaumont. Alton, UK: Dance Books, 2004.

O'Quinn, Daniel. "Jane Austen and Performance: Theatre, Memory, and Enculturation." In *A Companion to Jane Austen*, edited by Claudia L. Johnson and Clara Tuite, 377–88. Chichester, UK: Wiley-Blackwell, 2009.

Orel, Harold. *The Final Years of Thomas Hardy, 1912—1928.* London: Macmillan, 1976.

Page, Norman. *The Language of Jane Austen.* New York: Barnes and Noble, 1972.

Bibliography

Palmer, Sally B. "Screens and Screening in *Sense and Sensibility*." *Persuasions* 33 (2011): 154–71.

Park, Julie. "What the Eye Cannot See: Interior Landscapes in 'Mansfield Park.'" *Eighteenth Century* 54, no. 2 (2013): 169–81.

Parker, Rozsika. *The Subversive Stitch: Embroidery and the Making of the Feminine*. London: I. B. Tauris, 2010.

Parry, Sarah. "'Give My Love to Mary Jane': The Story behind the Austen Graffiti." *Female Spectator Newsletter (Chawton House)* 1, no. 3 (2015): 4–5.

Patel, Aniruddh D. *Music, Language, and the Brain*. Oxford: Oxford University Press, 2008.

Patten, Robert L. "Isaac Cruikshank (1764–1811)." In *Oxford Dictionary of National Biography*. Oxford: Oxford University Press, 2016.

Pendle, Karin, ed. *Women and Music: A History*. 2nd ed. Bloomington: Indiana University Press, 2001.

Plantinga, Leon. "The Piano and the Nineteenth Century." In *Nineteenth-Century Piano Music*, edited by R. Larry Todd, 1–15. New York: Routledge, 2004.

Pointon, Marcia. *Hanging the Head: Portraiture and Social Formation in Eighteenth-Century England*. New Haven, CT: Yale University Press, 1993.

———. *Strategies for Showing: Women, Possession, and Representation in English Visual Culture 1665–1800*. Oxford: Oxford University Press, 1997.

———. "'Surrounded with Brilliants': Miniature Portraits in Eighteenth-Century England." *Art Bulletin* 83, no. 1 (2002): 48–71.

Pool, Daniel. *What Jane Austen Ate and Charles Dickens Knew*. New York: Simon and Schuster, 1993.

Potter, Tiffany, ed. *Women, Popular Culture, and the Eighteenth Century*. Toronto: University of Toronto Press, 2012.

Rajan, Rajeswari. "Austen in the World: Postcolonial Mappings." In *The Postcolonial Jane Austen*, edited by You-Me Park and Rajeswari Sunder Rajan, 3–25. New York: Routledge, 2000.

Raphael, Linda. *Narrative Skepticism: Moral Agency and Representations of Consciousness in Fiction*. Madison, NJ: Fairleigh Dickinson University Press, 2001.

Reich, Nancy B. "European Composers and Musicians, Ca. 1800–1890." In *Women and Music: A History*, edited by Karin Pendle, 147–74. Bloomington: Indiana University Press, 2001.

Richardson, Alan. "Byron and the Theatre." In *The Cambridge Companion to Byron*, edited by Drummond Bone, 133–50. Cambridge: Cambridge University Press, 2004.

Riley, Noël. *The Accomplished Lady: A History of Genteel Pursuits c. 1660–1860*. Huddersfield, UK: Oblong, 2017.

Roberts, Stephen K. "Conclusion: County Counsels: Some Concluding Remarks." In *The County Community in Seventeenth-Century England and Wales*, edited by Jacqueline Eales and Andrew Hopper. Hatfield, UK: University of Hertfordshire Press, 2012.

Robillard, Valerie K., and Else Jongeneel. *Pictures into Words: Theoretical and Descriptive Approaches to Ekphrasis*. Amsterdam: VU University Press, 1998.

Robinson, Terry F. "'A Mere Skeleton of History': Reading Relics in Jane Austen's *Northanger Abbey*." *European Romantic Review* 17, no. 2 (2006): 215–27.

Bibliography

Robson, Martin. *A History of the Royal Navy: The Napoleonic Wars.* London: I. B. Tauris, 2014.

Sabor, Peter, ed. *The Cambridge Companion to Emma.* Cambridge: Cambridge University Press, 2015.

———. "Godmersham Park Library: Jane Austen's Paradise Regained." *Persuasions: The Jane Austen Journal* 39 (2017): 31–44.

———. "Reading with Austen." [Digital Re-creation of Godmersham Park Library] McGill University Burney Centre. www.readingwithausten.com.

———. "'Staring in Astonishment': Portraits and Prints in *Persuasion*." In *Jane Austen's Business: Her World and Her Profession*, edited by Juliet McMaster, 17–29. Basingstoke, UK: Palgrave Macmillan, 1996.

"The Strategic Withdrawal from Ekphrasis in Jane Austen's Novels." In *Icons—Texts—Iconotexts: Essays on Ekphrasis and Intermediality*, edited by Peter Wagner, 213–35. Berlin: de Gruyter, 1996.

Said, Edward W. *Culture and Imperialism.* New York: Vintage, 1994.

Sales, Roger. *Jane Austen and Representations of Regency England.* London: Routledge, 1996.

Santesso, Aaron. "William Hogarth and the Tradition of Sexual Scissors." *Studies in English Literature, 1500–1900* 39, no. 3 (1999): 499–521.

Scarth, Kate. "It-Narratives, Thing Theory, and 'Trivial Things': Sophie Gee's *The Scandal of the Season* and *The Rape of the Lock*." In *Pope's "Rape of the Lock" 300 Years On*, edited by Don Nichols, 151–66. Toronto: University of Toronto Press, 2015.

Schneider, Ana-Karina. "*Mansfield Park*." In *The Literary Encyclopedia*, 2008.

Scott, John M. "'If Art Could Tell': A Milton Reading of *Pride and Prejudice*." *Persuasion On-Line* 37, no. 1 (2016).

Selwyn, David. *Jane Austen and Leisure.* London: Hambledon, 1999.

Sheehan, Collen A. "Jane Austen's 'Tribute' to the Prince Regent: A Gentleman Riddled with Difficulty." *Persuasion On-Line* 27, no. 1 (2006).

———. "Lampooning the Prince: A Second Solution to the Second Charade in *Emma*." *Persuasion On-Line* 27, no. 1 (2006).

Shell, Alison. *Oral Culture and Catholicism in Early Modern England.* Cambridge: Cambridge University Press, 2007.

Showalter, Elaine. *A Literature of Their Own: British Women Novelists from Brontë to Lessing.* Princeton, NJ: Princeton University Press, 1977.

Silver, Sean. *The Mind Is a Collection: Case Studies in Eighteenth-Century Thought.* Philadelphia: University of Pennsylvania Press, 2015.

Simonton, Deborah. "Threading the Needle, Pulling the Press: Gender, Skill and the Tools of the Trade in Eighteenth-Century European Towns." *Cultural History* 1, no. 2 (2012): 180–204.

Sloan, Kim. *A Noble Art: Amateur Artists and Drawing Masters C. 1600–1800.* London: British Museum Press, 2000.

Smethurst, Paul. *Travel Writing and the Natural World, 1768–1840.* London: Palgrave Macmillan, 2012.

Smyth, Gerry. *Music in Contemporary British Fiction: Listening to the Novel.* Basingstoke, UK: Palgrave, 2008.

Bibliography

Soltes, John. "Interview: American Repertory Ballet Stages New Ballet Based on 'Pride and Prejudice.'" *Hollywood Soapbox* (2017). Web.

Southam, Brian, *Jane Austen and the Navy*. London and New York: Hambledon and London, 2000.

———. *Jane Austen's Literary Manuscripts: A Study of the Novelist's Development through the Surviving Papers*. Oxford: Oxford University Press, 1964.

———, ed. *Jane Austen's Sir Charles Grandison*. Oxford: Clarendon, 1981.

———. "Sanditon: The Seventh Novel." In *Jane Austen's Achievement*, edited by Juliet McMaster, 1–26. London: Macmillan, 1976.

Spekke, Arnolds. *The Ancient Amber Routes and the Geographical Discovery of the Eastern Baltic*. Stockholm: M. Goppers, 1967.

Spongberg, Mary. "History, Fiction, and Anachronism: Northanger Abbey, the Tudor 'Past' and the 'Gothic' Present." *Textual Practice* 26, no. 4 (2012): 631–48.

Sprayberry, A. Marie. "Sex, Power, and Other People's Money: The Prince Regent and His Impact on Jane Austen's Life and Work." *Persuasion On-Line* 33, no. 1 (2012).

Stanley, Eric Gerald, "Jane Austen's *Mansfield Park* and Kotzebue's *Das Kind der Liebe, Lovers' Vows*: 'that we should have such a scene to play!'?" *Archiv für das Studium der neueren Sprachen und Literaturen* 157, no. 2 (2005): 300–317.

Stewart, David. "Political Ruins: Gothic Sham Ruins and the '45." *Journal of the Society of Architectural Historians* 55, no. 4 (1996): 400–11.

Stovel, Nora Foster. "'Every Savage Can Dance': Choreographing Courtship." *Persuasions* 23 (2003): 29–49.

———. "An Invitation to Dance and a Proposal of Marriage: Jane Austen's *Emma* and Two Film Adaptations." *Persuasions On-Line* 28 (2007).

Streatfield, David C., and Alistair M. Duckworth. *Landscape in the Gardens and the Literature of Eighteenth-Century England*. Los Angeles: William Andrews Clark Memorial Library/ UCLA, 1981.

Styles, John. "Georgian Britain 1714–1837." In *Design and the Decorative Arts: Britain 1500–1900*, edited by Michael Snodin and Styles, 281–307. London: V & A Publications, 2001.

Styles, John, and Amanda Vickery. *Gender, Taste, and Material Culture in Britain and North America, 1700–1830*. New Haven, CT: Yale University Press, 2007.

Sutherland, Kathryn, ed. *Jane Austen: Writer in the World*. Oxford: Bodleian Library, 2017.

———. *Jane Austen's Textual Lives: From Aeschylus to Bollywood*. Oxford: Oxford University Press, 2005.

Tanner, Tony. *Jane Austen*. Cambridge, MA: Harvard University Press, 1986.

———. "Jane Austen and 'the Quiet Thing': A Study of *Mansfield Park*." In *Critical Essays on Jane Austen*, edited by Brian Southam, 136–61. London: Routledge, 1968.

Tave, Stuart. *Some Words of Jane Austen*. Chicago: Chicago University Press, 1973.

Temperley, Nicholas, ed. *Musicians of Bath and Beyond: Edward Loder (1809–1865) and His Family*. Suffolk, UK: Boydell, 2016.

Thompson, Allison. "Dancing at St. James." *Persuasions On-Line* 33, no. 1 (2012).

———. "The Felicities of Rapid Motion: Jane Austen in the Ballroom." *Persuasions On-Line* (2007).

Thompson, A. Hamilton. *Netley Abbey*. London: Her Majesty's Stationery Office, 1953.

Thompson, Sarah. "Recycling Ruins: The Critical Reception of John Aislabie's Work at Fountains Abbey and the Changing Function of the Gothic." *Third Text* 25, no. 6 (2011): 675–86.

Thrush, Nanette. "A Picture's Worth a Thousand Lies: Portraits in Victorian Literature." In *Auto-Poetica: Representations of the Creative Process in Nineteenth-Century British and American Fiction*, edited by Darby Lewes, 195–202. Lanham, MD: Lexington, 2006.

Todd, Janet, ed. *The Cambridge Introduction to Jane Austen*. Cambridge: Cambridge University Press, 2012.

———, ed. *Jane Austen in Context*. Cambridge: Cambridge University Press, 2005.

Tomalin, Claire. *Jane Austen: A Life*. New York: Random House, 1997.

Tomko, Michael. *British Romanticism and the Catholic Question: Religion, History and National Identity, 1778–1829*. New York: Palgrave, 2010.

Toner, Anne. "Landscape as Literary Criticism." *Critical Survey* 26, no. 1 (2014): 3–19.

Townshend, Dale. "Improvement and Repair: Architecture, Romance, and the Politics of the Gothic." *Literature Compass* 8, no. 10 (2011): 712–38.

———. "Ruins, Romance and the Rise of Gothic Tourism: The Case of Netley Abbey." *Eighteenth-Century Studies* 37, no. 3 (2014): 377–94.

Treitel, G. H. "Jane Austen and the Law." *Law Quarterly Review* 100 (1984): 549–86.

Trilling, Lionel. "*Mansfield Park*." In *Jane Austen: A Collection of Critical Essays*, edited by Ian Watt, 124–40. Englewood Cliffs: Prentice-Hall, 1963.

Troide, Lars E., ed. *The Early Journals and Letters of Fanny Burney*. Montreal: McGill-Queens University Press, 1988.

Tully, Catherine L. "The Choreography of Understanding: Edward Liang's 'Age of Innocence' at the Joffrey." *Joffrey Ballet News Archive* 26 (2012).

Turner, Simon. "Samuel William Fores." In *Oxford Dictionary of National Biography*. Oxford: Oxford University Press, 2017.

Upfal, Annette. "A Taste for Cruel Humour: Jane Austen's *The History of England* and James Gillray's Bawdy Caricature of Charles James Fox." In *Home and Away: The Place of the Child Writer*, edited by David Own and Lesley Peterson, 217–37. Newcastle upon Tyne: Cambridge Scholars, 2016.

Urda, Kathleen E. "Why the Show Must Not Go On: Real Character and the Absence of Theatrical Performances in *Mansfield Park*." *Eighteenth-Century Fiction* 26, no. 2 (Winter 2013/2014): 281–302.

Valihora, Karen. *Austen's Oughts: Judgment after Locke and Shaftesbury*. Newark: University of Delaware Press, 2010.

Vick, Robin. "The Sale at Steventon Parsonage." *Jane Austen Society Report for 1993* (1993): 295–98.

Vickery, Amanda. *Behind Closed Doors: At Home in Georgian England*. New Haven, CT: Yale University Press, 2009.

———. *The Gentleman's Daughter: Women's Lives in Georgian England*. New Haven, CT: Yale University Press, 1998.

Villaseñor, Alice. "Edward Austen Knight's Godmersham Library and Jane Austen's *Emma*." *Persuasions* 29 (2007): 79–87.

Volz, Jessica A. *Visualization in the Novels of Austen, Radcliffe, Edgeworth, and Burney*. London: Anthem, 2017.

Bibliography

von Erffa, Helmut, and Allen Staley. *The Paintings of Benjamin West*. New Haven, CT: Yale University Press, 1986.

Wall, Cynthia Sundberg. *The Prose of Things: Transformations of Description in the Eighteenth Century*. Chicago: Chicago University Press, 2002.

Wallace, Beth Kowaleski. "'Penance and Mortification for Ever': Jane Austen and the Ambient Noise of Catholicism." *Tulsa Studies in Women's Literature* 31, no. 1/2 (2012): 159–80.

Wallace, Robert K. *Jane Austen and Mozart: Classical Equilibrium in Fiction and Music*. Athens: University of Georgia Press, 1983.

Ward, Bernard. *The Dawn of the Catholic Revival in England, 1791–1803*. London: Longmans, Green, 1909.

Weickmann, Dorion. "Choreography and Narrative: The *Ballet D'action* of the Eighteenth Century." In *The Cambridge Companion to Ballet*, edited by Marion Kant, 53–64. Cambridge: Cambridge University Press, 2007.

Wells, Julliette. "In Music She Had Always Used to Feel Alone in the World." *Persuasions* 26 (2004): 98–110.

———. "A Harpist Arrives at Mansfield Park: Music and the Moral Ambiguity of Mary Crawford." *Persuasions* 28 (2006): 101–14.

———. *Reading Austen in America*. New York: Bloomsbury Academic, 2017.

———. "'Some of Your Accomplishments Are Not Ordinary': The Limits of Artistry in *Jane Eyre*." In *The Brontës in the World of Arts*, edited by Sandra Hagan and Juliette Wells, 67–80. Aldershot, UK: Ashgate, 2008.

Wendorf, Richard. *The Elements of Life: Biography and Portrait-Painting in Stuart and Georgian England*. Oxford: Clarendon, 1990.

———. *Sir Joshua Reynolds: The Painter in Society*. Cambridge, MA: Harvard University Press, 1996.

Wheatley, Harry Benjamin, and Peter Cunningham. *London Past and Present: Its History, Associations, and Traditions*. 3 vols. London: John Murray, 1891.

White, Laura Mooneyham. *Jane Austen's Anglicanism*. Burlington, VT: Ashgate, 2011.

White, Laura Mooneyham, Carmen Smith, Brian Pytlik Zillig, et al. *Austen Said: Patterns of Diction in Austen's Major Novels*. http://austen.unl.edu.

Wijitsopon, Raksangob. "A Corpus-Based of the Style in Jane Austen's Novels." *Manusya: Journal of Humanities Regular* 16, no. 1 (2013): 41–64.

Wilson, Cheryl. *Literature and Dance in Nineteenth-Century Britain: Jane Austen to the New Woman*. Cambridge: Cambridge University Press, 2009.

Wilson, Margaret. *Almost Another Sister: The Story of Jane Austen's Favourite Niece*. Maidstone, UK: George Mann, 1998.

Wood, Gillen D'Arcy. *Romanticism and Music Culture in Britain, 1770–1840: Virtue and Virtuosity*. Cambridge: Cambridge University Press, 2010.

Wright, Carrie. "'Unbearably Fine': The Socio-Political Powers of Jewelry in Jane Austen's World." *Persuasions: The Jane Austen Journal On-Line* 36, no. 1 (2015).

Zelicovici, Dvora. "The Inefficacy of *Lovers' Vows*." *ELH* 50 (1983): 531–40.

Zionkowski, Linda, and Miriam Hart. "'Aunt Jane Began Her Day with Music': Austen and the Female Amateur." *Persuasions* 37 (2015): 165–85.

Zunshine, Lisa. "Why Jane Austen Was Different, And Why We May Need Cognitive Science to See It." *Style* 41, no. 3 (2007): 276.

Contributors

Elaine Bander, retired from the English Department of Dawson College (Montreal) since 2008, has published numerous essays on Austen in *Persuasions: The Jane Austen Journal* and *Persuasions On-Line* as well as essays on Frances Burney in the *Burney Journal* and *Age of Johnson*. Her essay "Jane Austen and the Uses of Silence" was published in *Literature and Ethics: Essays Presented to A. E. Malloch* (1987). In retirement she has assisted Stewart J. Cooke in preparation of volume 2 of *The Court Journals and Letters of Frances Burney* (2011) and volume 1 of *Additional Journals and Letters of Frances Burney* (2015).

Anna Battigelli, Professor of English at SUNY Plattsburgh, is the author of *Margaret Cavendish and the Exiles of the Mind* (1998) and has coedited with Laura M. Stevens a special-topics double issue of *Tulsa Studies in Women's Literature* titled "Eighteenth-Century Women and English Catholicism."

Barbara M. Benedict, the Charles A. Dana Professor of English at Trinity College, is the author of *Framing Feeling: Sentiment and Style in English Prose Fiction, 1745–1800* (1994); *Making the Modern Reader: Cultural Mediation in Early Modern Literary Anthologies* (1996); and *Curiosity: A Cultural History of Early Modern Inquiry* (2001). She is also coeditor, with Deirdre Le Faye, of *Northanger Abbey* (2006). She is working on a book about collecting, collections and things in the early-modern literary imagination, and editing a handbook of literature and science for Palgrave.

Natasha Duquette, Professor of English at Tyndale University College in Toronto, is the editor of Helen Maria Williams's *Julia, a novel interspersed with poetical pieces* (2009). With Elisabeth Lenckos, she coedited *Jane Austen and the Arts: Elegance, Propriety, and Harmony* (2013). Her articles on Jane Austen have appeared in the journal *Persuasions On-Line*, and, with Elisabeth Lenckos, she coedited *Jane Austen and the Arts: Elegance, Propriety, and Harmony* (2013). Her monograph *Veiled Intent: Dissenting Women's Aesthetic Approach to Biblical Interpretation* was published in 2016.

Contributors

Marilyn Francus, Professor of English at West Virginia University, is the author of *The Converting Imagination: Linguistic Theory in Swift's Satiric Prose* (1994) and *Monstrous Motherhood: Eighteenth-Century Culture and the Ideology of Domesticity* (2012). She is the editor of the *Burney Journal*, and chair of the International Visitor Program for the Jane Austen Society of North America.

Jocelyn Harris, Professor emerita of English at the University of Otago, is the author of *Jane Austen's Art of Memory* (1989); *A Revolution Almost beyond Expression: Jane Austen's "Persuasion"* (2007); and *Satire, Celebrity, and Politics in Jane Austen* (2017).

Miriam Hart pursued her Ph.D. at Ohio University after twenty years of touring as a singer, recording with the Allman Brothers as well as with her group, The Local Girls; she has performed at the White House, on *A Prairie Home Companion*, and elsewhere. Her dissertation, "Hardly an Innocent Diversion: Music in the Life and Writings of Jane Austen" (1999), included the first complete photographic archiving of Austen's songbooks. With Linda Zionkowski, she has published several articles on gender and musical performance in Austen's writing; they are also coediting a collection of essays on women and music in Georgian Britain.

Nancy E. Johnson, Associate Dean of the College of Liberal Arts and Science and Professor of English at SUNY New Paltz, is the author of *The English Jacobin Novel on Rights, Property and the Law: Critiquing the Contract* (2004); editor of *Impassioned Jurisprudence: Law, Literature and Emotion, 1760–1848* (2015); scholarly editor of *The Court Journals and Letters of Frances Burney, 1790–June 1791*, vol. 6 (2019); and editor, with Paul Keen, of *Mary Wollstonecraft in Context* (forthcoming).

Tonya J. Moutray, Associate Dean and Professor of English at Russell Sage College in Troy, New York, is the author of *Refugee Nuns, the French Revolution, and British Literature and Culture* (2016). Her work has also appeared in the *European Romantic Review*, *Victorian Literature and Culture*, and *Studies in English Literature, 1500–1900*.

Deborah C. Payne, Associate Professor at American University, is the editor of *The Cambridge Companion to English Restoration Theatre* (2000); *Four Restoration Libertine Plays* (2005); and, more recently, *Revisiting*

Contributors

Shakespeare's "Lost" Play: Cardenio/Double Falsehood in the Eighteenth Century (2016). Professor Payne just completed "The Commodiluxe Stage: A New Material History of Restoration Theatre."

Peter Sabor, a Fellow of the Royal Society of Canada, is Professor of English and Canada Research Chair at McGill University, Montreal, where he is also Director of the Burney Centre. His publications on Jane Austen include an edition of her early writings, *Juvenilia* (2006), *Manuscript Works*, coedited with Linda Bree and Janet Todd (2013), and *The Cambridge Companion to Emma* (2015).

Juliette Wells, the Elizabeth Conolly Todd Distinguished Professor of English in the Center for the Humanities at Goucher College in Baltimore, Maryland, is the author of two books on Austen reception history: *Reading Austen in America* (2017) and *Everybody's Jane: Austen in the Popular Imagination* (2011). For Penguin Classics, she prepared two-hundredth-anniversary deluxe annotated editions of Austen's *Persuasion* (2017) and *Emma* (2015). She coedited *The Brontës in the World of the Arts* (2008) and has published widely on women novelists and their cultural legacies.

Cheryl A. Wilson, Dean of the School of Humanities and Social Sciences and Professor of English at Stevenson University in Maryland, is the author of *Fashioning the Silver Fork Novel* (2012) and *Literature and Dance in Nineteenth-Century Britain: Jane Austen to the New Woman* (2009). Her work on Austen has appeared in *Eighteenth-Century Theory and Interpretation, Persuasions,* and *Literature/Film Quarterly*. Her recent book is *Jane Austen and the Victorian Heroine* (2017).

Linda Zionkowski, Professor of English at Ohio University, is the author of *Men's Work: Gender, Class, and the Professionalization of Poetry, 1660–1784* (2001); coeditor, with Cynthia Klekar, of *The Culture of the Gift in Eighteenth-Century England* (2009); and author of *Women and Gift Exchange in Eighteenth-Century Fiction: Richardson, Burney, Austen* (2016). With her collaborator Miriam Hart, she has published several articles on the musical culture of Austen's novels, and is editing a collection of essays on women and music in Georgian Britain

Index

abbeys, 15, 165–88; Catholic identity of, 15, and ecologic integrity, 170; and English landscape, 168–73; and history, 175; and improvements, 169–70, 175; in literature, 171–84; and national feeling, 183; and nature, 168–73; and ruins, 167–70; and sacrilege motif, 172–73; as tourist destinations, 171, 173. *See also under names of individual abbeys*

Ackermann, Rudolph (publisher), 9, 10, 232, 234; *The Repository of the Arts*, 10, 232

acting, 51, 53–54; depicted in literature, 49, 51, 53–57, 60n51, 78–81, 87–90

aesthetics, 13–14, 44–60, 146–62, 179–84

Alexander, Christine, 28

American Repertory Ballet, ballet adaptation of *Pride and Prejudice*, 104

Andrews, James (portraitist), 27

annotations. *See* marginalia

Armstrong, Isobel, 33

Arne, Thomas (composer), 79

artistic proficiency, and women, 2, 12, 49–50, 52, 189, 206–23, 222nn14, 15

artlessness, 14, 44–60

art, as deception, 27–41; and moral philosophy, 44–60, 201; psychological benefits of, 2, 4, 17; and unmarried women, 4; and women's education, 2, 206–23. *See also* aesthetics; Austen, Jane, and hermeneutic uncertainty

Astley's (theater), 78, 95

Austen, Anna (JA's niece), 1, 26, 77, 109–10, 116

Austen, Cassandra (JA's sister), 1; copy of Morland's *Pedlars*,25; paintings by, 24–30; portrait of Edward IV, 28; portrait of Fanny Knight, 25, 26; portrait of Henry V, 30; portraits of JA, 25–26, 27, 190

Austen, Cassandra Leigh (JA's mother), 1

Austen, Charles (JA's brother), 10; gift to JA of topaz cross, 146–52

Austen, Francis (JA's brother), 10, 11, 37

Austen, George (JA's father), 1, 109–10; library of, 79–80, 109–10, 121nn2,3

Austen, Henry (JA's brother), 28, 78–79, 234; and drawing lessons, 24; "Memoir of Miss Austen," 27, 167, 193, 224

Austen, James (JA's brother), 109

Austen, Jane: on acting, 51, 57, 60n51, 78–81, 87–90; on artlessness, 44–60; and caricature, 224–38; and Christianity, 146–64; 165–88; and dance, 93–108; and drama, 76–92; dramatic tastes of, 78; and drawing, 1–2, 24; and the English novel, 17, 47; and gender, 126–45; and Henry Austen's gift of topaz cross, 146–50; and hermeneutic uncertainty, 24–43, 50, 189–205; juvenilia, 27–30, 77, 80, 116, 208–11, 228, 234; and landscape design, 165–88; language and style of, 3, 33, 150; and legal arts, 61–75; and marginalia, 109–25; and music, 206–23; musical proficiency of, 207; and physicality, 13, 93, 96–103; portraits of 25–27; and portraiture, 24–43, 189–205; reading practices of, 14, 109–25; and sexual innuendoes, 17, 131, 134–38, 212, 214–16, 234–35

Austen, Jane, works by:
— *Catharine, or the Bower*, 30, 208
— *Emma*, 9, 12, 15–17; abbeys depicted in, 165–67, 179–84; and artistic proficiency, 44, 50, 213–14; and Cruikshank, 232; and idealizing tendency o;f art, 227; and material culture, 133–34, 141; and music, 208, 213–14; and portraits, 34–35, 189–205; and reading, 111–12; and women's dress, 141; and women's work, 133–34

261

Index

— "Frederic and Elfrida," 208
— "Henry and Eliza," 209
— "The History of England," 27–31, 111, 168
— *Lady Susan*, 11, 82, 232
— "Lesley Castle," 209
— *Love and Friendship*, 82
— *Mansfield Park*: and artistic proficiency, 5–9, 206–7, 214–16, 219–20; and artlessness, 46–57, 216, 219–20; and books, 9, 128; and caricatures, 230; and Christianity, 147–52; and drama, 77, 82, 84–89; and elegance, 147–64; and the estate, 4–7, 9, 152, 156; and the English Reformation, 165–67; and greed, 126–28; and jewelry, 146–64; and music, 206–7, 214–16, 219–20; and portraits, 8, 33–34; and seduction; 138, 141–42; and sentimentalized objects, 33–34, 126–27, 132; and substitution of riches for morality, 136; and slave trade, 152–53, 158, 232; and wastefulness, 134–35
— *Northanger Abbey*, 6–7; abbeys depicted in, 15, 165–66, 169, 173–77, 179–80; and artlessness, 44–47, 50–52, 57, 210; and consumer goods, 11, 137, 141–42; and narrative, 84; and the picturesque, 14, 140, 166–67, 173–77; and Alexander Pope, 131; and portraits, 8, 15, 35–36; and political satire, 231
— *Persuasion*, and artistic proficiency, 50; and *The Baronetage*, 63–66; and books; 128; and the estate, 66–70; and gendered authority, 11–12, 61–75; and home, 4; and judgment, 62, and law, 61–75; and music, 214; and narrative, 84, 85, and paintings, 9, 38–40; and political satire, 230, 233; and Alexander Pope, 130–31; and portrait miniatures, 16, 31–32, 36–38, 41, 190; and portraits, 8–9, 38–41; and rhetoric, 62, 70; and sexual scheming, 138
— "Plan of a Novel," 47
— *Pride and Prejudice*, 4, 12, 13; and artistic proficiency, 189, 211–13; and books, 15, 16, 128–30; and domestic arts, 134, 217; and dress, 137; and landscape, 140; and paintings, 226; and pedantry, 211–13; and picturesque, 167, 211–13, 217, 226, 230, 233; and Alexander Pope, 138; and portrait miniatures, 32–33; and portraits, 32–33, 226; and stage dance, 97–103; 106–7;
— *Sanditon*: and books, 10, 128, 137; and portrait miniatures, 40–41; and portraits, 40–41, 225
— *Sense and Sensibility*, 3, 5, 9, 12; and artistic proficiency, 190, 208; arts and emotional development in, 216–19; arts and marriage in, 208; and books, 132, 134; and Catholic refugees, 166, 179; and consumer goods, 138; and domestic arts, 190; and free indirect discourse, 83; and language, 30; and London, 229–30; and music, 12; and needlework, 166, 179; and picturesque, 167; and Alexander Pope, 10, 126; and portrait miniatures, 31–32, 133, 190; and portraits, 190; and taste, 54
— *The Watsons*, 141
Austen family, 1; and books, 109–25; and theater, 94–95

Badiou, Alain, 83
ballerina, rise of, 13, 94, 100–101
ballet, 13; in dramatic performances, 94; influence on Austen, 94–103; as narrative, 95–96; rise of, 93–94, 100–101
Ballet d'action, 95–6, 100, 106
Ballet Fantastique, production of *Pride and Prejudice*, 103–4
ballrooms, 93, 96–97
Barbauld, Anna (poet and literary critic), 6
Baronetage of England, 61–75; as physical book, 63; and social order, 64–65
Battaglia, Beatrice, 176
Beckford, Charlotte-Maria (Austen's friend), 228
Bermingham, Ann, 8, 9
Bertelsen, Lance, 225
Blackstone, Sir William (jurist), 66

Index

Blair, Hugh (clergyman and rhetorician), 113
Blank, Antje, 36
Bonaparte, Napoléon, 229
book culture, 109–25
books, 2, 4, 9–10, 109–25. *See also* Austen, George (library of); Godmersham Park library; reading
Boydell, John (print-dealer and publisher), 225
Bradbrook, Frank W., 126
Bray, Joe, 8, 15, 33
Bree, Linda, 77
Brown, Bill, 127
Brunton, Mary, *Self-Control*, 118–19
Bullock's Liverpool Museum, 226
Bunberry, Henry, *Recruits*, 28–29
Burke, Edmund, 67, 149, 159, 167
Burney, Charles (composer, music historian, and musician), 12
Burney, Frances, 83, 177 *The Wanderer*, 48–49, 53, 84, 119, 120, 129, 177
Butte, George, 85
Byrne, Paula, 57, 77, 79, 89, 94, 132, 146–47
Byron, George Gordon, Lord, 38, 81

Canning, George, 231–32, 233
caricatures, 17, 39, 51, 224, 224–38
carriages, 62, 68–71
Catholicism, 15, 130, 139, 149–50, 165–88
Catholic Refugees, 166, 177–79
Chapman, R.W., 26, 27
Chapone, Hester, 206
Chard, William (organist at Winchester), 207
Christianity, 147, 149–52; and prayer, 147, 151–52, 159
Clark, Lorrie, 14
Cohen, Selma Jeanne, 97
Coleridge, Samuel Taylor, 81
Commons, House of, 64
Constable, John (painter), 173; *Netley Abbey by Moonlight*, 174
Conway, Alison, 8
Copeland, Edward, 54, 140
Cowper, William, 132
Cruikshank, Isaac, 229, 233

dance, 13, 93–103; and female physicality, 13, 96–97, 106–7; manuals, 97; social, 93–95; stage, 13, 93–103. *See also* ballet
Davis, Tracy C., 83
Dighton, Robert (engraver, printseller, and portrait miniaturist), 232
domestic arts: in daily life, 2; commercial use of, 9; and gender, 10–11, 50, 201; in novels, 134–35, 190, 217–18, 220, 227; psychological benefits of, 4
domestic space, symbolic use of, 8, 40, 53, 69–71, 86, 97–98, 101–2, 156, 165, 193, 198, 219
Donkin, Ellen, 83
drama, 76–92, 94; and the novel, 82–89; in Regency England, 76–77; 78–80
drawing, 1–2, 10, 24, 33–34, 49–51, 189–201, 201n2
Duckworth, Alistair, 66
Dummer, Thomas, 173

Edgeworth, Maria, 48, 80, 207
education, 2, 44–60, 105, 120, 130–31, 160; artistic, 52, 206–20; through books, 9, 109–20, 128; moral, 56, 150–62, 189, 206–8; musical, 12, 206–20
ekphrasis, 191, 196
elegance, 13–14, 146–64, 215, 220
Emsley, Sarah, 150
Engelhardt, Molly, 100
English Landscape, 6, 7, 15–16, 55, 86–87, 140, 155–58, 165–77
Englishness, 15, 17. *See also* English landscape
English Reformation, 15, 150, 165–77, 179–80
estate, the, 4–7, 66–72; as represented by rooms, 69–70
Evans, Jessica, 104–5

Felton, Henry, 113
female accomplishments, 2, 46–60, 189, 206–23. *See also* artlessness; education
Fores, Samuel William (caricaturist, printer, and print shop owner), 229, 230, 234
Fountains Abbey, 168–70, 172–73
Fraiman, Susan, 153
free indirect discourse, 3, 7, 19n18, 35, 84–85, 89, 125, 158–59

Index

Frieman, Jacob (German artist), 37
Fruman, Jacob (German artist), 37
Fuller's Temple of Fancy, 9

Gatrell, Vic, 227
Gay, Penny, 89
gender, 10–12, 61–72, 103, 126–45, 191–92, 213
Gillray, James (caricaturist), 17, 228–34
Gilpin, William (artist and Anglican clergyman), 6, 15; influence on Austen, 165–84; *Tintern Abbey I* (1782), 171; *Tintern Abbey II* (1782), 171; *Tintern Abbey I* (1800), 182; *Tintern Abbey II* (1800), 183
Godmersham Park Library, 15, 80–81, 110, 117
Goldsmith, Oliver: *History of England*, 27–29, 125n27, 125n33
Goodwin, Sarah Webster, 212
gothic architecture, 66, 165–66, 169, 173–76, 180–81, 184
gothic novel, 6, 15, 176–77
Gray, Thomas, 173

Hall, Samuel (clergyman), 56
Halperin, John, 77
Halsey, Katie, 117, 119
harp, 47–48, 49, 52–53, 214, 215
Harris, James, 113
Harris, Jocelyn, 37, 64
heroines: and artistic proficiency, 12, 34, 48–49, 54, 190–201; and artlessness, 14, 44, 46–57; and judgment, 11–12, 14, 44–46, 53–57, 62–72, 151–52; physicality of, 96, 97–103, 106; and reading, 5, 53, 76, 106, 109, 112, 128, 130, 176, 195, 209, 210, 219–20; in sentimental novels, 9, 47–51, 131, 160–61; and taste, 14, 44, 50–57, 86, 140–62, 211–20
Hisamori, Kazuko, 31
Hoeveler, Diane Long, 176
Holland, William (printseller and bookseller), 234
Home, Henry, Lord Kames, *Elements of Criticism*, 56
Honan, Park, 26–27
Honychurch, Lennox, 161
Hume, David, *History of England*, 111–13

Humphrey, Hannah (printseller and bookseller), 230, 231, 234

Inchbald, Elizabeth, *Lovers' Vows*, 5, 13, 45, 51, 53, 82, 86, 87, 94–95
inheritance, 65–66
interiors. *See* domestic space
"intimate portrait," 16–17, 189–205

jewelry, 10, 13, 14, 129, 132, 141–42, 146, 148, 150; and portrait miniatures, 9, 32, 37
Joffrey Ballet, *Age of Innocence* (Austen-inspired ballet), 103
John Crook, Son, and Besford (haberdashers), 233
John Johnston's (print shop), 233
Johnny Fairburn's (print shop), 233
Johnson, Claudia, 213, 218
Johnstone's Commercial Guide and Street Directory, 229
Jones, William Naunton (editor), 233
judgment, 10–12, 14, 44–48, 53–57, 61–75, 102, 148, 192–93, 207, 212
Justice, George, 126

Kames, Henry Home, Lord, 56
Kauffman, Angelica, 154, *Self-Portrait*, 155
Kean, Edmund, 78–79
Kelly, Helena, 89
Kernick, David, 82
Keymer, Thomas, 63
Kindred, Sheila Johnson, 147
Kirkham, Margaret, 27
Knight, Edward Austen (JA's brother), 15, 110, 117, 121n3
Knight, Fanny (JA's niece), 24, 25, 26, 224
Knight, Richard Payne (scholar, theorist of picturesque), 55, 59n35, 167
Knox, Vicesimus: *Elegant Extracts*, 110–18, 130
Krieger, Murray, 191

landscapes (in nature), 4, 6–7, 15–16, 55, 86–87, 140, 155–58, 165–77; and Catholicism, 15, 173–77; and Englishness, 4, 6–7, 15–16, 55, 86–87, 140, 155–58, 165–84;
landscapes (as paintings), 15, 190, 196, 217

Index

law, Anne Elliot as figure of, 61–68, 72
Le Faye, Deirdre, 27
Lefroy, Anna (JA's niece), 1, 26, 77, 109–10, 116
Leighton, John, 193
Leppert, Richard, 206, 213, 214
Liang, Edwaard, *Age of Innocence*, 103
libraries, 10; George Austen's Library, 79–81, 109–10, 121n2; circulating libraries, 9, 128, 137; Godmersham Park Library, 15, 117, 119, 121n3, 128–30
Lloyd, Stephen, 16, 190, 193, 194
Looser, Devoney, 89
Losano, Antonia, 200
luxury goods, 9, 127–35, 140, 154, 161

Macaulay, Catherin: *Letters on Education*, 206–7, 220
MacGregor, Neil, 193
Marginalia: and Austen family book culture, 109–25; and education, 111, 113; photographs of, 111, 112, 113, 114, 118, 120; and Alexander Pope, 117–18; as readerly resistance, 112–13; and states of mind, 119
McKendrick, Neil, 127
Memoir of Jane Austen (1870), 27
Miall, David S., 170
Mitchell, W.J.T., 191
Mitford, Mary Russell (author and dramatist), 227
monasteries: Dissolution of, 166, 167–73
Moore, Roger E., 150, 173, 176
More, Hannah (religious writer), 2, 49, 50, 51, 119, 207, 216
Morland, George, *Pedlars*, 24–25
Murray, Ann, *Mentoria*, 116
music, 1, 4, 9, 12, 44, 47–52, 55–57, 189–90, 206–23
Myer, Valerie Grosvenor, 27

Napoléon, 36, 225, 229, 231, 233
Napoleonic Wars, 36, 65, 67, 74n26,
narrative: in ballet, 93–103; fixedness of (compared to drama), 77–90, 97; and interiority, 13, 76–92; and landscapes, 173–77, 179–84; and perspective 1, 7, 8; and portraits, 191–94; readerly experience of, 6; and women's work, 3. *See also* free indirect discourse
Nattes, John Claude (watercolorist), 1
natural world: appreciation of, 7, 51–52, 55–56, 59n35, 86, 148, 223n29
nature, 67, 100, 119, 140, 154–55, 165–77, 181–84. *See also* natural world
The Navy List, 11, 61–75
needlework, 5, 10, 17, 134–35, 166, 179
Netley Abbey, 168, 172–74
Newton, Richard (caricaturist), 234
Nightingale, Joseph (writer and preacher), 230
Nigro, Jeffrey, 215
Nokes, David, 26
novel: and Austen family reading habits, 116–20; Austen's feminist revision of, 61–75; Austen's narrative innovations in, 9, 11–12; Austen's preference for over drama, 13, 76–92; ballet's influence on, 93–108; and caricature, 225–26, 234–35; as commodity, 129–30; and cultural anxieties, 207–8; and ekphrasis, 191; and gothic landscape, 165–88; and sentimental novel, 47–57
Noverre, Jean Georges (French dancer and choreographer), 95–96, 100, 105–7

O'Quinn, Daniel, 87

painting (as activity), 16–17, 25, 38, 171–77; and aesthetics, 52, 55–56; and Cassandra Austen, 24–30; in domestic arts, 220; dress for, 154; on screens, 134–35,
paintings (as objects), 10, 15, 25; as depicted in novels, 33–41, 189–92, 194–201, 213, 217. *See also* portrait miniatures; portraits
Palmer Sally B, 217
Park, Julie, 86–87
Perrot, Jules, 97
piano, 1, 2, 12, 44, 47, 50, 52, 106, 159, 206–23
picturesque, 6, 8, 14–15, 50–51, 55–56, 140, 165–73, 179–84, 225; and *Emma*, 15, 166–67, 179–84; and *Mansfield Park*, 8, 14, 50–51; and *Northanger Abbey*, 14, 140, 166–67, 173–77; and *Pride and Prejudice*, 6

Index

Piozzi, Hester Thrale, 178
Platinga, Leon, 12
Pointon, Marcia, 8, 16, 31, 190–92, 194
Political Satire, 17, 229–31
Pope, Alexander, 173; *Elegy to an Unfortunate Lady*, 131; Epistle *to Bathurst*, 117–18, 138–39; *Epistle to Burlington*, 118, 130, 140–42, 154–56; *Epistle to Dr. Arbuthnot*, 135; *Epistle to a Lady*, 118, 135–36, 140; *Essay on Criticism*, 130; *Essay on Man*, 130; as portrait collector, 136; *The Rape of the Lock*, 10, 126, 131, 136
"portrait contract," 16, 190–201
portrait gallery, 137; as depicted in novels, 32–33, 137, 190
portrait miniatures, 9, 16, 31–38, 40–41, 136–37, 190, 193, 196–97; in Austen's self-description, 3; as 225; as jewelry, 9, 32, 37; in *Persuasion*, 16, 31–32, 36–38, 41; in *Pride and Prejudice*, 33; in *Sanditon*, 40–41; in *Sense and Sensibility*, 31–2, 133
portrait shops, 225
portraits, 7–8, 15–17, 24–43, 69, 154–55, 200, 225, 228; in *Emma*, 34–35, 189–205; in "The History of England," 27–30; in *Mansfield Park*, 33–34; in *Northanger Abbey*, 35–36; in *Persuasion*, 38–41; in *Pride and Prejudice*, 33; in *Sanditon*, 40–41. *See also* portrait miniatures
portraiture. *See* portraits
Price, Uvedale (landscape theorist), 55, 167

Radcliffe, Ann, 178
Rajan, Rajeswari, 153
reading aloud, 1, 53
reading: Austen's reading of drama, 76, 79–87; Austen's reading of novels, 83–84; Austen's reading of Pope, 126–45; Austen family habits of, 1, 14–15, 109–25; and female education, 49, 207–8; of portraits, 33, 191–94; reading as depicted in novels, 5, 33, 53, 97–103, 105–6, 128–31, 166, 174–77, 195–96, 199–200, 209–10, 219–20; and resistance to, 15, 111–12. *See also* books; book culture; marginalia; narrative, readerly experience of

Reformation, 15, 150, 165–77, 179–80
Regency satire. *See* caricatures
religion. *See* Christianity
Repton, Humphry, 6, 55
Reynolds, Sir Joshua (painter), 16, 33, 223, 226–27, 234, 236n13
Richardson, Samuel, 83
Robertson, William, *History of Scotland*, 111
Robinson, Terry F., 174
Robson, Martin, 67
rooms. *See* domestic space
Rousseau, Jean-Jacques, 14, 51

Sabor, Peter, 79, 109, 110, 225
Said, Edward, 152–53
satire, 17; Austen's ambiguous use of, 176; and caricatures, 234–38; of consumerism, 10, 154; of domestic arts, 134–35, 211–20; in juvenilia, 28–30, 116, 208–11, 228; political satire, 17, 229–31; of Alexander Pope, 117–18, 128, 130–31
satiric prints, 17, 39, 51, 224, 224–38
Schimmelpenninck, Mary Anne, 160–62
Schneider, Ana-Karina, 153
Scott, Sir Walter, 38, 49, 82; *Marmion*, 80; *Waverley*, 47–49
sewing, 3, 10
Shaftesbury, 3rd Earl of (Anthony Ashley Cooper), 14, 51, 54–56
Sheehan, Colleen A., 232
Shell, Alison, 172
shops: and amateur artists, 9–10; portrait shops, 225; print shops, 17, 228–29; as social venues, 10, 230–31, 232, 234
silhouettes, 1
slave narratives, 152
slave trade, 152–53, 158, 232
Sloan, Kim, 16, 190, 193–94
Smethurst, Paul, 181
Smith, Adam (economist and moral philosopher), 14
Smith, Charlotte (poet and novelist), 47
Society of Painters in Oil and Water Colours, 226
Soni, Vivasvan, 54, 153
Southam, Brian, 10, 25, 61, 69, 77, 147, 149
Spongberg, Mary, 176
Sutherland, Kathryn, 27

Index

Tanner, Tony, 69
taste, 4, 14, 50–57, 130, 137, 139–42, 146, 148–49, 162, 192
Tattersal's (auction house), 64, 68
Tegg, Thomas (bookseller), 233
theater. *See* drama
The Three Brothers of Gotham, 228
Thrush, Nanette, 191
Tintern Abbey: in art, 17, 34, 165, 168–73, 182, 183–84: as a place, 168–69, 181–84
Todd, Janet, 32, 36, 77
Townshend, Dale, 168
Turner, J.M.W.: *Fishing Boats Entering Calais Harbor*, 38–39; *Tintern Abbey*, 171–73

Urda, Kathleen E., 13

Valihora, Karen, 54
Vestris, Auguste (French dancer), 95

Wallace, Beth Kowaleski, 177, 179, 183

Wallace, Robert, 207
Wedgewood, Josiah, 9, 141
Weickmann, Dorion, 95, 99
Wells, Juliette, 215
West, Benjamin, *Christ Healing the Sick*, 227, 234; *Christ Rejected by the Elders*, 227, 234
White, Gabrielle, 153
White, Laura Mooneyham, 147
Williams, Charles (caricaturist), 229
Wilson, Margaret, 25
Wollstonecraft, Mary, 2, 14, 159–60
Woodward, George Murgatroyd (caricaturist), 234
Wordsworth, William, 81
Wright, Carrie, 146

Young, Edward, "Night Thoughts," 118

Zelicovici, Dvora, 87
Zoffany, Johann, *The Family of Sir William Young*, 161–62
Zunshine, Lisa, 85

www.ingramcontent.com/pod-product-compliance
Lightning Source LLC
Chambersburg PA
CBHW021349300426
44114CB00012B/1152